A Chief Lieutenant of the Tuskegee Machine

Florida A&M University, Tallahassee
Florida Atlantic University, Boca Raton
Florida Gulf Coast University, Ft. Myers
Florida International University, Miami
Florida State University, Tallahassee
University of Central Florida, Orlando
University of Florida, Gainesville
University of North Florida, Jacksonville
University of South Florida, Tampa
University of West Florida, Pensacola

Charles Banks, 1911

A Chief Lieutenant
of the Tuskegee Machine

Charles Banks of Mississippi

❦

David H. Jackson Jr.

University Press of Florida

Gainesville · Tallahassee · Tampa · Boca Raton
Pensacola · Orlando · Miami · Jacksonville · Ft. Myers

Copyright 2002 by David H. Jackson Jr.
Printed in the United States of America on recycled, acid-free paper

07 06 05 04 03   6 5 4 3 2

The map on page xvi is reproduced from *The Most Southern Place on Earth:
The Mississippi Delta and the Roots of Regional Identity* by James C. Cobb,
copyright 1992 by James C. Cobb. Used by permission of Oxford University
Press, Inc.

Library of Congress Cataloging-in-Publication Data
Jackson, David H., Jr.
A chief lieutenant of the Tuskegee Machine : Charles Banks of Mississippi /
David H. Jackson, Jr.
p. cm.
Includes bibliographical references and index.
ISBN 0-8130-2544-3 (cloth : alk. paper)
1. Banks, Charles, 1873–1923. 2. African Americans—Biography. 3. African
American political activists—Biography. 4. Washington, Booker T., 1856–
1915—Friends and associates. 5. Tuskegee Institute—Biography. 6. African
Americans—Mississippi—Politics and government—20th century. 7. African
Americans—Education—Mississippi—History—20th century. 8. African
Americans—Mississippi—Social conditions—20th century. 9. Mississippi—
Politics and government—1865–1950. 10. Mississippi—Race relations.
I. Title.
E185.97.B216 J33 2002
976.2004'96073'0092—dc21
[B]   2002072628

The University Press of Florida is the scholarly publishing agency
for the State University System of Florida, comprising Florida A&M
University, Florida Atlantic University, Florida Gulf Coast University,
Florida International University, Florida State University, University
of Central Florida, University of Florida, University of North Florida,
University of South Florida, and University of West Florida.

University Press of Florida
15 Northwest 15th Street
Gainesville, FL 32611–2079
http://www.upf.com

Dedicated to
My mother and father,
My wife, Sheila, and our children,
David III and Daja.

Contents

List of Figures   ix

Preface   xi

1. The Early Life of Charles Banks: "Where I First Saw the First Light of Day"   1

2. History of Mound Bayou: "A Negro Metropolis"   25

3. Charles Banks, Booker T. Washington, and the Mound Bayou Connection   41

4. Leader, Organizer, and Promoter: "On My Job All the Time and Doing the Best That My Ability Will Allow"   59

5. The Business League: "Being Worked to the Limit"   90

6. Fund-Raiser for Negro Education: "Going Ahead Endeavoring to Meet the Conditions as Best We Can"   104

7. On Matters Political: "I See That 'Sambo' Is Left Out"   129

8. "Wizard" of Finance: "Never Running Away from Battle"   154

9. Mound Bayou Cotton Oil Mill: "The Largest and Most Serious Undertaking . . . in the History of Our Race"   170

10. After Booker T. Washington: "A Tempest in the Teapot"   187

11. Conclusion: "The Most Public-Spirited Citizen in the History of Mississippi"   204

Abbreviations   217

Notes   219

Bibliography   259

Index   273

Figures

1. Map of the Yazoo Mississippi Delta, showing location of Mound Bayou   xvi

2. Charles Banks in 1911   79

3. Charles Banks in 1909   80

4. Charles Banks and Isaiah T. Montgomery   80

5. Cashier's office at the Bank of Mound Bayou   81

6. Home of Charles and Trenna Banks   82

7. Officers of the Bank of Mound Bayou and their families   83

8. Mr. and Mrs. Simon Gaiter   84

9. Bethel African Methodist Episcopal Church   84

10. The Bank of Mound Bayou   85

11. The Carnegie Library at Mound Bayou   85

12. The Mound Bayou Oil Mill and Manufacturing Company   86

13. Booker T. Washington speaking at oil mill dedication   86

14. Charles Banks ca. 1905   87

15. The Mound Bayou Consolidated Negro School   88

16. The Mound Bayou Oil Mill under construction   88

17. Booker T. Washington during his tour of Mississippi, 1908   89

Preface

An analysis of the life of Charles Banks is long overdue. Many books and essays have been written about his mentor Booker T. Washington and about the Tuskegee Machine. Historians have also written about Washington's National Negro Business League (NNBL) and the search that took place for black leaders after his death. This, however, is the first treatment of Charles Banks, one of Washington's "lieutenants" who played a critical role in the Tuskegee Machine. Louis Harlan has described the Tuskegee Machine as "an intricate, nationwide web of institutions in the black community that were conducted, dominated, or strongly influenced from the little town in the deep South where Washington had his base."[1] Organized in a pyramid structure, the Tuskegee Machine placed Washington at the top, his state lieutenants below him, local leaders on the third level, and the masses of his followers on the bottom. Charles Banks, lieutenant for Mississippi (a state with a large population of Negroes), became responsible for carrying out Washington's program there. The machine, wrote Harlan, was "broadly based throughout the black middle class, had powerful white allies and many recruits even from the Talented Tenth, [and] made rewards and punishments a central feature of its recruitment and retention of its followers." Washington, Banks, and other Tuskegee men, moreover, used the machine to exercise influence over the black press, to control black (and sometimes white) political patronage, to determine who received white largesse, and for a variety of other purposes.[2]

There is no question Booker T. Washington became the preeminent black leader of his day, but it is often assumed he rose to this position on his own.[3] If it were not for lieutenants like Banks, who were stationed throughout the states, Washington would not have been nearly as effective. Banks communicated with the masses of black people in Mississippi on a regular basis, and he persuasively promoted Washington's agenda.

In return for his support of the Tuskegee Machine, Banks gained access to Washington's white philanthropic resources, access to expertise from others in the Tuskegee Machine, and political influence. He also received untiring support from members of the machine, which helped him consolidate power as a black leader. Banks, therefore, wielded a considerable amount of power and influence throughout the country. He was the prototype of the lieutenants Washington had in his organization. In examining Charles Banks, one better understands Washington's effectiveness as a leader. Moreover, an analysis of Banks's life shows he frequently employed a "black survival strategy," as did other Tuskegee men, in which he appeared on the surface to be deferential and conciliatory toward whites. Yet, he only acted in this manner to manipulate whites for his own purposes.

This study traces the life of Charles Banks from his birth in 1873 to his death in 1923. Banks's power became inextricably linked to the success of the Tuskegee Machine, and as Washington rose to national prominence near the turn of the century, Banks's power increased accordingly. For more than fifteen years, he served as first vice-president of the NNBL and president of the Mississippi Negro Business League (MNBL). He also became an influential Republican in Mississippi for years. Through his organizational affiliations and endeavors, Banks worked with some of the most powerful blacks and whites in the country, and he became, arguably, the most influential black person in Mississippi from 1905 to 1915 and clearly the state's foremost black business leader.

There are several purposes for writing this biography on Charles Banks. The first is to give scholars a fresh interpretation of Booker T. Washington and the Tuskegee Machine that mitigates the image of the machine as being conniving, heavy-handed, intolerant, and ruthless. Louis Harlan's seminal work on Booker T. Washington paints this image, especially when describing how Washington dealt with his detractors.[4] The second is to provide an insider's perspective on the workings of the Tuskegee Machine. Third, the biography discusses the benefits received by members of the machine, such as capital, expertise, national exposure, and political power. And fourth, the biography will show that working with the machine turned out to be mutually beneficial for Washington, Banks, and other Tuskegee supporters.

In addition, this study seeks to present a typical Washington lieutenant, Charles Banks, and show that if it were not for such key men, Washington would not have been nearly as effective as he was. Moreover, this study illustrates that lieutenants like Banks were not mere puppets of

Washington but men who had considerable latitude in their decision making. Although Washington disagreed with Banks on different occasions, Banks did not fall out of the Tuskegee leader's favor. The study will also show that there were Negro businessmen during Washington's time who were wealthy, competent, and successful in their endeavors. Last, the study will provide perhaps the most complete history to date of Mound Bayou, Mississippi, especially during its golden age, 1900–1915.

Charles Banks lived the American dream to the extent that he rose from poverty to prominence at a time most blacks could not imagine doing so. Although very little has been written about him, Banks dedicated most of his life to carving out a place in society for Negroes during the nadir, or lowest point, in African American history. This is what Washington and other members of the Tuskegee Machine called constructionalism. Constructionalists believed in carving out a place in society where they could develop economically, socially, educationally, and politically notwithstanding the forces working against them. Despite the vicissitudes he contended with, Banks found ways not only to survive but also to thrive.

The book is organized by topic, and each chapter is divided into sections and arranged chronologically. *Negro* is used frequently throughout this work to describe African Americans because Banks, Washington, and others of the time used the term when they referred to themselves. The term *black* is used synonymously with *Negro* because they used it as well.

Major sources consulted in compiling this work were the Booker T. Washington Papers, the National Negro Business League Papers, the Tuskegee Institute News Clippings Files, the Robert Russa Moton Papers, and the Benjamin T. Montgomery Family Papers. These sources served as invaluable tools of research, especially the Washington and Moton papers, for Banks corresponded with Tuskegee almost daily for many years. Even when Banks wrote to people who did not live in Tuskegee, he commonly sent carbon copies to Washington, Emmett Scott, and Moton to keep them apprised of his work.

While these sources served as useful tools for studying Banks's life, the fact that his personal papers are currently unavailable has limited this study. To some extent, the available data forced me to look at Banks in terms of his association with Bookerites and Tuskegee. Moreover, since Emmett Scott's papers are closed indefinitely, it became difficult to ascertain information about Banks's personal life after 1917 that may be tucked away in the Scott collection at Morgan State University. I have sought to provide more information about Banks's family, especially his wife and his siblings, but the lack of documents prevented me from doing so.

Notwithstanding these limitations, I hope to present a comprehensive study. I also hope this book will do more than shed light on the subject; I hope it will inspire others to research and write on other obscure African Americans of the era who were equally committed to racial uplift but whose stories are yet untold.

Acknowledgments

This study grew out of a research seminar taken at the University of Memphis in the fall of 1993. Professor David Tucker came into class with a list of names for students to choose from for research topics for the semester. There were two African Americans on the list—D'Army Bailey and Charles Banks. Although I had never heard of either, I randomly chose Charles Banks. Little did I know that the next nine years of my life would be spent studying him. After I submitted my paper, Professor Tucker wrote encouragingly on the last page that I should pursue Banks as a dissertation topic. For that suggestion, I say thank you.

I incurred many debts as a result of this study. I am truly appreciative of the guidance, encouragement, comments, and suggestions given to me by my mentors and friends: Kenneth W. Goings, professor of history and chair of the African-American and African Studies Department at Ohio State University, and Charles W. Crawford, professor of history at the University of Memphis. They codirected a significant portion of this study as a doctoral dissertation and helped guide the overall structure of the work while helping me fine-tune my research skills.

I am also very thankful for the invaluable insights provided to me by Beverly Bond, assistant professor of history, University of Memphis; Margaret M. Caffrey, associate professor of history, University of Memphis; F. Jack Hurley, professor of history, University of Memphis; and Randolph Meade Walker, associate professor of history, LeMoyne–Owen College. Each read my manuscript carefully and provided me with critical but helpful suggestions on how it could be improved. A number of other scholars read all or part of the manuscript at various stages: Maceo Dailey, associate professor of history, University of Texas at El Paso; Neil McMillen, professor of history, University of Southern Mississippi; Ted Hemmingway, professor of history, Florida A&M University; and especially Larry E. Rivers, distinguished professor of history, Florida A&M University, who provided encouragement and guidance throughout the process. All gave me important comments on my work. My research assistants Michael Woodward, DeShauna Keown, William Hicks, Will Guzman, and Anthony Dixon enthusiastically and efficiently found information for me. Franzetta Fitz, Reginald Mitchell, and Sonya Bridges provided me with technological assistance. Of the individuals I interviewed about Mound Bayou, Milburn J. Crowe and Kemper Smith were especially helpful. I must also truly thank my good friend Kever Conyers, who, in addition to general encouragement, willingly shared his accounting expertise and helped me analyze several financial documents relating to Banks. I also offer a word of gratitude to Kenneth Pratt for copyediting early drafts of this manuscript and Jean C. Lee, the copy editor who made final revisions. In addition, I am grateful to Meredith Morris-Babb and the rest of the staff at the University Press of Florida for guiding this work to publication.

Cynthia Wilson, curator of the Tuskegee University Archives, was most helpful in allowing me to access freely the materials in her care. A special thanks goes to David Beito, associate professor of history, University of Alabama, for sharing relevant newspaper articles for this study. I would like to thank Keith Simmonds, professor of political science, and Gary Paul, associate professor of political science, who served as former and current chair, respectively, of the Department of History and Political Science at Florida A&M University, for helping shape my schedule so I would have time to complete this project while teaching four classes a semester.

To the ancestors, from Africa to America, whose spirit and guidance gave me the fortitude, tenacity, determination, and inspiration to complete this project: specifically, my grandfather Leroy Jackson Sr.; my grandmother Oless Redmond Jackson; my father, David H. Jackson Sr.; and historians (past and present) Carter G. Woodson, W. E. B. Du Bois, Charles Wesley, Rayford Logan, Joel A. Rogers, John Hope Franklin, Yosef Ben-Yochannan, and John Henrik Clarke. They, along with other unnamed African ancestors, sacrificed themselves in the struggle and in many other ways to make my aspirations not just a dream but a reality. I realize that, am grateful, and will never forget it.

Last, none of my efforts would have been possible without the support and encouragement of my sisters, Tammy and Belinda, and my mother, Vera, whose expectations throughout my life have given me the drive to set lofty goals. Also, my wife, Sheila, has been patient and made many sacrifices over the years while still encouraging me to finish this project. For that I am most grateful and dedicate this work to her and our children, David III and Daja.

Although I was given assistance by others with this study, all errors contained herein are mine.

Fig. 1. The Yazoo Mississippi Delta, showing the location of the town of Mound Bayou. From James C. Cobb, *The Most Southern Place on Earth: The Mississippi Delta and the Roots of Regional Identity* (New York: Oxford University Press, 1992).

The Early Life of Charles Banks

"Where I First Saw the First Light of Day"

On November 25, 1912, Booker T. Washington stood before a crowd of at least 15,000 black men and women in Mound Bayou, Mississippi. There to give the keynote address for the dedication ceremony at the opening of the Mound Bayou Cotton Oil Mill, Washington spoke to black people not only from Mound Bayou but also from other cities such as New Orleans, Memphis, and Jackson. Indeed, this turned out to be a grand occasion because the Mound Bayou Cotton Oil Mill was one of the largest of its kind in the state and it became a symbol of black self-help and black self-sufficiency. The oil mill reputedly cost $100,000 to erect, and its promoters publicized it as being an enterprise totally owned and operated by Negroes.[1]

One woman who attended the opening of the oil mill probably represented the dominant view of those in attendance when she stated: "Well, Lord, here I is. I are sho' ready to lef' dese lowgrounds. I has hearn Booker T. . . . I has seen de ile mill, de big wheels an' all dat." She noted further that what once was "ain't now, fer us cullud folks is gwine ter see de cotton after it's done picked in the fiel' and 'fo' we buys it back 'cross de counter."[2] Her words express her joy at seeing that black people had moved from just picking cotton in the fields to manufacturing it in the mill. Sharecroppers, who were less than fifty years from slavery, viewed this as being a significant achievement.

After Washington finished his speech, he pulled the cord that sounded the whistle for the symbolic opening of the mill.[3] "The opening of this Oil Mill," said Washington, "marks a unique and distinct step in the progress of the Negroes of America." To him the oil mill represented "the largest and most serious undertaking in a purely commercial and manufacturing enterprise in the history of our race."[4] Charles Banks became the primary organizer and promoter of this enterprise. Banks's role in making the mill a reality was indicative of an enterprising person, one whose reputation would become legend in Mississippi.

Black Life in Mississippi

The excitement at the opening of the oil mill surely departed from the typical experiences of black Mississippians during the era. In fact, the time period covered in this study, 1873–1923, falls well within what historian Rayford Logan called the nadir, or lowest point, in African American history.[5] After making some advances during Reconstruction, black people in this time struggled and suffered on all fronts, political, social, educational, and economic.[6]

During most of Banks's life, Mississippi Negroes lived in what one historian has called "the heartland of American Apartheid."[7] Racial discrimination so prevailed in Mississippi at the end of Reconstruction that some white Mississippians thought Jim Crow legislation was completely unnecessary. Although Mississippi boasted that it had some prominent black political officials, many black Mississippians knew their "place."[8] Blacks and whites in Mississippi were kept apart in public and private hospitals and were prevented from using the same entrances to state-funded health-care facilities. Black criminals were not even incarcerated in the same prison cells with whites.[9]

Racial segregation in Mississippi, therefore, became largely a matter of custom. "Mississippi seems to have had fewer Jim Crow laws during the entire segregation period than most southern states," noted one writer.[10] In other words, since blacks knew their "place," legislation was not needed. Carter G. Woodson, the father of black history, summed this up best: "When you control a man's thinking you do not have to worry about his actions. You do not have to tell him not to stand here or go yonder, he will find his 'proper place' and will stay in it," Woodson asserted. Moreover, he said, "you do not need to send him to the back door. He will go without being told. In fact, if there is no back door, he will cut one for his special benefit."[11] Although some Negroes deviated from this pattern, the type of thinking described by Woodson typified that of many blacks in Mississippi at the turn of the century. This is not a condemnation of blacks' behavior; the behavior was learned over hundreds of years of enslavement, and blacks knew that violations of "social etiquette" often resulted in murder.[12]

Wherever they turned, black Mississippians faced segregation. More often than not, Jim Crow customs required not merely separation but exclusion. At funerals, weddings, courtrooms, public facilities, and other places of social gathering, habit dictated the races would never integrate. The racial code prohibited any form of interracial activity that might have implied equality. Nevertheless, blacks were not as concerned about integration as they were about having access to the facilities.[13]

Ironically, the early part of the 1870s has been viewed as a time of optimism for Negroes in Mississippi. Reconstruction in the state produced some of the most prominent black politicians of the day. Within the state, John Roy Lynch served as speaker of the house for Mississippi in 1872 and Thomas W. Cardozo was superintendent of education from 1874, a year after Charley Banks's birth, to 1876. Alexander K. Davis served as lieutenant governor, and James Hill became the secretary of state in 1874.[14]

Mississippi also produced black politicians at the national level. Hiram R. Revels and Blanche K. Bruce served terms in the U.S. Senate, an accomplishment that would not be repeated for more than eighty years. If these achievements represented the best of times for black Mississippians, the worst of times were soon to follow. By the time President Rutherford B. Hayes effected the Compromise of 1877, when Charley Banks was four years old, many of the gains made during Reconstruction were slowly but surely being stripped.[15]

After 1877, blacks' political rights were taken away through fraud, intimidation, and outright murder. In 1890, Mississippi legislators called a constitutional convention to disfranchise blacks, and that is exactly what they did. They imposed poll taxes, literacy requirements, and prohibited voting for those who had been convicted of theft, perjury, arson, bribery, or burglary. Following Mississippi's lead, other southern states began enacting similar laws to deny suffrage to Negroes.[16] The decision in *Williams v. Mississippi* (1898) added to the political impotence of black Mississippians. With this case, Mississippi courts legally paved the way for the segregation and disfranchisement of Negroes in the state.[17] This was a significant difference from the times of Revels and Bruce. Economically, blacks were confronted with conditions similar to those they faced during slavery. The old planter class worked diligently to maintain an economic system that kept black people dependent as before. Under sharecropping, this is precisely what happened. In short, the economic situation for blacks remained about as bleak as it had been before the Civil War.[18]

The educational picture looked as bad for young Charley Banks as the political and economic ones. Although blacks paid a disproportionate share of public school expenses, they received little in return. Mississippi held the dubious distinction of being the southern state that spent the least amount of money on black education. By 1900, black children received only 19 percent of the state's funds for education although they accounted for some 60 percent of the school-age population. Whites realized that if they could limit the educational achievements of Negroes, they could also stifle their political, economic, and social aspirations.[19]

There were some instances, nevertheless, in which black Mississippians worked closely with whites in the post-Reconstruction period. When William C. Handy, father of the blues, visited Clarksdale, Mississippi in 1903, he marveled that the white Clarksdale bank had a black assistant cashier. He noted that he "had never seen [anything like this] before in all my travels."[20] Such situations, however, were the exception rather than the rule. In most cases, the place of black Mississippians was carefully proscribed and fully understood by both races.

Neil McMillen states that the years between 1889 and 1919 were "among the most repressive in Mississippi history."[21] On numerous occasions, a breach in the code of racial etiquette by Negroes led to swift and severe punishments. Blacks in Mississippi met with "indescribable cruelties" from white mobs. Some were drowned, torched, bludgeoned, dragged to death behind automobiles, tortured to death with hot irons, or publicly burned at "Negro Barbecues." Others had fingers and ears chopped off, eyes gouged out, and pieces of their flesh pulled from their bodies with corkscrews as they were tortured to death before crowds of thousands.[22] On June 11, 1900, the *Houston Daily Post* described the fate of Henry Askew and Ed Russ, two black men who were victims of a Mississippi mob. Askew and Russ had been in the vicinity where a thirteen-year-old white female was murdered. Although no conclusive evidence linked the men to the murder, a mob gathered, overpowered the sheriff, and murdered them both. "The Negroes were tied back to back and swung up to the same tree," the newspaper noted. After this, "their bodies were riddled with bullets, and after death ensued, were set on fire." Observers said that "the nauseating smell of the burning flesh could be smelt for miles around." Apparently the only crime these two men committed was being in the wrong place at the wrong time.[23]

The time between 1890 and 1930 was one of the most dangerous periods for Negroes in the United States. During this time, approximately four thousand black men and women were lynched.[24] To be sure, many black men and women were executed during this time for being assertive and for deviating from expected behavioral norms. Nevertheless, in this violent period the Mound Bayou Cotton Oil Mill was constructed and set into operation. It was also the time Charley Banks lived in the Magnolia State.

Born in 1873 in a time of promise, Banks lived through an era in which many dreams of black people were dashed away. Despite this, Banks rose to a position of prominence in the state of Mississippi and became a person whom few would equal. His work was just as weighty and his position more enduring than that of black politicians. He exerted considerable influence in Mississippi from about 1905 to 1920 and became one of the leading black figures in the state and in the nation.

Family Background

Banks's family deeply influenced his development and ambitions. He was born March 25, 1873, in Clarksdale, Mississippi, to Daniel A. and Sallie Ann Banks. His parents had been slaves in Mississippi during the antebellum period. The 1880 census listed Sallie as thirty-eight years old and her husband as thirty. Daniel had a relatively large household. According to the 1880 census, nine people lived in the Banks's home, including four children: Joeannia, eleven; Charley, seven; Mary, five; and G. Joseph, one. Fifty-year-old Marriah Holley, Charley's maternal grandmother, also lived with them. Everyone in the household was born in Mississippi except for Virginia-born Sallie and her mother. By the time of the 1880 census, Marriah Holley had become a widow.[25] Described as "penniless" by one writer, the Bankses in 1880 had two boarders: Georga White, a twenty-two-year-old black female and native of Tennessee, and Dan Jinning, a twenty-four-year-old black male also from Tennessee. Both Georga and Dan were reported as single by the 1880 census.[26]

Daniel Banks worked as a farmer and Sallie Banks worked as a housekeeper and cook. White was listed as a housekeeper by the census while Jinning worked as a laborer. Sallie's job frequently required her to be away from her family and home. All of the household members' jobs were low-paying. Most black men had to take seasonal jobs, which often paid less than thirty dollars a month, and many cooks were expected to work seven days a week for as little as twenty-five cents a day.[27] However, by the time of Charley's birth, the Bankses had gained the favor of the most prominent white family in Clarksdale, John and Eliza Clark.

John Clark was born in 1823 to a well-known British architect in Ashton, England, named James Hawkins Clark. After working briefly in Nova Scotia, James Clark moved his family to Philadelphia. James later received a commission to work in New Orleans and took his son along with him. Unfortunately, James Clark died of yellow fever while in New Orleans in 1839. John Clark, therefore, had to decide whether to go back north to Philadelphia or try his hand at survival in the South. The younger Clark decided on the latter and moved to Coahoma County, Mississippi, where he became a very successful farmer and lumberman. In fact, he saved enough money to purchase 101 acres of government land in the Delta for $1.25 an acre. This land would later become Clarksdale's business district.[28]

John Clark married Eliza Jane Alcorn in 1854. Although they started married life in a log cabin, they later had a two-story house constructed in 1859. John refused to use slave labor for the construction of his home so he hired workmen from the North. This approach, however, deviated from the norm, for one of the Clarks's closest neighbors, Major Napoleon Bonaparte Leavell, who had lived south of the Clarks since 1845, reportedly owned 150 slaves.[29] Since John and Eliza were said to have refused to use slave labor to build their home, it is unclear if they ever owned slaves. Thus no evidence clearly points to whose plantation the Bankses worked on before emancipation.[30] The Clarks had real estate totaling $50,000 in 1870 and personal assets of $12,000. Their family was fairly large also. In addition to John and Eliza, there were J. Hawkins, twelve; John Jr., eleven; Walter, nine; Eugene, seven; Blanche, five; and Charles, two.[31]

After emancipation, Sallie Banks worked as a cook for the Clarks for several years. In general, black cooks commonly worked from early morning until about eight at night, which meant they could not see their children or other family members until late evenings. In return for the hard work and to compensate for low wages, some cooks helped themselves to what they called the boss's "service pan"—leftover food, which they took home to their families.[32]

Though tension frequently existed between mistress and cook, in some cases a loving relationship existed between the two, which appears to have been the situation with Sallie Banks and Eliza Clark. Consequently, Sallie could have worked fewer hours and been better compensated than many black cooks. The Clarks, unlike many employers, even allowed Sallie to bring her children to work. In fact, Charley Banks was born in a "shack later used for a chicken house" on the property of the Clarks.[33] He boasted that he "first saw the first light of day" on the homestead of the Clarks.[34]

Charley Banks's exposure to a successful businessman like John Clark may have influenced his future aspirations. He may have learned much about being an entrepreneur and about business management from observing the Clarks. If so, what he observed paid great dividends to him as he matured.

Early Education

When he was very young, Banks's parents made him aware of the importance of education. Daniel Banks could read but could not write. The rest of the adults in the household, Sallie, Marriah, Georga, and Dan, could neither read nor write; Charley did not follow this pattern. While it is unclear whether any of his siblings attended school, it is certain Charley received his elementary education in the Coahoma County school system.[35]

During this time, many black people throughout the nation thirsted for education, had an opportunity to receive it, and pursued it with great vigor. By the time of the 1880 census, eleven-year-old Joeannia, like her father, had learned to read, although she could not write. Eliza Clark, Sallie's employer, who worked as a private tutor in Clarksdale, became known as the "mother of Clarksdale schools." More likely than not, she assisted the Banks children with their education.[36]

The Freedmen's Bureau worked tirelessly in the South to establish schools and teach black children. Many northern white churches sent missionaries south for the same reason. In 1870, the Mississippi legislature designated Coahoma County as a school district. With financial assistance from the state and from local poll taxes, the district operated in four-month terms. The first public school in Clarksdale, however, did not open until 1884, with eight students in attendance.[37]

Relationship with the Clarks

Charley and his family appear to have been very attached to the Clarks, and over time the Clark family seems to have grown especially fond of Charley. Perhaps he showed signs of promise. In any case, it seems he left an impression upon the Clarks during his youth.[38] The relationship between the Bankses and the Clarks was long-standing, and it affected Charley's views on race relations. For blacks, a certain amount of social status came with being "favorites" of prominent white families. This certainly happened with southern blacks whose families had been enslaved. Being favorites distinguished them from other black families and supposedly showed whites they were different.[39]

In a letter Banks wrote to Booker T. Washington in 1910, he noted that the relationship that existed between his family and the Clarks demonstrated "it is possible for the kindliest of feeling to exist between people though of different races."[40] The letter was precipitated by a newspaper article Banks had read about Leland Hume of Nashville, who was described as a southerner of the "old and genuine antebellum aristocracy stock." In the article, Hume recounted pleasant experiences he had with black people over the years, which seemed to mirror Banks's experiences. "I am like the younger generation of whites," Banks noted, however, "in that I do not fully understand 'The Black Mammy and Old Massy' ties."[41] This statement reveals that Banks wanted to distance himself from the paternalistic relationship his parents were accustomed to, thereby showing that he was a "New Negro."

Nevertheless, referring to Hume's relation of an incident when the children of an elderly black woman who had worked for Hume some years earlier visited him and greeted him warmly, Banks stated he had "the same feeling for the Clarks, who founded Clarksdale."[42] It is clear, then, that Banks really felt close to the Clarks. When speaking of his early life in Clarksdale, Banks frequently mentioned the warm relationships he had with white friends in that town, especially the Clarks.[43] He continued to believe black and white Americans could maintain cordial relations.

In the same letter, Banks reminded Washington of his Atlanta Exposition speech, in particular the part where he encouraged Negroes to "let down your buckets where you are," while also pointing out that blacks and whites "could be separate and distinct as the fingers of the hand in matters social, yet firm friends, and all working for the common good." While Banks understood the social standing of black people in Mississippi and the South at that time, he thought good relations could exist between blacks and whites outside of social mingling, particularly when it came to business affairs.[44]

Banks concluded the letter to Washington with this statement about race relations:

To my mind no great[er] workers for the needs of the hour are there than they who are earnestly, conscientiously, faithfully and intelligently working for peace and amicable relations, and a better understanding with those among whom we live.[45]

Banks maintained contact with the Clarks for many years after he moved from Clarksdale. Eliza Clark wrote Banks in December 1911 and inquired about the health of his grandmother Marriah Holley. Eliza said Holley had been ill, but felt better and expected to recover fully. In his reply, Banks wrote that it was "very kind beyond expression to note the interest you have manifested in her through all these years." He told Eliza further that he had visited his mother and grandmother and they were doing fine. They had, he said, "plenty of fuel and supplies, [and] as the weather was getting cool I sent her some additional underwear."[46]

Eliza Clark had expressed concern about Sallie Banks. In fact, she seemed nearly distraught that she had not seen Sallie in a while. "I am sorry my mother has not been able to come to see you as requested," Banks wrote, but "I am sure she will come as soon as the weather permits." He also apologized for not seeing the Clarks during a 1911 visit to Clarksdale. Banks did assure Eliza, however, that he would see her during the Christmas holidays if not sooner. He also reminded her that she and her family were very dear to his family. "Ever praying Gods' choicest blessings upon you and all the Clarks," Banks expressed his "high appreciation of the interest manifested by you and the rest of [your] family in our family."[47]

Banks thought people who did not live in the South could not appreciate the relationships that existed between whites and blacks.[48] While he may have been romanticizing about these "relations," his optimism about whites had been shaped largely by his early experiences with them.[49]

The *Clarksdale Daily Register* at the end of 1912 published an article by Eliza Clark that also portrayed the close and enduring relationship between the two families. In the article, she praised Banks's grandmother. Clark's comments were so full of praise that Washington after reading the article told Banks, "one can well understand how successful you have been when he reads of the stock from which you come."[50]

Washington paid Banks a great compliment with this remark. One's "stock" was indicative of one's status, and members of the "old black elite," usually mulattos, frequently placed a lot of value on the stock from which they came. For the elite, good stock meant free status during the antebellum period, privileged slave status during that time, or kinship to white relatives. One's stock frequently was part of the criteria for admission into the old black elite. Last, a person's stock spoke to the individual's general abilities and potential for advancement in society. In other words, success depended on bloodline.[51]

Banks at Rust University

Banks, with assistance from the Clarks, attended Rust University in Holly Springs, Mississippi, a school founded by the Methodist Episcopal Church through its Freedmen's Aid Society.[52] Founded in 1866, Rust was the oldest black college in Mississippi, and one black educator of that day viewed it as "one of the leading institutions of learning in the Southland."[53]

Originally named Shaw University, Rust initially opened as an elementary school. A northern minister, the Reverend A. C. McDonald, founded the school and became its first president. The faculty at Rust consisted of predominantly white northerners, who viewed themselves as missionaries. Rust provided students with instruction at all grades and levels, including elementary in the school's early years. For a short while before World War I, Rust even offered training in medicine and law. Nevertheless, the school remained basically a secondary institution until after the war.[54]

Ida B. Wells–Barnett, black activist and antilynching crusader, attended Rust. At this school she "had the guidance and instruction of dedicated missionaries and teachers who came to Holly Springs to assist the freedmen."[55] The education she received at Rust must have followed a sufficient curriculum because after she left, Wells passed several teacher examinations. She taught in a school district about six miles from Holly Springs, in Shelby County, Tennessee, and in the Memphis school system.[56]

Banks attended Rust University from 1887 to 1890 but apparently left school before he graduated.[57] Nonetheless, by the time he left Rust, Banks, like Wells–Barnett, had clearly received a sound liberal arts education.[58] A white writer of the day who held the same biases about blacks as many other whites, commented on Banks's command of the English language: "If one placed him behind a screen, so that he could not see his color, and listened to his conversation, he would imagine that he was hearing the speech of a college-bred American." The writer probably meant that Banks's diction and clarity of speech sounded as if he had attended a prestigious college in the North.[59] Among black aristocrats, the ability to speak and write proper English was essential.[60] Whether Banks realized it or not, he began to become part of the black aristocracy.

As a student at Rust, Banks became acquainted with the northern missionaries' view of education as it related to black Americans. They maintained that a classical liberal education would be the equalizer for blacks in social, political, and civil life. They thought that education would allow black people to assimilate into white society, cause whites to erase stereotypes of black inferiority, and also prompt them to accept blacks as whole people. Moreover, according to Cynthia Neverdon-Morton, black "colleges instilled in these students a lasting sense of responsibility to utilize the education they had been so fortunate to receive, not simply for personal advancement but to enhance the future possibilities of all Afro-Americans."[61]

The aim for equality through education proved to be idealistic and never materialized as predicted. However, many college-educated blacks carried out the charge to "uplift the race." These views influenced Banks's ideas about what college-educated blacks should do to elevate the race. While a student at Rust, Banks "made the most of his opportunities to prepare himself for the career of usefulness and success" he later pursued.[62]

Banks's choice of Rust University perhaps indicates his family's lack of financial resources to send him to a northern college. It is fairly certain the Clark family assisted him financially.[63] Many southern blacks who had money at that time, especially the so-called aristocrats of color, sent their children to schools in the North because they believed it was a means to keep or gain access to the inner circles of the black elite.[64]

Banks possibly chose Rust because of its proximity to his home and because of his familiarity with Holly Springs. Perhaps most impressive is that Banks went to college at a time most black Americans did not receive any education. The fact that he attended college at all, regardless of whether he graduated, carried a great amount of prestige, particularly in the black community.[65]

Early Work Experiences

Banks made exceptional gains in the working world soon after he left Rust in 1890. Upon leaving college, he served as a census enumerator for one year.[66] Around the same time, at about age seventeen, he opened a mercantile business in Clarksdale. It seems that early on, Banks knew what it took to become a successful entrepreneur. In the mercantile business, Banks "met with a measure of success that must have flattered his most sanguine expectations," notes one writer. Banks later invited his brother-in-law to be an associate in Banks & Bro. The general merchandise store grew so successful that some believed it a credit to all the people of Clarksdale, black and white.[67]

Banks had always manifested a fascination with business, an interest that perhaps grew from spending time at the Clark residence and witnessing John Clark's business success. Whatever the case, Banks displayed promising signs of business savvy early in life. "He always liked the jingle and clink of the dollars of commerce," notes one writer, "and their sound is as pleasing to [his] ears as the rhapsody of a Beethoven sonata."[68]

Banks's preference for business over farm work could have also stemmed from his desire to distance himself from work associated with slavery. Many blacks tried to distance themselves from so-called "nigger work," yet most in the South were employed in manual or domestic labor. They worked as cooks, house servants, farmers, gardeners, and laundresses. In 1900, a black worker was typically thought of as a low-wage, unskilled laborer.[69]

Occupational stereotyping was fairly typical throughout the South, and it definitely became the norm in Mississippi. Regardless of the legal status of black people, the planter class tried to retain the basic features of slavery. Leon Litwack summarizes the attitude of the black masses when he states that although many southern blacks did the same type of field work they had done during slavery, "scores of freedmen refused to resign themselves to the permanent status of a landless agricultural working class." Moreover, Litwack says, "like most Americans, they aspired to something better and yearned for economic independence and self-employment. Without that independence, their freedom seemed incomplete, even precarious."[70]

Family Background of Trenna Banks

In 1893, when Banks turned twenty, he married Trenna Ophelia Booze of Natchez, Mississippi. A light-skinned woman, Trenna was born in Natchez in 1870 to Henderson and T. M. Louise Booze, both of whom had been slaves and were fathered by their owners in Natchez.[71] The Booze family resided in the household of Trenna's maternal grandmother, R. Sullivan, a fifty-four-year-old housekeeper who was widowed by 1880. Sullivan, a mulatto, had moved to Mississippi from Kentucky. In all likelihood, she became the mistress of the white man who would be Trenna's grandfather. The 1880 census listed Trenna's father as black and Trenna's mother as mulatto. Born in Mississippi in 1849, Henderson Booze worked as a gardener, and his wife, Louise, born in 1853 in Mississippi, worked as a washerwoman.[72]

Gardening, housekeeping, and laundering were all low-paying occupations. However, in terms of domestic work, washerwomen ranked highest on the scale. Although they were paid relatively little for their work, washerwomen were afforded the benefit of working at home, where they did not have to worry about becoming sexual prey. They could also spend more time caring for their families. Notwithstanding, washerwomen were not guaranteed payment for their services. For instance, if they damaged the clothing of a customer or if a customer simply refused to pay, they had no recourse. This often placed washerwomen and their families in economically precarious situations. If their occupations are proper indicators, the Booze family had only modest financial resources.[73]

Both Henderson and Louise Booze could read and write, while Louise's mother could do neither. The Boozes had been provided with an education by their owners during slavery. After marrying, they had eleven children; Sullivan, who was listed as head of household, and two other people also lived in their home.[74]

With its proximity to New Orleans, Natchez became a city where "miscegenation was probably more pervasive than in any other Mississippi community."[75] Light-complexioned families, such as the Johnsons, the Fitzgeralds, and the Winns, "constituted an elite circle whose cultural and social pretensions approximated those of upper-class whites." Some of these same families even owned slaves during the antebellum period.[76] Others gained wealth from property and money they inherited from white relatives. The upper-class blacks of Natchez, for the most part, isolated themselves from people outside of their clique. A rigid color line as well as bloodline, or stock, was used to maintain this circle of isolation.[77]

Race relations in Natchez were different from the rest of the state. According to Jacqueline Rouse, "Many of the horrors of slavery were avoided in Natchez because of the extensive intermixture of the races." "Mulattos of these interracial unions," she continues, "were extremely conscious of their white heritage."[78] Many of the mulattos of Natchez chose to pass for white, and those who did not tended to measure themselves by the percentage of "white blood" in their veins.[79]

While the Booze family may have reaped some benefit from being mulatto in Natchez, they still lived very modestly. They do not appear to have had the wealth of members of the Natchez black elite. Nonetheless, the Boozes still provided their children with an education.

Education of Trenna Banks

As for most black people after the Civil War, schooling seems to have been important in the Booze household. Henderson and Louise had been granted the opportunity to receive an education during the antebellum period by their owners. By 1880, all the Booze children who were of age had started school and could read and write.[80] An incident involving Eugene Parker Booze, one of Trenna's younger brothers, confirms the value her parents placed on education. In 1886, at the age of eight, Eugene started a successful newspaper, magazine, and shoeshine stand. After he worked for four years and simultaneously attended school, his father made him close the business. Henderson offered "strenuous objection" to Eugene working "because of its interference" with his son's education. To compensate for this interference all along, "regular lessons were given [to Eugene] at night . . . by his mother and older sister, Trenna," according to one writer. His father later arranged for him to move to Saint Louis, Missouri, with Barry Parker, his godfather, where he attended school full time and completed sixth grade. The Boozes likely realized their children's education, along with their light complexion, could pay great dividends later in life.[81]

Trenna Booze attended Natchez Baptist College, founded by the Negro Baptist Convention of Mississippi in 1885. Some considered it "the Pride of the Race" and the most important semi-independent school established by the Negro Baptist Convention of Mississippi.[82] Although an observer called it "one of the leading educational institutions of the State of Mississippi," the school basically provided its students with an elementary education.[83]

Women like Trenna Booze realized the importance of educating black women, not only to increase their status but primarily because most of them had to work. Black men generally believed women should stay in the home where they could raise their children. However, at the same time:

> The men seemed to ignore the fact that conditions in the South generally did not allow the black man to provide adequate financial support for his family so that the women could remain at home. Many black women were forced to work in order to supplement the family's income.[84]

Negro women were restricted for the most part to either domestic work or teaching in black schools. Education improved their quality of life and shielded black women from sexual harassment faced in many white homes.[85]

Teaching was a highly revered occupation for black women because "it implicitly involved a commitment to social and political activism."[86] Many black women also worked as teachers because they embraced the Victorian idea that women were "naturally" better than men with children. Both black and white cultures still adhered to belief in the moral superiority of women. Black women believed that if they could reach the children, they would be uplifting the next generation of black people. And as Mary Church Terrell, a prominent club woman, pointed out, by working as teachers, black women could "escape from the limitations that the society imposed on women."[87]

Negro women who did not have an education were frequently forced to choose between not working in white homes and having their families live in abject poverty or working in those homes and submitting to the sexual desires and harassment of white men. Many uneducated black women worked as cooks, housekeepers, and laundresses to supplement their family's income. Although its pay was mediocre, domestic work often was the only work available to black women.[88]

After leaving Natchez College, Trenna worked as a schoolteacher in Mississippi for several years. Southern black female teachers were paid very little. They earned no more than thirty dollars a month, which equaled what some black women earned as washerwomen in Mississippi.[89] Although it is uncertain what subjects Trenna taught, black teachers in the South were responsible for instructing students in many subjects, including biology, cooking, homemaking, English, Latin, dressmaking, and history. Some people viewed Trenna as a highly refined and intelligent woman despite her modest beginnings, and after she married, she rose to a position of leadership among black women in her state.[90] Charley's and Trenna's lifestyle mirrored other southern black middle-class families.

Like many other upwardly mobile black middle-class families, Charley and Trenna had no children, and no stigma attached to them for this.[91] Many middle-class black women were involved in the business of trying to uplift the race, and they channeled their energies fully toward that pursuit. At the same time, they did not disdain procreation and proliferation of the race; they viewed both roles as essential.[92]

The few sources that mention Trenna Banks note that she supported her husband in his business endeavors and contributed greatly to the success of his career. A devoted wife for many years, she supported Charley and helped him "steer clear of the Scylla and Charybdis of business misfortune." This devotion is not surprising; it was expected among black Victorians. One writer praised Trenna Banks's "genuine hospitality" and "domestic accomplishments," two attributes widely respected among women in the black middle and upper classes, the black elite.[93]

The Black Elite

Trenna took on many of the manners and values of the black elite, as the former observations by her contemporaries attest. Like other members of the black aristocracy, she lived by strict rules that guided her etiquette, manners, and dress. The Bankses were part of the rising black middle class, or new black elite, who devoutly adhered to Booker T. Washington's philosophy of self-reliance and self-help. While they may not have qualified as "elites" by the standards of the old black elite, they certainly maintained similar values and decorum. Overall, their behavior accorded perfectly with Victorian ideals prevalent during that time.[94]

For acceptance in the old black elite, factors such as education, wealth, occupation, and skin color (the latter because many of these people were light-skinned blacks or mulattos) were considered. One's ancestry and family heritage was also important. If a person had family members who were free during the antebellum period or who fought ardently against slavery and made names for themselves, it often meant acceptance into the old black elite. Many of the old guard placed less emphasis on economic status, although most of them were wealthy. They believed if they placed less emphasis on wealth, they could keep out "unrefined" black people who had acquired some degree of financial success through hard work.[95]

The criteria for the new black elite differed. The new black elite were mostly self-made men and women who were usually less articulate and less educated than the old elite and who vigorously upheld Washington's philosophy of self-help. Complexion did not matter nearly as much as economic security, business achievement, and income. Many of these men figured prominently in Washington's NNBL.[96]

Physical Appearance

By the time he married, Banks had clearly made the physical transition into manhood. He would henceforth call himself Charles or Chas. instead of the more youthful-sounding Charley.[97] He stood six feet tall, had broad shoulders, had a "coal black" complexion, and was said to be of "pure African stock." Charles grew to be "a big-bodied man, with a shiny round head, [and] quick, snapping eyes," as described by Washington. "I never appreciated what a big man Banks was," Washington continued, "until I began to notice the swift and unerring way in which he reached out his long arms to pick up . . . a pen or to get . . . the attention of an acquaintance."[98] Banks was so big it seems he had very little difficulty in reaching anything he wanted. Because of this, Washington said, "there was a certain fascination in watching him move."[99] Washington also said Banks had the build of Jack Johnson, a famous Negro boxing champion.[100]

Others cited Charles Banks as a model for the potential and intelligence of dark-skinned blacks who appeared to be of "pure African stock." Many times when black people made gains in society and were successful in different endeavors, whites tried to attribute their success to white blood being in their veins. This explains how many whites rationalized the prominence of Frederick Douglass and Booker T. Washington, since both men had white fathers. However, Charles Banks was so dark, that reasoning would have been ludicrous. "Mr. Banks has not a high percent of Anglo-Saxon blood in his veins, as every one knows," said prominent Memphis educator Green P. Hamilton, "therefore, the Negro race is entitled to receive full credit for his enterprise, genius and brains."[101] Washington often singled out Banks and Robert R. Moton, Washington's successor at Tuskegee, to make the same point. On one occasion when he described the accomplishments of these men, Washington carefully noted that both Moton and Banks were "full-blooded" black men.[102]

In contrast to Banks's "coal black" complexion, his wife, Trenna, had very light skin. While light-skinned blacks usually looked for mates of the same complexion, dark-skinned men who were upwardly mobile frequently took wives who were of a lighter hue, and Charles Banks followed this pattern. His marriage to the light-skinned Trenna, as many black men thought, carried with it a certain amount of prestige.[103]

The idea of "white" being better than "black" generally permeated the thinking of black Mississippians during this era. Many fair-skinned blacks placed a premium on light skin and believed that if they mixed with someone of a darker hue they might "taint" the color of their offspring. In some cases, lighter-skinned blacks even tried to separate from the black masses. However, many were eventually forced to reevaluate their position after realizing that as far as white people were concerned, "one drop" of black blood qualified them as "niggers." Regardless of their complexion, they would be treated exactly the same as "niggers" who were "coal black."[104]

Several members of the Booze family were very light-skinned; some were so light they could easily have passed for white. Eugene Booze, the blue-eyed younger brother of Trenna, was so light one would find it almost "impossible to distinguish him from one of the white race." On one occasion, he was referred to by some black residents of his community as being a "half-white niggah."[105]

By the time Charles married Trenna in 1893, he had become a fairly well-established businessman. His mercantile business had successfully operated for four years. So Trenna might have seen him as a good provider. On the one hand, his financial status may have eclipsed the issue of his complexion for Trenna; on the other hand, she may have accepted him because her father was black and because she simply loved him. Paula Giddings has noted that for many college-educated women of that time, "marrying men of achievement was also an integral part of their determination to fulfill themselves as women."[106] This may have been another of Trenna's considerations, since she came from a family with meager financial resources.

When women married men who were prominent and economically secure, they had the flexibility of doing and saying things "without reference to dire economic need, or concern that they might threaten their husbands' self-worth." Women such as Ida B. Wells-Barnett, Mary Church Terrell, and Margaret Murray Washington followed this pattern. Echoing this point, Fannie B. Williams, a progressive black leader of the day, noted that "every colored man who succeeds in business brings his wife . . . a little nearer to that sphere of chivalry and protection in which every white woman finds shelter."[107] This was the desire of many black Victorians, such as Trenna Banks.

Home of the Banks

In 1908, Charles and Trenna built a house in Mound Bayou, Mississippi, said to be "the most palatial residence in the delta section of the state."[108] Indeed, the house had a gazebo and wrap-around porch. It also had two stories and at least two fireplaces for heating.[109] Such amenities were extravagances many blacks could not dream of owning.

Since having a nice home was so important to the social life of black aristocrats, they spent what often appeared to others a disproportionate amount of their resources on the homes.[110] In a letter to C. C. Buel, Charles Banks boasted that his "residence cost in construction, and furnishing nearly ten thousand dollars."[111] A house in 1910 that cost that amount was considered expensive by most standards and was almost unheard of for Negroes in the South. One observer described the Banks's home as being "commodious enough to house a small-sized army. . . . The rich barons of olden times did not live in more real comfort and security."[112]

In keeping with the values of the black elite, the Bankses realized they needed a nice home for several reasons. First, many black people could not secure hotel accommodations in the South, so guests commonly stayed with friends when traveling. If a prominent person came to visit, a leading family in the town would have them stay at their home. Second, considerable status came with owning a nice home. One could look at a person's home and draw certain conclusions about him.[113]

Other than church-related events, many of the social and fraternal activities of black aristocrats took place in their homes. Their homes were also used to host weddings, receptions, small dinners, and so forth. Mayme Louise Booze, Trenna's sister, was married at the Banks's residence on March 28, 1911.[114] The Bankses sent invitations to the event and were obviously proud to be able to host it at their home. Trenna Banks probably hosted some of the meetings of the Silone Yates Federation (SYF), a local black women's club, at her home as well. In fact, the federation was founded in the home of one of Mound Bayou's most prominent black women, L. E. Stringer.[115]

A genteel performance was expected from these families at receptions or small dinners, and they conformed to the prevailing rules of social etiquette without deviation.[116] Women usually served as hostesses at these functions, and Trenna Banks became "noted for her many domestic accomplishments and for her genuine hospitality."[117] Her activities demonstrated that she believed in upholding the values of the black elite.

Church Affiliation

The Bankses also followed the pattern of the black elite in their church affiliation. They attended Bethel African Methodist Episcopal Church (A.M.E. Church) in Mound Bayou, the town's second largest church in terms of membership. Banks and his wife followed a trend typical of many of the new black elite, especially the light-skinned ones, in trying to distinguish themselves by the church they attended. In some cases, people with dark skin could not attend mulatto-dominated churches.[118] The old black elite typically joined Presbyterian, Congregational, Episcopal, Methodist Episcopal, or Catholic churches. The old elite viewed the Episcopal Church as the most prestigious, followed by the Presbyterian.[119]

Many black people resented the elite for trying to distance themselves from their own people. Working-class blacks thought this showed that elite blacks were trying to become white. Washington frequently told an amusing story about the elite. He said that one Sunday an older black woman in Mississippi went into an Episcopal church and took a seat near the back. During the service, the lady started clapping her hands and moaning. An usher quickly came over to her to see if she was ill. "No sir, I'se happy; I'se got religion. Yes, sir, I'se got religion!" The usher looked at her in shock and responded, "Why, don't you know that this isn't the place to get religion."[120] Washington won the laughter of many black people with this story. He intended to show how far Episcopal worship services were from the typical black church services.

The division in the black community over church affiliation to some degree can be attributed to a difference in interpretation. Carter G. Woodson states that there were widely different opinions "in their ideas as to the importance of the church in the life of the community, in their attitudes as to the relation of the church to the individual, and in their standards of public conduct." Most of the masses believed "the individual should sacrifice all for the church." By contrast most old black elite, usually those of lighter hue, thought the church should only be "a means for making the bad good," and they saw no purpose in sacrificing all for the church.[121]

In some cases the particular church attended was more significant than the denomination, which was the case for the Bankses. The A.M.E. Church, the African Methodist Episcopal Zion Church, and the Baptist Church all had elite members. When the elite attended these churches, however, the preachers were generally well educated and the status of the members exceeded that of the Negro masses.[122] In Mound Bayou, there were two prominent churches, Bethel A.M.E. Church and Green Grove Baptist Church, the largest in terms of membership. Other smaller churches dotted the town, but they probably were attended by the common folk. Bethel and Green Grove were elitist (conservative) in the conduct of their services. "As a rule the services are well attended and intelligently conducted," noted a town resident, and their "ministers, generally speaking, are men of high character and well qualified for the leadership to which they have been called."[123]

Nevertheless, Mound Bayou had its denominational strife. When Eugene Booze, brother-in-law of Charles Banks, tried to establish an Episcopal church in Mound Bayou, it was a miserable failure. He secured $2,500 and a small plot of land, but the church did not draw many members. Led by the Reverend S. A. Morgan, Trinity Episcopal Mission did not exist for long. Town residents knew the church "had definitely been established for residents with lighter-than-average complexions," which they resented. This move prompted many of them to dismiss Booze as a "half-white niggah." Some blacks saw this as an attempt by the light-skinned residents to separate themselves from the masses.[124]

Although the opportunity presented itself, particularly with the Trinity Episcopal Mission, Banks never defected from the A.M.E. Church. There are two possible reasons for his unwavering fidelity. He may have stayed at Bethel because it had an elitist congregation and met his bourgeois expectations. Or he may have been committed to the A.M.E. Church because he had been a member of the denomination since his youth and because he had attained prominence and respect there. While in Clarksdale, Banks attended Friendship A.M.E. Church and served as Sunday school superintendent.[125]

Banks was very active in the A.M.E. Church. He figured prominently at the national level, and in 1896, before he moved to Mound Bayou, he served as a delegate to the General Conference at Wilmington, North Carolina. From that date on, Banks was chosen as delegate for his district for more than nineteen years. Even though Banks remained a layman, one of his contemporaries related that he was viewed as "one of the pillars of Methodism in his State, and his loyalty and fidelity to his branch of the great Christian Church have meant much to its welfare and progress."[126]

National Association of Colored Women

In addition to being active in the church, the Bankses were active in the community.[127] Trenna worked with the National Association of Colored Women (NACW), an organization whose motto stated its members were "lifting as we climb."[128] Founded in 1896, by 1917 the NACW consisted of more than one thousand clubs and represented some fifty thousand women in twenty-eight federations. Compared to other organizations in the black community, the NACW displayed a strong commitment to the idea of service to the race.[129] Most of the members were middle-class educated women, who worked diligently to uphold Victorian and Protestant mores. More than 65 percent of the club women, including Trenna, worked as educators. Some of them worked as hairdressers, clerks, seamstresses, or businesswomen. Seventy-five percent were married, but only about 25 percent had children.[130]

The main purpose of the NACW was to help elevate the black masses, because if they did not, members feared they risked being pulled into the lower class.[131] The social standing of many of the club women led them to adopt snobbish, condescending, and maternalistic attitudes toward the disadvantaged and the poor. Gerda Lerner notes that the welfare activities of the NACW "show[ed] strong class prejudices on the part of club women and reflect[ed] a patronizing, missionary attitude in dealing with the poor."[132] But while most of the women were elitist and maternalistic, the work they did to uplift the race clearly overshadowed these faults. Black women, moreover, seem to have been more successful than white women in bridging class lines.[133]

Most of these clubs engaged in a variety of activities, depending upon the immediate needs of the community. Some established and operated medical clinics, settlement houses, reading rooms, day-care centers, and homes for delinquent children. Others worked to outlaw lynching and established schools, orphanages, kindergartens, and homes for the elderly. The work of the NACW and its affiliates showed that its members believed they needed educational advancement to eliminate prejudice against blacks.[134] The state and Mound Bayou affiliates of the NACW were the Mississippi State Federation of Colored Women's Clubs (MSF) and the SYF respectively.[135]

Mississippi Women's Club

Like her husband, who held a high-profile position in Mississippi with the Mississippi Negro Business League (MNBL), Trenna Banks served as the president of the MSF, organized in 1903. Many prominent black women throughout the state, many of whom were married to influential or successful black men, were members. The goals and ideals of the organization were certainly geared toward racial uplift. Its stationary plainly stated, "the object shall be the binding together of our women for social, moral, and religious betterment, with the fundamental object of improvement in our homes."[136]

The state federation celebrated its annual meeting October 27 and 28, 1921, in Mound Bayou. More than fifty clubs were represented, with over one thousand members in attendance. Keynote addresses were given by prominent leaders, including Robert R. Moton, principal of Tuskegee; Henry Boswell, director of field sanitariums for Negroes and whites; and C. B. Thompson of the National Association for the Advancement of Colored People (NAACP). During the meeting, Alice Carter Oliver, who guided extension work for the state, directed "a pageant on correct and incorrect methods of dress presented by the delegates and local talent."[137]

Grace Allen Jones of the Piney Woods School in Braxton, Mississippi, in 1921 served as president of the federation, a position previously held by Trenna Banks. Jones outlined the goals she and her administration wanted to achieve: First, she urged the federation to cooperate with the Mississippi Department of education and the state teachers association in a campaign to "explain the compulsory education law to our people and encourage compliance with it." Second, she asked the women to organize more mothers clubs, establish a statewide education day, work with the state health department in the fight against tuberculosis, and introduce laws regarding child labor. Last, she encouraged the women to support the national organization in its effort to make a national shrine of the Frederick Douglass home.[138]

Trenna Banks also served as president of the SYF, organized in February 1909 in Mound Bayou. The organization was named after Josephine Silone Yates, who served as the second president of the NACW from 1901 to 1906.[139] The SYF in Mound Bayou was affiliated with the state federation, which ultimately connected it with the NACW. For a woman to join SYF, she had to be of good moral character and willing to work for the social and civic betterment of the community. The moral character of black women became especially important since whites frequently called it into question to justify or explain white men's sexual assaults on black women. The Mound Bayou club, which probably met weekly or biweekly, was "the intellectual organization of the town." The members were some of "the brightest women of the race in the state."[140]

Following the general trend of other local clubs, the women of SYF, under the leadership of Trenna Banks, made it "a part of their duty to visit the sick, the aged and worthy indigent," as a resident of the town observed, "and to administer to their necessities in every material way."[141] The women typically carried their Bibles and hymnbooks along with other items when they visited the sick and the shut-in. The club engaged in fund-raising for many reasons. For instance, they raised money to build a fence around and beautify the cemetery in Mound Bayou at a time when many black cemeteries in the state were not well kept. The work of the members of the SYF certainly adhered to the motto of the national organization: "Lifting as we climb."[142]

The work done by Trenna Banks shows that she upheld and believed in many of the ideals cherished by the black middle class.[143] The members of her women's clubs held her in high esteem, as evidenced by her election to leadership positions. She seems to have led the organization beyond rhetoric to active participation in improving the race. At the same time, she continued to conform to the role of the black elite.

History of Mound Bayou

"A Negro Metropolis"

It Isn't Your Town, It's You
If you want to live in the kind of a town
Like the kind of a town you like.
You needn't slip your clothes in a grip
And start on a long, long hike.
You'll only find what you left behind,
For there's nothing that's really new;
It's a knock at yourself when you knock your town.
It isn't the town—it's you.

Real towns are not made by men afraid,
Lest somebody get ahead;
When everyone works and nobody shirks,
You can raise a town from the dead.
And if, while you make, your personal stake,
Your neighbors can make one, too.
Your town will be what you want to see,
It isn't your town—it's you.
—**R. W. Glover**[1]

Mound Bayou's Founder

Charles Banks arrived in Mound Bayou at the end of 1903. Mound Bayou's history is both interesting and peculiar. It is interesting because of its rich history and evolution and peculiar because of its identity. Mound Bayou's founders claimed it was the oldest all-black town in the United States.[2] Since towns are made up of more than just structures, learning about the history of Mound Bayou and the kind of people Charles Banks worked with there helps one understand its critical role in his development as a leader. As an all-black town, Mound Bayou gave Banks an opportunity not afforded many other Negro leaders. Although he resided in the South, Banks lived in a safe haven, which shielded him from many of the trials and tribulations experienced by black southerners. This critically affected his role as a Negro leader.

Founded in 1887 by two men from Mississippi, Isaiah Tecumseh Montgomery and Benjamin Titus Green, Mound Bayou came into existence twenty-two years after the passage of the Thirteenth Amendment. Green, born a slave, grew up with the Montgomery family. He moved in with them at age thirteen and stayed there until he turned twenty-six. Montgomery was born May 21, 1847, at Davis Bend (the name for the Hurricane and Brierfield plantations) in Warren County, Mississippi, about thirty miles from Vicksburg. His father, Benjamin, was a favored slave of Joseph E. Davis, owner of three hundred slaves and older brother of Jefferson Davis, president of the Confederacy.[3]

According to Booker T. Washington, a friend of Isaiah Montgomery, "it was the express wish of Mr. Joseph E. Davis, after the close of the [Civil] war, that all of his ex-slaves should remain on the plantation that had been their home and the home of their children."[4] The Montgomerys agreed to purchase the 4,000–acre plantation from Davis for $300,000 in gold at a 6 percent interest rate per annum ($18,000).[5] They managed this property successfully and met their financial commitments to the Davises for years. During this time, Montgomery gained firsthand experience with large-scale people and property management. Benjamin Green, Isaiah's cousin, also played a prominent role in managing the Davis property.[6] Montgomery and Green were exposed to the concept of establishing an all-black community at a fairly young age while still at postbellum Davis Bend, and this profoundly affected their future aspirations.[7]

The "Exodus" movement, or what Montgomery called the "Kansas Hegira," of many of Davis Bend's tenants to Kansas in 1879 caused a severe labor shortage and sealed the fate of the experiment.[8] Twenty families, a total of about seventy people, left Davis Bend at this time.[9] However, many of the "exodusters" were disappointed with the poor conditions they found when they arrived in Kansas. In addition, many became ill from drinking water from the Missouri River, some contracted pneumonia, and about ten people died. Naturally, these conditions caused grave concern among the Mississippi immigrants, and some of them wanted to return to Mississippi; they called on Montgomery for assistance. Montgomery went to Kansas in 1879, where he witnessed the disheartening conditions. For those who wanted to return, he paid their way.

Perhaps the most important thing that occurred for Montgomery, however, happened in Lawrence, Kansas. While there, he saw about ten families from Davis Bend living as a community. After witnessing this, he focused on the idea of starting an all-black town composed of people from the same part of Mississippi. About ten years later, Montgomery's dream became a reality.[10]

The Founding of Mound Bayou

In 1872, one year before Charles Banks's birth, Montgomery married Martha Robb, whose family had been slaves of the Bridges family. Isaiah and Martha had twelve children, but only six girls survived.[11] Several years after the collapse of Davis Bend, Montgomery moved his family to Vicksburg, Mississippi, where he opened a general store and a restaurant. At that time, George W. McGinnis, a white land commissioner for the Louisville, New Orleans, and Texas Railroad (L, NO & T), approached James Hill, a prominent black Republican leader in Mississippi, about settling undeveloped land in the state. McGinnis wanted to discuss these issues with Hill because he worked for the railroad. Like many whites at that time, McGinnis believed black people were immune to diseases common to that area, such as malaria, and that they could work more effectively under extreme heat and humidity than white immigrants. Hill, already acquainted with the Davis Bend experiment, in turn referred McGinnis to Montgomery.[12]

McGinnis informed Montgomery that the railroad company wanted to open sparsely settled lands in Bolivar County, Mississippi, to black farmers.[13] When Montgomery first visited the site, however, he was not impressed. According to Washington, Montgomery said, "I gazed north and south along the railway . . . through the forest and jungle." Then Montgomery observed that "on either side were impassable barriers of cane which stood twenty-five feet high, interwoven with briers and thickly studded with mighty trees, some of them one hundred feet in height." Nevertheless, after assessing the land, Montgomery remarked, "This will do." He then told an engineer to "draw a plat of these lands . . . [then] send me one to the land office and make a duplicate. That will be notice, when it reaches me, that your task is done and mine is begun."[14]

To entice Montgomery even more, McGinnis promised him that the settlers would receive timber rights to the area and even more important, the railroad company would not cancel contracts with black settlers as long as they showed some potential for success. In addition, if a time came when one of the farmers did fail, Montgomery would be given an opportunity to find another Negro to move onto the land. From the very beginning, Montgomery and McGinnis intended this to be an all-black settlement.[15]

Excited by the news from McGinnis, Montgomery quickly contacted his cousin Benjamin Green, who had relocated to Newton, Mississippi, where he was conducting a successful mercantile business. Despite the horrid conditions in the Delta, Montgomery, Green, and seven other people managed to clear 90 acres of land in the fall of 1886. The site Montgomery chose sat in the eastern part of Bolivar County on the main line of the L, NO & T, twenty-seven miles from Clarksdale. In other words, Mound Bayou sat about halfway between Memphis, Tennessee, and Vicksburg, Mississippi.[16]

When the early settlers began to move to Mound Bayou, there were no houses or anything else. The entire territory, composed of about 30,000 acres, had dense forests and swarms of mosquitoes. Montgomery named the site Mound Bayou because of the large Native American burial mounds situated between two merging bayous, which ran through the town and served as a drainage system for the area. The founders viewed the land as fertile and ripe for raising cotton although it had not been used previously for that purpose.[17]

In the meantime, Montgomery began work as a land agent for the railroad and arranged a deal whereby settlers could buy small tracts of land, usually 40 to 80 acres, from the railroad company at inexpensive prices.[18] Although one observer stated that Montgomery "had no difficulty in getting enough people to cultivate" the land at Mound Bayou, the fact is that it took a lot of encouragement by Montgomery to convince Negroes to migrate there.[19] Fortunately, Montgomery apparently mastered the art of persuasion. He started by approaching his relatives and other people who had lived and worked on the Davis Bend plantation.

On several occasions while attempting to sell tracts of land to prospective buyers who did not necessarily care for the location, Montgomery made compelling speeches, appealing to their sense of racial pride and stressing the virtue of self-help and economic opportunity:

> You see this [land] is a pretty wild place. But this whole country was like this once. You have seen it change. You and your fathers for the most part performed the work that has made it what it is. You and

your fathers did this for some one else. Can't you do the same for yourselves?[20]

On another occasion he asked his doubtful prospects a series of questions to stimulate their racial sensibilities:

Why stagger at the difficulties that confront you? Have you not for centuries braved the miasma and hewn down forests like these at the behest of a master? Can you not do it for yourselves and your children unto successive generations, that they may worship and develop under their own vine and figtree?[21]

Booker T. Washington stated that after Montgomery finished preaching to these prospects, "the men picked up their axes and attacked the wilderness."[22]

Factors other than Montgomery's persuasive messages convinced settlers to move to Mound Bayou. The prevalence of "whitecapping" throughout the state was one of the most pressing issues considered by Mound Bayou immigrants. Although the term *whitecap* denoted any number of crimes perpetrated by whites against blacks, in Mississippi, the term referred specifically to an attempt by whites to "force a person to abandon his home and property; it meant driving Negroes off land they owned and rented." Many white brigands paraded throughout the southern counties of Mississippi, constantly threatening blacks and forcing them from their homes. Whitecaps would beat and burn Negroes indiscriminately and, according to Montgomery, they were especially hostile toward blacks who were farm owners or who rented land to black patrons. Therefore, many immigrants to Mound Bayou realized they needed a safe haven to survive and prosper. In a letter to Washington, Montgomery complained about instances of whitecapping in his state. "Thomas Harvey runs a neat little Grocery [and] he kept a Buggy and frequently rode [it] to his place of business," said Montgomery, but the whites resented this so much that "he was warned to sell his Buggy and walk [instead]."[23]

The Reverend C. A. Buchanan from West Point, Mississippi, who owned a successful printing business and published a Baptist newspaper, *The Preacher and Teacher's Safeguard*, suffered a similar fate. Whites forced him from his home because he owned a horse and buggy, which his daughter drove to and from work, and because his family had a nice home and a piano. Whites believed that the lifestyle practiced by the Buchanans "had a bad effect on the cooks and washerwomen, who aspired to do likewise, and became less disposed to work for the whites." Consequently, a mob of about one hundred white men went to Buchanan's office on a Saturday to order him to close his business and move his family from town by the following Tuesday. Luckily, Buchanan was two hundred miles away in Natchez at the time. However, the mob notified him by wire that he would be killed if he returned. His family and employees were forced to flee from the town and were not allowed to carry any of their possessions with them. Buchanan wrote the leaders of the mob "begging to be allowed to return to pack his belongings," but to no avail.[24]

Whites went to all sorts of extremes to force out blacks who, in their opinion, were setting bad examples for other Negroes in the state. They even posted threatening signs. "If you have not moved away from here by sundown tomorrow, we will shoot you like rabbits," read one of these notices, and the threats were not idle. While many blacks did not succumb to these threats and acts of violence, others did, as evidenced by the great number of Negroes from southern Mississippi who migrated to Mound Bayou and out of the state entirely.[25]

Mound Bayou resident Aurelius Hood commented on the "heavy tidal wave of immigration" of Negroes from Natchez, hometown of Charles Banks's wife.[26] A white reporter who visited the town also noted that "a score of White-Cap victims fled to the colony [of Mound Bayou] from the southern counties of the State."[27] Another Negro reportedly left his home and moved to Mound Bayou after being warned that he could not employ his children as laborers or sell or rent his land to other blacks on a share-cropping basis.[28] These assaults suggest that many whites feared competition from black businessmen and that they felt threatened by the potential of black success and independence.[29]

Montgomery tended to shy away from politics.[30] However, he served as a member of the Republican Central Committee in Bolivar County for several years and as the only black representative at the Mississippi constitutional convention of 1890. At this convention, under what became known as the Second Mississippi Plan, whites were determined to disfranchise blacks. The racist James K. Vardaman (who later served as governor of Mississippi, 1904–8, and as a U.S. senator, 1913–19) expressed the sentiment of most whites in his state when he unabashedly stated that "Mississippi's constitutional convention of 1890 was held for no other purpose than to eliminate the nigger from politics; not the 'ignorant and vicious,' as some of those apologists would have you believe, but the nigger. . . . Let the world know it just as it is."[31]

Even before the convention, the purpose was clear. Montgomery earned a dubious reputation for voting against black enfranchisement. He stated that it would be beneficial to reduce the Negro vote to less than that of the white vote via property and literacy requirements but implied simultaneously that this would make blacks want to secure wealth and education, thereby permitting them to gradually regain the franchise.[32] Montgomery apparently believed Negroes needed to establish themselves economically before becoming too involved in politics. He also believed that accumulating wealth would ultimately allow blacks to gain the franchise. Still, Montgomery's remarks may have been made for selfish and strategic reasons. They surely endeared him to whites and subsequently provided him with white support for his new town, only three years old in 1890.[33]

While conservative white Mississippians praised Montgomery for his actions, blacks throughout the country railed at him. T. Thomas Fortune, fiery editor of the *New York Age*, stated, "No flippant fool could have inflicted such a wound upon our cause as Mr. Montgomery has done in this address."[34] Many other Negroes referred to him as a "Judas" and a "traitor." Henry F. Downing, president and manager of the United States African News Company in New York, noted that Montgomery's "surrender of the rights of 123,000 Negroes upon the altar of expediency is an act [that is] unprecedented." Montgomery, however, believed that economic development, not political involvement, would advance Negroes.[35] Ultimately, the Mississippi Plan paved the way for other states to start disfranchising blacks. In some respects, Montgomery's remarks at the convention seem to have been a precursor for Washington's "Atlanta Compromise" speech. About fifteen years later, however, Montgomery conceded he had made a grave mistake in voting against black suffrage.[36]

Mound Bayou became incorporated in 1898, with Montgomery serving as its first mayor. Reverently called "The Honorable" by people in the town, "a harsher, truer title" for Montgomery, Saunders Redding said, "would have been Boss of Mound Bayou." By 1904 there were approximately 400 residents in the town proper and about 2,500 inhabitants on its periphery. From a business perspective, Montgomery and Green took advantage of being among the first settlers, opening the first three businesses there—a lumberyard, a general merchandise emporium, and a burial business—all of which were profitable. They also became land speculators and large-scale cotton producers. Whether they initially planned to become rich from settling Mound Bayou is uncertain, but Montgomery and Green certainly increased their personal fortunes as new settlers continued to migrate to their town. Montgomery also became the town's principal realtor. Montgomery was turning a profit of $8,000 a year, and one writer said he was the "only Negro in the United States who could put his hands on fifty thousand dollars 'cash money' in an hour's notice." Until an 1895 court order began to lessen their privilege, the families of Montgomery and Green maintained an economic hegemony over other town colonists. Nevertheless, by this time, there were more than ten businesses in the town, and in 1900 the L, NO & T built a new depot in Mound Bayou.[37]

Green and Montgomery had different visions about the growth and development of Mound Bayou. Montgomery wanted to create an ideal community that did not have class conflicts and that revolved around the family, schools, and churches. His vision focused on the economic and social development of the community, and he wanted the town to expand beyond its current borders. Green, who did not care much for white people, had a more limited vision. He envisioned a town with a few general stores, a permanent cotton gin and sawmill, and an economic concentration in cotton and lumber production.[38]

By the early 1890s, Montgomery overextended himself financially. He purchased an amount of land in 1892 that seriously tightened his cashflow. Consequently, he had to borrow about $10,000 from the owners of the L, NO & T to remain solvent. By 1895, he had fallen in arrears in making repayments to the L, NO & T, which had been purchased by the Illinois Central Railroad Company and its Yazoo and Mississippi Valley (Y & MV) Railroad subsidiary. Montgomery went bankrupt and his real estate was placed in receivership. Fortunately for Montgomery, the officers of the railroad worked out a deal with him, because he had "rendered the company good service" and was their best ally in Mississippi "so far as the selling of land to negroes is concerned."[39]

These financial problems created an unbridgeable rift between Montgomery and Green as early as 1892. All along, Green had thrived, becoming the town's principal economic leader. This added to the tension between the men because Montgomery felt he was the legitimate town founder and felt threatened by Green's increasing prominence. In addition, Green began to complain that Montgomery "consistently drew off the larger share of profits" from the businesses they jointly owned. So Green dissolved the partnership with Montgomery, and from that point on, enmity and mistrust bred.[40]

To the surprise of many, Green was shot and killed on January 24,

1896, after arguing with a customer over "five cents worth of rivets." One of Green's contemporaries estimated his estate to be worth $35,000 to $50,000 at the time of his death. The murder shocked town residents, because safety had been a major selling point and serious crimes were virtually nonexistent. In fact, many of the town leaders bragged about the strict moral code and low crime rate in Mound Bayou, which they believed showed that Negroes did not naturally have immoral or criminal tendencies. When couples moved to the town, they had to marry, and illegitimacy was not tolerated. One person who visited the town was advised that there were:

> limits to the sex freedom tolerated and when these limits are reached the violators feel unmistakably the disapproval of the group. Social disapproval is certain and severe upon the men who abuse the social arrangement by refusing to assume any responsibility whatever. The community places its disapproval upon "fast women" (women who try to take another woman's husband).[41]

Authorities later charged Richard Henry from Baton Rouge, Louisiana, with Green's murder, but never captured him. Henry had moved to the town from Baton Rouge and had been working for Richard H. McCarty for about two years. Nevertheless, for years after the Green shooting, crime in Mound Bayou did not increase significantly, but Green's murder would set a strange precedent among the town's elite.[42]

Regardless of his rhetoric in 1890, Montgomery became involved in politics when there were financial gains to be made. Upon Washington's recommendation, Montgomery, whom Washington believed to be "a colored man of first class order," received an appointment as federal receiver of public moneys for Mississippi from 1901 to 1903.[43] However, in 1903 a special federal investigator found evidence of financial irregularities. Montgomery had placed public funds in his personal bank account. "I have it from good authority," Charles Banks wrote Washington from Clarksdale in June 1903, "that it is rumored that the inspector for the department has recommended a change in the office of Receiver of Public Money in this state, charging irregularities in the management of same." Banks had not been able to discuss this matter with Montgomery because the latter was in the North when the allegations surfaced. Yet Banks did not contact Washington to defame Montgomery but to request that the Tuskegee leader help secure another black man to fill the position. Banks realized that the state's white referee, who was responsible for filling the position, already had several of his family members on the state payroll and "would not be averse to placing his brother in the place, should there be a vacancy." Ultimately, this would mean "shutting out the last that is left us at Jackson," said Banks.[44]

Amid these allegations, Washington had his secretary Emmett Jay Scott meet Montgomery in New Orleans to ask him to resign from the office. At first, Montgomery vigorously denied charges of wrongdoing and refused to resign, but Scott did not debate with him and eventually changed Montgomery's mind. Scott said, "He cannot now seek 'to save his face,' [and] . . . he ought to feel mighty glad 'to save his neck.'" After Scott became insistent, Montgomery finally agreed to resign.[45] He also repaid the missing $4,700 to the government before being prosecuted for embezzling federal funds.[46]

The affair did not sit well with Washington; he had recommended Montgomery for the position and the incident greatly embarrassed him. Scott summed up Washington's sentiment when he stated: "It is a pity that you have been betrayed by one whom you had trusted, but, but—it is the fates *again*!!"[47] Edgar S. Wilson, a white man who served as a referee for all presidential appointments in Mississippi from 1902 to 1910, was also disappointed by Montgomery's actions. Although Wilson had initially endorsed Montgomery, he later called him "a traitor to his race" and wondered how he could find another Negro to fill the position, "when I have endorsed him as the best, and the ideal man?"[48] Montgomery tried to redeem himself, telling his side of the story to Washington in a series of letters, but a disgusted Washington refused to respond. He had Scott "tell him that I have no power to change the decision of the Administration: I merely acted as a go-between, and as a shield for him." Washington further showed lack of confidence in Montgomery when he advised Scott to "be careful how you word your letter, as Montgomery is likely to show it to someone."[49] Washington's distrust of Montgomery made it easier for him to later support Banks as the leader of Mound Bayou.

Mound Bayou Enterprises

By 1912, after Banks had lived there for almost a decade, Mound Bayou had grown to be the largest Negro town in the United States. There were approximately 1,000 blacks residing in the town proper and about 8,000 living in its periphery. By this time, Mound Bayou had also grown in structures and businesses, with twenty-two mercantile houses, that is, dry goods and grocery stores, which did at least $600,000 in business annually. As the town continued to grow, many other types of businesses were also established. There was a weekly newspaper, the *Mound Bayou Demonstrator*, a post office, three blacksmith and wagon repair shops, three restaurants, two real estate companies, three shoe shops, several pharmacies, three barber shops, two watch and clock repair shops, a hotel, a cemetery, a telephone exchange, an electric power plant, a brick factory, a cotton oil mill, an ice plant, two cotton gins, and two saw mills. Mound Bayou also had an artesian well, six churches, three schools, a photographer, physicians, attorneys, a dentist, several lumber dealers, an undertaker, a tailor, several seamstresses, and a bank. Charles Banks in 1904 founded the bank, which the residents viewed as the lifeblood of the town. It provided them with the capital they needed to finance their homes and businesses; therefore, it became a key ingredient to the success of most of the town's businesses.[50]

The townspeople of Mound Bayou participated in a number of fraternal organizations, including the Masons, the Odd Fellows, the Knights of Pythias, the Household of Ruth, and the Order of the Eastern Star. A variety of other clubs for adults existed in the town, such as the Mound Bayou Business League (an affiliate of the NNBL), the Ministers' Union, the SYF, the Baptist Women's Union, and the Society of Renovators—the last three for women of the town. There were also societies for young people such as the Baptist Young People's Union and the Allen Endeavor League, named in honor of the founder of the A.M.E. Church, Richard Allen.[51]

Many prominent Mississippi Negroes filled the membership rolls in Mound Bayou's societies. In addition to Isaiah Montgomery and Benjamin Green, there was Joshua P. T. Montgomery, a cousin of Isaiah and the first attorney to practice in Mound Bayou; William T. Montgomery, older brother of Isaiah, vice-president of the Bank of Mound Bayou, and president of the Mound Bayou Loan and Investment Company; the Reverend Auger A. Cosey, pastor of the Green Grove Baptist Church, the largest in the town; Gertrude A. Jones-Bryant, principal of the public school; James A. Booker, Tuskegee graduate and special agent of the Farmers' Cooperative Demonstration Work of the U.S. Department of Agriculture; James B. Garrett, private secretary of Charles Banks; Thomas W. Cook, engineer and designer of the Mound Bayou Library and of the oil mill; Columbus R. Stringer, businessman; B. Howard Creswell, businessman and mayor; Eugene P. Booze, businessman and brother-in-law of Banks; Mayme Louise Booze, bank stenographer and Banks's sister-in-law; John W. Francis, local undertaker, businessman, and president of the Bank of Mound Bayou; Mrs. M. A. Lee, graduate of the Normal Department of Atlanta University, successful financier, and property owner; Benjamin A. Green, son of Benjamin T. Green, the first child born in Mound Bayou, lawyer, and future mayor of the town; J. H. Roby, physician; Clyde Lee, graduate of Meharry Medical College and physician; Scott Harris, another graduate of Meharry and a physician; Benjamin F. Ousley, principal of Mound Bayou Normal and Industrial Institute; Thomas M. Campbell, district agent for the U.S. Department of Agriculture, Bureau of Plant Industry; J. W. Covington, editor of the *Mound Bayou Demonstrator*; and Charles Banks, businessman and cashier of the Bank of Mound Bayou.[52] Based on various records, it seems that all these men and women were accorded high social status in the town.

Social Status

Businessmen and property owners in small black towns usually had the highest status.[53] Status in Mound Bayou, like other black towns, was predicated on family membership, educational attainments, occupation, and length of residence. Educational attainments alone did not guarantee acceptance into the town's elite. The ideology of these towns emphasized knowledge of practical skills; thus, economic stability, income, and business assertiveness were more important than just formal education.[54] Mound Bayou's artisans, small farmers, and laborers composed the bulk of its middle class. These people, however, deferred positions of leadership to the town's more "polished" and articulate professionals. In many black towns, ministers, land promoters, merchants, and bankers were the dominant leaders because these people (with the possible exception of the ministers) had capital and were in a position to extend credit to community residents. More often than not, however, the banker (cashier) wielded the most power in these towns.[55] Norman Crockett explains:

> in most cases the banker, through the allocation of capital in the form of credit and loans, came to be recognized as the premier citizen. In addition to their investments and financial control, the power of such individuals quickly spread to all aspects of town life. They presided over school boards and town councils, funded local newspapers, influenced churches, and organized lodges and fraternal so-

cieties. In a few instances bankers even displaced the original town promoter as the actual leader of the community.[56]

Within a few years of his arrival at Mound Bayou, Banks clearly exhibited most of the characteristics described above, that is, his influence touched all aspects of town life.

Women such as Trenna Banks, Martha Montgomery, and the wives of other town leaders, like their spouses, maintained a high status in the community. They assisted their husbands in setting the tone for the town and carrying out their agendas. These women worked in local community service clubs and labored diligently in the churches and schools. Their activities included hosting parties and receptions and coordinating town celebrations and charities. The SYF, mentioned earlier, is a good example of a Mound Bayou local club controlled by the wives of the elite.[57]

Without question, the most prominent persons in Mound Bayou carried the family names of Banks, Francis, Montgomery, Booze, and Green, and all conformed to the proscribed roles of the black elite discussed earlier.[58] Since they resided in Mound Bayou, this elite did not have to meet certain elitist requirements, such as strict ancestral credentials, needed in larger cities like Washington, D.C. In fact, the status of these families in Mound Bayou clearly placed them in the upper class, whereas if they had lived in larger cities, they probably would have been considered progressive middle-class Negroes. Nonetheless, if blacks moved to Mound Bayou and were successful in their endeavors, they were accorded a certain amount of status regardless of previous conditions. Persons related to members of the town's upper class or involved in business with them were also accorded high status in the community.

Many members of the prominent families intermarried. Eugene Booze, brother of Trenna Banks, married Isaiah Montgomery's daughter Mary. John W. Francis, business partner of Banks, married Ben Green's widow one year after his murder. Francis had worked as Green's store manager prior to the murder, but he took over the business after Green died. After the marriage, Francis became one of the most successful merchants in the town. Mayme Louise Booze, Trenna's sister, married James Garrett, Charles's personal secretary. Since Mayme worked as Banks's stenographer, it is possible she and Garrett met and cultivated their relationship in the workplace. Through intermarriage, the most progressive families in Mound Bayou were related to each other in some form or fashion. Early on, this helped unify the town leaders' vision and cut down on internal conflicts.

Most residents of small black towns like Mound Bayou did not attain the success and prosperity of the small elite class. Most Negroes living in and around Mound Bayou were poor, illiterate farmers who were working to better themselves and provide a decent living for their families. Unlike many other black southerners, however, they had the advantage of being landowners rather than sharecroppers. Most Negroes in Mississippi and the South in general had moved from slavery to peonage after the Civil War. By contrast, the average Mound Bayou resident typically purchased and lived on 40–acre plots of land, which they cultivated for profit. With cotton the major export of the town, most farmers were engaged in cotton production in some form or fashion. The average Mound Bayouan also did not have to worry about the financial exploitation endured by most black sharecroppers throughout the South.

Benjamin F. Ousley noted that many of the immigrants to Mound Bayou were poor former slaves who descended "from slave parents brought directly from Africa." He further describes these citizens:

As ex-slaves it is not strange that superstitions of Africa linger in the colony. It was only yesterday that two women told us how one had been "hurt" or "tricked" years ago, and how the daughter of the other had been "hurt" recently. Of course, there are would-be "doctors" who assert their ability to "take off the spell."[59]

While "some of the homes of the townspeople are substantial, and a few have very tasteful residences for a country town," the average citizen lived in a small cabin with two to four rooms, depending on the size of the family and its economic situation.[60]

Simon Gaiter and his family typify the experiences and vicissitudes of the average Mound Bayouan. Gaiter had been a slave on the Davis plantation with Isaiah Montgomery during the antebellum period. After being approached with the Mound Bayou proposition by Montgomery and Green, he moved to the town in 1887 and purchased a 40–acre plot of land. When he and his family moved to Mound Bayou, they had assets totaling $175. It took $165 to make a down payment on the land and to pay moving expenses, thus Gaiter only had $10 left after the payments were made. He cleared a small plot of land, built a log house, and planted a garden. Initially, he worked for Montgomery and Green, clearing land for the town at the rate of $4 an acre. His wife, Annie, and his children also worked, picking cotton and clearing lands. By 1890, a white family outside of Mound Bayou, contracted Simon to cultivate four acres of their land on a sharecropping basis.[61]

As newcomers to the town, the Gaiter family experienced hardships. Simon recalled that "many times we had bread only to eat and water alone to drink with it." Often they did not even have grease to cook their meals. They went without eating meat "sometimes for two and three months in succession" even though they hunted possums and coons on a regular basis. Notwithstanding these circumstances, the Gaiter family did well for themselves within a short time. By 1900, they had paid for their initial 40 acres of land and purchased an additional 40. Simon readily acknowledged that part of his success should be attributed to his wife: "I want to confess that I should not have succeeded, even as well as I have done but for the congenial disposition and willingness of my wife to assume on every occasion her full share of the mutual responsibility." He also praised her for "uncomplainingly submit[ting] to the hardships we were forced to undergo and the privations we had to endure."[62]

Wealth in Mound Bayou was unequally distributed and the town had a rigid class system. Much of the rhetoric spouted by Montgomery about the opportunity for success in Mound Bayou sounded good, but no one could guarantee the promise would be fulfilled. Montgomery did not always level with prospective buyers about what to expect if they moved to his town. Life for some new arrivals to Mound Bayou, such as the Gaiter family, was so arduous they found it difficult even to secure food.[63]

Still, no matter how bad conditions were for the residents, all-black towns were a welcome relief from the assaults and segregation experienced by Negroes in most predominantly white communities in the South. If blacks worked hard and had some degree of luck along the way, their chances for success were more than illusory. "The negro colonist of Mound Bayou owns his land, or rents it at standard cash rentals from negroes," noted a white Memphis reporter. "He hauls his cotton to the gins of Mound Bayou, stores it in the warehouses, and sells it in the market of Mound Bayou." Moreover, "he buys his fertilizers and his live stock in the town, and his building materials he gets at the Mound Bayou lumber-yard." He also "purchases his calico, his jeans, and his furniture from the Mound Bayou emporium."[64] These things are what made all the difference for Mound Bayou residents. The fact that the merchants as well as the patrons were Negroes generally ensured that residents did not have to deal with racial prejudice and discrimination on a daily basis.

Black professionals found this important because they had difficulty practicing in a discriminatory environment. Black attorneys in Mississippi, for example, knew they would not be accorded respect and that their clients would not receive fair hearings in Jim Crow courts. Considering this, many black people chose white attorneys when problems arose because they knew whites on the jury and on the bench would be more inclined to listen to "their own kind." Other blacks chose white attorneys because they thought they were smarter and better qualified than black attorneys. After 1900, some black lawyers could not even sit inside the railings with white attorneys in Mississippi courtrooms and others were not allowed to approach the bench. Still other black attorneys had to present their cases from the galleries. Because of the lack of clientele and income, many black doctors and lawyers looked to employment outside their practice as their major source of income. To ensure the success of Mound Bayou's business community, town residents were encouraged to support their own businesses.[65]

Living in Mound Bayou had both physical and psychological advantages and drawbacks. However, the positives far outweighed the negatives. After Banks moved to Mound Bayou, Isaiah Montgomery was relegated to the role of the town patriarch and Banks quickly became its "leading citizen." This troubled Montgomery, but ultimately he recognized the work done by Banks bettered what Banks called their "Negro Metropolis."[66]

Charles Banks, Booker T. Washington, and the Mound Bayou Connection

Philosophy of Banks

The philosophy of racial uplift advocated by Charles Banks guided the development of Mound Bayou. Many of Banks's philosophical ideals were virtually identical to those of Booker T. Washington. Both men had a deep respect for the other's work and ideas, especially during the time from about 1900 to Washington's death in 1915. When Washington attended Hampton Institute, the teachings of school founder Samuel Chapman Armstrong profoundly affected him. Armstrong placed emphasis on land acquisition, home ownership, and the development of vocational skills by Negroes.[1]

By the time Washington graduated from Hampton, he had become certain that the solution to the crisis in black life was economic independence, that is, Negroes producing goods and/or providing services people needed and wanted. If Negroes did these things, Washington believed, others would deal with them regardless of their color. He also thought white Southerners needed to be convinced that educating Negroes served the overall interest of the South. He taught that Negroes should be law-abiding and should cooperate with whites in maintaining peace. Moreover, Washington believed industrial education would create an economic niche in society for blacks without antagonizing or threatening Southern whites.[2]

Whites generally accepted Washington because they believed his message condoned segregation of the races. Washington made his position clear at the 1895 Cotton States International Exposition in Atlanta. Whites sincerely embraced his message that "in all things that are purely social we can be as separate as the five fingers, yet one as the hand in all things essential to mutual progress."[3] Southern whites also agreed with his public pronouncements that placed little emphasis on political rights, civil rights, or higher education for Negroes. White northerners believed Washington's teachings made for peaceful relations between the races in the South while providing economic stability for blacks and overall economic development in the South.[4]

Similarly, white southerners thought that by discouraging political and social activism, Washington encouraged Negroes to stay in their "place." In other words, they believed his teachings would ultimately keep blacks in an inferior economic and social position in the South, which is why some of Washington's detractors later called his speech the Atlanta Compromise. However, behind the scenes, Washington often financed efforts to undermine legal segregation. He acquiesced publicly as a strategy to keep the support of the white majority and possibly to protect himself.[5]

There were serious flaws in Washington's philosophy, some of which are probably more apparent today than then. Washington embraced the dominant American business philosophy of the time. He believed that if blacks could provide inexpensive essential products and services, whites would support them, because those things were needed. But by 1900 the theory of free competition and political individualism was becoming increasingly chimerical, and Washington underestimated the magnitude of white supremacy. Carpenters, brick masons, blacksmiths, and the like were still needed but not as much as before. Many of the vocations encouraged by Washington were rapidly vanishing. He did not realize that costly equipment put most black farmers at a serious disadvantage. One scholar commenting on this phenomenon asserted that Washington "utterly failed to see the relation of the laboring class to the Industrial Revolution and counseled an approach to the labor problem that had the effect of perpetuating the master-slave tradition."[6]

Recent scholarship has called for a reassessment of Washington, using his own words as a means of analysis. In the past, some scholars called him an "Uncle Tom" or an "accommodationist." August Meier and Louis Harlan accept the term *accommodationist* to describe Washington's behavior. Maceo Dailey, however, asserts that Washington considered himself a "constructionalist," and it is on this ground that the effectiveness of his program should be assessed.[7]

Constructionalists, such as Banks, Washington, and his supporters, believed they should "construct policies and programs to deal with the imposition and problems of racism, rather than react with mere words or with the threat of retaliation." Constructionalists, moreover, "viewed their task as constructing a community and carving out space in a country inclined to keep them at the bottom of the social, political, and economic ladder," according to Dailey. Washington and his personal secretary, Emmett Scott, even referred to themselves as constructionalists. Ultimately, Tuskegee loyalists believed that individual uplift, personal achievement, and steadfast allegiance to the struggle for Negro advancement would result in uplifting both the race and themselves.[8] To them, this program was more practical than theoretical and it moved far beyond the alternative, which often amounted to rhetorical discourse.

Records show that Banks and Montgomery, like Washington, were deferential toward their white neighbors and often pretended that race relations between Mound Bayou and surrounding white communities were satisfactory. At times, their seeming contentment with the maltreatment blacks received encouraged some whites to continue injustices. It also suggested to some black leaders that they accepted the often-repeated charge of Negro inferiority. A white reporter who visited the town expressed surprise at witnessing the "entire frankness and complacency with which they regard the fact . . . that they are in reality an inferior race."[9]

Many times Banks and Montgomery avoided being outwardly critical of racism and prejudice, especially of whites from surrounding communities. On one occasion, someone asked Montgomery if he was "afraid that from the whites who surround the colony a party of lawless men may raid your town?" His response indicated he felt Mound Bayou residents had nothing to worry about: "the better class of whites in Bolivar [County] know what we are doing here [and] if a raid was made on Mound Bayou, the [white] sheriff of the county could get enough deputies among the best [white] people in Mississippi to protect us."[10] Montgomery's apparent confidence in the goodness of whites is further illustrated in his response to a question about whether he believed there would ever be a race riot in northern Mississippi. He emphatically answered in the negative, because, he said, "up here our people are being guided by the wisdom of the best negroes in the State. And the whites understand this."[11]

Montgomery had good reason for thinking this way and for being so confident. The possibility of a white assault on the town occurred about 1913 when an unknown Negro in Mound Bayou shot and killed Riley Griffin, a white man. Griffin and his son had been drinking, and they attacked the Negro, who had been selling tickets at the town carnival. According to the *Memphis Commercial Appeal*, "Wednesday night was one of feverish anxiety among many of the negroes of this town, who feared nearby towns would attempt to retaliate." Fortunately, whites agreed the killing had taken place in self-defense, and "both negroes and white citizens of this county have joined to suppress any intimation of violence since the crime." Mound Bayou's leaders also requested the protection of the sheriff.[12]

While blacks and whites rarely joined together in such a situation, a more "unusual happening for the south—a really unheard of thing [occurred] in Mississippi." At the graveside of Griffin, "just before 'Ashes to ashes and dust to dust' was solemnly said, the white minister called upon Isaiah Montgomery . . . to make some remarks which he did, speaking appropriately." In addition, many prominent Negroes from Mound Bayou attended the funeral and Mayor Creswell assisted in digging the grave at the request of the Griffin family. According to the newspaper, after Griffin's burial, "peace and tranquility" returned to Mound Bayou and the surrounding towns, "and the best white people and the best negroes are working harmoniously together for mutual good and mutual progress."[13]

Several years later, another unusual event occurred in the all-black town. A fire had broken out in Mound Bayou's business district during the early morning hours. The conflagration was more than the citizens of the town could handle, so they called for help from Cleveland, Mississippi, about twenty miles away. The fire alarm sounded in Cleveland around 1 A.M. and "resulted in nearly the entire fire-fighting force of that town, all white men, coming to the rescue of the Negro town as quickly as fast-moving autos could bring them."[14] The strategy employed by the town's leaders continued to work to their advantage. If they had been viewed as radicals or as troublemakers, it is almost certain neighboring whites would not have assisted.

Publicly, Banks's view of whites who lived nearby was similar to that of Montgomery. He said their white neighbors laid "no barriers in the way of the effort to build up a substantial and creditable Negro town and colony."[15] He once stated that for economic reasons "the whites of [Mississippi] show a disposition to encourage and help this town and community." Banks believed that people who learned about race relations in the South from newspapers and politicians "fall far short of knowing what really is possible for the Negro in the South." Moreover, he said, "if there is any preference shown to Negroes any where, it seems to be to us [here in Mound Bayou]." Likewise, in a letter Banks wrote he stated that "the best feeling exists in this section between the races and always has."[16] These comments, however, were made to white men. His tone on similar issues differed significantly when he wrote to black friends. Banks realized the importance of "wearing the mask," as Paul Lawrence Dunbar wrote, when dealing with whites, so he said such things for white consumption.[17]

On another occasion, Banks expressed similar views to W. L. Park, vice-president and general manager of the Illinois Central Railroad: "the Negro problem . . . is being . . . well handled by the white man in the south," and "the thoughtful and right thinking Negro co-operates [with the white man] necessarily." Banks also told Park that if he observed the work taking place at Mound Bayou, he would "most likely conclude that it has not only been worth while to the Negroes who have done the work here, but to the white neighbors as well who encouraged and helped us to gain this footing." In this case, as in numerous others, Banks knew that most southern whites did everything but encourage and help them. But rather than reveal his true feelings about race relations in the South, Banks sought to convince Park to invest in one of his enterprises at Mound Bayou.[18]

Another time, when Banks invited whites to a ceremony in Mound Bayou, he expressed conciliatory views in a circular letter. He noted that while Negroes in the town were making progress and doing positive things, "the thinking ones among us realize that this progress could not have been made without the aid, indulgence, kindly feelings and help of our white friends." Furthermore, he said, "in many respects what we have done here is as much a compliment to the white man under whose supervision and direction we are, as it is to the negro." Banks used a lowercase *n* when spelling Negro in this circular because it went to whites. He generally did not do this when writing to blacks or to friendly whites.[19]

Banks believed that he, Washington, and other Tuskegee men were being criticized by some black leaders for two main reasons: for their policy of "preaching harmony and peace among the races" and for "holding aloof from politics." However, Banks made no apologies for holding these positions. "We know that a policy that makes for peace and goodwill between the races is best for all concerned . . . it is best for the commonwealth . . . the Negro has all to gain and nothing to lose by making friends with his white neighbors right here at his very door," he argued. To Banks, "the policy of the radicals, thought out a thousand miles from the scene is not to be compared with one intelligently and deliberately planned on the scene." In the final analysis, he believed that when poverty and illiteracy decreased, the philosophy and policies he supported would "be approved by sober judgement."[20]

An analysis of many personal and confidential letters written by Banks indicate that he said many of these things only to pacify and placate whites. Evidence suggests that he did not really believe them. He used this strategy to manipulate whites and to achieve his goals. This can be called a "black survival strategy" and it was often janus-faced. The tactic may have been Machiavellian, but as long as the end justified the means, Banks considered it proper. He explained to Washington, "I have adopted the policy of making the white man feel that he shares in the credit of what the Negro has done here at Mound Bayou." Banks went on to say that he wanted the white man to feel "that it is as much a compliment to him as it is to the Negroes of Mound Bayou for us to have been able to accomplish as much here as we have."[21]

Banks left no doubt about why he often courted and acted deferentially toward whites. The main reason he praised whites and took a conciliatory posture on certain issues, he said, was simply "to strip him of any fear or suspicion of what such a progress means to him." Banks realized he lived in a time when white jealousy could result in egregious crimes. Because Banks sought to avoid this, he often tried to convince whites that "it is [of] more real value to the commonwealth and to the business people of our distributing points to have thrifty, energetic and productive people like these who live here at Mound Bayou."[22]

Although he did not object to Negroes filing lawsuits when situations warranted such, Banks did not see repeatedly seeking legal recourse to address grievances, especially against certain white companies, as beneficial to blacks. Other black leaders thought just the opposite. S. Douglass Russell, a black leader in Langston, Oklahoma, argued that since legal segregation existed throughout the state, Negroes should demand accommodations equal to those of whites. Consequently, Russell filed a complaint with the State Corporation Commission charging that Negroes were not receiving equal treatment on the railroads in Oklahoma. Banks did not particularly care for Russell's tactics and claimed that Negro travelers from Memphis to Vicksburg were receiving equal accommodations. "There is a great tendency on the part of some of our people to institute suits against railroads for every little imaginary thing to say nothing of real causes," said Banks.[23]

Banks viewed these methods as counterproductive, because, he said, "we could hardly expect the highest and most favorable consideration from those whom we desire to reach when it is understood that we perniciously and indiscriminately harass the companies with law suits without merit or foundation." Banks believed these actions would offend many white supporters, so he suggested to Washington that they find some way of discouraging such actions by Negroes.[24] Washington, not surprisingly, completely agreed with Banks on this subject, commenting that "it will not do to have the railroad authorities get the idea that we are disposed to harass them with suits for damages in connection with every little difficulty which may arise." He went on to note that he would do whatever he could "toward discouraging such suits whenever opportunity offers."[25]

Another incident illustrates how Banks could manipulate the thinking of whites to suit his own purposes. While on a trip, Banks gave an interview to a white man. In return for the interview, Banks was offered money to cover his expenses. He refused the money, however, stating he "felt it would be out of place, or unjust to . . . accept." The interviewer was shocked, Banks said, because the "Southern Negro had been pictured to him as loving the coin so well. . . . [However], as Franklin says in his Almanac, I may have paid a high price for the 'whistle' but I think it worth the while." Banks did not refuse the money just because he thought it the proper thing to do. He felt that by doing so he could alter the man's views of the southern Negro. Banks, later commenting on the effectiveness of his strategy, asserted that the results were "drammatical and just what I aimed to do."[26]

If their public statements are interpreted literally, it appears Banks and Montgomery believed whites in Mississippi were genuinely concerned with their progress in Mound Bayou. However, this interpretation seems fallacious. More likely, the two men used this strategy to pacify whites and keep them from raiding the town.[27] If they could stay on the good side of influential whites, Banks and Montgomery reasoned, it would benefit the town in the long run. The riots in Tulsa, Oklahoma, in 1921 and Rosewood, Florida, in 1923 show how white fury and vengeance could totally destroy black communities. In both cases, white mobs overran and destroyed the community for crimes allegedly committed by one Negro.[28] It seems the whites were looking for an excuse to eliminate the communities because they were a source of economic competition. Thus, the white patronage strategy of Banks and Montgomery allowed them to accomplish their goals. Whites never came to Mound Bayou to molest blacks.

The strategy of Mound Bayou's leadership was similar to that employed by Washington, where he kept the support of his white patrons while behind the scenes he fought against segregation.[29]

As a result of this black survival strategy, many of Mound Bayou's leaders won the respect of a number of influential whites and they had an unusual amount of confidence when dealing with whites in general. In addition, a number of "good whites" supported Mound Bayou's leaders. In March 1912, Thomas Owen, a prominent attorney in Cleveland and Rosedale, Mississippi, stated that the work carried on by Banks and others "meets the approval of the best white people and unquestionably is calculated to do great good among the negroes." Owen thought Banks's approach to racial uplift would make Negroes "more useful citizens and [allow them] to engage in work that they are qualified to do as well as qualifying them for the work they will have to do." He closed by stating that "it is useless for me to say that the better class of white people of the state will endorse and do endorse the work that you are doing."[30]

In April 1912, L. K. Salsbury, president of a business in Memphis, said he had high regard for Banks's judgment when it came to financial matters and to "the needs of the negroes in the South." "I consider your judgment and ability and high standing not on[ly] with the colored people but with the white people in the South," said Salsbury. He also said that he believed Banks's leadership "is equal to, if not greater, than is that of Booker Washington." He went on to say that Banks's work in Mound Bayou and throughout the South helped "to harmonize the white people and the negro, and to show to each that it is to their interest to teach the negro not only to farm scientifically, but to save his money and plan ahead for a rainy day . . . and is working wonders along that line."[31]

Considering these statements, it becomes clear why the leaders and residents at Mound Bayou did not worry about assaults in their "Negro Metropolis." Currying favor worked. Ultimately the desired results, staving off white assaults and gaining the support of "good whites" in various endeavors, were achieved. Many of the leaders in Mound Bayou consequently were able to step beyond their "place." They had nice homes, carriages, clothing, and numerous other things that would have been considered "uppity." These were a serious breach in the code of racial etiquette and would not have been tolerated if the people had lived in most predominantly white communities in Mississippi and other southern states.

Banks also shared his thoughts about the growth of Mound Bayou. He had a broad vision of the town, as did Montgomery, especially when it came to expansion. In a letter to Scott in 1910, Banks noted that Mound Bayou consisted of thousands of acres of land and as it continued to grow, there was "quite a bit of adjacent [land] to be had." He wanted to devise a plan to "buy up all the contiguous territory available, and sell out [the land] to settlers in forty acre tracts [which] would help greatly our whole scheme here." He made clear his intentions for the growth of the town: "You have an idea what it would mean for us to ultimately control this corner of the county as we now control Mound Bayou."[32] On another occasion Banks stated that Mound Bayou's leaders always intended to have a community totally owned and controlled by Negroes, but "by 'enlarging the Mound Bayou proposition' I meant to enlarge the general idea of those who founded Mound Bayou." Now, he said, "we mean to have a larger and more pretentious town, and instead of owning and controlling 30,000 acres, we mean to own and control all the land that can be brought under our influence, and connect [it] to this which we already have."[33]

Philosophy of the Talented Tenth

Charles Banks and Booker T. Washington had many detractors among the Talented Tenth because of differences over how the Negro should gain advancement. Members of the Talented Tenth such as William Monroe Trotter and W. E. B. Du Bois, both Harvard University graduates, believed Washington's emphasis on vocational training rather than a rigorous classical education harmed the overall progress of Negroes. By the term "Talented Tenth," Du Bois meant a group of blacks who were educated and committed to racial uplift and who would lead the masses of Negroes to full liberation.[34] Washington's philosophy did not endear him to certain members of the old black elite. Some felt threatened by his teachings, particularly his emphasis on economic development. If common Negroes acquired substantial wealth, too many "unpolished Negroes," who lacked proper ancestral credentials, would try to enter the society of the black elite. If this happened, members of the old elite reasoned, they would no longer be able to use economic attainment as a major part of their selection criteria.[35]

W. E. B. Du Bois, who had earned a Ph.D. at Harvard, became Washington's foremost adversary. Du Bois believed Washington's emphasis on economic development would not help black men defend their rights and that ultimately Washington's "programme practically accepts the alleged inferiority of the Negro races."[36] Du Bois also argued, "if we make money the object of man-training, we shall develop money-makers but not necessarily men; if we make technical skill the object of education, we may possess artisans but not in nature, men." If Negroes conformed to the teachings of Washington, Du Bois believed, they would be giving up their self-respect, and he contended that "self respect is worth more than land and houses, and that a people who voluntarily surrender such respect . . . are not worth civilizing."[37] These remarks were leveled at men such as Banks and other Washington supporters in the NNBL. But Du Bois did not categorically reject industrial education for blacks. In fact, he stated, "after we have sent our most promising to college, then not only the rest, but the college men too, need training in technical schools for the actual technique."[38]

The Talented Tenth and Washington shared common ground on some other issues. Like most of the black elite, Washington was paternalistic toward the Negro masses. He also conformed to the rules of home life, dress, and decorum of the black aristocrats. Some members of the black elite supported Washington because they were dependent on his recommendation for federal political appointments. Washington's influence could literally make or break Negroes in public life.[39]

Banks's Relationship with the Tuskegee Machine

Banks established a close relationship with members of the Tuskegee Machine. He won the favor and confidence of Washington, the most powerful Negro in the country, shortly after he moved to Mound Bayou. It is unclear how long Banks had been acquainted with the philosophy and teachings of Washington, but in 1900 the men formally met in Boston at the first meeting of the NNBL. Banks, who lived in Clarksdale at the time, accompanied Montgomery to the meeting. Washington's belief in self-help, racial solidarity, and economic development must have struck a deep chord with Banks.[40]

Banks's correspondence with Tuskegee in the early 1900s shows his efforts to establish relations with Washington and his associates. For example, in a May 1903 letter to Washington, Banks closed by saying, "I have the honor to be your friend."[41] After he established a close relationship with Washington, however, Banks rarely ended his letters in this fashion. Early on, the correspondence between these two shows they were trying to feel each other out. Banks took steps to curry favor with Washington. Other leaders in black towns likewise courted Washington because he emphasized economic development and this jibed with their ideas about self-reliance and economic growth. They also realized that Washington, like many other black aristocrats, had influence and connections with white philanthropists and that those philanthropists had resources that could benefit the towns. Philanthropists such as Andrew Carnegie, John D. Rockefeller, and Julius Rosenwald frequently sought Washington's endorsement and advice before contributing to projects undertaken by Negroes.[42]

The plethora of correspondence between Banks, Washington, and Scott indicates that they were close friends who trusted and relied on one another. Banks purchased almost all of north Mound Bayou, made it into a subdivision, and named the principal streets after Washington, Scott, T. Thomas Fortune, Fred Moore, and himself, all in honor of the NNBL. Flattered by this gesture, Washington thanked Banks "for the compliment implied in naming streets after me and other friends."[43]

Banks believed whites supported the Tuskegee principal because of "the known saneness of your position on all public questions affecting the races and the South." He also thought most Negroes supported Washington. "You are deservedly popular with the great majority of our people, in fact, all of them," Banks asserted in October 1907, "with perhaps the exception of the chronic knockers and grumblers, who neither do nor approve anything."[44] The exceptions Banks referred to probably included Du Bois, Trotter, Jesse Max Barber, and other Negro critics of Washington.

Banks frequently defended Washington against his detractors. The National Negro Suffrage League, Trotter's militant organization, met in Boston, where they adopted the following resolutions criticizing Washington:

Inasmuch as Booker T. Washington has glorified the revised Constitutions of the South, has minimized the Jim Crow car outrage, has attacked the wisdom of the fourteenth and fifteenth amendments to the Constitution; has deprecated the primary importance of the ballot; has preached to the colored people silent submission to intolerable conditions and makes his people a by-word and laughing stock before the world, he is not a fit leader for the colored race, and no

President who recognizes him as a political leader should receive the colored vote of the North.

Therefore, since President Roosevelt has given him charge of the appointment of all negroes of whatever state in the Union, and has made him the negro adviser as to all policies affecting colored Americans, in the interests of our race we call upon President Roosevelt to dispense with Washington as our political spokesman.[45]

When these sorts of criticisms were leveled against Washington, his supporters frequently responded to the charges, often upon the Tuskegeean's request. This kept Washington from having to respond personally and also showed he had Negro supporters who appreciated his program and disagreed with his adversaries. Once when a magazine article criticized Washington, Banks sent a rebuttal to several newspapers in Vicksburg, Jackson, and Memphis, replying "to this unjust attack." Washington was pleased. "I felt quite sure that you could satisfactorily meet the allegations set forth," he said. "I am very glad you have done so, so convincingly."[46]

Banks realized that it benefited him to look out for Washington. While on vacation in Colorado Springs one time, he wrote Washington that he "ran across something which I think can be made of some value to you." Banks had met General W. J. Palmer, founder of Colorado Springs and builder of several railroads. Palmer, said Banks, was "reputed to be worth twenty or thirty millions . . . [and] has recently given that city a park valued at more than one million." Banks found out that Palmer respected Washington's agenda, and he wanted to coordinate a meeting between the two. He said he knew Washington would "grasp the meaning of this suggestion and take whatever course that seems best." Whether Washington followed up on this opportunity is not known. Banks also reminded Washington that he would do anything to help him: "If I can in any way serve you, I shall be pleased to do so."[47] Washington was assured he could count on Banks as a loyal ally, one committed to his philosophy of racial uplift.

Washington also trusted Banks to do special favors. On one occasion, he asked Banks to have a Chicago surgeon invited to the meeting of the Colored Medical Association of Mississippi: "In your own way I wish very much that you might arrange to have Dr. George C. Hall invited to the meeting." But Washington did not want it known that he was orchestrating the effort. "Do not use my name in connection with it," he told Banks, and he knew that he could depend on him to keep his anonymity.[48] Another time, Washington wrote to Banks, "Please let me have the facts regarding Meridian. . . . Be sure that no one in Meridian knows that I am seeking this information."[49] Banks clearly served as Washington's primary agent, or lieutenant, in Mississippi, and Banks told Washington who he could or could not trust on a regular basis. In responding to an inquiry about the Reverend E. P. Jones of Vicksburg, Banks advised Washington, "Rev. Jones is one of our good friends, and supports us strongly in all our messages." When Banks had visited Vicksburg, he found the Reverend Jones "trying to do the best he could for Tuskegee."[50]

Likewise, Washington looked out for the interests of Banks. Once when Banks sent a circular letter, Washington received comments about it from one of his friends in Washington, D.C. He quickly advised Banks, "there is much personal advertising of yourself." However, he said, "Of course you will know how to take the hint and be guided accordingly in case you think there is any foundation for such criticism."[51]

Washington frequently spoke highly of Banks, in letters, in speeches, and in the books and articles he wrote. On one occasion, he told Montgomery, "I have the fullest confidence in your fellow-worker and fellow-citizen, Mr. Charles Banks, and have the highest respect for him." He further noted, "I have not only respect for him but a deep affection for him."[52] In *My Larger Education*, Washington said that while Banks may not be the wealthiest Negro in Mississippi, "he is the most influential businessman in the United States." And although there were eleven black banks in the state at the time, Washington believed Banks "was the leading Negro banker in Mississippi." Banks is discussed in two chapters of Washington's book, and about ten pages in one chapter are devoted entirely to Banks and the Mound Bayou proposition. Washington saw Banks as more than a prominent businessman: "he is a leader of his race and a broad-minded and public-spirited citizen." Moreover, even though Banks did not hold a public office, Washington said, there are "few men, either white or black, in Mississippi to-day who are performing, directly or indirectly, a more important service to their state."[53]

Washington also credited Banks with being "the moving spirit of Mound Bayou." He advised potential visitors to the town, "Should you have reason to make any inquiries whatsoever, and especially touching any business or town politics, you will invariably be answered 'see Banks.'" The Tuskegee leader stated that under many different circumstances, he could not "recall that he [Banks] ever in any way seemed at a loss or in the slightest degree puzzled as to what to do in a crisis." Washington, more-over, said he believed that if the Negro businessmen in the state were ever brought together for the purpose of finding a leader, "a burst like that of a political nomination will rend the air with 'Banks! Banks!'"[54]

In light of the fact that Banks headed the MNBL for almost two de-cades, Washington's assessment was probably true. Like himself, Wash-ington viewed Banks as a man who "contributes toward the softening down of prejudice and the establishing of genuine confidence between the races."[55] Furthermore, "I have learned much from studying the success of Charles Banks. Before all else he has taught me the value of common-sense in dealing with conditions as they exist in the South," asserted Washington. "I have learned from him that, in spite of what the Southern white man may say about the Negro in moments of excitement, the sober sentiment of the South is in sympathy with every effort that promises solid and substantial progress to the Negro." Washington's remarks con-firm the respect he had for Banks. They also helped provide Banks with a number of white allies inside and outside the South.[56]

More important, Banks's role as a lieutenant made him the most influ-ential Negro in Mississippi during most of the Washington era. If any Negro in Mississippi wanted to secure the attention or services of Wash-ington, they were directed to Banks. If a black leader there wanted Wash-ington to speak in their city or wanted philanthropic assistance, they were in most cases referred to Banks. He in turn would consult with Washing-ton or Scott, then respond to the request. It became apparent to people in Mississippi that the only way to get to Washington was through Banks. And they could all but forget about receiving assistance from the Tuskegee Machine if they were Banks's enemies. His role as lieutenant gave Banks an enormous amount of power, primarily in Mississippi but also at the national level.[57]

Banks dealt primarily with agrarian workers, and most Negroes in Mis-sissippi inclined toward Washington's philosophy of economic uplift be-cause it appeared more relevant to their everyday lives. But if people such as Banks had not worked so hard at the grassroots level on a daily basis, Washington's influence would not have been as strong. The fact that Washington astutely chose influential men in different states to act on his behalf indicates that he realized the importance of allying himself with powerful Negroes whose philosophy of racial uplift came close to his own.

Banks established perhaps an even closer relationship with Scott, Washington's confidant and personal secretary. Correspondence between

Banks and Scott on occasion reached as much as two or three letters a day. As a matter of fact, the two became best friends. Besides ending letters with phrases such as "I am your friend," the correspondence shows in other ways how close they were.[58] On January 1, 1907, Banks wrote his first letter of the year to Scott, and he continued in this fashion until he died. Although this may seem a simple gesture of goodwill, Scott felt it an "admirable practice which I so cordially appreciate," that is, your custom "of writing me the first letter on the first of January each year."[59] Scott also wrote to Banks on the first day of the year for many years. [60]

Whenever Scott wanted information about people and places in Mississippi, he went to Banks. On September 13, 1916, he asked Banks to let him know confidentially whether Clarksdale Grade School, headed by George H. Oliver, was a "white or a colored institution."[61] Apparently, Oliver had gone to Scott trying to secure financial assistance for the school from either the Rosenwald or the Anna T. Jeanes Fund.[62] Two days later, Banks informed Scott, the "Clarksdale Grade School . . . is a colored school, and, of course, Mr. Oliver is a colored man." Providing Scott with more information than he requested, Banks said he had personally known Oliver for years and found him to be "trustworthy" in every respect and "a good man to work with in his line."[63]

Scott could not provide assistance to Oliver. However, Scott asked Banks to "explain to him that I have tried to help his cause by getting in touch with Dr. Dillard of the Jeanes Fund." [64] If he did not already know, this showed Oliver that Banks was being fully informed about his affairs and that he probably should communicate directly with Banks. Instances such as this helped establish Banks as an influential black leader throughout Mississippi.

Banks also did other investigative work for the Tuskegee Machine on request from Scott and Washington. For example, Scott asked Banks to find some information about Ray Stannard Baker, a leading reporter at the *American Magazine*. According to Scott, Baker had taken an interest in race relations in the South after the 1906 Atlanta race riot. Baker was said to be "setting forth racial relations in the South with a great deal of intelligent peculiarity" in articles, so Washington wanted to establish a relationship with him. At the same time, Scott worried "that the 'Trotterites' are seeking to guide Baker, so far as any favorable reference to Dr. Washington of Tuskegee is concerned." He asked Banks to write a letter directly to Baker to look into the situation. "Of course, it will not be wise, in the slightest [way] for you to mention" the request, Scott cautioned.[65]

In the letter Banks wrote to Baker, he suggested that "Negroes efforts at race building . . . [should] have some point in the articles." He also suggested that Baker mention Washington's role in keeping race relations in the South in a state of calm. Moreover, he said the work Washington personally engaged in and his work through the Tuskegee Institute were worth noting. Banks went on to explain that "the best white people" throughout the South approved of Washington's policies while the agendas set forth by his detractors were often futile and ill-received. Most of Banks's points ultimately were included in Baker's widely-read book *Following the Color Line.*[66] Scott made similar requests of Banks on a frequent basis. "I cannot afford to have you feel that I am taking the advantage of the friendship which has already been generous beyond my deserts," Scott said, after acknowledging how often he solicited Banks's help.[67]

Just as Banks did favors in response to Scott's requests, Scott made efforts to assist Banks. In fact, Scott became Banks's guardian angel at Tuskegee. They became so close that if someone wrote Washington a derogatory letter about Banks, Scott often intercepted the letter and kept it from Washington's knowledge. Scott must have believed it would be best for Washington to keep a pristine image of Banks. Scott also frequently forwarded these letters to Banks so he could respond directly to the complainants. This probably shocked many complainants. For all they knew, Washington was forwarding the letters to Banks. This sent a direct message that Banks served as a key player in the Tuskegee Machine and that backstabbing would not be tolerated.[68]

Scott also made Banks privy to personal and confidential issues taking place inside and outside of Tuskegee. "In sending you the enclosed letter," he once told Banks, "I am doing it in entire confidence and I shall ask you to respect my faith in you by not showing this letter to anyone whatever. As soon as you have read it, I shall be glad if you will return it."[69] On another occasion, he told Banks he had a letter Banks might want to see: "Of course, I send it to you in confidence, and [hope] you will not intimate or indicate that you are apprised of . . . the matter."[70] Scott also did other things to assist Banks in consolidating power. He found places to have Banks's articles, such as "The Negro Question," published. Banks had written this article in response to the 1906 Atlanta race riot and mounting racial tension throughout the South. He told Scott that although the essay "is not radical, neither is it conservative to a point that might be considered ridiculous." He believed that newspapers like the *Memphis Commercial Appeal* would either "'boil it down' or perhaps out it out." Ultimately, he wanted the article published in a northern magazine. After some maneuvering, Scott arranged to have the essay published in the *Tradesman* in Chattanooga, Tennessee, and reprinted by *Colored American Magazine*, which provided Banks an opportunity to express his ideas to a wider audience and receive greater public exposure.[71]

Scott also invested in many enterprises undertaken by Banks, including the Bank of Mound Bayou and the Mound Bayou Cotton Oil Mill. Scott's father even moved to Mound Bayou and worked for Banks as a supervisor in the oil mill and for the Masonic Benefit Association (MBA). Like Washington, Scott eventually had a vested interest in the growth of Mound Bayou in general and the business interests of Charles Banks in particular. A biographer of Scott noted the differences between Washington and Scott when it came to their friends. Washington rarely let his personal loyalties or friendships blind him to the weaknesses of his associates. By contrast, Scott on many occasions went to extreme lengths to assist his friends, including Banks, even when failure seemed imminent.[72]

On occasion, the spouses of the three men also associated with each other, which further sealed the bond between the men. Trenna Banks communicated with and visited both Margaret Washington and Eleonora Scott. Likewise, these women visited Trenna at Mound Bayou. In October 1912, Trenna visited Tuskegee. Although explicit details of the trip are unavailable, Charles Banks told Scott, "you know I appreciate what you are doing, and I am sure that Mrs. Banks will have no reason to regret, being at Tuskegee among our warmest and best friends." Scott gave Banks some idea of what his wife and the other ladies were doing one evening at Tuskegee: "The Madam [Mrs. Banks] is riding this afternoon with Mrs. Scott." Washington also noted that they had a reception for Trenna when she visited Tuskegee. Her trip seems to have been a pleasant one, because when she arrived back at Mound Bayou, Banks wrote Scott that she came back "loud in her praise for you and the good people at Tuskegee." Those at Tuskegee were thrilled to learn that Trenna enjoyed her trip so much and stated that "she certainly made a fine impression on all of our people."[73]

Washington came to view Mound Bayou as more than a town. It reminded him of a school, a place where a Negro, he said, "may get inspiration, by seeing what other members of his race have accomplished, but a place, also, where he has an opportunity to learn some of the fundamental duties and responsibilities of social and civic life." When boasting about Mound Bayou, Washington quickly mentioned that "black men cleared the land, built the houses, and founded the town."[74] He became so attached to Mound Bayou that in a letter to Montgomery he stated that next to Tuskegee, he could not think of any other place in the world in which he "was so deeply interested." Moreover, he said, "there is no community whose success would bring me more happiness outside Tuskegee, and there is no community whose failure would bring me more sorrow outside of Tuskegee than is true of Mound Bayou."[75]

Like Washington, Banks believed in racial uplift through economic development, racial cooperation, and self-help. He thought that with the assistance of a small number of good whites, Negroes could take full advantage of their segregated station in life. Perhaps more than anything else, ideologically, Washington appreciated that Banks "recognizes that, behind everything else, is the economic problem" and that he vigorously channeled most of his energy to that area of the struggle for racial uplift.[76] Living in Mound Bayou, then, helped Banks pursue his philosophy of racial uplift and at the same time gave him a platform from which to promote his agenda.

Leader, Organizer, and Promoter

*"On My Job All the Time and Doing the Best That
My Ability Will Allow"*

State and Local Leader

Throughout most of his life Charles Banks worked as a community and
race leader. Of the many attributes that aided him in his endeavors, his
leadership abilities stand out. Banks became affiliated with a number of
organizations in Mississippi and the nation. He joined the Masons, the
Knights of Pythias, the Odd Fellows, the National Negro Bankers Association, and the Negro Bankers Association of Mississippi, and in many of
these organizations he held positions of leadership.[1]

When events occurred affecting Negroes in Mississippi, people frequently contacted Banks for guidance. For example, when someone assas-
sinated E. D. Howell, cashier at the Peoples Bank in Hattiesburg, and
robbed the bank of $4,000, Banks was called to assist. After the robbery,
Louis K. Atwood, attorney and president of the Southern Bank and the
Mississippi Negro Bankers Association in 1908; Sidney D. Redmond,
lawyer, physician, and president of American Bank of Jackson; Charles
Banks; and other prominent black Mississippians called a special meeting
of the executive committee of the Negro Bankers Association of Mississippi to devise a means of restoring the bank.[2] It turned out that Howell,
who was also the owner of a furniture store and another business in
Hattiesburg, had been killed by his close friend Joe Williams. The trial
lasted for three years. An audit, however, revealed that Williams had stolen $12,000 from the Peoples Bank just a few days before he murdered
Howell.[3]

In another instance, H. J. Hutton, a black businessman in Oklahoma, wrote to Banks asking for his advice and assistance in establishing a Negro Business League for the state. "Knowing of your ability as a leader," Hutton told Banks, "I commit myself to your feet for proper steps."[4] Washington also asked Banks to go to New Orleans "for the good of the cause" and to help the Negroes there establish a state league.[5]

Washington and Scott went to great lengths to help Banks become the preeminent Negro leader in Mississippi, and their efforts brought reciprocal rewards. In July 1913 Perry W. Howard, a prominent black attorney and political boss in Jackson, Mississippi, informed Banks that William H. Holtzclaw (graduate of Tuskegee) wanted Washington to speak at Jackson in November for the Mississippi Negro State Fair and for "Negro Day." Banks thought Atwood was really the person "engineering" the event and felt that if they wanted Washington to speak, they should have consulted him. Banks told Scott that "in order to strengthen our friends there, if he is to go at all, [and] before he is committed to it, I would like to see that the fellows at Jackson, or the ones who are trying to get him to come, be referred to this end of the line." Banks knew Scott would understand that this would make it crystal clear that Banks was Washington's chief in Mississippi. "If he is to go at all, our friends should control the situation, and in this case, I should like to give [Perry] Howard as much consideration as circumstances will warrant," Banks said. Scott, of course, accommodated the request and even told Banks in a handwritten note on the bottom of the letter that Washington was "not going there . . . in any event!"[6] This incident is significant because it shows that through Banks's help and assistance Howard amassed power in Jackson. Banks helped Howard in this manner on several other occasions.[7]

About three years later, Howard wanted to secure Washington as the keynote speaker for the Mississippi Negro State Fair in Jackson, but unlike Holtzclaw or Atwood, Howard followed proper protocol. "I want to ask you now and in time to get in touch with Dr. Washington," he informed Banks, "and have him speak for us on the 3rd day of November." After Howard heard back from Banks, he planned to send Washington an official invitation. Furthermore, since Howard was in charge of the program that year, he asked Banks to introduce Washington on the program and help him in other ways: "I am going to depend upon you to do this for me. . . . I am absolutely depending on you." Washington did not attend this affair because of his failing health. Notwithstanding, influential black leaders in Mississippi routinely turned to Banks when they wanted access to Washington and favors from the Tuskegee Machine.[8] Banks undoubtedly understood that by controlling access, he increased his own power.[9]

As a leader, Banks confidently spoke out on behalf of the citizens of his beloved Mound Bayou. Part of his confidence emanated from the fact that he lived in an all-black town and did not have to worry about the haranguing he might have received if he had lived in a mostly white community. When the American Express Company published an article in the spring of 1907, stating that "no honest negro can be found to do the work for the company" in Mound Bayou, Banks promptly responded. Officials at the company apparently published the article because G. C. Kettering, a Negro superintendent, had been dismissed for stealing funds. To Banks, however, the article indicted all Negroes in Mound Bayou, and that infuriated him. He responded to the charge vehemently. "It is but fair to the Negroes of Mound Bayou to let the public know that he (the discharged agent) was not a Mound Bayou Negro," Banks said, "but one who had been in the employ of the Express Company, as an express wagon driver at Clarksdale, and brought here by them."[10] To drive his point home, Banks went on to say that "the public should know that when a few leading business men of Mound Bayou offered a real Mound Bayou Negro, one whom they knew to be honest, and competent, their recommendation was turned down." Banks took umbrage at the company's remarks not only because they misrepresented the people in the town but also because such statements could have adversely influenced potential investors and settlers. Banks closed his letter by telling the company that it "should at least let the facts bear them out before charging that an honest Negro cannot be found here to handle their business."[11]

On another occasion, H. R. Beale of the advertising department at Oliver Chilled Plow Works in South Bend, Indiana, wrote a letter to Columbus R. Stringer, president of C. R. Stringer and Company of Mound Bayou, soliciting a list of farmers' names so the firm could send booklets to them displaying the company's equipment. Stringer sent Beale a list of farmers he worked with in Mound Bayou. A few days later Stringer received a note back from Beale stating that "what we wanted was only WHITE farmers." Beale further advised that "the advertising matter that we send out is very expensive and we do not think it would be appreciated by the Negro population in the southern states, if, in fact, the large portion of them could read the booklets at all." Therefore, he instructed Stringer to be particular "in making up any lists for us . . . [so] . . . they contain only the names of WHITE men." If the lists already received included any "colored men," Beale asked Stringer to advise him accordingly so he could "return it to you for correction."[12]

Stringer must have resented the letter from Beale because he too was a "colored man." Stringer did not respond but forwarded the letter to Charles Banks. About a week later, Banks wrote to the Oliver Chilled Plow Works. He told the owners of the company that perhaps they "did not know that Mound Bayou, the town in which Mr. Stringer does business, is comprised entirely of Negroes." Quite likely he shocked them when he related that "Mr. Stringer is himself a Negro . . . [and] upon what you base your conclusion that the advertising matter would not be appreciated by Negroes here is not clear to me." He informed them that "the farmers of the community are distinguished because of their progressiveness, and have shown such a desire for up-to-date farming equipment that the United States Government has seen proper to place a [farm] demonstration agent here." Banks believed the owners of the company might be surprised to learn that the farmers at Mound Bayou were "really in search of more light on farming." He had his personal secretary forward an article about Mound Bayou, which had been published by *Planters Journal*, a white-owned magazine based in Memphis, Tennessee. Banks realized that an article written by whites would be more convincing to the company. He also sent the company a copy of the town newspaper, the *Demonstrator*, and other advertising materials about Mound Bayou showing how progressive it was.[13]

Banks cared about the progress of black farmers throughout Mississippi. Since Mississippi's economy was based largely on agriculture and since Negroes were heavily involved in farming, black farmers, especially in the Delta, were Banks's primary constituents. In a message to them at the beginning of 1910, Banks recapped their many achievements of the previous year. He praised farmers who had grown their own meat, corn, and hay and who had produced a surplus to turn a profit. However, he urged them to consider the coming year: "What of 1910? Will you not start out to do even better here in Mound Bayou this year? Won't you start farming earlier, and get the advantages which an early start gives?" He also felt there were other things they could do with their time which were also germane. "Straighten up your fences, whitewash the farm houses, paint the house, build new out-houses and otherwise improve your premises and make farm life attractive and pleasant," advised Banks.[14]

Banks had no problem chastising black farmers who did not keep up with advances in the farming industry. Once he told farmers:

Will you not subscribe for a least one farm paper . . . and keep up with what advanced thinkers on farming are saying or doing? I know some of our people think they know all about farming and do not appreciate any new steps in their line, but the fact that you have been farming, some of you since freedom, and still have practically nothing, living out of stores instead of living at home, having the merchant or banker lend you money instead of being able to lend them money, ought to convince you that your methods are unsound. . . . Raise enough of what you need and have something to sell.[15]

Banks believed that his advice was key and said that if black farmers followed his suggestions, they would "have a splendid opportunity this year to enter on the highway to success."[16] Washington admired the way Banks counseled the farmers in his state and thought that Banks's efforts were bound to accomplish great good.[17] Banks also went to extraordinary lengths to make the farmers familiar with the latest advances and to provide them access to persons who could give them technical information.

Farm Demonstration Agent

Around 1908, Booker T. Washington assisted Charles Banks in securing a farm demonstration agent for Mound Bayou and the surrounding area. Banks realized that if black laborers left the South, it would spell disaster for Mound Bayou. By securing a farm agent, he would be helping to keep black labor in the South. The farm demonstration program was begun after a pamphlet "How to Build Up Worn Out Soils," written by Tuskegee scientist George Washington Carver, caught the attention of Frederick T. Gates, who worked for John D. Rockefeller. Gates wanted to learn more about how southern soil could be saved, and he planned to use money from the General Education Board (GEB) to assist in the effort. About the same time, Seaman A. Knapp started a demonstration farm in Texas for the U.S. Department of Agriculture to show farmers how to plant and harvest cotton to minimize the effects of the dreaded boll weevil. Gates, who already had an interest in Knapp's work, wanted to see Carver's suggestions on soil preservation expanded to include farmers throughout the country. Eventually, the GEB and the Department of Agriculture agreed to pay Knapp to head a project to teach new methods to farmers throughout the South. Knapp in turn proposed that a Negro be placed on the farm demonstration staff.[18]

Thomas M. Campbell was the person selected. Campbell hailed from Bowman, Georgia, and his family had been so poor that at age fifteen he walked three hundred miles to attend Tuskegee. When he arrived, he had only fifteen cents in his pocket and only one change of clothes. Campbell began studying at Tuskegee in the lowest grade and completed all his studies there in seven years. He graduated on May 26, 1906, and became demonstration agent for the Bureau of Plant Industry, U.S. Department of Agriculture, that fall. By March 1908, he received a promotion to district agent, with four local agents working under him. His territory included Alabama and Mississippi, and he had a local headquarters at Mound Bayou, although he worked primarily from Tuskegee. A large share of Campbell's work consisted of introducing the study of agriculture in Negro schools throughout Alabama and Mississippi.[19]

As a result of Banks's efforts and Washington's influence with Republican Party leaders, the U.S. Department of Agriculture placed a full-time demonstration agent at Mound Bayou by December 1907. The agent worked under the direction of Campbell and Knapp. Washington said he considered Knapp "a very fine man [who] is doing much to help our people in agricultural directions."[20] That was not altogether true, however. Although Knapp provided support for some Negro agents, he did not commit proportional agency resources to black farmers.[21] Nonetheless, Banks liked having an agent in his town for demonstration work and assured Washington that they would "endeavor to lend all help and encouragement needed" to make the person successful.[22]

Ultimately, James A. Booker became the demonstration agent at Mound Bayou. Born in 1875, Booker hailed from Cannelton, West Virginia, where he attended public school. He later attended and graduated from the West Virginia Colored Institute. Booker completed the curriculum for the Normal and Agricultural Department of the West Virginia Institute in 1903, and in 1904 he returned there to teach. Two years later, he entered the Tuskegee Institute where he ably completed a two-year post-graduate course in agriculture in only one year. In 1908, he was appointed as a special agent for the Farmers' Cooperative Demonstration Work of the U.S. Department of Agriculture, located at Mound Bayou.[23]

Banks often served as a liaison between the farmers and Booker, and he approved of what Booker was doing for the farmers in and around Mound Bayou.[24] The agent was required to "make demonstrations of the best methods of farming and to teach practical things along the line of agricultural economy."[25] Farmers were very receptive. "Our farmers all speak encouragingly of the work," Banks told Booker. Still he suggested Booker call a meeting at one of the churches, "so that we may all have a testimonial meeting, and get additional inspiration to go forward in the work yet before us."[26]

The demonstration work went so well in Mound Bayou that in January 1909, Banks told Knapp that Tuskegee was sending a Jesup Agricultural Wagon to assist the demonstration agent in his work. Banks realized that this would be an incentive that would encourage black laborers to stay in Mound Bayou. Developed by Booker T. Washington in 1904, the mule-drawn Jesup Wagon was an agricultural school on wheels, designed to spread the "gospel of 256 improved methods of farming." The Jesup Wagon stood twelve feet high by twelve feet long with a movable canvas that could be adjusted in case of rain. As a mobile school, it became a convenient way to teach Negro farmers about improved farming methods and implements.[27] The wagon was named for Morris K. Jesup, a New York banker, philanthropist, and contributor to Tuskegee who provided the funds needed to build, supply, and operate the wagon, including a mule and harness. Washington convinced Jesup to provide Mound Bayou with a wagon, and Tuskegee and Mound Bayou received a grant from the Slater Fund, directed by James Dillard, to cover operating expenses.[28]

Early on, Banks requested that Campbell, who had considerable experience with the mobile school, come to Mound Bayou and assist Booker in getting the wagon started.[29] Washington approved Banks's request. By May 1910, Washington became concerned about whether Booker was using the Jesup Wagon at Mound Bayou frequently enough. He cautioned Banks that the town might lose the wagon and its funding.[30] Nevertheless, on May 31, Washington told Banks he had a thousand dollars at Tuskegee for the Mound Bayou wagon.[31] Notwithstanding, Banks felt compelled to discuss the issue with Booker. Booker later apologized to Washington for not using the wagon more frequently, and he promised to start using it again in June 1910. In fact, he specified seven dates the wagon would be used and announced that new features would be added.[32]

Meanwhile, Banks worked hard to provide access to new and different farming methods for the farmers in his community. He had Campbell assist Booker with the first Bolivar County Negro Fair. Impressed with Campbell's contributions, Banks told Washington that Campbell had helped make the fair the best ever held in the county. In addition, he said that Campbell had helped spur a greater sense of competitiveness among the Negro farmers of Bolivar County, something they wanted for a long time.[33] Overall, Banks observed, Booker's "efforts to have our people farm better, raise more for home consumption, and otherwise increase the pleasure of farm life have had large and beneficial results." Moreover, he thought that Booker and the Department of Agriculture should be acknowledged for their contribution to the prosperity the farmers in his vicinity were enjoying.[34]

About three years later, however, Banks asked Washington to help him find another person to take Booker's place, because he feared Booker had "served his usefulness."[35] In compliance with Banks's request, Washington arranged for Booker to be replaced by the end of 1911.[36] It appears that a Mr. Beck filled the slot.[37] However, shortly after Beck took the job, Banks expressed displeasure with his performance. Such matters often kept Banks busy on the home front. In fact, he confessed to Washington that he felt "fully loaded down with mammoth proportions" from handling so many different things.[38] Nonetheless, problems continued to abound for Banks. For instance, he discovered that Campbell had requested Beck to provide him with some exhibits for the demonstration work but that Beck had not complied. "This is the first intimation I have had that exhibits were wanted," Banks told Campbell, "and I have seen Mr. Beck constantly every day but he has never mentioned the matter to me." Furthermore, Banks said:

> I think Mr. Beck makes a good speech but as a hustler and worker among the people whom he is intended to help, it begins to look as though he is even more wanting than the man whom he succeeded.

> Up to the present my experience has been that these fellows are more anxious to find a place where they can be on a pay roll and draw more money than they are to do the real work.[39]

Banks did not want Campbell to think he had problems with all the men sent to help in Mound Bayou. "I am here on my job all the time and doing the best that my ability will allow and I am satisfied that only such a spirit can be of genuine, effective help here," he said, and that "unless a fellow means to get to work in real earnest with a view of doing what his hands finds to do, there is but little use to send him here." If better people were not found to fill the job, Banks worried, those funding the project would be greatly disappointed with the results. In closing, Banks told Campbell that he wrote him frankly so they could resolve his concerns about Beck and get some real good out of Tuskegee's efforts to help them.[40] Banks sent a copy of the letter to Washington and Scott to inform them of his dissatisfaction with the agents.[41]

Organizer and Promoter

One of Charles Banks's greatest assets was his ability to organize and promote. For example, after securing 40,000 acres of land south of Pine Bluff, Arkansas, Banks, along with J. A. Patterson, founded another Negro colony in a sawmill community called Peace. Banks never moved there, however, and Patterson became the patriarch of the settlement.[42]

In March 1907, Washington asked Banks him to help him collect money to keep the Frederick Douglass home in Anacostia, D.C., from being closed. Banks responded accordingly and began to solicit funds throughout Mississippi.[43] As a result of the fund-raising efforts of Banks, Washington, and many others, the Douglass home was kept open.

Washington knew of Banks's superior organizational skills and frequently solicited his support. Perhaps the best example of Banks's skills is his coordination of Washington's tour throughout the state of Mississippi in October 1908. Washington had taken similar tours through other states, including Arkansas and the Oklahoma and Indian Territories, and those had won considerable support for his agenda. Through these tours, Washington said, he wanted "to meet the masses of my people and to instruct them as far as I can through speaking and to help them in their industrial and moral life."[44] By mid 1908, Banks had organized a full schedule to ensure that as many Mississippians as possible, both black and white, would be exposed to Washington. The schedule was as follows: Holly Springs, October 5; Jackson, October 6; Natchez, October 7; Vicksburg, October 8; Greenville, October 9; Mound Bayou, October 10; and Helena, Arkansas, October 11.[45]

After being given the task of coordinating the tour, Banks began to collect information about each city he scheduled Washington to visit and gave him the names of prominent people who lived in each. Banks briefed Washington about Thomas W. Stringer of Vicksburg, who served as a presiding elder of the A.M.E. Church. Stringer served as the leader in church and lodges in the state, and he founded the Masonic order in Mississippi as well as the Knights of Pythias. Then Banks told Washington that "a reference to him is easily a great hit anywhere in Mississippi, and especially Vicksburg." In addition, Banks provided Washington with information about key landmarks in the state.[46] Banks also negotiated reduced rates from the railroad. This took a tremendous amount of bargaining, but in the end, Banks secured very inexpensive fares for Washington and his entourage. Furthermore, those interested in hearing Washington could receive twenty-five-cent fares from stations within a fifty-mile radius of each city at which he spoke.[47]

Banks became the major promoter of this tour, which ultimately brought publicity to himself and to Mound Bayou. "Get hold of the leading white papers in every community where I am to speak," Washington told Banks, and "arrange for the attendance of as many white people as you possibly can at the places where I am to speak."[48] Banks began writing newspaper editors asking them to publicize Washington's tour.[49] Banks also wrote Howard in Jackson, requesting that he use his influence to make sure the leading white people were invited to hear the address of "Dr. Booker T. Washington."[50]

Banks wanted to show Washington how much he and other Mississippians appreciated his coming to the state. Although Washington did not plan to charge a fee for the tour, Banks began to solicit money from fellow Mississippians. He asked them to have their "local committees raise and tender to him [Washington] a purse equivalent to the amount expended by him in going from place to place." The amount Banks estimated each committee would need to raise ranged from $75 to $100. Banks made it clear, however, that he was requesting the money without Washington's "knowledge or consent . . . because I believe it right and proper . . . [and] I understand that similar courtesies were shown him on similar trips."[51]

When Washington found out about Banks's actions, however, he told him point-blank: "Don't do this." Emmett Scott reiterated the point to Banks on two occasions. The first time, Scott told him that "the Doctor very earnestly objects to propositions of purses being raised by local committees." The second time, the tone was stronger, enough for Banks to realize that he should cease his efforts. According to Scott, "the Doctor rather feels that no obligation should be put upon the people to tender him a purse of any kind. . . . Will you call off the whole business at once?" Scott related further that Washington had suggested he wire this information to Banks instead of writing, which would have taken longer.[52]

After receiving this stern message, Banks felt compelled to explain his actions to Washington, to let him know why he inaugurated the "movement for the purse" in the first place:

> The railroad will require fares paid for eighteen [people] in addition to the charge for tourist sleepers. As we will have to get about ten or

twelve more besides those who will come with you, and they must be selected and invited, I thought to have them feel that they were your guests on the car in full, and at the same time have our local committees raise amounts equivalent to the entire expense of the car.[53]

After reflecting on his plan, Banks noted that he felt "inclined to think this method would give color, rather than detract from the beauty of the trip." Nevertheless, he assured Washington that he had ceased his fundraising. However, Banks explained to Washington, although he had dropped his requests for money from the local committees, the railroad still would be expecting a payment of fares for eighteen people from each place. Thus, he wanted to know how Washington planned to handle this.[54]

Banks apparently had more insight as to what was needed to cover expenses for the trip and had, perhaps, thought out the matter more thoroughly than Washington or Scott. Only six days after Banks wrote Washington about canceling the purse, Scott sent Banks a letter requesting money for the trip: "Will you not, at your convenience, let Dr. Washington know at Tuskegee, just exactly what you and the local league of Mississippi can do in the way of bearing any part of these expenses. . . . We wish to know this as far in advance as possible so that we shall know just exactly what to depend upon."[55]

Banks was puzzled by Scott's request, and although Scott asked him to keep the request secret from Washington, Banks decided to go directly to the latter, telling Washington that he was "somewhat at sea regarding Scott's letter." This gave Banks an opportunity to show his plans were correct in the first place. "Mr. Scott asks what the local league of Mississippi and myself would do in the way of helping out on the R.R. expense," he said, but "you will doubtless remember wiring me to recall my letter requesting local committees to . . . cover your expenses." Banks went on to say that while he had initially received favorable responses from people he had written, after he received the telegram, he immediately wrote back to them stating that they would not have to cover any expenses. To maintain his credibility, Banks said, he could "hardly now go back to them with the suggestion as given me by Mr. Scott."[56] Banks made it known, however, that he would still personally give as much as possible. Eventually, Washington ended up soliciting funds from other sources; for instance, J. T. Harahan, president of Illinois Central Railroad was asked if he would do anything to help reduce his expenses.[57]

Scott had placed Banks in a precarious position by asking him to go

behind Washington's back to solicit funds again from the local committees. However, Banks stood up for himself and addressed the matter directly with Washington. Although he wrote his letter directly to Washington, he sent Scott a copy. This let Scott know that Banks did not intend
to undermine him by going behind his back. At the same time, Scott could
have intercepted Banks's letter and prevented Washington from seeing it.
Despite all this, Banks continued to make arrangements for the tour.

When Washington arrived in Holly Springs on October 5, a crowd of
three thousand greeted him. While there, he spoke at Rust University and
at the Theological and Industrial Institute, founded by Bishop Elias
Cottrell of the Colored Methodist Episcopal Church. At Rust, Washington spoke to a gathering of about eighteen hundred and had an even larger
crowd waiting for him outside the assembly room. Washington gave basically the same speech in all the cities he visited. Throughout the oration,
he was frequently interrupted by bursts of thunderous applause, which
affirmed that his audience agreed with his views on race relations, education, and economic development. Washington started the speech at Rust
slowly: "I have but one objective in view in coming here and that is to see
for myself some of the progress of my own race and to say what I could
. . . in the direction of helping to improve their industrial, educational,
moral, and religious life and to strengthen friendly relations between the
white race and the black race." Then Washington moved into the sub-
stance of the speech. One observer commented, "Dr. Washington delivered plain, inspiring and practical talks which the people warmly received." Later that evening, Washington and his entourage attended a
dinner and reception at the home of Bishop Cottrell.[58]

A distinguished coterie accompanied Washington throughout the tour,
including Emmett Scott, his personal secretary; Nathan Hunt, his stenog-
rapher; Major Robert R. Moton, commandant of Hampton Institute,
Hampton, Virginia; Hightower T. Kealing, editor of the *A.M.E. Church
Review*, Philadelphia, Pennsylvania; Roscoe Simmons, editor of the *National Review*, New York; Josiah T. Settle, attorney, Memphis, Tennessee;
Charles Stewart, newspaper correspondent, Chicago, Illinois; Wayne W.
Cox, cashier of the Delta Penny Savings Bank, Indianola, Mississippi;
Bishop Cottrell; and, of course, Charles Banks. The fact that these people
accompanied Washington is significant not only because it shows they
supported his agenda but also because it demonstrates that he enjoyed the
support of progressive Negroes throughout the nation.[59]

Washington stopped in Jackson on October 6. As in Holly Springs, he impressed the crowds, speaking to a group of about three thousand, of which around three hundred were white. About three minutes after Washington concluded his speech, the platform on which he was standing collapsed. Pandemonium erupted in the auditorium, and about fifteen people were injured, including a few whites. Some people broke down doors to get out; others jumped from windows. Washington received no injuries and exited the building with little inconvenience. No sabotage was ever found.[60]

Washington moved on to Natchez, where he observed that the white people were so interested in hearing him "that they expressed a desire to pay for the opera-house in which I spoke." At Vicksburg, he spoke in a large building, formerly used as a skating rink. So many people came that hundreds still could not fit into the building. In Greenville, Washington delivered a speech at the courthouse. Once again, the building was too small to accommodate the people who wanted to hear him. At the sheriff's request, he gave a second speech to the crowd that had gathered on the outside steps of the courthouse.[61]

Washington stopped last at Mound Bayou, where, he asserted, "the largest and most successful meeting of the trip was held." He observed that the audience there was so large it "extended out in the surrounding fields as far as my voice could reach." Not surprisingly, Washington stayed at the home of Charles Banks. He gave two speeches in the town, one at a church and one at the site of the cotton oil mill, where six thousand people were in attendance. In addition to scheduled visits to towns in Mississippi, Washington made a few whistle stops at places such as Leland, Port Gibson, and Shaw, where he spoke to voluminous crowds from the balcony of the train. Other people could only catch a glimpse of Washington as he passed by on the train and graciously waved at them.[62]

In the end, the trip proved to be a stunning success. Washington estimated that he spoke to between forty thousand and fifty thousand people during his journey through Mississippi.[63] Banks received thank-you notes from numerous attendees from both in and out of the state. Washington certainly was pleased with the way Banks organized and promoted the tour, telling Banks: "I cannot find words to express the deep feeling of gratitude which all of us owe you for the magnificent manner in which you planned and carried out this trip through Mississippi." "No one could have done it better," Washington asserted.[64] In addition, Washington was pleased with the overall progress Negroes were making in the Magnolia State. He commented that he believed more had been accomplished by

Negroes in Mississippi in the past ten years than had been done since the Civil War. He went on to say that "the colored people have learned that in getting land, in building homes, and in saving their money they can make themselves a force in the communities in which they live." These points were totally in line with his constructionalist views.[65]

"The trip through Mississippi was a splendid ovation for the Doctor from beginning to end," Scott told Banks. "You more than met every expectation and simply overwhelmed the Doctor with a series of receptions not to be duplicated anywhere close in all the country." Even more impressive, Scott continued, "every detail seemed to have been worked out and the various incidents occurred with clock-like precision."[66] An editorial in the July 9, 1908, issue of the New York Age stated that even black people in northern states such as New York, Illinois, Massachusetts, and Connecticut could not equal the progress of their sisters and brothers in the Magnolia State. Other editorials and articles about the tour were published in numerous newspapers and magazines, including the Christian Recorder, the Charleston (West Virginia) Advocate, the Star of Zion, the Memphis Commercial Appeal, the New Orleans Picayune, the Odd Fellows Journal, the Southern Workman, and the A.M.E. Church Review. Roscoe C. Simmons, editor of the National Review, perhaps best summarized the opinion about Banks's organizing and hosting of the tour. In short, he said, "we all feel greatly helped and inspired by all we have seen and heard during this instructive and delightful tour."[67] Banks received national exposure for coordinating the tour, which benefited him and Mound Bayou.

Even though Washington spoke so highly of the progress being made in Mississippi, he still felt compelled to hire a private detective, F. E. Miller of the Pinkerton Detective Agency, to accompany him on the tour. He had received several death threats before the trip through Mississippi and continued to receive some throughout. Hiring a detective, however, was not unusual for Washington. In 1905 he had hired two Pinkerton detectives to travel with him as he toured Arkansas and the Oklahoma and Indian Territories.[68] As early as September 22, 1908, J. Matony of Cynthia, Mississippi, warned Washington, "It has been said that you will never leave in peace but in corpse or some other way, but not like you came." Although Washington seemed impressed by the fact that about 73 percent of the Negroes in Jackson owned or were buying their homes and that there were two black-owned banks in that city, he still had to be concerned about the threats made against him, particularly in Jackson.[69] Scott had Detective Miller assess the sentiment of the people in Jackson concerning Washington's visit before the entourage arrived. Miller interviewed both white and black people in Jackson and found that "the colored all were very much pleased" to have Washington visit them. And while Miller found some whites who would not openly state their opinions, he "found a great many anxious to see and hear him [Washington]." And he "did not find any one who was opposed to his visit."[70]

Nonetheless, the lynching of two men, Frank and Jim Davis at Lula, Mississippi, on October 11, illustrates the climate in which Washington's lectures were taking place. The men had gotten into an altercation with J. C. Kendall, a conductor for the Yazoo and Mississippi Valley Railroad, and one of them allegedly shot Kendall two times with his own gun. Although the Davis brothers escaped initially, they were captured not long after and incarcerated in the Lula jail. A short time later, an irate mob of white citizens stormed the jail and lynched the two inmates. Their bodies were left hanging all night on Sunday, supposedly so Washington could see them as he passed through the state.[71]

Emmett Scott teased Banks about the incident when he got back to Tuskegee. "I was rather amused at the way you scampered home after that lynching happened," Scott said. "We were afraid that we would receive a warm reception from the citizens of Lula," and he continued, "I was rather happy when I found myself in the confines of Memphis." After Scott got past the humor, he complimented Banks on the splendid job he did in organizing and promoting the trip.[72] Banks's success in this endeavor led to other requests for his help as promoter and organizer.

Robert R. Moton, Washington's successor at Tuskegee, received an invitation from Banks to speak at Banks's hometown, Clarksdale, on July 11, 1920. Although Moton said he would work with other leaders in the area, he especially wanted Banks's support: "Whatever you put your hand on . . . will succeed."[73] Moton had accompanied Washington's entourage in 1908.

Banks extended the invitation so Moton could address nearby residents as they celebrated the opening of the Mound Bayou Consolidated Negro School. Since whites in the Delta were supposedly "looking towards the improvement of racial relations," especially those in Clarksdale, the dedication ceremony was held there.[74] Moton agreed to speak.[75] Banks was excited not only because of the dedication but also because the affair gave him an opportunity to shine in his hometown.

Banks primarily coordinated the trip for Moton. He publicized the event by telling community members that Moton was not charging a fee for the address. He informed them that Moton agreed to speak mainly for the good he might contribute to Mississippi and assured them that the affair was going to be "on a higher plane than what they had been used to."[76]

Days before Moton arrived in Clarksdale, Banks advised him of some things he should talk about in his address. Moton appreciated the pointers because it helped make his speech more relevant to the people in the Delta. At the dedication ceremony, Banks gave a "forceful" introduction of the Tuskegee principal. While the text of Moton's address is unknown, he apparently did a satisfactory job. Banks later told him that he had "made a fine impression and much good" would result from his message.[77]

In Clarksdale, Moton addressed an audience of seven thousand people, both black and white. He spoke on the subject of interracial cooperation and did so "eloquently and convincingly," according to a newspaper report. Many influential people were in attendance: representatives from the Chambers of Commerce of Helena, Arkansas, Greenwood, Mississippi, and Memphis, Tennessee, were present; and even the president of the Memphis Chamber of Commerce, George R. James, with his delegation. Banks's friend C. P. J. Mooney, editor of the *Memphis Commercial Appeal*, also attended and delivered a "splendid address."[78] Moton's tour proved to be a stunning success, and again Banks distinguished himself as a successful promoter.

Isaiah Montgomery wanted Moton to stop over in Mound Bayou the day after he spoke in Clarksdale for the celebration of the town's thirty-second Founders Day.[79] However, since Banks and Montgomery were not on the best of terms, Banks discouraged Moton from participating in the Mound Bayou celebration. "As to the Founders Day for Mound Bayou, out that out. . . . At this time, no advertisement that would detract from the Clarksdale meeting, which is only twenty-eight miles from here, should be permitted," Banks advised. Banks suggested, "just simply arrange so that you will have to go elsewhere on the 12th, see?"[80]

Albon Holsey, Moton's secretary, responded to Banks's suggestion and let him know that Moton appreciated "the significance of your suggestion and will govern himself accordingly."[81] Moton also liked the "tactical way" Banks handled the situation.[82] Sure enough, Moton sent Montgomery a letter a few days later advising that he would not be able to attend the festivities at Mound Bayou because he had to be back at Tuskegee the morning of the twelfth for the opening of the National Federation of Women's Clubs.[83] Up to this point, Moton, the new head of the Tuskegee Machine, still respected the advice of Banks when it came to the affairs of Mississippi.

On at least on one other occasion Moton solicited Banks's help to coordinate a tour through Mississippi. However, when Moton toured Mississippi at the end of October 1921, Banks was not the key organizer. The main person arranging the tour was William H. Holtzclaw, principal of Utica Industrial Institute. Banks served as coordinator for only the northern Mississippi region. Other black leaders worked the rest of the state.

As mentioned earlier, Holtzclaw, a Tuskegee graduate, had tried in 1913 to get Washington to speak at Jackson for the state fair and on Negro Day. However, Banks had blocked the effort because he felt Holtzclaw had not followed proper protocol and because he believed Atwood was the person "engineering" it. That is, they were trying to by-pass him to get to Washington. Relations between Banks and Holtzclaw were cordial; the latter probably never realized that Banks had blocked Washington's going to Jackson.

Holtzclaw apparently proposed the tour to Moton, so he took the lead and served as chairman of the invitation committee. Since Banks had received such acclaim for his organizing skills, this had to have been disappointing. Nonetheless, he felt compelled to work with Holtzclaw, as he did not want Moton to think that he would not support the effort because he was not controlling the entire tour.[84]

At Holtzclaw's request, Banks made suggestions for Moton's tour, which he sent to the Utica principal. Holtzclaw knew of Banks's tremendous skills as an organizer, so he too went to Banks for his help in putting together the tour. Banks very openly obliged:

My first suggestion is . . . that a careful itinerary be made. 2. That the towns visited extend to us a written invitation which we can present to Dr. Moton. 3. That we ask Senator Percy, Mr. Stone, Mr. Wilson, Mr. Hilburn, Bishop Bratton and Mr. Bolton Smith of Memphis to join us in this good will campaign and to form themselves into a committee that shall be in control of the campaign. 4. It should be suggested to this white committee that they try to raise the money through their friends to [de]fray the expenses of the small committee of leading Colored men who will form a part of the party. This committee of Colored men, seems to me, should not exceed a dozen.[85]

He closed by telling Holtzclaw, "if there is any thing else that I can do, write or wire me and I shall take pleasure in responding to your request."[86]

On another occasion, Banks even suggested the travel itinerary for Moton. Holtzclaw agreed with the way Banks had things laid out as compared to other proposals he had seen. "My opinion is that the itinerary submitted by Charles Banks . . . may seem best suited to the occasion, [and] would be far more satisfactory; and this I would like for Dr. Moton to know," he wrote to Holsey.[87] However, not all of Banks's recommendations for the tour were followed. Banks wanted Moton to end the tour in Mound Bayou, because the MSF was going to be in session on October 28th. But Moton had to be back in Tuskegee that night for an engagement the next morning.[88]

Banks continued to work with Holtzclaw in coordinating the tour. "Everything is working smoothly and harmoniously from Chas. Banks in the north to J. E. Johnson in the south," Holtzclaw informed Holsey.[89] While matters seemed to be moving along smoothly, there were some divisive issues along the way. On September 22, 1921, a disturbing article about the tour appeared in a newspaper: "Dr. Moton comes to Mississippi at the invitation of Charles Banks of Mound Bayou, Vice-President of the National Negro Business League." Holtzclaw said he and other committee members were aware of the article and had discussed it at the last meeting of the committee, of which Banks was a member. "No one seemed to know anything about it and I am at a loss to know where it came from," Holtzclaw asserted. "The invitation goes to Dr. Moton not only from a Committee of Negroes but from various organizations, white and black, in the state of Mississippi."[90]

Problems erupted again among committee members at the end of September. At that time Banks received a letter from Dr. Redmond of Jackson, the finance committee chairman, stating that he [Redmond] had been appointed to raise $300 from Greenville and $200 from Mound Bayou to defray expenses for Moton's tour. "In soliciting these funds from Mound Bayou and Greenville I would suggest that you tell them that it has been definitely decided that the doctor will include these cities in his itinerary," Redmond said. However, Redmond advised Banks to tell them, "that their inclusion will depend upon their contributing their allotment of the expenses."[91]

Banks did not understand why Redmond needed to raise so much money for the tour. He became skeptical and reluctant to pursue the course. "I cannot understand the meaning of this, there is nothing involved in the way of expense except Dr. Moton's railroad fare over the State and perhaps his secretary," Banks told Holtzclaw. Furthermore, he said, "I handled Dr. Washington's tour before and no request was made for funds whatever on any place visited." Then Banks severed his ties: "I am writing to say now that I will not undertake this and if this is the program, I prefer to be left out of the arrangements or to be held in any way responsible for the success of the trip." Banks sent a copy of his letter to Moton, so Moton would know what was going on and understand Banks's position on the matter.[92] In a surprise move, however, Banks also sent copies of the correspondence to Fred Moore of the *New York Age*. His purpose here is unknown, unless he wanted to discredit the efforts of Redmond, whom he had clashed with before, and Holtzclaw.[93]

Ultimately, Banks turned over all of his correspondence to Holtzclaw and asked him to keep things going. Although Banks took this step, Holtzclaw reported to Moton's secretary that "he is joining heartily with us to make the visit a grand affair."[94] Banks did continue to work with them although he disagreed with their approach to raising funds for the trip. When the committee issued its press releases, the list of people responsible for organizing the tour still included Banks's name.[95] Moton even sent Banks a generic letter thanking him for cooperating with Holtzclaw and other members of the committee "in making possible my visit, and in working up interest in the forthcoming meeting."[96]

On October 16, Holtzclaw conceded to Holsey that he was having a hard time securing money for the trip, but that did not place a damper on his enthusiasm.[97] The next day he wrote Moton, "there has been some little mix up in regard to financial affairs, but we have everything straight now."[98] Apparently, some alternative was found to the plan proposed by Redmond.[99] In fact, it appears that Banks, Montgomery, Redmond, Holtzclaw, and others ended up lending money to the committee to cover some of the expenses. Records show that Banks and Montgomery may have jointly lent up to $150.[100] This had to have placed a strain on both, considering that Mississippi was in the midst of a cotton depression.

Ultimately, Moton visited Brookhaven, Hattiesburg, Meridian, Jackson, Utica, Lorman, Greenville, and Mound Bayou on the tour. Also, the MSF adjusted its meeting schedule so Moton could speak to them on October 27, the day he visited Mound Bayou.[101] This arrangement pleased Banks as it satisfied his earlier request for Moton to speak to the federation. In the end, the trip was a success. A distinguished group of gentlemen accompanied Moton, ranging from educators and doctors to businessmen and lawyers. Banks was part of Moton's entourage on the tour, along with Isaiah Montgomery and others.[102] Moton spoke to thousands of people, both black and white, on the tour. One observer optimistically noted that Moton "brought together in helpful, friendly, [and] sympathetic relations thousands of white and colored citizens who were impelled by the spirit of common interest, mutual respect, and goodwill."[103]

In the end, Moton wrote Banks another thank-you letter. This time the letter was more personal and sincere. "I want to thank you . . . for your large share in the Mississippi trip," he told Banks. "I am glad of the conference we had. I had hoped we could sit down together alone and talk out many things. . . . It was a pleasure to be at Mound Bayou again and to see the improvement in every way." Moton also told Banks that he was "not blind either to the large share you had in that improvement."[104]

Fig. 2. Charles Banks in 1911, when he was thirty-eight. From *Beacon Lights of the Race*.

Fig. 3. Banks in 1909, one year after he coordinated Booker T. Washington's educational tour of Mississippi. From *The Negro at Mound Bayou*.

Fig. 4. Banks *(seated)*, the "leading citizen" of Mound Bayou, and Isaiah T. Montgomery, the town's founder. From *Progress of a Race*.

Fig. 5. Cashier's office at the Bank of Mound Bayou. Banks *(seated, right)* founded the bank in 1904. From *The Negro at Mound Bayou.*

Fig. 6. Home of Charles and Trenna Banks, built in 1908 at a cost of $10,000. Charles
standing in front of the house, and Trenna is shown in the inset. From *Beacon Lights of the R...*

Fig. 7. Officers of the Bank of Mound Bayou and their families. Banks (*second row, far left*); Mont-
mery (*second row, far right*). Courtesy of Milburn J. Crowe.

Fig. 8. Mr. and Mrs. Simon Gaiter were among the first settlers to Mound Bayou in 1887. Simon had been a slave on the Davis Plantation with Montgomery. From *The Negro at Mound Bayou.*

Fig. 9. Bethel African Methodist Episcopal Church, the second largest church in Mound Bayou, attended by the Bankses and other elite families. From *The Negro at Mound Bayou.*

Fig. 10. The Bank of Mound Bayou became the heart of the business community. This two-story redbrick building was constructed in 1907 at a cost of $5,000. Courtesy of Milburn J. Crowe.

Fig. 11. The Carnegie Library at Mound Bayou, completed in 1910, was built at a cost of $4,000. It was designed and constructed by Thomas Cook. Courtesy of Milburn J. Crowe.

Fig. 12. The Mound Bayou Oil Mill and Manufacturing Company, designed by Cook, was completed in November 1912. Courtesy of Milburn J. Crowe.

Fig. 13. Booker T. Washington speaking at the dedication of the mill on November 25 1912. Fifteen thousand people attended the ceremony. Courtesy of Milburn J. Crowe.

Fig. 14. Banks ca. 1905, after he founded the
Bank of Mound Bayou. From *Voice of the Negro*.

Fig. 15. The Mound Bayou Consolidated Negro School, a three-story brick building desig by M. M. Alsop, opened in 1920. Courtesy of Milburn J. Crowe.

Fig. 16. The Mound Bayou Oil Mill and Manufacturing Company under construction. Ce tesy of Milburn J. Crowe.

g. 17. Booker T. Washington and associates in Mississippi during his tour of the state in
08. (*Seated, left to right*): Emmett Scott, Robert Moton, Booker T. Washington, and (*far
ht*) Bishop Elias Cottrell. (*Standing*): William H. Holtzclaw (*second from left*) and Charles
nks (*fifth from left*). From *Booker T. Washington: Builder of a Civilization.*

The Business League

"Being Worked to the Limit"

Serving the NNBL

Banks attended the first meeting of the NNBL at Boston in 1900, where he first met Booker T. Washington. The following year, Banks became third vice-president of the league at its annual meeting in Chicago. After dutifully serving in that position for six years, he was elected first vice-president of the organization in 1907, second in command only to Washington. League members had confidence in his leadership abilities, and he was consistently reelected to that post for sixteen years. By 1909, Banks and his wife, Trenna, were both life members of the organization.[1]

Banks worked very closely with Washington and Scott to build the NNBL into an effective organization. Washington and Scott contacted Banks for advice and he reciprocated accordingly. Without lieutenants such as Banks, Washington would not have been as effective as he was with the NNBL in furthering his message.[2] Moreover, through this organization, Banks promoted himself and his enterprises and gained national recognition, because influential businessmen and women throughout the country were affiliated with the league.

The NNBL was organized in a pyramid structure, with Washington at the top level, state presidents on the second level, local presidents were below them, and the general members on the bottom. Broadly speaking, the local presidents reported to the state presidents and the state presidents reported to Washington.[3] Men and women from a number of professions, ranging from farmers and carpenters to businessmen and doctors, were members of the NNBL. Most of the leaders of the league were also key players in the Tuskegee Machine.

Washington established the national organization for many reasons. According to a program distributed at its third annual meeting, held in Richmond, Virginia, August 25–27, 1902:

> The object [of the League] is to inform, as best we may, the world of the progress the Negro is making in every part of the country, and to stimulate local business enterprises through its annual meetings and in any other manner deemed wise; to encourage the organization of local business for the purpose of furthering commercial growth in all places where such organizations are deemed needful and wise.[4]

Economic development and independence, racial pride, and self-help, evinced by the league's members, were the general aims of the organization.[5]

Banks served in many capacities to advise, to promote, to stabilize, and to perpetuate the aims of the national organization. He actively sought persons of influence to sit on the executive committee and/or fill other leadership positions in the league. In a letter to Robert Owen of Los Angeles, California, who appears to have been a man with clout, Banks assured him that he would do all he could to make sure he served on the executive committee.[6] When Phillip J. Allston of Boston, the fourth vice-president of the league, died in December 1916, Scott went to Banks to see if he agreed with his choice for replacement. Scott suggested Watt Terry for the post: "What do you think about having [him] . . . to succeed our friend, Mr. Allston?"[7]

On numerous occasions Washington and Scott asked Banks to help them secure prominent speakers for the league's national conventions. Banks took charge of this responsibility for the 1910 convention. Washington asked Banks to try to secure the services of Senator James Gordon of Mississippi. Banks turned to W. D. Frazee, a U.S. district attorney in Mississippi, to help persuade Gordon to serve as keynote speaker. "I think you will agree with me that your fellow townsman and distinguished citizen, Senator Gordon, by reason of his broad remarks and conservative attitude on ethnic as well as other subjects before the Senate and during his sojourn in the North," Banks averred, "has been of inestimable value towards the ends which our best white citizens of the South, irrespective of party, so much desire, i.e., peace, harmony, [and] a better understanding between the races as well as classes."[8]

To encourage his support, Banks informed Frazee that former president Roosevelt would possibly be in attendance at the meeting. He also assured him that all of Gordon's expenses would be covered and any other compensation "the Senator might be willing to accept." In closing, Banks assured Frazee that no radicals would be at the meeting: "You know me well enough to know I would not be party to a move that would in the least embarrass you or him and trust you will take this matter up with him personally and at once."[9]

Although Banks wrote these generous words about the senator to Frazee (a white man), he did not have that much confidence in Gordon. In a private letter to Washington, Banks said frankly that he viewed the senator as being "rather old, somewhat childish and in some measure to be taken as a joke."[10] Ultimately, Banks believed Gordon would be too "risky" and that someone else should be found to deliver the keynote address. On the one hand, this suggests that as first vice-president, Banks assisted the national organization by securing prominent speakers for the conventions. On the other hand, this scenario displays another instance of "black survivalism." It demonstrates that he, like other members of the Tuskegee Machine, said patronizing things to whites to manipulate them and get what he wanted from them.

Despite Banks's concerns, Washington still wanted to "take a chance" on Gordon, but he asked Banks "to be responsible for him." Washington had some concerns because he believed that many people were interested in Gordon and that anything Gordon said during a presentation would receive national attention. So Washington wanted Banks to make sure Gordon limited his remarks to "relations of the race as outlined in his speech in the Senate." "Your main job," he told Banks, "would be to get him to not occupy too much time. If you could give him some definite facts as to the progress of the colored people in Mississippi, it would help him out."[11] Although Banks eventually secured Gordon as the keynote speaker, Washington changed his mind and asked Banks to find a prudent way to withdraw the invitation. Somehow, this is precisely what Banks managed to do. He advised Washington on August 1, 1910, that he had found "an honorable way out [of] the Senator Gordon proposition."[12]

Washington relied on his lieutenants to carry out his wishes. He realized that because Banks had worked with numerous influential people in Mississippi, he had a good chance of securing the services of other Mississippians such as Senator Gordon.

Washington and Scott frequently checked with Banks to see whether he agreed with their ideas about the national meetings of the league, especially if those ideas concerned anyone from Mississippi. Once Emmett

Scott considered asking Eugene Booze, Banks's brother-in-law, to give a presentation at the 1914 meeting in Muscogee, Oklahoma, but first he consulted Banks.[13] Banks gave his endorsement.[14] With Banks's approval, Scott invited Booze to participate. Scott also checked with Banks to make sure he agreed with the other Mississippians Scott selected to participate in the program, namely W. W. Cox and W. A. Attaway.[15] This power to "pick and choose" helped establish Banks as the most powerful black leader in Mississippi.

Banks also exerted influence over people outside of Mississippi who participated in the League. For instance, he prodded Scott to add M. W. Dogan, president of Wiley University in Marshall, Texas, to the Muscogee program. A former classmate of Banks at Rust University, Dogan graduated while Banks was still a student. Although Banks suggested someone from outside of Mississippi, he felt "sufficient merit" warranted his actions.[16]

Banks did more than secure speakers for league meetings. As first vice-president, he also presided over many of the sessions at the annual conventions and made motivational presentations to league members over the years. League members discussed any number of issues at the annual meetings. For instance, at the 1910 meeting held in New York City, Banks did a presentation on "How to Succeed" at the banquet, where "bisque tortoni: à la Mrs. Charles Banks" was served.[17]

When Washington wanted to drum up attendance for the 1914 meeting, he turned to Banks for help in making the convention a success. Banks started contacting league members in Florida, Georgia, Alabama, Mississippi, and Tennessee, emphasizing the importance of attending the coming meeting. He sent a poignant circular letter to NNBL members. Impressed by the letter, Scott told Washington he regarded it "as very effective and is probably worth your reading."[18] In the letter Banks told members that "from all indications this [meeting] promises to be in many respects the most [interesting?] session in the history of the League." He also reminded them:

the scope and influence of the work of the National Negro Business League among our people has long ago shown itself in the growth of enterprises and the gospel of hope and encouragement along these lines that is preached by its worthy President . . . has had its effect for good beyond sanguine expectations of its strongest supporters, and as the years go by, we are warranted in predicting continued larger usefulness of that great agency, the National Negro Business League."[19]

Banks also helped Washington select the dates and locations for the annual meetings.[20] As simple as this sounds on the surface, choosing a location for the meetings was very political, as different state leagues inevitably vied to host the event. This clearly happened after the Muscogee meeting. For some reason, league members did not agree on a location for the 1915 meeting while at Muscogee. Washington, therefore, went to Banks for suggestions. "There are several points [affiliates] that are making a vigorous request for the meeting of the League in August," he related, "but before acting I should like to get your own views and wishes as to the next meeting place."[21] Banks replied that he thought it a bit early to deal with the question and told Washington he would give his views on the matter at the beginning of the next year.[22]

Over the years, one of the most vexing concerns of the organization was finances, and Banks assisted in this area in all ways he could. Nevertheless, it proved a difficult task to keep the league out of the red. On different occasions, Banks, along with other leaders of the league, met with philanthropists, such as Andrew Carnegie, to try to obtain subsidies.[23] Apparently, Washington felt he needed Banks at one such meeting. It was important for Banks to be there, he said, "otherwise, I fear we shall miss securing any money this year from Mr. Carnegie for the Business League."[24]

One way the group addressed its financial problems was to have a national organizer who could find funding. Initially, Washington served in this capacity, but he ultimately envisioned a national organizer who would one day make the league a self-supporting organization, independent of white largesse. As secretary of the league, Scott found himself spending a considerable amount of time in all facets of the organization. Over the years Washington became disturbed about this because it took Scott away from his official duties at Tuskegee. Eventually, Washington intimated to Scott that the time had come for a "regular organizer who will live at Tuskegee and not just [be] there incidentally," to work for the league. Washington wanted a salaried person to serve in that role full time.[25]

Eventually, Ralph Tyler served as national organizer of the NNBL, helping raise money and coordinate the affairs of the organization. As national organizer, Tyler visited Mississippi around November 1913 to take inventory of affairs there, and Banks made his trip such a success that

Washington praised Banks for his efforts. "I thank you most heartily for the thoroughgoing manner you have gone about arranging for Mr. Tyler's visit," he said. "You have carried the state most thoroughly, and I feel quite sure he will be well received and finely treated."[26] Banks even arranged for Tyler to receive a 1,000–mile ticket book to cover his travel expenses in Mississippi.[27] Washington liked this because it saved the national organization at least fifty dollars. "I am especially grateful to you for the donation of the . . . ticket book to cover his itinerary in the state," Washington said. "Mr. Tyler's trip could not have been worked out better than it was, by you and your associates."[28]

After Washington died in November 1915, the financial problems of the league grew worse. During Washington's life the association had gained many supporters because of his personality and the relationships he established, but with him gone, there were concerns whether the money from these sources would dissipate.[29] As early as December 1915, Scott wrote to Banks that he needed to secure at least $1,500 to $2,000 from two or three of Tuskegee's trustees for the NNBL, which they had contributed in the past. However, he said, "I am not sure that I shall succeed, but I want you to know that I am making the effort."[30]

By January of the next year, Scott shared with Banks a message he received from Charles H. Anderson of Jacksonville, Florida, treasurer of the NNBL, concerning the league's finances. He told Banks that the organization's general account was "now overdrawn to the extent of more than $300." The financial woes of the league even factored into whom Scott and Banks considered for leadership positions in the group. When Scott recommended Watt Terry for fourth vice-president, he did so because he believed Terry would be "willing to do something in the way of helping to finance the organization." Scott said recruiting people with money to serve as officers was imperative, because it was the "only way we shall be able to make it go in the future . . . we shall have to have it financed by some individual or group of individuals." Scott had arrived at this conclusion because the local leagues were not contributing to the organization as expected.[31]

Banks and the MNBL

Perhaps Banks's most significant contribution to the NNBL was his creation of the first state affiliate, the MNBL. Banks put out a call for the state organization around March 1905. He felt that although the national organization was doing much to help uplift the race, "it could not fully accomplish the aims of its illustrious founders . . . without the organization and hearty cooperation of State Business Leagues as auxiliaries." Washington was pleased Banks took the initiative to start the organization, which led to the development of many other chapters throughout Mississippi and eventually the rest of the country.[32] This may be one reason he moved so quickly from third to first vice-president of the NNBL shortly after the creation of the MNBL.

Banks sent letters to men in his state trying to interest them in the MNBL meeting.[33] He made clear his philosophy concerning the MNBL, which coincided with that of the national organization. "Not only does it hope to arouse, encourage and strengthen the merchant," he said, "but the farmer, the lawyer, the doctor, the shoemaker, the barber, in fact, every honorable pursuit in which the Negro is engaged or should engage finds a warm friend in the Business League."[34] Isaiah Montgomery had no problem acknowledging that Banks brought about the state meeting. He told Washington that because of Banks's efforts, he was "assured that the gathering will be of considerable magnitude, and well calculated to exercise a broad influence."[35]

Planning for the 1905 Greenville meeting, Banks asked Emmett Scott to deliver the keynote address. Scott declined because he had too much work to do at Tuskegee and because, he said, he greatly feared that "as a speaker I shall prove a positive disappointment."[36] Like Scott, Washington was really pleased to hear about Banks's efforts, in terms of pushing the interests of the business league. Although Washington was pleased with Banks's efforts to establish the business league, telling Banks that "the idea of a state organization and a state meeting are very good," he did not agree to speak either.[37]

Later, Banks consulted Washington about the speech he, Banks, planned to make at the Greenville meeting. He realized his words would be "watched closely by the white press, as well as our own people," so Banks sent the Tuskegeean a copy of the speech with the hope that Washington would use his "'blue pencil' freely on what should be left unsaid."[38] Washington apparently appreciated Banks sending him the draft. "I think you have very carefully summed up the whole situation," he responded, "and I think what you say will be productive of great good. I have no criticisms to submit."[39]

At Greenville in June 1905, Charles Banks became president of the MNBL, a position he held for more than fifteen years. The MNBL was the first and reputedly the strongest state league in the association.[40] According to Scott, Mississippi represented the "best organized and most enterprising of the State Business Leagues."[41] Banks applauded the work of the Sherman, Mississippi, chapter of the MNBL. Headed by the Reverend A. J. Hall, a man committed to carrying out the aims of the organization, the chapter purchased more than 1,600 acres of land. It also planned to purchase an additional 220 acres in the near future. The Sherman league was "trying to do more in a concrete way than perhaps any league in [this] state," Banks told Scott. To Banks, this was constructionalism, not rhetoric. Consequently, he asked Scott to write the Reverend Hall a letter of praise for their accomplishments under Washington's name. Scott complied with Banks's request, but sent a draft of the letter to Banks for him to review and edit before it was sent to Hall.[42]

Early on, it seems Washington and Scott underestimated the value of having state chapters affiliated with the national organization. Initially, Scott even believed that a state organization might cause Banks, who served as third vice-president at the time, and others to neglect the national organization.[43] Their view changed, however, thanks largely to Banks. In March 1908, Banks explained to Scott how he believed the NNBL could become an even more effective and powerful organization. He told Scott, "The Nat'l League will grow and become potent in proportion to the relative strength of the Local League and State Organizations." Furthermore, he said, "I think that a representative of the Nat'l Organization should meet and talk with each Local League at least once a year. The work would [then] be harmonized, closer relations established between the parent and off-spring, and the Nat'l League would be correspondingly helped."[44]

Over time, Washington and Scott embraced Banks's idea. On this matter, Banks's vision reached beyond Washington's and Scott's. Also, the pyramid structure of the league can be largely attributed to Banks's initial organizing of the MNBL, which mushroomed into numerous local affiliates. Banks also helped organize various state and local affiliates. For example, S. K. Kinwood of Hattiesburg, Mississippi, wrote Banks that he and several other businessmen had organized a local business league and that they wanted information so they could become official and permanent members of the state and national association.[45] Another time, H. A. Wisher of Leland, Mississippi, wrote Banks stating that men in his area were interested in starting a local league. "We understand you are president of the State League," he said, "and if you can assist us by letting us have a copy of your by-laws and constitution, we would be very grateful to you for same."[46] The process would be duplicated in other states, sometimes with Banks's assistance. A black businessman from Oklahoma wrote Banks asking for help in starting a state business league, and Washington later asked Banks to go to New Orleans to help the Negroes of Louisiana start a league.[47]

As president of the Mississippi league, Banks actively promoted Washington's and his own personal agenda. Charles Banks and lieutenants in other states made it possible for Washington to be an effective and influential leader nationwide. According to John H. Burrows, Washington recognized that the NNBL "functioned viably through its race contacts," therefore, "he maintained significant and lengthy contact with Negro leaders whose prominence in League activity was needed." Burrows further states that Washington "sought to expand his influence among selected black leaders through gratuitous actions which included offers of financial assistance." This seems to have been the case with Washington and Banks, but their relationship was mutually beneficial.[48]

Likewise, Banks and others who worked and communicated with Negroes on a daily basis at the grassroots level served as conduits for Washington's program. One of Banks's contemporaries noted that "his wise and aggressive leadership has done much to encourage and stimulate business enterprises among the members of the race, not only in the State of Mississippi, but throughout the South."[49] Significantly, the positions Banks held as first vice-president of the NNBL and president of the MNBL allowed him to lead, hobnob, and work with some of the most influential Negroes in the nation. His role in these positions also gave him national exposure on many occasions.

Mississippi Day

Perhaps one of Banks's proudest moments as head of the MNBL occurred in 1909, one year after he orchestrated Washington's tour of Mississippi. As stated earlier, the Mississippi chapter of the NNBL was reputedly the strongest in the league. "From the beginning it has been one of the strongest links in the chain of local and state Negro Business Leagues which give the parent organization strength and potentiality," a newspaper reported. "It has walked in the vanguard and never brought the lagging rear." [50] Washington must have been impressed by the progress he witnessed Negroes making when he toured the Magnolia State in 1908. One month after his visit, he suggested to Banks that they have a Mississippi Day at the next general convention of the NNBL in 1909 to showcase to the nation the progress Negroes were making in Mississippi, a Deep South state.

Naturally, Banks was flattered by the invitation. Though he had previously confided to Scott that he was being "worked to the limit," he still took this opportunity to showcase his state and the MNBL.[51] It seems Banks had only one concern about the request. He did not want other league members to feel that he and Washington were "Mississippizing" the league too much.[52] This, however, did not concern Washington.

A Mississippi Day would obviously boost Banks's status in Mississippi and help spotlight him as the head Negro leader in the affairs of black Mississippi. As time moved on, Washington informed Banks that he was anxious about Mississippi Day and that he wanted it to be a great and model affair:

I wish you and your helpers and advisers in the state to study very carefully the whole situation and so present a program that will take into consideration every place of business conducted by our people in your state, perhaps letting the old man come at the night session. Perhaps Thursday would be the best day for this, arranging it so that one and perhaps two or three Mississippi men will preside at different times during 'Mississippi Day.'[53]

The 1909 meeting took place in Louisville, Kentucky, from August 18 to 20, with Thursday, August 19 designated Mississippi Day. Instead of the normal routine of people from throughout the country making presentations about their business endeavors, on this day all the presenters were from Mississippi. The Mississippians also had a large exhibit of photographs of their businesses so all present could marvel at their accomplishments. At the start of the program, Washington resigned the chair in favor of Banks, who introduced the Mississippi delegation. A number of subjects were discussed, including farming, merchandizing, banking, pharmacies, management of a cottonseed oil mill, fraternal insurance, and blacks in the professions. At one point during the program, at least fifty Mississippians "occupied a section facing the rostrum."[54]

C. W. Gilliam of Okolona discussed his dry-goods business, which conducted $40,000 in sales annually. Banks introduced W. P. Mackintosh, who had the distinction of being the only black merchant in the Magnolia State who had been in business continually for twenty-five years. S. Cox, a successful farmer of Eutaw, discussed how he managed to start his business with a five-acre farm despite beginning his life in slavery and never attending school. By 1909 he owned 722 acres in the Delta and another farm of 200 acres near Mound Bayou. He estimated his property to be worth at least $20,000.[55]

Dr. E. P. Brown, a physician from Greenville, explained how he saved $50,000 from his profession and cultivated over 1,000 acres of land he owned. Banks then introduced Willis E. Mollison, a leading lawyer from Vicksburg. Mollison, who like Cox, had been born into slavery, credited his mother for his success. He served as clerk of the circuit and chancery courts for eight years and later had the distinction of being appointed district attorney by a Democratic judge. E. P. Jones of Vicksburg spoke about fraternal insurance in Mississippi. In introducing Jones, Banks reminded his audience that "the great life insurance companies of the country discriminated against the Negro," thus "it was necessary to organize companies among themselves to procure protection."[56]

John W. Strauther, president of the Greensville Savings Bank, took the platform next and discussed banking in Mississippi. Mississippi blacks bragged about this, for the Magnolia State had eleven black-owned and black-operated banks, more than any other state in the Union, north or south. Perry Howard of Jackson discussed the accomplishments of the MNBL. He took pride in noting that in the MNBL "all walks of life are represented." A. A. Cosey presented information on the Mound Bayou Cotton Oil Mill and Manufacturing Company. Cosey reported that the mill "will employ from sixty to seventy-five persons paying them from $1.25 to $5 per day."[57]

The last presenter was Bishop Elias Cottrell of Holly Springs. He gave a presentation about the overall achievements of Mississippi blacks. He informed the audience that he viewed religion as a business. "If studying religion as a business the clergy are enabled to help the people along business lines, as the clergy are more often heard by the people than any other profession, it is easier for them to instill business ideas into them," he insisted. "The solution of the negro problem lies in work." After the last presentation, Banks turned the chair back to Washington.[58] Mississippi Day brought Banks a tremendous amount of national recognition. It also served to reinforce and boost his power and influence in Mississippi. By this time, Charles Banks had become the most influential Negro in Mississippi.

NNBL Meeting of 1916

The 1916 meeting of the NNBL was one of the most significant in the history of the organization. It was the first meeting held after the passing of its founder, Booker T. Washington. For a number of reasons (discussed in detail later), Banks decided not to run for the presidency of the league. In a December 1915 letter to Richard W. Thompson, a Tuskegee Machine press contact, Scott told him pointedly that "Mr. Banks, Mr. Napier and I are all agreed that Mr. Napier shall stand for the Presidency of the Business League."[59] A few months before the August meeting, Banks told Scott that while he did "not want to be continued as President" he did want to "keep some place with the Organization, perhaps, on the Executive Committee." He also assured Scott that either way he would continue to work "as faithfully and persistently in the future as I have in the past."[60] James C. Napier, a successful businessman and prominent leader from Nashville, Tennessee, had been Banks's friend for a long time. He had served as chairman of the executive committee for years and was probably the number three man in the organization after Banks. Moreover, in 1903 Washington had asked Napier to head the league, but Napier declined.[61] Ultimately, Banks retained his position as first vice-president of the league.

Notwithstanding this, Banks and Scott pretty much set the agenda for the 1916 meeting. Since Banks served as first vice-president, Scott wanted him to preside over the program. By June 1916, Scott asked Banks to recommend persons for the business league program. Scott thought it would be wise to have Robert Moton, the new principal of Tuskegee, Napier, the newly chosen president of the business league, and a few others, but before he finalized these plans Scott wanted to make sure Banks approved of his selections.[62]

Meantime, someone suggested to Scott that Mrs. John W. Francis of Mound Bayou be added to the program. Again, Scott wanted to make sure she met with Banks's approval. "Please let me know what you would recommend in this matter," he asked, "and also let me have the names of any other persons you would suggest."[63] Scott turned to Banks quite a bit for help in coordinating the meeting. Banks even chose the topics program participants were to speak about. When Minnie M. Cox of Indianola, Mississippi, was invited to speak, Scott did not know what to ask her to talk about, so he went to Banks. "It occurs to me that some subject such as 'My experiences as a business woman' will give Mrs. Cox an opportunity to bring out just what would be most helpful to her hearers," Banks replied. Ultimately, Minnie Cox turned down the request.[64]

The 1916 meeting took place from August 16 to 19 in Kansas City, Missouri, and was the fourth time the convention had met west of the Mississippi River. At the opening, attendees sang "The Battle Hymn of the Negro," written by William H. Davis to the tune of Julia Ward Howe's "Battle Hymn of the Republic." Fortune J. Weaver, president of the Greater Kansas City, Missouri, Business League called the convention to order and delivered the opening address. After welcoming the members, he turned the gavel over to Charles Banks, who served as permanent chairman of the convention.[65]

The first night session was devoted to memorial exercises in honor of the late league president. At all of the previous national conventions, Washington had delivered an annual address on opening night. Thousands of people, black and white, attended the memorial to listen and pay tribute to Washington's memory. At the memorial session, Banks reiterated the reasons Washington had organized the league. In response to allegations that Negroes were making no progress in terms of education or the business world and that ending slavery had been a mistake, he said that the Tuskegee Wizard organized the league to promote Negro thrift, industry, and business enterprise. Banks received hearty applause when he told the crowd Washington "knew that the best way for individuals or a race to win the confidence and support of other people, was to prove to them that we were trying to help ourselves."[66]

Scott, secretary of the league, gave the main address, which one observer called a "masterpiece." Banks gave Scott a warm introduction:

No one is better fitted, and no one could be more appropriately selected to deliver the principal eulogy on this occasion than that splendid and loyal young man who, for a long term of years, was closer to Dr. Booker T. Washington than another other man in America—I refer to his confidential Secretary, Mr. Emmett J. Scott. For many years past Mr. Scott has been Secretary of Tuskegee Institute and Secretary of the National Negro Business League, and as Dr. Washington often said he never knew a man who could work harder, who could accomplish so much and who, in connection with the work of this league, could get out and discover so many successful Negro business men and women as Mr. Scott.[67]

In paying tribute to Washington, Scott said he was an honest man, a true friend and a brave, courageous person who fought valiantly in the struggle for "the liberation of humanity."[68]

Banks apparently did a fine job in chairing the meeting. About one month later, after Scott had some time to reflect, he told Banks: "I feel more and more pleased that everything went off so satisfactorily. Your presiding was ideal and . . . everyone remarked upon the smooth running of our proceedings."[69] For many years, Banks continued to serve as first vice-president of the NNBL.

Fund-Raiser for Negro Education

"Going Ahead Endeavoring to Meet the Conditions as Best We Can"

Orations for Education

Negroes in Mississippi found their educational situation abysmally poor at the turn of the century, especially in terms of state support. Of all southern states, Mississippi held the dubious distinction of being the one that spent the least amount on Negro education. Moreover, there were great disparities in the education provided for black and white children. Although black children accounted for 60 percent of the state's school-age population around 1900, they received only 19 percent of school funds. Such gross inequities were commonplace in the South and posed a challenge for Negro leaders in the state.[1]

Negroes in Mississippi needed educational resources, from books to schools. Most of Banks's efforts were geared toward fund-raising for Mississippi schools through philanthropic foundations. Banks also worked at the grassroots level to help young people secure an education. Ultimately, he met the challenge of educational neglect as best as he could.[2]

Charles Banks diligently served the state of Mississippi in many capacities when it came to Negro education. He worked as a trustee at three black schools, two in Mississippi and one in Ohio. He became a trustee at Campbell College, Jackson, Mississippi, which according to one observer was "one of the leading educational institutions of the A.M.E. Church."[3] He also served as trustee at another A.M.E. school, Wilberforce University, Wilberforce, Ohio, and at Utica Normal and Industrial Institute in Utica, Mississippi.[4] In addition, Banks frequently gave addresses at various Negro colleges. In May 1910 he spoke at Alcorn College, where he shared the stage with Senator James Gordon from Mississippi. In May

1913, Banks gave the commencement address at Campbell College. Although the text of Banks's speech is unknown, Emmett Scott said if it came close to other speeches Banks had given, it was "right up to snuff."[5] A Dr. Vernon also wrote Banks praising him for the "fine" address he gave at the commencement.[6]

On several occasions, Washington invited Banks to give speeches to help raise money for Tuskegee: "If in any way you can connect the work at Mound Bayou with the work at Tuskegee, showing any helpful influence that Mound Bayou has gotten from Tuskegee, it will be all the more valuable for the purpose of raising money for the school."[7] Banks also helped William H. Holtzclaw secure funds for his school. In commenting on the men who helped his school, Holtzclaw noted that Banks "is ever ready to do something for Utica, as he is for every other good cause."[8] Perhaps because Banks gave speeches and solicited funds for educational purposes on such a frequent basis, Governor Edmund F. Noel of Mississippi recommended Banks as a delegate to the Negro Educational Congress, which took place on July 15, 1912, in Saint Paul, Minnesota.[9]

Although Banks supported industrial education for Negroes, he worked just as diligently to provide some means of standard education for the children in and around his community. Members of the Tuskegee Machine were not one-dimensional. Too often the literature about Booker T. Washington and his supporters has emphasized a dichotomy between Washington and Du Bois, minimizing the similarities in their work.[10] Influenced by the education he received at Rust University, Banks, with the support of Washington, secured money for liberal arts schools in and around Mound Bayou. Banks also contributed to Negro education by providing students with scholarships.

The Banks Prize

In 1905, Banks decided to give a twenty-five dollar annual scholarship to Tuskegee, as he nurtured his relationship with Booker T. Washington and the Tuskegee Machine. Called the Banks Prize, the scholarship was given to an outstanding student who studied at the Phelps Hall Bible Training School.[11] Washington awarded the prize at the Tuskegee Institute's graduation ceremony. Twenty-five dollars was a fairly generous award considering that some students at the school only earned three dollars a month for work-study. "Let me . . . thank you for your . . . desire to establish a prize at Tuskegee," Washington wrote when Banks first suggested the idea.[12]

Ultimately, Banks believed in supporting Negro education in all ways. He believed that the more resources Negroes obtained, the more they should give to further the race's education.[13]

Banks continued to send money to Tuskegee for the award even during difficult financial times. For example, by May 2, 1913, Washington wrote Banks: "I am sure you will forgive me for writing you again with reference to the prize you offer." He was concerned because the prize was to be awarded at the commencement ceremony on May 29. Banks responded accordingly and sent a check to Tuskegee. To prevent this from occurring the next year, Washington asked Banks in February if he planned to continue the prize. Banks responded that it would give him great "pleasure to continue the Banks Prize for the students of the Phelps Hall Bible Training School this year as in the past," but to make sure he did not forget, Banks asked Washington to "kindly have Mr. Scott to bring this to my attention again sometime around the middle of April." This is precisely what Scott did. On April 17, 1914, Banks was sent a reminder. Based on their correspondence, Banks made the 1914 contribution without delay.[14] Records show that as late as 1918, Banks continued to send money to Tuskegee for the Banks Prize. By that time, Robert R. Moton had become principal of the Institute and he appreciated Banks's "continued loyalty and help to the school," he wrote.[15]

Encouraging Youth Achievement

Though Banks gave money for the prize to Tuskegee, he frequently sought favors in return. Perhaps because he did not have children of his own or because he just wanted to support black children and Washington's school, Banks worked hard to have several of his relatives and other young people admitted to Tuskegee Institute. He also assisted them in securing scholarships or work-study to help defray expenses.

Banks's nephew, Leon Carter, is one example of a family member he assisted. Carter first attended Tuskegee during the 1905–6 term. As Carter returned to Tuskegee for his second year, however, Banks seemed concerned about Carter's ability to pay for his schooling. "I desire to have him work out part of his schooling, if it can be arranged, as I want him to be as much self-sustaining as possible," Banks told Emmett Scott. Simultaneously, Banks sought assistance for a friend's child. "I have a friend, who has a boy, Dexter Montgomery, who will likely accompany him," Banks announced. Montgomery's mother wanted Banks to find out if her son could work to defray part of his educational expenses also. Scott forwarded Banks's letter to a Mr. Arrington at Tuskegee and told him to accommodate Banks's request: "I should be happy if you would—in our office—answer this letter & tell him we'll look after these boys. Banks does everything he can for us."[16]

Three days later, Scott told Banks he was delighted Carter would be returning to the school along with Montgomery. More important, Scott wrote that the school would give the boys an opportunity to work off as much of their expenses as possible. He went on to tell Banks that if Montgomery "can meet the requirements of the night school and wishes to enter that department, we shall be glad to admit him there. Of course, as you know, in the night school, students are able to work out a great deal more of their expenses than in the day school."[17] Banks's ability to secure support for his nephew and his friend's son showed others he had useful connections at Tuskegee, which helped him gain continued respect as a leader. Consequently, some Mississippi Negroes got the impression they should "go to Banks" if they wanted to get their children into Tuskegee or secure financial support for them.

Banks had two other nephews, Charles Moore and his younger brother, Malvin, who both attended Tuskegee Institute from around 1910 to 1914. Banks had them visit Scott upon their arrival in the fall of 1910 so Scott could advise them.[18] Although available records do not mention Charles's academic interests, they show that Malvin studied veterinary science. Scott arranged for Malvin to have his work-study in the horse barn, "where he will have [the] special opportunity to study . . . and have his theory lessons, even now with the veterinarian." If Malvin took the job, he would have earned about $3.00 to $3.60 a month as a day-school student. Malvin could have earned more money if he attended night school, but Scott told Banks he thought "it desirable for him to remain in the day school, unless you object." Banks decided to abide by Scott's judgment. To assure Banks that his nephews were being taken care of, Scott told the boys to visit him on a regular basis so he could help them if necessary.[19] Based on the correspondence between Banks and Scott, Malvin seems to have been a very focused student. However, the same cannot be said for his older brother, Charles.

In November 1910, Banks received a letter from Washington: "I regret to have to write you that your nephew, Charles Moore, is not giving full satisfaction in his conduct as a student." Unlike Malvin, Charles did not "seem to be interested and seems to have no definite purpose in view," opined Washington. He went on to say that Charles "neglects his duties and has become very troublesome." Washington assured Banks the administrators had spoken with the young man and were trying to help him in every way possible. None of this appeared to have worked, however, so Washington suggested Banks write his nephew to encourage him to do better, "to make the best of his opportunities here."[20]

Scott also advised Banks to write to his nephew. "He has been troublesome in certain directions and has not been wholly amenable to discipline," Scott averred. Because they were close friends, Scott told Banks he would "talk with him from time to time and shall try to keep him in the straight and narrow way." This embarrassed Banks, especially since he had helped the young man get accepted into the school and worked to secure financial assistance for him. To a member of the black elite, this kind of behavior was not acceptable, especially from people in their bloodline. Banks wrote young Charles "strongly" and hoped it would have a positive effect.[21] Whatever Banks told Charles must have worked, at least for the rest of the 1910–11 school year, because there were no more letters from Tuskegee concerning problems with the young man. However, that did not last long.

Charles Moore seems to have been prone to trouble at Tuskegee. In the spring of 1912, J. B. Ramsey, commandant at Tuskegee, sent a disturbing letter to Washington. "I am notifying you that we have three small boys who are guilty of stealing from the Commissary," he said. Ramsey retrieved the stolen goods and locked them in the attic of one of the offices on campus. The stolen merchandise totaled about $50, which was an offense great enough to result in a suspension. Ramsey named the perpetrators. "The boys are as follows: William [sic], Thomas Forest, and Charles Moore."[22]

For several days, Scott refrained from writing Banks about the matter. When he finally did write, he advised Banks that Charles's conduct would "likely . . . lead to his dismissal from the Institute." Scott had delayed writing Banks, he said, because he wanted "to get the matter in some kind of shape, looking to [save] the boy if possible." "Dr. Washington and I both regret most sincerely the . . . of sending you such unfavorable news, but we thought we had better notify you in advance of final action," Scott added.[23] He also sent Banks a copy of the letter written by Ramsey outlining the charges. However, about three days later Scott told Banks in a personal letter he felt sure that Charles would be reinstated after he had been out of school a while and assured Banks he would help make it possible.[24]

In the end, the Tuskegee Executive Council decided to suspend Moore and the other boys. "Moore is in a more or less unenviable position here now being suspended and being kept in custody at the school," Scott told Banks. Rather than keep the boy in custody, however, Scott told school officials he would have Banks arrange for Charles to be transported home as soon as possible. "I have no doubt . . . that . . . the Executive Council will be disposed to consider his return after he has been out a while," Scott reminded Banks. Scott noted that it had also been his policy in the past not to consider readmitting suspended students as long as they were still on school grounds.[25]

One can only wonder what Banks said or did to his nephew when he finally got the chance to see him. On March 26, 1912, Banks wrote Scott thanking him for the manner in which he handled the situation and noted that he had sent Charles a money order for fifteen dollars, "advising him to go to his mother."[26] Three days later Moore was on his way home. "Young Moore started for home yesterday," Scott informed Banks, "a through ticket was bought for him to Memphis, and the balance of the money was given to him."[27]

In the meantime, Malvin Moore continued to work hard in school, making his uncle and the rest of his family very happy. By June 1914, he graduated from Tuskegee with a distinguished record. Scott told Banks:

> I am sure you will be pleased to know of the fine record that Malvin has made here at Tuskegee Institute. It is a record of which you have every reason to feel proud. I think you will be interested also to learn that his company, Company "1" of the Institute Battalion in the presence of the student body, officers of the school and a large crowd of visitors, won the prize competitive drill contest, Wednesday, May 27th. The winning of this prize means that his name and the name of his company will be engraved on the silver loving cup to be preserved in the archives of the school for all time.[28]

Scott said his son, Emmett, served as a second lieutenant in Malvin's company. Last, he assured Banks he had continued to lend his support to Malvin to the very end. That is, he had "arranged for Malvin to secure his diploma without confusion on Commencement Day."[29]

Banks also helped young men and women who were not family members attend Tuskegee. In 1917, he assisted Thomas Williams of Clarksdale. "I am personally interested in him, have known his parents for many years, and will appreciate anything that can be done" to help him financially and otherwise, Banks wrote Moton.[30] Moton responded by telling Banks that as long as Williams was "able bodied, strong, healthy, willing to work and far enough advanced in his studies to at least pass the entrance examination for the C Preparatory Class," Tuskegee would be glad to admit him into night school and "give him an opportunity to work out the whole of his expenses for board." At that time, board cost $11 a month. Moton asked Banks to have Williams bring a letter from Banks to present when he arrived at Tuskegee. This undoubtedly signaled to Williams and others that Banks had some clout at the Institute. Without the letter from Banks, the terms arranged by Moton would be null and void.[31]

On some occasions, Banks even went out on a limb for people who were not academically prepared for Tuskegee. In October 1920, Banks recommended Wilson Lee of Memphis for admittance on scholarship. Banks even filled out the admission application for him. In this case, however, the registrar sent word to Banks that Lee had only reached the fifth grade and "is unable to pass our entrance requirements." Nonetheless, the administrator told Banks that Lee would "probably be able to pass the examination next year, and we will keep his application on file if it is agreeable to you."[32]

Others Banks assisted in this way included Arthur Harris; Tyree Felder, daughter of the Reverend S. B. Felder; a son of Minnie Jordan; a son of Delia Vanbiber; and a son of B. S. Stone, a professor who hailed from Africa.[33] Banks helped the young people get accepted into college, secure financial aid, and better themselves so they could also one day contribute to the race. Banks also had people trained at Tuskegee so that upon their return to Mound Bayou they could help ensure its growth and survival. Yet this does not fully explain his contributions to the educational uplift of Negroes. Most of his efforts were spent on securing badly needed funds from various philanthropic sources.

General Education Board

On the home front, much needed to be done to improve the educational facilities at Mound Bayou. Until about 1916, the town had three educational institutions: the Baptist College, the Mound Bayou Normal and

Industrial Institute, and a public school. After that point, other schools were gradually added. However, even with three schools, Charles Banks recognized the educational resources in Mound Bayou could "not be said to be up to the rest of the progress being made" in the town. The schools had very little outside help and did not have "any real first class school buildings or dormitories," according to Banks. Because of the community's efforts, the schools had buildings worth about $5,000, located on about eight acres of land.[34]

Nevertheless, the people in Mound Bayou were suffering "very much because of the lack of one to push the educational side of our work," Banks said, and he believed that to improve the town's educational facilities, the support of philanthropists was needed.[35] Banks also realized that Mound Bayou would attract more settlers if its educational resources were improved. This is one reason his connections at Tuskegee were so important. By doing favors for Washington and Scott, Banks hoped for favors in return.

In June 1907, Banks wrote Scott soliciting the support of the Tuskegee Machine in securing contributions from the GEB. The GEB was an organization connected to the Southern Education Board (SEB), also called the Ogden movement. The SEB had been established to improve the public school system for all children throughout the South. Although Washington worked as a paid agent of the SEB, its members never invited him to join the board because of his race. He worked closely with several northern SEB members, including Robert C. Ogden, a trustee at Tuskegee; Wallace Buttrick, executive secretary of the GEB; George Foster Peabody, contributor to Tuskegee; and William H. Baldwin, chairman of trustees at Tuskegee.[36] But these contacts were not enough to force southern board members to accept Washington; in fact, Washington could not even attend the meetings. One historian who assessed Washington's relationship with the SEB has concluded that it turned out to be "one of the most frustrating of his life."[37]

In seeking help for his town, Banks reminded Scott that Mound Bayou "had nothing . . . that approaches anything like respectability or in any degree adequate and commensurate in an educational way." "If there is any place in Miss., that should have strong educational facilities and backing, for our people," Banks asserted, "Mound Bayou is that place." He asked Scott to help him secure the needed support. "I sincerely trust you can see your way clear to take the matter up with the proper officials, and push it to the desired end," Banks told Scott.[38] Scott wrote back to Banks intimating he would give his untiring support concerning the town's school situation and said he hoped he could advise Banks favorably in the near future.[39]

Shortly afterward, Banks solicited the help of Ogden, president of the GEB, for funding assistance. After providing Ogden with some demographic and geographic information on Mound Bayou, Banks informed him that there was "no educational institution of consequence here, and in fact, in no part of the Delta, for the education and training of the Negroes." Banks may have exaggerated the situation somewhat to elicit Ogden's support. After explaining the town's needs, Banks concluded by telling Ogden that if he had any questions about the merits of the cause, he should contact Washington, B. G. Humphries, their congressman, or R. W. Millsaps, founder of Millsaps College, for references.[40]

After discussing matters with Scott, Banks went to Washington and told him he had submitted a formal application to the GEB for financial assistance. It just so happened that Ogden was one of Washington's contacts, and he probably would not have made a contribution without consulting Washington. Banks apparently realized this, which explains why he filtered his requests through Tuskegee. Of course, Washington gave Banks a favorable response, and the latter thanked Washington for the "assurance that you are willing to help us in our school matters here."[41] About two months later, Banks followed up with Washington on the education issue. "As stated to you in a former communication," Banks reminded Washington, "we need one good school here, that will serve the purpose of this and adjacent territory. Again it is my opinion that Northern Capitalists can find it [a] good investment by cooperating with us." Although Banks believed that white largesse would "go far towards a realization of what we all desire," he made sure Washington understood that Mound Bayou's leaders were "not waiting for outside assistance, but going ahead endeavoring to meet the conditions as best we can."[42]

By October 1907, Scott provided Banks with the name and address of the executive secretary of the GEB, Buttrick. He told Banks to type his proposal and application and forward them to Tuskegee, after which he would personally pass them on to Buttrick. "As I told you at Topeka," Scott reminded Banks, "I want to help every movement of yours I possibly can. I know Dr. Buttrick pretty well, certainly sufficiently well to address him in your matter and I shall be glad to do it."[43] As requested, Banks sent the materials to Scott. Scott in turn worked with Washington's ghostwriter and white friend Robert Park, a sociologist, and prepared a letter for Banks to submit to the GEB. Scott sincerely wanted to assist Banks. "I want to help you, not only in this, but in all other matters possible," he told Banks.[44]

Similarly, Banks appreciated all Scott had done and felt the letter prepared by him and Park would help greatly.[45] Unfortunately, the board denied Banks's request.[46] The rejection did not altogether surprise Banks considering the board's largely southern membership and its consistent pattern of discrimination. Even Washington had very little luck with the GEB and ultimately realized that the board focused more on assisting white than Negro public education.[47] Undaunted, Banks began pursuing funding from other sources.

Rockefeller and Carnegie Funds

As Banks understood, there were several other philanthropic sources the Tuskegee Machine had access to. Banks worked very hard to secure monies from the Rockefeller and Carnegie funds. "I am writing to have you start a campaign to have Mr. Rockefeller or Mr. Carnegie, or some other philanthropist build a Y.M.C.A. building, a library building, or a school building for the Negroes of Mound Bayou," Banks told Scott in November 1908. He believed that such a contribution would benefit all Negroes in the Mississippi Delta. He also felt that the lack of educational resources in that part of the South was inexcusable, especially since Negroes outnumbered whites in the Delta by four to one. Making a final plea in his letter, Banks asked Scott to "please take this up with a view of having some of them give us a good building here for educational purposes."[48]

Next, Banks wrote a letter to John D. Rockefeller expressing the need for a religious or educational institution at Mound Bayou. One of Rockefeller's assistants, a Mr. Murphy, followed up with Banks, but like the GEB, the foundation did not approve the application. According to Murphy, "among the large number of applications which come to Mr. Rockefeller, there are, of course, a great many worthy objects which he nevertheless feels it would be unwise for him to take up." In light of this, Murphy regretted to say that "the matter which you present is one of these, and for that reason cannot be favorably considered."[49] Upon receiving this letter, Banks forwarded it to Washington. Maybe he thought Washington might be able to have the application reconsidered, or maybe he just wanted to inform Washington that this, the second request, had been denied so Washington would assist more vigorously with others.[50] In response, Washington suggested John J. Goldwire of Griffin, Georgia, and Sumner George of Langston University in Langston, Oklahoma, as possible sources of help. Meanwhile, Washington said, he would speak to Andrew Carnegie personally about securing money for an educational building at Mound Bayou.[51]

A few days later, Washington, who had probably already spoken to Carnegie, contacted Banks and assured him that Mound Bayou would receive a library. "While I have no official authority to say so . . . I feel rather sure that if your board of Aldermen will agree to appropriate enough money each year to maintain a library in proper shape," Washington advised, "Mr. Carnegie will give the money for the building . . . [but] he will require that you appropriate ten per cent annually of the amount which he gives." Washington explained in detail this meant that if Carnegie gave the town $2,000, it would be required to come up with $200 annually for the expenses of the library. These expenses were for books, maintenance, and so forth. Considering the terms, Washington cautioned Banks and the town council: "You can decide what amount of money you can invest safely in a building and also what amount you are able to give annually toward its support."[52]

Banks was excited when he received the message. "It goes without saying that our municipal board will do anything they can to secure a [library] building," Banks told Washington four days later. At that point, however, he did not know how much money the town would be able to appropriate each year. In fact, he tried to have the percentage Mound Bayou citizens would have to pay for the upkeep of the library reduced because he had other plans for the town's money. "You have been here and know just what is before us," Banks told Washington. The town boosters were already in the process of purchasing an artesian well for Mound Bayou, and they also needed to improve its lighting and sanitation. "This will tax us quite heavily, and yet I do not want to let the opportunity pass to secure the library building," Banks stated. Although one Mound Bayouan believed the municipal council accepted the conditions set forth by Carnegie "unhesitatingly," all along Banks tried to strike a compromise to Carnegie's terms. Banks believed they could secure a custodian and maintain the library for less cost than in larger cities. Thus, he asked "if it would be possible to arrange our maintenance at a five percent basis instead of ten." With those terms, Mound Bayou would be able to maintain a library that cost between $5,000 and $10,000. Last, Banks assured

Washington that he asked for these favors only "because I know you are in sympathy with our work, and will judge it rightly."[53]

A shrewd leader and negotiator himself, Washington would not acquiesce to Banks's plea. "I hardly think it wise to ask Mr. Carnegie to change his general rule," Washington informed Banks, because it was clear "he does not like to do so." Furthermore, he said, "I believe that it would cost you ten percent of the money to put into the building to keep it up." He also explained that Carnegie had worked hard to come up with his ten-percent principle and that after giving it much thought, Carnegie "is convinced that his conclusion is right." Washington agreed that since Mound Bayou was a small town, upkeep might indeed be cheaper; likewise, he thought that other expenses might be smaller. Hence, Washington judged Banks's point moot. Finally, in reference to Banks's concern about the artesian well, street lights, and sewer system for Mound Bayou, Washington said, "a sewerage system as well as the improving of your streets are . . . of the greatest importance." If he had to choose between those things and a library, the library would have to wait.[54]

Meanwhile, after consulting Washington, Scott advised Banks of the approach he should take to secure Carnegie's support. First, he advised Banks to write Carnegie, calling his attention to complimentary remarks made about Mound Bayou and its leaders by President Roosevelt. Second, he suggested Banks mention that Washington had visited Mound Bayou and could "give them definite information with regard to what you are doing there." If Banks did these things, Scott believed Washington would be in a good position to take up the matter. Assuring Banks of his efforts to help, Scott said, "I am particular[ly] anxious to help you get a building, and I think this will help us to get it."[55] In giving him this guidance, Scott not only assisted Banks in the particular endeavor but also effectively introduced him to the procedures and operations of the Tuskegee Machine.

Though he failed to negotiate a compromise to Carnegie's terms, Banks did not let the opportunity to secure a library pass. Despite Mound Bayou's need for improved sanitation and lighting, Banks was "convinced that we must do more than we have done here to prepare our citizenry here for their singular task." Moreover, he said, "it is the necessity of this preparation that moves me to in some way increase our school and auxiliary facilities, hence, the library . . . movement." And while their educational facilities were unsatisfactory, Banks asserted that he could "hardly be contented without doing my best to assist in relieving the situation."

Banks finally agreed that if Carnegie would provide a library, the town would come up with 10 percent for maintenance on a building that cost about $4,000. Lastly, Banks wrote Washington, "if not troubling you too much, [I] shall be pleased to leave the matter of negotiations and etc., in your hands."[56]

Washington pulled some strings with Carnegie shortly afterward. At the end of December 1908, Banks wrote a letter to Andrew Carnegie but routed it through Tuskegee, having Scott send it on.[57] In the letter, Banks informed Carnegie the town council at Mound Bayou had agreed "to provide an amount equaling ten percent of the cost of the building for maintenance annually" and that it could afford a building that cost about $4,000.[58]

In the meantime, Washington continued to take up this business with Carnegie on Banks's behalf. In the process, he discovered Banks had not fully completed the application, leaving blank the space stating how much the town would "appropriate annually for the support of the library." Washington told Banks that he "took the liberty from memory to fill in this space as $400. This means, in case Mr. Carnegie agrees, that you would get $4,000." Maybe sensing that Banks's error on the application might have been intentional, Washington reminded him that he could not guarantee Carnegie would grant the request. "Of course the matter has not been formally and definitely passed on yet," Washington told Banks, "but I think you will hear from it within a few days."[59] Later, not having heard from Carnegie, Banks contacted Scott for an update on the status of the application, but at that point Scott had not heard anything either. However, he cautioned Banks not to be too impatient, because, he said, "they move rather slowly . . . in that office."[60]

Good news finally arrived about February 16, 1909. In a circular letter, Banks announced that "through the influence of Dr. Booker T. Washington, Mr. Andrew Carnegie has agreed to pay the full amount for the erection of a library building at Mound Bayou, Mississippi." He also noted that a site had been secured and that plans were underway to construct the building.[61] By October 1909 construction had begun, and Banks started sending out pictures so others could see the Carnegie Library being erected. After seeing the picture, Washington commented that he could tell it was going to "be a good, substantial building." The fifty-by-sixty-foot brick structure was located diagonally across the street from the Mound Bayou Normal and Industrial Institute. Mound Bayou's own engineer, Thomas Cook, planned and constructed the library.[62]

By March 1910, Cook had almost completed the library. By then, Banks had become interested in finding publishing companies that would place the library on their mailing lists so they could receive complimentary copies of different publications. He told the publishing companies that if reading materials were provided, they would be greatly appreciated by the people in Mound Bayou.[63] Banks also had Emmett Scott place Mound Bayou's library on Tuskegee's complimentary mailing list for two of its publications, the *Southern Letter* and the *Tuskegee Student*.[64]

Next, Banks tried to secure chairs by soliciting donations from different people, especially members of the MNBL, for which he served as president. "We are arranging seats for our new Carnegie Library," Banks informed members of the Mississippi league, and "we will [need] chairs, and I desire that all our friends help us by paying for one chair, the price of which is 50 cents."[65] In addition to members of the MNBL, many other people responded to Banks's request; for example, Emmett Scott agreed to pay one dollar for two chairs. Washington also sent Banks a dollar for two chairs and said he regretted he could not send more.[66] The library opened in December 1910.[67]

Unfortunately, by the end of 1911, it appears the town council at Mound Bayou reneged on its obligation to pay the 10 percent for upkeep. However, the council seems to have been using the building for meetings, smokers, and banquets to raise money to meet its obligation, rather than strictly for educational purposes. This is not altogether surprising since Banks, on several occasions, had tried to maneuver out of paying these expenses when he applied for the grant, maybe sensing that the town would have problems paying its ten percent. Banks did not want to look bad before Carnegie. But as his enemies found out the library was not being used for its intended purpose, they tried to make sure Carnegie and Washington were aware of that fact.[68]

In January 1912, someone sent a complaint about the library to Washington, but Scott intercepted the letter. Scott felt compelled to discuss the issue with Banks. "A report has been made to Dr. Washington which I have held up but which I, nevertheless, beg to call to your attention," he told Banks. The letter stated that while the town council had promised to pay $400 annually for the upkeep of the library, "it is not at all being used for that purpose." The complaint asserted that instead the library was being used as a headquarters for the MBA, a benevolent organization for which Banks served as secretary-treasurer.[69]

According to Scott, the letter went further to "state that there are no books in the library and nothing whatever to indicate that Mr. Carnegie's generosity is being used in the way intended." The unidentified writer also stated he felt certain that "Mr. Carnegie would resent Mr. Washington's interest in Mound Bayou if he should learn that the library matter is being treated in this manner."[70] Scott's letter to Banks had an uncharacteristically strong tone. It seems Scott presumed Banks was guilty of the allegations.

Two days later, after reflecting on the tone of his letter, Scott wrote Banks again, noting he had written "somewhat hastily Saturday with reference to the use of your Carnegie Library for other purposes than for the library alone." Tactfully assuming responsibility for the crassness of his letter he told Banks: "I do not know whether I properly placed before you my own position in the matter. . . . I am anxious for you to understand that this complaint came here in the regular way, but instead of bringing it to Dr. Washington's attention, I thought I would bring it to your attention first of all." Then he assured Banks he felt "quite sure that the matters mentioned will receive your attention."[71]

In a handwritten note to Scott, Banks said he wanted "to see the report and have name of party making the charge [and] complaint."[72] In response to Banks's request to see a copy of the letter, Scott explained he "did not place on file the complaint which came here regarding your library." He did seem to remember, however, that the letter came anonymously and opened by saying: "I am sure you will be more than interested to learn whether the facts which follow are true than in learning the name of the writer."[73] The following is a brief recreation of the complaint letter by Scott:

> I only have to say now that I have [recently] been to Mound Bayou and am well acquainted with the facts as they related to the library secured by you for that place. . . .
>
> Of course, I quite appreciate, as you do, that both Tuskegee and Mound Bayou and other thriving enterprises must bear their share of [camelot?] and misrepresentation.[74]

Scott served as a guardian angel for Banks at Tuskegee. Scott could have called the matter to Washington's attention, but instead he informed Banks of the charges and discarded the letter to make sure Washington never saw it. Scott also made sure Banks knew why he wrote to him about the matter. "I wrote you so that you might know that the 'watchman was on the town!' when this complaint came here," Scott said.[75] Scott helped strengthen Banks's power and prestige through such acts because when complaints or derogatory information about Banks were sent to Tuskegee, the complainants rarely received responses, and Banks's relationship with the Machine was not weakened. This may have shown the "knocking," "envious," and "jealous" Negroes that they were wasting their time trying to discredit Banks to Washington.

On January 23, 1912 Banks responded fully to the charges relayed by Scott. "It is true that we use a portion, about one sixth of the library building for the Masonic Benefit Association office," Banks declared. But the library benefited, he said, because "the town receives a rent for this part that assists in paying the custodian and janitor." This meant that the funds generated from the rent were being used to help meet the $400 obligation. To keep Scott from being alarmed about the MBA renting the library space, Banks told him the organization planned to construct its own building in Mound Bayou within the next year.[76]

Regarding the charge about the reading materials or lack thereof, Banks said, "it is true that we have no books." But he pointed to "the campaign I have been waging through the *New York Age* for books." He confirmed that the building "is not fully up to the standard of [a] library, but our plans are working rapidly to that end. All public lectures, etc., are held in the building, and it is certainly filling a particular need along the line that is adapted to Mound Bayou." On the latter score, Banks was certain "the substantial citizens" of Mound Bayou would support him in the assertion.[77] Then Banks explained why he believed someone sent such a derogatory letter to Washington:

> There seems to be more envy and jealousy on the part of the Negroes against Mound Bayou than is shown by the whites fighting us from money angles. I suppose Tuskegee knows the depths to which the knocking, envious, jealous Negro will descend in order to impede or improve the work of those who are trying to do things.[78]

Banks closed, however, by assuring Scott of one fact: "We have nothing to hide and all our work is on the level." In all likelihood, Banks's remarks were truthful; Scott's father lived in Mound Bayou and worked for the MBA, which made it possible for him to verify the truth.[79]

Mound Bayou Normal and the Rosenwald Fund

Mound Bayou still needed educational resources in addition to the Carnegie Library (especially since the library had few or no books), and Charles Banks worked hard to help secure them. The leaders at Mound Bayou also realized that sound educational facilities would make their town more attractive to potential settlers. Many town leaders, like Banks and Montgomery, were dissatisfied with the county's management of the public school system. Their frustrations emanated from the fact that 20 percent more Negro children than white children attended the county's segregated public schools, but the white schools received 58 percent more money annually than their black counterparts. This outraged Banks because the taxes Negroes paid far exceeded the amount of money their schools received.[80] Such disparity did not only occur in Mound Bayou or Mississippi. Charles L. Coon, superintendent of schools in Wilson, North Carolina, demonstrated the prevalence of this problem throughout the South. In a 1905–1906 North Carolina state school report, Coon showed statistically that blacks paid more in taxes than was spent on their schools. And in 1909, he expounded on these findings with statistics from other states.[81]

The situation improved somewhat for Mound Bayou in 1912, when it became officially recognized as a town instead of a village. That change gave Banks and other town leaders the leverage they needed to establish a separate public school system.[82] Banks solicited the support of his white friends. He wrote to Thomas Owen, a prominent attorney from Cleveland and Rosedale, Mississippi, and asked him to assist in taking up "the matter of having Mound Bayou made a separate school district." "You know conditions here, and just what we are and can do," Banks wrote Owen, "and I trust you will put forth your usual splendid efforts to have this brought about."[83]

These efforts by Banks and others did not provide immediate results. About a year and a half after he first wrote Owen, Banks noted that Mound Bayouans were "still at it here" trying to secure control of their public school. He explained that they were doing voluntarily what Governor James K. Vardaman advocated: "attempting to support our public school with tax paid by us."[84] Unfortunately, these efforts would not result in major improvements for Mound Bayou, as white southerners never intended to divert a proportional share of tax funds to Negro schools.

Nonetheless, Banks worked vigorously to obtain funding for the

Mound Bayou Normal Institute, one of two private schools there. The Reverend Benjamin F. Ousley, a graduate of Fisk University, former missionary to Africa, and former teacher at Alcorn College, served as principal of the school. Established in 1892, Mound Bayou Normal sat on eight acres of land donated by Isaiah Montgomery and Benjamin Green. In terms of normal education, this school became one of the best in the Delta. Its students came from all over the area, some walking four miles "over muddy roads" to get there. These same students bypassed the public schools near their homes to attend Mound Bayou Normal. There were many advantages to attending the school. For instance, while the public schools met for only four or five months a year, Mound Bayou Normal Institute met for nine months. Students who stayed in school twice as long would likely be twice as far ahead in terms of academic preparation.[85]

The buildings that housed the school had been constructed by the American Missionary Association (A.M.A.) of New York City, a white organization that contributed to the development of private Negro schools after the Civil War. Mound Bayou Normal consisted of two buildings, one with four rooms and the other with two. The smaller, two-room building cost about $900 and the larger frame building cost about $2,000. Twenty additional acres of land were also purchased for the school for the purpose of industrial and agricultural training.[86] The A.M.A. provided two-thirds of the operating costs for the school, and students paid the other third. Students were required to pay $9 a year ($1 a month) for tuition. To show their appreciation for the donations, the trustees of the school deeded the institute's land to the A.M.A.[87]

According to Ousley, Mound Bayou Normal intended to "put within the reach of every boy and girl of the Mound Bayou district a good common school education, based upon Christian character." While the instruction given at the school was not intended to be denominational, the school still aimed "to be thoroughly Christian," because "the most careful moral and religious training is considered to be of the utmost importance," Ousley wrote. The school had four departments: Primary, Intermediate, Grammar, and Normal, and it took twelve years to complete the course of study there and receive a diploma. They had approximately 135 students at various grade levels and six teachers. Even though it received some money from the A.M.A., the school urgently needed "funds to enlarge its work," Ousley said, stating that "a girls dormitory and home for single women teachers and also a boys dormitory would add much to the growth and efficiency of the school." It also needed an industrial building and a carpentry shop for industrial training.[88] Ousley realized that introducing industrial training into the curriculum would make the school more appealing to Washington and white philanthropists.

Ousley went to Banks to see if anything could be done to help the situation. Banks in turn went to Washington. In a September 1, 1912 telegram, he asked Washington for $1,000 from the Julius Rosenwald Fund for Ousley's school. Rosenwald made major contributions toward improving the educational facilities for Negroes in the South. He had begun extending his philanthropy to Washington with a relatively small donation of $25,000. Rosenwald instructed Washington to use the money for small schools that were patterned after Tuskegee. He was so pleased with Washington's handling of the funds that he later began to fund other endeavors pursued by the Tuskegee leader. Banks told Washington he believed that Mound Bayou Normal deserved help because "the school is doing splendid work."[89]

Banks requested financial help from the Rosenwald Fund, he said, because Mound Bayou was "getting practically no assistance in our efforts in our school work except for what little comes from the county." Banks said the $1,000 would cover the improvements Ousley wanted. Significantly, the citizens of Mound Bayou were not idly waiting for others to do for them what they could be doing for themselves. They had already purchased land costing about $800, which they intended to add to the school grounds, and they were making other improvements to the school as well.[90]

Washington had many questions when he received Banks's request. "What is the condition of the school, how large is it . . . how many pupils does it have, what is its history," asked Washington.[91] Banks sent Washington all of the information he requested, including a history of the school, written by Ousley. Banks seems to have had some reservations in approaching Washington about help for the school because it did not offer technical training, which usually was the case for schools that received money from the Rosenwald Fund.[92] However, the Tuskegeean contacted Rosenwald, and presumably he helped Banks secure money for the school to establish an industrial training workshop.[93]

Jeanes Fund

Banks also worked to secure money for Mound Bayou Normal from the Anna T. Jeanes Fund. A wealthy Quaker, Anna Jeanes lived in Philadelphia, Pennsylvania. Before she died at the end of 1907, she gave $1 million to Washington and Hollis Frissell, one of Washington's white allies, to be used for the development of rural black schools. Washington and Frissell selected a board of trustees, modeled after the board at Tuskegee, to handle the distribution and management of the fund. James Hardy Dillard, a former dean and classics professor at Tulane University in New Orleans, administered the fund. Dillard, a white southern educator, was respected throughout the country.[94] Washington wanted to use the money to generate concern for the development of Negro schools. Dillard wanted to use it more directly rather than to try to convince whites to support black schools.

Ultimately, Dillard won out and he used the Jeanes Fund to hire "supervising teachers." He selected an experienced teacher named Virginia Randolph to serve in this capacity. Randolph had already been a county superintendent for Henrico County, Virginia. As supervising teacher, she traveled to different schools and provided new teaching methods, introduced simplified forms of manual training, and guided overall development. Moreover, while visiting these schools she learned about the problems and conditions the people had to contend with. Dillard and Randolph eventually developed an extensive network of supervising teachers, starting in Virginia and later expanding throughout the South. Ultimately, the Jeanes Fund placed 134 supervising teachers in southern counties, often paying one-half a teacher's salary while the county paid the other half.[95]

Banks had asked Dillard to assist him in securing money to finance the construction of a library in Mound Bayou before Carnegie agreed to build it.[96] However, after this unsuccessful bid, Banks asked Dillard to arrange to have a Jeanes Fund teacher placed at Mound Bayou. "If you kindly arrange for the teacher here, we can easily . . . cooperate with your school work here in a very profitable and satisfactory way," Banks declared.[97] Dillard wrote Banks on March 15, 1909, and asked him if the citizens of Mound Bayou needed anything else at that moment, but Banks said no. Banks wanted to know, however, if Dillard would be able to help them during the next school year and if he would specify exactly what the Jeanes Fund would provide for them: "I think . . . it would be well for us to know definitely just what you will do for us, and that the matter of securing [a] suitable person be under consideration as soon as possible." At that time, Banks said, he did not have any "special recommendation," but he stated that Washington would help them secure a person who would be a good fit for the job.[98]

According to Banks, he and Dillard were "getting on finely" up to that point. "He has asked me to name what we wanted," Banks told Scott. Dillard also suggested, declared Banks, "that I go ahead and make a selection of teachers." Banks then asked Scott to recommend someone for the position.[99] Scott began searching for a "strong industrial teacher" to fill the position, but he needed to know if Banks wanted the person immediately or for the next fall.[100] Unfortunately, Banks and Dillard had miscommunicated somewhere along the way. Dillard had not gotten approval for Banks's proposal although Banks thought he had. "I had gotten the impression that you desired that I should go ahead looking up [a] suitable person to carry out the county work," Banks told Dillard, "and am making some searches and investigations with a view of having the person at work no later than October." Before he continued, Banks said, he wanted to be sure these steps were in accordance with Dillard's wishes.[101]

By the fall of 1909, Dillard provided the citizens of Bolivar County with funds for a Jeanes supervising teacher, who would be paid $50 a month over a nine-month period. John St. Anthony Green, the oldest son of the late Benjamin T. Green, served in this capacity. John Green attended Alcorn A&M College for two years, after which he attended Fisk University, earning a degree from that institution in 1909. He had just finished college when he took the supervising teacher position. Not surprisingly, some people objected to his having the job for that reason, and some also objected because he did not have a county teacher's license. After complaints by several "little tight headed county school keepers," Green took the required examination and passed it with a ninety-five.[102] After holding the position for one year, Green resigned and took a job at Wilberforce University in Ohio.[103] Sydney J. Brown followed Green. However, Banks did not like Brown's performance, especially in comparison with John Green, and he would later ask Dillard to replace Brown.[104]

Unhappy with Brown, Banks asked Washington for recommendations, telling him the citizens of Mound Bayou had reached the stage "where we need real top notches for this work."[105] In May 1911, Washington suggested Jessie O. Thomas, a senior at Tuskegee, saying he felt confident Thomas could get the job done.[106] Banks then recommended Thomas to Dillard.[107]

However, as Banks recommended Thomas, a Mr. Pearman, the superintendent of education for Bolivar County, began lobbying for Brown to keep the position. Pearman, who had also been communicating with Dillard, boasted that Brown had been of great service to the schools in Cleveland, Mississippi, and said he could not think of a better person for the job. When Scott learned of this, he sent a letter marked "confidential" to Banks, in which he stated he had "located a hitch with reference to the Jeanes Fund. I pass this information on to you for whatever use of it you may care to make." He told Banks that Pearman was "standing up for Sydney Brown, and our New Orleans friend [James Dillard] is thereby embarrassed." This placed Banks in a somewhat precarious position; this was not supposed to happen on his home turf.[108]

Shortly after receiving Scott's letter, Banks told Dillard he had heard through the grapevine that their county superintendent had lent his support to Brown. To protect Scott, however, Banks said, "As to the correctness of this . . . I do not know." Although he did not actually know Brown, Banks said, "I have the facilities for finding him out."[109] He had already found out plenty:

> . . . for your information and guidance I beg to advise that I find Brown, of such an unfit character for the place, that he was lately arrested for selling 'Blind Tiger' whiskey. I find also that he was implicated in juggling with school funds, and escaped an indictment by reason of fact that some of us did what we could to prevent the disgrace.[110]

To make sure Dillard knew what he thought of Brown, Banks stated further that "Mound Bayou does not stand for the tolerance of such a character as Brown." Even more damning, Banks asserted that Brown "is of no service to himself, and can hardly be of any service to any one else."[111] As Banks intended, after hearing these things, Dillard no longer felt embarrassed about rejecting Pearman's selection.

Banks did not stop at criticizing Brown. He asked Owen, his white attorney friend, to help keep Brown from being appointed. Banks informed Scott he had "referred Dr. Dillard's communication to my friend Mr. Owen who is the County Boss and makes [the] superintendents."[112] It seems Owen had the power to make or break Brown when it came to this matter, and it appears Owen lent his support to Banks in discrediting Brown. Banks's comments also imply that Owen had influence over Pearman, the county superintendent. Even more important, this communication shows that through his contacts, Banks at times could even assert authority over influential whites, such as Pearman.

Scott and Washington admired the way Banks handled the issue. Scott said that when he told Washington what Banks had done, Washington "had a quiet chuckle at the way in which you have gone about securing what you have started out to secure." Scott reacted similarly: "I have laughed just a bit myself at the fine way in which Mr. Owen handled this matter for you."[113]

For some unknown reason, Thomas did not take the position. Scott gave Banks the names of at least four other people he thought would do a good job.[114] Eventually, Banks recommended Gertrude A. Bryant, principal of the public school in Mound Bayou, for the job. Bryant held a teaching license and was exempt from taking any state teaching examinations. She received her education at Knox Academy in Selma, Alabama, and then at Cherry Street Public School in Vicksburg, Mississippi. She had taught in Bolivar County since 1902, and Banks saw her as a "suitable and competent person to do the work here." He also believed he could get the county superintendent to agree to her nomination.[115]

After about a month and a half, Banks became concerned because he had not heard anything from Dillard. He wrote Robert Moton, his colleague in the NNBL and a trustee for the Jeanes Fund, and expressed his concerns. "I have heard nothing from Dr. Dillard in a definite way about our teacher here," Banks told Moton. "He requested that I get [an] endorsement for her from our County Superintendent. This has been done and forwarded to him." Banks wrote to Moton because he thought Moton could get Dillard to give them a "definite understanding, so [we] will [know] where we are."[116]

Because of the large number of applications Dillard approved for the Jeanes Fund, he could no longer pay the entire salary for the teacher in Bolivar County. He suggested Banks ask the county superintendent "if the county would provide any part of the salary, and how much." He also requested that Banks send another letter of endorsement for his candidate from the county superintendent.[117] Banks believed he could get the letter of endorsement, but he did not think he could secure funds from the county, because the county did not want to take on new expenditures. To strike a compromise, Banks told Dillard that if he would inform him how much the Jeanes Fund could contribute, "Mound Bayou will most likely be able to supplement the amount to warrant Mrs. Bryant in taking up the work."[118]

Banks continued to pursue funding from this source relentlessly. Along the way Scott continued to give him assurance that his request would probably be funded.[119] However, by the fall 1913 school year, Mound Bayouans had not received funds for their Jeanes teacher. "I am hoping that you are now prepared to take favorable action in the matter and that our efforts here at self help appeals to you sufficiently to give us consideration which a number of other localities enjoy," Banks told Dillard.[120] Washington continued to assist Banks; in fact, he assured Banks he had "been at work pretty vigorously on Dr. Dillard" and that he felt "pretty sure something will be done from the Slater Fund or the Jeanes Fund" to help at Mound Bayou.[121] But by this time Banks was frustrated. "It looks like the good doctor [Dillard] is getting me ready for another fall down," Banks told Scott after reading a letter from Dillard.[122]

Dillard had written that he had hoped to be able to continue to appropriate funds for a Jeanes teacher at Mound Bayou, but he conceded he was "greatly embarrassed." The Jeanes Fund had fewer dollars in 1914 than in the previous year, so he regretfully informed Banks there was no more money to dispense. Dillard went on to state that he had been "particularly anxious" to consult Banks in "regard to the whole educational situation at Mound Bayou." "I should be very glad if at some time," Dillard said, "at your convenience you would let me have your views as to what ought to be done in the way of concentration and improvement."[123] Banks made another plea to Dillard in August 1914: "If you can in some way indicate to me just what appropriation could be allowed here, I would then be in a position to more intelligently advise as to cooperation."[124]

Banks secured funds for a Jeanes teacher sporadically over the years. Banks and other town boosters were also successful in obtaining funding from Jeanes for the Mound Bayou Normal and Industrial Institute on several occasions. In 1907, Banks and Montgomery, with the help of Washington, secured funding for the salary of an agricultural instructor at the school. And they secured money from the Jeanes Fund on at least two other occasions, in 1912 and 1914.[125]

Mound Bayou Consolidated Schools

Mound Bayou's leaders continued to take steps to establish a consolidated school district and construct a new school building. By 1917, Pearman was succeeded as county superintendent of public education by a person far more amenable to supporting Mound Bayou's effort to establish a separate school district.[126] Pearman seems to have been ardently opposed to such an idea because under his administration the all-white county government had complete jurisdiction over the entire Bolivar County Public School System and therefore he could directly influence whether or not Mound Bayou could establish a separate school district. Although the new superintendent still had jurisdiction over public schools in Mound Bayou, the town's leaders were given more flexibility.

By 1919, Mound Bayou had "six public schools and two graded or Normal Schools." The purpose of the new school would be to "follow . . . those institutions that have proved best adapted to meet the needs of our people under present conditions, and at the same time afford facilities for acquiring higher grades preparatory to courses on other Institutions."[127] In other words, the school would continue to provide students with technical training but also provide them with liberal arts education. By 1920, some Bookerites freely deviated from emphasizing technical training. Also, as conditions remained bleak for most blacks after World War I, to some degree they lost faith in the Tuskegee model of industrial training and they began to turn toward the liberal arts.

Supporters of the Mound Bayou Consolidated Negro School raised money to establish the institution by issuing bonds totaling $100,000. Mound Bayou citizens constructed a three-story brick building, designed by local black architect M. M. Alsop, that cost about $70,000. Town leaders estimated the new school would accommodate a minimum of 1,000 students and had the capacity to serve as many as 1,500 in the future.[128] Banks said the Mound Bayou Consolidated Negro School "is perhaps the largest proposition of its kind in the Country." Bolivar County whites contributed to the effort. "The bond issue aggregating $100,000 was handled for us faithfully by white friends and neighbors in the County," Banks said.[129] When the school opened its doors in 1920, it had "sixteen well-equipped class rooms, an auditorium seating 700, and an annual enrollment of 850."[130]

On Matters Political

"I See That 'Sambo' Is Left Out"

Early Political Activities

Banks's involvement and influence in national, state, and local politics were longstanding although he never ran for public office. As a matter of fact, he stated that "too much political activity . . . will hinder my larger and more basic purpose."[1] Still, like Washington, he expended a lot of time, effort, and money trying to prevent "lily-white" Republicans from completely taking over the GOP in the South. Banks's political career began as early as 1890 when he served as census enumerator for his district. Even at that time, he had gained the goodwill of the whites in Clarksdale, where he lived. Banks told Washington, with a bit of hyperbole, that "every white man in town endorsed his application for appointment."[2] Ethan A. Hitchcock, secretary of the interior, also appointed Banks as supervisor of the Twelfth Census for the Third District of Mississippi in 1900. Banks had begun to gain prominence as a Negro leader even before he met Washington.[3]

Banks worked as a member of the state executive committee for the Republican Party, and in 1904 he became a delegate to the Republican National Convention representing the Third District. He also served as a delegate at large at the Republican conventions of 1908 and 1912.[4] Like most Negroes of his era, Banks supported the candidacy and presidency of Theodore Roosevelt. Early on, he believed Roosevelt had the best interests of Negroes at heart.[5]

Three events convinced Banks and most other blacks that they had a friend in Roosevelt. The first event occurred in 1901, not long after Roosevelt had been in office. He invited Washington to a dinner at the

White House, where they discussed education and politics. This infuriated white southerners, many of whom could not imagine being invited to
the White House themselves. Over time, southern whites came to believe
the Tuskegee leader was influencing southern policy, which happened to
be true. Roosevelt used Washington as his patronage referee for the region partially so he could weaken Democratic control in the South while
he simultaneously built up the Republican Party.[6] In addition, Roosevelt
used Washington to wean the southern Republican Party from its attach-
ment to Mark Hanna, Roosevelt's most formidable challenger for the
1904 Republican presidential nomination.[7]

The second event that made Negroes throughout the country feel they
had a friend in the White House was the appointment of William D.
Crum, a Negro physician, as collector of the Port of Charleston. Many
white southerners resented a black person holding such a high official
post. They were especially troubled that this appointment came after a
time when white southerners had expended so much effort in eliminating
blacks from office holding throughout the South.[8]

The third event occurred even closer to home for Charles Banks. A
graduate of Fisk University, Minnie Cox had been postmistress in Indianola, Mississippi, since the Harrison administration, but bitter, jealous,
covetous whites would force her out of the position in 1902. Mississippi
Democratic senator John L. McLaurin expressed the view of many when
he asserted on the floor of the Senate that "the white people of Mississippi
don't want negro postmasters appointed to give them out their mail."[9]
Angry whites in Indianola started holding meetings, where talk of violence became commonplace. At that point, Cox resigned from the position and moved to Birmingham, Alabama.[10]

When President Roosevelt learned of the events in Indianola, he refused to accept Cox's resignation and demanded she be returned to office.
Whites in the area refused to honor the president's demand, so Roosevelt
eventually closed the post office. Indianola whites, in turn, had the mail
sent to Greenville, about thirty miles away, and hired a Negro to bring the
mail to Indianola.[11] Apparently whites did not mind blacks doing postal
work as long as they were performing menial tasks, but the idea of a black
person heading the post office repulsed them. Eventually, the white su-
premacists won out.

James K. Vardaman, a candidate for governor at the time, expressed the
sentiments of many Mississippi whites when he asserted that they were

not "going to let niggers hold office" there. He successfully played the race card to win the gubernatorial election.[12] Indeed, after Cox's commission expired in 1904, the post office reopened under a white postmaster, although it was reduced from a third-class to a fourth-class facility.[13] Strangely enough, after spending some time in Birmingham, the Cox family returned to Indianola where Minnie's husband, Wayne, opened the Delta Penny Savings Bank, which had a substantial white clientele.[14]

These three acts made many blacks, including Banks, believe Roosevelt cared about their well-being. However, blacks soon discovered that Roosevelt harbored some of the same views as extremists such as Vardaman. A major difference was that Vardaman was much more open and vocal. Roosevelt's feelings about blacks were expressed more in his public letters and through his political actions. For instance, he clearly acknowledged that during his administration blacks were given fewer political appointments than during the Harrison and McKinley administrations. Washington realized this, but he tried to excuse it by saying that although the "quantity" of black officeholders had been decreased, the "quality" had been increased.[15]

Roosevelt believed only a few privileged blacks deserved his support. He was committed to helping "individual blacks when political advantage coincided with ideology," states Thomas Dyer, but not Negroes as a whole. He believed most blacks should receive full citizenship gradually. Moreover, Roosevelt later regretted having invited Washington to the White House, and he never invited him to the White House for dinner again. He also later regretted his appointment of Crum.[16]

Charles Banks, like many blacks, began to pierce Roosevelt's veil on his view of race relations after the Brownsville affair. In 1906, a ten-minute shooting spree by unknown assailants took place outside of a club near Fort Brown in Brownsville, Texas. One police officer suffered wounds and one white man died. Consequently, several black soldiers, who were believed to have been retaliating for past offenses, were accused. They vehemently denied any involvement. Despite Washington urging against such a move, President Roosevelt ordered three companies of black soldiers discharged, excepting the white officers, without a trial. William Howard Taft, Roosevelt's secretary of war, at first held up the order, but ultimately he carried it out and became its arch defender.[17] A Memphis newspaper warned that "every negro leader of consequence in the state [of Mississippi] is either actively or passively opposing President Roosevelt and all other probable aspirants for the presidency who are supposed to represent his policies." These Negroes endorsed Senator Joseph B. Foraker's denunciation of Roosevelt's handling of the Brownsville affair.[18]

The discharge of the soldiers without a trial infuriated members of the black community and had lingering effects on political affairs for years to come—as presidential candidate Taft found out. Likewise, Roosevelt's decision placed leaders like Charles Banks, a loyal Republican, in a precarious situation because they had to rationalize Roosevelt's actions to themselves and to their constituents. Roosevelt wrote Banks at least three times between November and December 1908 for advice. Realizing that "the Brownsville business may come up again," he solicited Banks's help in trying to curb further negative consequences.[19] As a politician, Roosevelt took steps that were politically expedient, even when they went against some of his fundamental beliefs.[20]

Although Banks knew Wayne and Minnie Cox, it is unknown whether he was involved in the Indianola affair.[21] At that time he was not as influential in Mississippi politics as he later would become. However, after he moved to Mound Bayou in 1903, Banks regularly responded to similar situations on behalf of black political appointees with considerable resolve. Typically, he would churn out letters to Washington, members of the Tuskegee Machine, presidents, and others who could influence the outcome. Among other things, he went so far as to travel to Washington, D.C., and personally meet with presidents and their advisers in his efforts to correct injustices perpetrated against black people.[22]

Banks and President Taft

Banks became very involved in the 1908 presidential campaign. Early on, Washington solicited Banks's help in identifying Negro leaders in Mississippi who were not supporting Taft's nomination. Taft's political manager, Arthur I. Vorys of Indiana, wanted the names so he could invite the men to Washington, D.C., and possibly gain their support. Taft was suffering from a backlash over the Brownsville affair and other events. Taft and his supporters knew they needed as much help as they could get to gain Negro support.

Even though some blacks did not support Taft's nomination, one observer called Banks "the original Taft supporter" in Mississippi and said that "with voice and pen he did more than possibly any other man to turn popular support in the direction of Mr. Taft's candidacy." Banks himself stated that he "was really the first out and out Taft man" among Negroes in the Magnolia State. "We have had quite a battle in this state," Banks reported to Scott, explaining how difficult it had been to keep his position as a delegate at large to the Republican National Convention and simultaneously stay on good terms with the Negroes in Mississippi while supporting Taft. Even though Banks felt he had been mistreated at the state convention by Frank Harris Hitchcock, Taft's national campaign manager, he remained optimistic. "Out of it all I was master so far as the Negroes were concerned when it came to naming the delegation from the State at Large," Banks boasted.[23]

Out of all of the black delegates chosen for the Republican National Convention, Taft chose Banks to second his nomination for the candidacy, partially because of Washington's recommendation. The Tuskegee leader told Taft that Banks "is very black, has a pleasing appearance, is a good speaker and stands well with the strongest of both races in Mississippi."[24] However, according to one source, "for the sake of political expediency this honor was not conferred upon him."[25] This may be only partially true. Hitchcock blocked Banks from seconding the nomination because, he said, Banks "had been fighting him & could not accept him."[26] Ultimately, none of the Negroes recommended were allowed to second the nomination. This clearly disturbed Washington, who wrote his friend Charles W. Anderson of New York:

> The Foraker forces had no trouble in getting a Colored man to second his nomination, while the friends of Secretary Taft, of course, placed his Negro followers at the usual disadvantage in not providing such an opportunity. It would have been a tremendous advantage to the Secretary, if you, [William] Lewis . . . Banks or some other sensible Colored man had been asked . . . to prepare a second address. In some way, we shall have to try to bring these people to their senses.[27]

As the presidential elections approached, Banks realized that many blacks were unhappy with the Republican Party and were considering switching. However, he advised them that "changing from one party to another is useless. . . . Stand by the old party boys for out of that party came President Lincoln, and today we have one of the best Presidents that ever lived." No matter what Banks said, Mississippi Negroes were not convinced they would get a fair deal under Taft. They questioned his sincerity even though he promised Washington and other leaders he would not support "lily-whitism."[28]

After Taft won the election, Banks had the honor of participating in the inaugural parade, serving as colonel for one of Taft's staff members. Considerable pomp and circumstance accompanied the occasion: the colonels rode on fine horses and wore Prince Albert coats, silk hats, sashes, and rosettes.[29] Usually Negro participants in the inaugural parades were treated in a discriminatory fashion. Placed at the end of the parade, the Negro division had to pass after dark.[30]

After helping Taft get elected, Banks began to test the president's commitment to Negroes in the South. On April 1, 1909, Banks led a twelve-man delegation of black leaders from Mississippi to meet with President Taft. Banks stated in a letter to the president's secretary that the delegation wanted to find out "what little service we can [be] to the President and the administration in carrying out his policy as far as our State is concerned." Moreover, said Banks, they wanted "to know how best to serve him." But Banks clearly had other motives. While there, Banks showed Taft a newspaper article that stated that "all colored postmasters are to be removed." Taft, who was reportedly "jovial" in receiving Banks and the others, told them to "pay no attention to these reports."[31] The response seemed to satisfy Banks's primary purpose for meeting with the president, and his leading of this successful delegation helped establish Banks as one of, if not the most, influential black political leaders in Mississippi at the time.

On April 12, 1909, a Washington, D.C., newspaper article stated that President Taft had instructed the director of the census bureau to "disregard party lines" when selecting people for supervisor and other appointed positions, especially in the South.[32] Although Banks had said he could not and would not accept any appointed office, he became concerned after reading this article and wanted to have a hand in selecting the Negroes who would be appointed. In the 1900 census, Banks and Willis E. Mollison, a Vicksburg attorney, were the only Mississippi Negroes appointed as supervisors. Banks wanted to make sure that there were as many, if not more, in 1910. Washington suggested that Banks meet again with the president to explain his concerns. Banks took this advice.[33]

Banks became more and more concerned that Mississippi would have no Negro census supervisors appointed for the 1910 census and very few, if any, Negro enumerators.[34] Blacks outnumbered whites in Mississippi, and Banks believed they should be represented in some way. According to the 1900 census, Bolivar County had 31,197 blacks (88 percent of the total county population) and only 4,197 whites. Lonzo B. Moseley, Taft's white Mississippi national committeeman and also his patronage referee for the state, became a bitter adversary of Banks. By 1912, Moseley also held three federal offices in Mississippi: United States commissioner, clerk of the United States district court, and federal jury commissioner.[35] Once in 1908 Scott asked Banks to assume a conciliatory posture toward Moseley. "I want to say now that if the plan is to have me and those whom I represent deal through and at the direction of Mr. Moseley," Banks replied, "it will not suit at all."[36] Banks believed Moseley had headed the movement to prevent blacks from being appointed to positions though Moseley claimed the administration was averse to doing so. Hitchcock, one of Taft's managers and later postmaster general, also became one of Banks's political foes. Like Moseley, he oftentimes refused to cooperate with the black politicos and sympathized with "lily-whites."[37]

Banks wrote a letter to the president's secretary, Fred Warner Carpenter, expressing his concerns about the census matter. Carpenter did not respond, and five days later, when the census list came out for Mississippi, no blacks were included.[38] "The deal we are getting in this census matter is simply awful," Banks told Scott. "In this district alone for the last census there were 66 Negro enumerators [and] I doubt if there will be half this many in the entire State at this time."[39] Seeking an alternative, Banks began writing newspaper editors to persuade them to put his argument before the public.[40] He told Scott that the actions taken by the Taft administration have "dealt us a heavy blow" and that "the Negroes have lost heart, and feel that they have less friends about the White House than in 50 years." Banks realized blacks were slowly but surely being excluded from White House planning and decision making. "I see that 'Sambo' is left out," he complained to Scott.[41]

It appears Banks's protests had some effect on the administration by January 1910, because he was appointed special agent for Mississippi. As special agent, Banks was supposed to assist the supervisors in selecting and preparing "suitable Negro men enumerators."[42] However, Banks let Washington know that he did not consider the appointment a special honor, and "as to the pay," he said, "[I] have men in my employ whom I pay more than the allowance." Banks said he did not have time to do the work and "but for my duty to my country and a chance to serve my race, I would have positively declined the appointment."[43]

Also, Banks was now an assistant to the census supervisors, although he had previously served as a supervisor. But Banks was allowed to select at least forty-five black enumerators through this position, which continued his patronage power. Although this served as a form of self-promotion for Banks, he still did not like the treatment Negroes received in the census matter. He told Washington that even though he had done all he could for President Taft, "his public utterances touching the Negro have been of a kind calculated to drive them further away. Personally, I feel that he has done us more harm than good by what he has said."[44]

Banks did not care if the Taft administration knew how he felt. "It has cost me money, patience and time to reach a point with the Negroes of Mississippi where they trust me fully," Banks told Washington, and that "is a confidence I appreciate above ideas held by authorities and [I] cannot and will not play any part that is less than manly and courageous." "Now if this be 'treason, let treason be the most of it,'" Banks stated. Furthermore, he said he had "nothing to regret or withdraw" from what he had said and written.[45]

Meantime, Banks had learned that many Negro census applicants were not advised of the dates, times, and locations of the census exams, and, he said, "in a number of cases the examinations were started late, and time to do the work cut down seriously." Banks argued that the administration should address this grossly unfair practice.[46] Banks continued to work diligently on behalf of the Negro census applicants, which Washington and Scott believed was effective. Washington told Banks that when he stopped in the District of Columbia he found the census people "simply overjoyed by reason of your magnificent success. They say you set them all an example and demonstrated that they had no reason to be filled with fear as they were at first."[47]

Notwithstanding, no Negro supervisors were appointed for the 1910 census, and a smaller number of Negro enumerators were selected than in 1900. Banks became so incensed by the actions of President Taft and his administration that he claimed the Republican supervisors in Mississippi, in particular Moseley in Jackson, "gave the Negroes the rawest deal of all. . . . I hardly think they could have fared much worse under the rankest and most radical Democratic partisan." [48]

Political Patronage

Banks's political influence can be seen in his assistance to candidates who wanted to keep or receive judicial appointments and postal positions. Patronage dispensation was a critical resource for members of the Tuskegee Machine. Banks worked hard to secure a judicial appointment for his friend Thomas Owen, who Banks felt was the right type of white person for such a position. Some twenty-eight letters were written on Owen's behalf from people ranging from businessmen to judges. "Our candidate will come highly recommended by members of the bar throughout the state," Banks boasted, with "a number of Judges and Chancellors being for him and the almost certain next Governor, leaning his way."[49]

Around December 1910, Congress debated whether to appoint a new federal judge for Bolivar County. If it did so, Banks wanted to control the appointment. As he had done on many other occasions, Banks turned to the Tuskegee Machine for support.[50] He asked Scott to contact Charles Hilles, private secretary to President Taft, to make certain "nothing will be done without our knowledge." In addition, he asked Scott to follow these developments very closely with him. Both Scott and Washington agreed to lend whatever assistance they could. In February 1911, Scott planned to write to Frank Cole, secretary to the U.S. attorney general, about the matter. But first he wanted Banks to read and edit what he had written. In the letter, Scott did not mention Owen's name: "I have not mentioned the name of your candidate as I think [it] well to feel Mr. Cole out first before 'laying the cards on the table.'"[51]

On a previous occasion, Cole had invited Scott to discuss with him any matters relating to race, and Scott took this opportunity to assist Banks. He explained to Cole that a bill pending before Congress would create another federal judgeship in Mississippi. "The influential Negroes in that state are anxious to have appointed to this place a man likely to be sympathetic and well disposed toward them," Scott said. He asked that suggestions from "some of these colored citizens of worth and moment," be heard before a selection was made. Scott told Cole that blacks in Mississippi were making more progress than in any other southern state and for that reason they did not want someone appointed who would be "not so well disposed toward their progress."[52]

Banks continued to press members of the Tuskegee Machine for help, especially after it looked as if the bill would pass both the House and the Senate.[53] In the meantime, even within Mississippi, Banks started tapping his contacts to help Owen. "You have done an especially wise thing in securing . . . the earnest support of the best people in your state," Scott wrote Banks. Indeed, his tentacles even found their way into Governor Edmund F. Noel's office. Although the details of his letter and the response he received from the governor's office are unknown, Scott, Washington and Banks were impressed that the salutation read, "Dear Mr. Banks." Throughout the South, whites rarely addressed blacks as Mister, especially upper-class whites in Mississippi.[54]

But perhaps Banks misinterpreted the letter from the governor's office, because less than a month later, he reported to Scott that Governor Noel "is after the Judgeship which we want for our mutual friend, Mr. Owen." Apparently Noel had his own man in mind for the position if it materialized. Surprisingly, Banks was not overly concerned about this turn of events. "I don't think he [Noel's nominee] has any show," Banks said, "but I think it well to keep in touch with Mr. Hilles."[55] Banks had so much confidence in the effectiveness of the Tuskegee Machine that he felt at the federal level he had more Republican patronage power and influence than the governor of Mississippi.[56]

Before Scott contacted Hilles, he wanted to know the exact status of the judgeship. "I need to be in position to state that the bill has been introduced or will soon be introduced, that it has been passed or will soon be passed, etc.," he told Banks.[57] By March 1912, Banks wrote Hilles and informed him that the bill had passed. With more than a million Negroes in Mississippi, a majority of the state's population, Banks told Hilles he was "naturally interested in the whole matter." The new district would include the Black Belt of Mississippi, where Negroes outnumbered whites four to one, so "the new judge would mean much to us," Banks said.[58]

Banks had a serious concern that Democrats in Congress were plotting to delay the passage of the bill, hoping for a Democrat in the next election so they could name the judge. "It occurs to me that the present administration has all to lose and nothing to gain by allowing the measure to be deferred," Banks warned.[59] For whatever reason, Owen did not receive the appointment.

In 1912, Banks started pushing to have Phillip A. Rush, a "leading white lawyer" of Senatobia, Mississippi, appointed to either the State Department or the Department of Justice. In a letter to Scott, Banks noted he had "run across this opportunity" and asked for Scott's help while Washington was out of town. "Of course I know the Doctor is away, but I thought we might pull off this stunt while he is away," Banks joked.

Humor notwithstanding, Banks clearly realized that this appointment would help bolster his power as a federal patronage dispenser for Mississippi.[60]

Scott followed through with a letter to William H. Lewis, a black Harvard Law School graduate who served as an assistant attorney general for the Department of Justice. Lewis had landed this position through Washington's endorsement.[61] When Lewis received the letter from Scott he "rushed" to the attorney general's office with it and delivered it to the secretary, Frank Cole. Lewis had assured Scott that "Mr. Rush's application will have the most careful consideration of the Attorney General and the President."[62] In the meantime, Scott sent Lewis's response to Rush. The letter made it apparent to Rush that the Mississippi wing of the Tuskegee Machine (headed by Banks) had been working on his behalf.[63] Scott sent all of the letters to Banks for review. In the end, the president denied Rush's application and appointed his own man.[64]

Banks never gave up trying to help Owen become a judge. When federal judge Henry Niles died in 1918, Banks looked to Tuskegee again for help from the machine. Banks wanted to see an end to the economic exploitation of black labor, and judges greatly affected the outcome of such cases. "On account of peonage and other cases," he said, "we are interested in having a liberal Democrat like Judge Jones as [his] successor." Of course, the liberal he had in mind was Owen. Banks asked Moton, then principal of Tuskegee Institute, to help but to do so "cautiously." "What we want is no hasty action," Banks said.[65]

Moton went to Judge William H. Thomas of the Alabama Supreme Court, who gave Moton recommendations for persons he thought were "suitable" to succeed Judge Niles. Thomas suggested either Judge Jeff Truly or Judge J. S. Sexton, both of whom were already circuit or county court judges. After this, Moton asked Banks to tell him how he could be of service in securing the appointment of either man he wanted. "Judge Thomas is one of our most loyal friends, and I feel we may count absolutely on his judgement. He thoroughly understands the situation," wrote Moton.[66]

But Banks rejected both of Judge Thomas's recommendations outright. He knew both judges fairly well, he told Moton, and did not find either one "suitable." In fact, Banks reported that Judge Sexton participated in Mississippi's constitutional convention of 1890, which was held expressly to disfranchise black voters in Mississippi and which produced the dreadful Mississippi Plan. What is more, Banks said, he did not have the same confidence in Thomas as did Moton. He reminded Moton that when Thomas campaigned for governor, "part of his platform was 'Substitution of Negro Labor with Italian Labor.'" So, said Banks, he could not accept Moton's recommendations with good conscience. Instead, he recommended Owen, "who is," he said, "in many respects, one of the biggest and best men that I know of in all the Southland." In his opinion, neither person suggested by Thomas could be compared to Owen.[67]

Through the Tuskegee Machine, Banks had a voice in federal appointments all over Mississippi. Influential whites such as Owen and Rush realized they could benefit by working with members of the Tuskegee Machine. As Mississippi's chief lieutenant, Banks used patronage to exert influence over even powerful whites in the state.

For postal appointments, Banks lobbied on behalf of several Mississippians, black and white. He worked hard to help a white woman, Lillie W. Nugent, try to secure the postmaster job at Rosedale, although his adversary, Moseley, had someone else in mind.[68] Banks also worked to have another white woman, Vannie Jones, appointed postmaster at Beulah. Both the Rosedale and Beulah post offices served his county, and Banks thought "that it is but justice that we should name this appointment." Nine-tenths of the people in the county were Negroes, and they would be the ones patronizing the post offices.[69] "Business with the post office is made easier and more pleasant if those in charge of the office are anything like easy to approach," Banks stated. Moreover, he said, "as a rule we know pretty well those best suited in temperament for such places."[70] While it is unclear whether Nugent received the post at Rosedale, it is certain that Jones did not receive the post at Beulah.[71]

Thomas I. Keys, a Negro, is the postal worker Banks worked most vigorously to support. Keys had been postmaster at Ocean Springs for twelve years, under three Republican administrations, and he had the support of many white businessmen in his town, especially the mayor and a minister. Keys asked Banks for assistance when he discovered Moseley and his associates were trying to have him ousted. Banks was alarmed, he told Carpenter, because "some Negroes who have held Post Offices for several years in this State . . . are now being opposed for reappointment." Democrats believed if they stirred white resentment about Negroes holding these posts, they would not be reappointed under Taft's administration.[72] Banks eventually realized his complaints were falling on deaf ears. After receiving little or no response from Carpenter, Banks wrote directly to President Taft to plead his case, to no avail.[73]

Although he was crossing party lines, Moseley supported a white Democrat over Keys. Moseley told Keys the reason he did this was because of the "President's policy not to appoint any colored man in the South."[74] Consequently, Banks and Scott agreed to use the Keys matter to test the support of the Taft administration. "Ocean Springs offers the opportunity for the test of strength referred to by our Washington friend," Scott stated. Banks concurred about "making the Ocean Springs a test case."[75] Of course, Banks solicited the support of Washington and the Tuskegee Machine. "It seems to me to be grossly unfair to allow the referee in this state to use the President's name in forcing our people out of offices they have held for years without any trouble," Banks lamented to Washington.[76]

Meanwhile, events unfolded that reinforced Banks's belief that blacks had few, if any, friends in the White House. This really became apparent after Banks made a plea to Arthur I. Vorys, one of Taft's political managers, whom Banks had considered one of the allies of the Tuskegee Machine. Banks wrote to Vorys about the mistreatment in the Ocean Springs matter and provided specific details about Moseley's efforts to have Negro postmasters removed from office. Banks also remarked about having had trouble in the past bringing Moseley in line and expressed dissatisfaction with Hitchcock's handling of the Ocean Springs affair.[77]

The day after Banks sent this letter, Washington wrote Hilles in support of Banks. "It seems to me that now, if ever, is the time for Mr. Vorys to be of help to the man who lined up with him," Washington noted, "at a time when Moseley was absolutely obstructing the situation in Mississippi." Washington suggested that while Moseley continued to support Roosevelt, Banks had begun to support Taft. To really drive home his point, he reminded Hilles, "it is due more to Banks than anyone else that we were able to get out of Mississippi a Taft delegation."[78]

Interestingly, Vorys forwarded Banks's letter to Postmaster General Hitchcock, a political enemy of Banks and an ally of Moseley, claiming he did so because it would be a "means of removing any misunderstanding between you and him."[79] This shocked Banks, Washington, and Scott. Washington conceded that "Mr. Vorys' action in sending your letter to Mr. Hitchcock puzzles me more than anything I have run across in a long time."[80]

The Ocean Springs affair dragged on. According to a letter Banks sent Fred Moore of the *New York Age*, Moseley called Keys to a meeting in Jackson (at Moseley's office) in March 1910. While Keys was there,

Moseley asked for his resignation, saying it was the president's policy to not appoint Negroes to office in the South. But Keys refused to resign. Later that month, Keys received a letter from Moseley requesting him to meet in Washington, D.C., about the first of April. When Keys arrived, Moseley took him to the office of Postmaster General Hitchcock. Hitchcock reportedly told Keys that because of so much opposition in the South, he could not appoint him.[81]

In an effort to appease Keys, however, Hitchcock promised that if Keys would resign, he would "secure him a place in some of the depts. in Washington with a salary of $1,400 per year." Hitchcock also told Keys that in Washington, D.C., he could secure a good education for his children. Again, Keys refused, noting that despite what the postmaster general said, there was no opposition of consequence in Ocean Springs.[82] Regardless of the efforts of Banks and the Tuskegee Machine, Keys still did not receive the appointment as postmaster—the position went to a white Democrat.[83] Although members of the Tuskegee Machine were fighting to maintain influence within the Republican Party, they were losing the battle.

Taft explained his refusal to appoint Negroes in the South by claiming his actions were in the name of reform and in the party's overall interest. But blacks were not that naïve; they knew that Taft's acts were harmful to Negro progress. Blacks also realized that men like Moseley and Hitchcock were merely agents for Taft and that he condoned all they were doing.[84]

Election of 1912

In early May 1912, the *New York Times*, in a story entitled "Booker T. Washington working for Roosevelt," reported that Banks and Perry Howard, both Mississippi delegates, were going to support Roosevelt over Taft. The article also stated that Banks and Howard were members of the same "Business League" and were close friends of Washington.[85] Similar rumors began to spread throughout the country. For instance, Fred Moore reported to Washington that Taft, William Brown McKinley (a Republican congressman and Taft leader from Illinois), and Hilles heard that Banks had considered shifting his support to Roosevelt. Moore told Washington he would tell Banks that "it would be almost suicidal for him to go otherwise than for Taft in as much as the President told me that he was interested in Mound Bayou, and was trying to help them out in every way possible in their efforts to establish Mound Bayou."[86] Unbeknownst to Moore, Taft was lying. Moore advised Banks, "it is very necessary that our leading men stand out strong in support of Taft and not allow any suspicions to attach to them."[87]

Washington became concerned about these reports and told Banks that the media had "linked your name up with mine in connection with Mr. Roosevelt and Mr. Taft." "You can easily see," he said, "that if you should shift from Mr. Taft, it would be very embarrassing to me." Rumors even circulated that Washington had gone to Mound Bayou to try to convince Banks to stick with Taft. He presumed Banks had seen the newspaper articles, but he said he was "quite sure that these dispatches are fakes, hatched up in Washington." Washington informed Banks that the information was purportedly being sent out by Isaiah Montgomery, who remained loyal to Taft.[88]

When the Republican state convention met in Jackson, Mississippi, on March 28, 1912, it was a virtual powder keg waiting to explode. The party had split, with some Republicans supporting the incumbent, Taft, and others supporting Roosevelt. Most of the party leaders were Negroes, and those supporting Roosevelt understood that if he received the nomination, the position of national committeeman, held by Moseley, would be given to someone in their camp. This was very important; the national committeeman served as the chief dispenser of patronage in the state.[89]

When the convention was called to order, two factions were present, each with its own delegates. Moseley headed the Taft supporters, called the "regular faction," while Charles Banks, Sidney D. Redmond, and Perry Howard headed the "Roosevelt faction." Each group wanted control of the convention, which would determine which delegates would go to the national convention in Chicago that summer. Tension filled the air, and according to the *Memphis Commercial Appeal*, "while pistols may not have actually been drawn, there were numbers of delegates who let it be known that they were prepared to draw if the occasion required it."[90]

At least on one occasion, proceedings did turn violent. The *Chicago Daily Tribune* reported:

> In Mississippi L. B. Moseley, who is sitting as a Taft national committeeman, made out a temporary roll of the convention at large. When it met, Michael J. Mulvihill, the postmaster at Vicksburg announced that he had been designated as temporary chairman. . . . W[illis] E. Mollison, a delegate, then moved to substitute Daniel W. Gary, a Roosevelt man, as temporary chairman.

The motion was adopted by a vote of 3 to 1, but Mulvihill declared it lost and refused to permit a division. Thereupon Mollison moved that Gary be elected permanent chairman, which was done by a vote of 210 to 60.

When Gary [a Negro] ascended to the platform to take the gavel, M. H. Daly, United States Postmaster at Coldwater, pressed a pistol against Gary and threatened to kill him. Gary was surrounded by United States marshals, policemen, and others, pulled and hauled, and finally was thrown from the platform. Fortunately he was caught by some of his friends or he might have been seriously injured.[91]

Ultimately, Moseley's regular faction won out and chose delegates who would endorse Taft at the national convention. Dissatisfied with the results, the Roosevelt faction chose its own delegates and left it to the Republican National Committee to decide which were legitimate. Unfortunately for Banks, Howard, Redmond and other black Roosevelt supporters, Moseley served as the Mississippi representative on the national committee.[92]

By the time the Republican National Convention convened in Chicago in 1912, tempers had boiled over and street fights between Roosevelt and Taft men were a regular occurrence in the Windy City. In time, the national committee met and attentively considered the state of affairs in Mississippi. They heard about Gary's ouster from the platform at the state convention. Nonetheless, because of Moseley's presence and influence on the committee, it overwhelmingly ruled in favor of the regular faction.[93]

Although Banks had been elected a delegate at large to the national convention, as in 1908, he no longer operated as one. He became one of Taft's most vociferous critics at the convention. Banks, who a northern paper described as "an influential member of his race in Mississippi," caused a nationwide stir when he bolted to Roosevelt. Not only did he do this, he also wrote a letter to McKinley, Taft's national campaign director: "I am returning to you herewith the money placed in my hands, at your suggestion, to defray travelling costs of some of the delegates from Mississippi." The implications of this letter were clear to all—Taft's men had been trying to buy the delegate's support. Banks sent a copy of the letter to Roosevelt's campaign manager, Senator Joseph M. Dixon, who sent copies of the letter to the press.[94]

"It is apparent that someone connected with your campaign has been continually trying to discredit me before the country and with my people for some time," Banks told McKinley. A few weeks before the national convention, Banks had gone to Washington, D.C., to look into the judicial bill before Congress, and while there he was called to Taft's campaign headquarters. One of Taft's assistants, Banks claimed, "brought up the matter of expenses for delegates from my state. I told him then and there, in your presence, that so far as I was concerned, I would not accept any expense money for me whatever." Nonetheless, said Banks, "you then proposed that I take enough for the rest of the delegates. I stated to you that they were all men who could get to Chicago." Somehow Banks was persuaded to take the money for the other delegates.[95]

However, when Banks arrived at Chicago, he discovered some delegates had been told he had a considerable sum of money for them and for himself, which made it appear that Banks was holding on to or had spent the money earmarked for other Negro delegates. Banks resented these insinuations and he returned all the money to Taft's campaign manager. "The insinuations that I can be or have been bought are known to be untrue and unfounded by no one better than those connected with your campaign, as well as those of four years ago," Banks noted. "I have never asked any of you for one cent and never applied for an office." He stated that he was "a man worth $75,000 or $100,000 in his own right, elected by his own people to a position of secretary and treasurer [of the MBA], paying a fair salary, and handling nearly $200,000 a year." This showed that while they were suggesting impropriety on Banks's part, he was financially secure and the people of Mississippi had no problem with entrusting him with their $200,000 per year. Any man "with hundreds of people in his employ, either as tenants, wage hands, clerks, etc., and whose credit runs up in the thousands, is not apt to allow you or any set of men to buy him with a few hundred dollars," he said.[96]

To make his position crystal clear, Banks stated that his "dissatisfaction with the policy of the Taft administration is not of recent and spasmodic origin, but as early as April following the inauguration, I headed a delegation from Mississippi and called on the president." While at that meeting, Banks said, he protested "against any action . . . which did not mean to accord to us that which to us by right belonged, and by all the rules of the game." Ultimately, he went public at the convention, making it known that he would no longer support Taft but support Roosevelt instead. This affair embarrassed Taft and Moseley and added to the already charged political atmosphere.[97]

Banks did not show much concern about how Taft's forces would respond to his actions; he cared more about keeping the confidence of his people in Mississippi. In fact, he stated that no delegate from the state could honestly say he had been "elected on the strength of, or alliance with any particular candidate." By this, Banks meant he had not been paid off by either candidate before the convention. Black people in Mississippi, he concluded, "have trusted me more than once, they will trust me again, and I know whereof I speak when I say 90 per cent of the party in that state desire effective protests against some conditions prevailing there as well as in some other sections of the country."[98]

Initially, Taft supporters only gave a brief rebuttal to Banks's letter. "I hope every Republican will read the Banks letter with extreme care and then draw his own conclusions. Its disclosures are illuminating. Its issuance from the Roosevelt headquarters is significant," McKinley wrote.[99] Shortly after this, Taft's political managers, especially Moseley, started a vicious campaign to discredit Banks "with every Negro who visited them."[100]

In an effort to silence Banks, Taft's managers claimed they had information that would discredit him. Banks boldly urged them to publish whatever information they had but insisted they be able to vouch for the truthfulness of their report. They leveled several charges. First, they charged Banks with mishandling "a few hundred dollars." He responded that they were falsely accusing him to create a bad impression with the public and to mitigate the effects of his letter when he returned the money.[101]

Second, they alleged that Banks tried to "bribe delegates to desert Taft for Roosevelt." Taft's managers persuaded the Reverend W. H. Shumpert to say Banks tried to bribe him to leave Taft for Roosevelt. In response, Banks asserted that Shumpert had, in fact, come to see him because Shumpert needed help paying the mortgage on his home, which was "now long past due." Moreover, said Banks, "I have helped him before these days, and when he tries to create false impressions he knows better than anyone else that he does less than a man, saying nothing of being a minister of the gospel."[102]

Third, they produced an affidavit from a man named Buckley, who also alleged Banks tried to bribe him politically. Banks called the man's credibility into question, stating that Buckley "represents nothing" and suggesting that Taft's men handpicked him because the Republicans in his home district would not have elected him as their delegate.[103]

"And speaking of bribery," Banks stated, it was Buckley who said that "Mr. Moseley, the National Committeeman from Mississippi, has promised to allow him to name certain postmasters immediately after the convention is over." Not stopping there, Banks asserted that "this is most likely true because Mr. Moseley will make such promises. He has made similar promises to every colored man on the delegation."[104]

Banks enumerated his grievances against President Taft and his administration. First, he said he had never been satisfied with Taft's statements in his inaugural address about the appointment of Negroes in the South. "This he knows," Banks affirmed.[105] During that speech (which Theodore Roosevelt read and approved before Taft delivered it), Taft had stated he would not appoint blacks to positions in the South where it would cause friction between the races and thereby hinder productivity. This assured whites that if they raised a ruckus, Taft would remove black appointees from their posts, which is basically what he did. The practice became so common under his administration that some people referred to it as Taft's "Southern policy."[106]

"When he came into office we had four Negroes holding presidential post offices," said Banks, but "today we have none save in the exclusively Negro town, Mound Bayou." Banks said that the only reason a black held the post in his town was because no whites were there to fill the position. Referring to the president, Banks said he did not have "too much confidence in his promises regarding my people, for it is for them that I am battling." Moving beyond Mississippi politics, Banks berated Taft for lying to Walter Cohen, who had served as receiver of the New Orleans land office. "Mr. Taft promised in my presence to retain Walter Cohen in his place at New Orleans," said Banks, but "the president did not make good on his word."[107]

Banks also exposed the fact that during a recent senatorial campaign in Mississippi, a prominent white Democrat who was well respected in his party, "announced from Washington that the President would soon remove the remaining Negro postmasters in south Mississippi." In response to this announcement, Banks said, he had written to President Taft and his advisers. They had told him, "they would not be removed." Nonetheless, each and every one was removed, said Banks, "and in all cases [they] had the support of black and white reputable citizens in their community." Banks even revisited the Thomas Keys affair. He explained how Keys had been summoned to Moseley's office, where he was told "that on account of being a Negro, he could not have him appointed again but would try to get him a place in Washington. Against all of this I protested all the time, but of no avail."[108]

On a broader level, Banks talked about how the Republican conventions in Mississippi were a sham. "Mr. Moseley is opposed to and fights bitterly any man of color in Mississippi who shows any manliness and independence in politics," Banks related. Moreover, Banks claimed, Moseley had never led a delegation to a Republican Convention that he had not "selected." Banks refused to say "elected," because the convention members were comprised mainly of "officeholders, janitors, [and] professional jurors of his selection." "One of his delegates selected to come here cannot even write his name," Banks charged. Even more damning, Banks said that at the Republican conventions in Mississippi, white police officers, who were Democrats, were stationed at the doors and on the floor and that no one could enter without a ticket with Moseley's name stamped on it. This deeply angered Banks: "Moseley may as well tell the delegates to remain at home and send them word whom he has selected."[109]

According to Banks, Moseley was stifling the Republican Party in Mississippi, which would lead to a loss of credibility with both blacks and whites. Moseley, Banks argued, "has an office holding trust, himself an office holder, and all of his relatives, from the postmaster at Jackson down." Indeed, Moseley did hold three federal offices in Mississippi. Ultimately, Banks blamed President Taft for the problems blacks were having with lily-white Republicans like Moseley: "I have told the President in the White House of these conditions, and our objections. He knows about them, and yet Moseley is continued the absolute boss, before whose scepter I refuse to bow . . . ," asserted Banks.[110]

Four years earlier, Banks reminded, he was "the original Taft man in Mississippi," but even then in 1908, he had made it clear he expected certain conditions to be improved for blacks in his state and Taft had agreed. "The net result, however, is that we are now worse off in Mississippi than ever since emancipation," Banks proclaimed. Banks firmly believed that Moseley and other Taft managers would do anything to destroy any Negro who was "independent in thought and action." He made it clear he did not desire to have his work validated by Taft or his managers: "My work for and among the negroes of Mississippi does not depend upon the certificate of Mr. Moseley, not even upon that of the President himself."[111]

Speaking out as he did certainly took courage. What he said about the president and his managers at the convention could have easily led to his death upon his return to the Magnolia State. Blacks in Mississippi were killed for much smaller offenses than this. Despite the danger involved, Banks felt obligated to speak out on behalf of black Mississippians and black Republicans everywhere.

When the presidential election of 1912 came, Banks, Howard, Mollison, Gary, and other black Mississippi leaders broke rank with Booker T. Washington, opposed Taft's nomination, and bolted to Roosevelt.[112] Although Washington had told Banks that "if you should shift from Mr. Taft, it would be very embarrassing to me," Banks could not force himself to be conciliatory in the matter.[113] Out of deference to Washington, Banks did not immediately defect from Taft. However, other black Mississippi political leaders, such as Howard and Redmond, immediately joined the Roosevelt exodus to establish the Progressive, or Bull Moose, Party. Ultimately, Banks and other black Roosevelt supporters were dismayed when Roosevelt barred southern Negroes from serving as delegates at the Bull Moose Convention, claiming they were part of the reason he did not receive the regular Republican Party nomination. They were also disappointed by his decision to make the southern wing of the Progressive Party "lily-white."[114]

Other prominent Mississippi blacks, including Louis K. Atwood and Isaiah Montgomery, continued to support Taft. These leaders, however, were out of touch with most blacks in Mississippi. Nevertheless, Banks believed he had more than enough reason to abandon Taft, whom Banks said had set Negroes back at least fifty years.[115] In his mind, Banks had to choose between two evils, and the lesser evil was Roosevelt.

After Washington realized Banks intended to defect, he informed him that he was not upset but that he still planned to remain neutral. "You are free, as you know without any [approval] from me, to act in any way that your own judgment and conscience dictates," Washington said.[116] In the end, Woodrow Wilson, a southern Democrat, was elected president. Indeed, some blacks, among them W. E. B. Du Bois, were so disgusted with both Taft and Roosevelt that they decided to support Wilson. Despite the support of blacks, Wilson ended up moving the nation further in the direction of segregation.[117]

Under Wilson's administration, the Tuskegee Machine's political apparatus all but vanished. Even Washington only communicated directly with Wilson on a few occasions. Washington, Banks, and other members of the machine lost much of their patronage power under the Wilson administration because as Republicans they could not recommend appointments. Banks, like other black leaders in the South, continued to lose influence too within the Republican Party as it increasingly became lily-white and conservative. Meanwhile, Democrats were dutifully eliminating Negroes from the overall political scene.[118]

Election of 1916

About a month before Washington died, Banks wrote him a lengthy letter "on matters political." Referring to patronage, Banks stated that the Republican Party hardly existed in the South "when there are no offices to give." The coming campaign, he said, offered an opportunity for blacks to assist northern Republican managers in strengthening the party in the South in a way that would help them as well as the Negroes. But, he cautioned, "it is folly for the managers at the North to look for any real building up of a party here by dealing through the office holding Republicans whose only interest is entrenching themselves for dispensing patronage."[119]

Although Banks said he would work with the GOP when the goal was to provide something "worthwhile to us as a people," he rejected the Republican Party's mistreatment of its Negro constituents. "The idea that the way to build up a party in the South, as held by some, is to equal or out do the Democrats in ostracizing and curbing the Negro is erroneous and not bourne out by past events," Banks told Washington. This approach, he said, was "unsound, un-American, does not deserve to succeed and will not make lasting success."[120]

When it came time for the state and national Republican Conventions in 1916, Banks believed "that the Negroes of the South will have a difficult time this year in getting what should be ours in the coming . . . conventions." So in January, Banks started laying the groundwork for the April conventions. He wanted to make sure three things occurred: first, that black Republicans in the South be accorded proper recognition at the conventions. Second, that black Republicans continue to hammer away at lily-whites within the party. And third, that they continue to fight "against the policy . . . of having affairs in the hands of a class of men in the South who really do not want to deal squarely with the colored men of importance, and who will not take orders from them." Banks sent letters expressing his ideas to prominent black Republicans in Texas, Tennessee, South Carolina, Georgia, Louisiana and Arkansas, in hope that they would work with him.[121]

By this time, Washington had died, so Banks turned to Scott for assistance in mustering political support. "I am writing you on matters political," he said, "and think that you can be of effective service to me, and through me to the boys of our State generally." Many of Banks's complaints about the Republican Party were similar to those he made years earlier during the Taft administration:

> You, perhaps, know that in nearly all of the states of the South, the handful of men who call themselves the Republican Party among the Whites, are nothing more than an office holding crowd and are pretty well all opposed to election as delegates of Negroes who are really representative, who have opinions of their own and who are independent in thought and action. They have done nothing to keep the Party alive and while they try to impress the white leaders of the North that they are doing something in this direction, yet, as a matter of fact, they do nothing and will never do anything except band themselves together for the Control of Post Offices during Republican Administration. This is particularly true of Mississippi.[122]

At the 1916 Republican National Convention, under a new apportionment, Mississippi was to have twelve delegates. According to Banks, "the chances are that our boys can elect at least one-half of these if we can be assured of recognition when we reach Chicago." Banks asked Scott to put him in touch with some of the influential and prominent managers and candidates from the North "who will see that we are treated right by the Committee on Credentials and that we stand for and will receive due recognition."[123]

Banks also informed Scott that he favored Roosevelt for the Republican nomination but that he would "work with any available line-up." Though Banks had kept in touch with Roosevelt over the years, his goal was justice for Negroes. When Banks wrote to Scott, he did not know whom the latter planned to support. But he told Scott that "when it comes to a matter of seeing that our people get what is their due in this section or any other section, you and I stand on the same platform."[124]

Scott agreed with Banks about supporting Roosevelt. "I have reviewed the whole field myself," he said, "without being able to see anybody on the horizon but the Colonel." But as for placing Banks in contact with influential northern Republicans, Scott said Banks had been keeping closer contacts with Roosevelt's advisers, such as George Perkins, chairman of the Republican Party, than he had. In fact, he said, he had not kept in touch with any but Roosevelt himself. And Roosevelt had refused to discuss his campaign with Scott.[125]

When the Mississippi Republican Convention took place, the lily-whites, headed by the national committeeman, Moseley, prevented Banks and his longtime political ally Mollison from being elected to the state delegation. Moseley obviously had not forgotten how Banks lambasted him and Taft at the previous national convention. Meanwhile, Banks and Mollison threatened to contest the delegates at large at the coming national convention. Bad blood continued to exist between the two, and they were never reconciled. Moseley died in 1917, and Michael J. Mulvihill of Vicksburg, a man of the same ilk, replaced him.[126]

Banks attended the Republican National Convention in Chicago and again put his support behind Roosevelt. Unfortunately, Roosevelt did not receive the nomination. Instead, it went to Charles Hughes, former governor of New York and U.S. Supreme Court justice.[127]

In 1919, a large contingent of Negroes, under the leadership of Howard, sought recognition at the Republican National Committee meeting in Saint Louis and also at the Republican National Convention in Chicago. However, both times they were unsuccessful. They were defeated by the forces of Mulvihill, the new national committeeman. Early on, Mulvihill had the support of Isaiah Montgomery and Eugene Booze, but when he refused to appoint any blacks to significant positions in the party, even these supporters defected. In 1920, Howard unsuccessfully challenged Mulvihill for the position of national committeeman for Mississippi. In 1924, he ran against Mulvihill again and with almost unanimous Negro support, Howard defeated Mulvihill and became the first black to serve on the Republican National Committee in the twentieth century.[128]

Throughout the South, black Republicans fared much the same. Lily-white factions continued to gain strength in the party while the role of blacks diminished.[129] Intraparty conflicts continued to plague the GOP. In the end, Wilson was elected to a second term, so most blacks expected and received no improvements politically. Wilson remained in office until 1921, two years before Banks died.[130]

Although Banks continued to communicate with presidents, by 1921 virtually all of his power as a patronage dispenser had disappeared.[131] Later in life, Banks realized that undying party loyalty did not benefit the Negro. In a letter to Robert Moton he related:

it is far better to have high class Democrats in such places than to have the professional office holding type, characteristic of the average Southern white Republican. The one [Democrat] is sure of his ground socially and otherwise and has the courage to give us a reasonably square deal under the circumstances, [and] does not attempt to take both the organization as well as the office.[132]

By contrast, Banks believed the Republican "usually tries to 'out Herod, Herod.'"[133] Moton agreed with Banks's assessment: "Good, high class Democrats are infinitely safer and more acceptable to colored people than half hearted, professional Lilly-white Republicans who are with the Republican Party in the last analysis, for the 'loaves and fishes.'"[134]

As the political and racial climate in America changed, blacks received less and less sympathy from each administration. In all likelihood, this reinforced Banks's belief that the solution to the Negro problem in America did not fall within the realm of politics. Though he had tasted the political power of patronage, Banks did not advocate political agitation to the same extent as did leaders such as Du Bois and Trotter.

Although Banks never ran for political office, he certainly wanted to influence and choose those who did. But mounting discrimination in politics encouraged him to promote economic development over political activism. After Negroes developed a sound economic base, he believed, they would find it easier to achieve their political rights.

"Wizard" of Finance

"Never Running Away from Battle"

Various Business Ventures

Charles Banks was an entrepreneur and business promoter throughout most of his life. Notwithstanding, some scholars have suggested that his business enterprises, particularly the Mound Bayou Oil Mill, which was capitalized at $100,000, were dismal failures.[1] This interpretation needs to be reconsidered. Banks started Banks & Bro., a mercantile business, when he was about sixteen. From then until his death in 1923, Banks supported himself and his family through various ventures. More than his other endeavors, Banks's entrepreneurship was his greatest success and was one reason Washington admired him. In *My Larger Education*, Washington called Banks "the most influential businessman in the United States."[2] For Washington, Banks served as a living model of what the Negro could accomplish through business development. He overcame extreme poverty as a youth and accumulated some wealth through the principle of economic uplift.

By 1911, Banks served as a director of two insurance companies, the Union Guaranty Insurance Company of Mississippi in Jackson and the Mississippi Beneficial Life Insurance Company in Indianola. He also was a banker, general manager of the Mound Bayou Oil Mill, and owner of a cotton brokerage company, a blacksmith shop, and a laundry. In addition, he owned stock in most of the eleven black banks in Mississippi and stock in several other businesses, including the Farmer's Cooperative Mercantile Company, run by his brother-in-law, Eugene Booze. Moreover, Banks formed a partnership with the undertaker in Mound Bayou, John W.

Francis, in 1907, which dealt in land speculation, building supplies, and lumber sales, and they also operated a mercantile business together. Banks also owned substantial property in Memphis, Clarksdale, and other surrounding towns. He held the titles to at least 250 lots in Mound Bayou, estimated to be worth $7,000, and owned over 1,000 acres of land in Bolivar County. He also purchased more than 2,000 acres of land in the Saint Francis Basin in Arkansas.[3]

Banks's businesses provided jobs for "hundreds of people," as clerks, tenants, wage hands, and so forth, and was one of his contributions to racial uplift. At a time when some Negroes were earning $20 a month, Banks paid the manager of his cotton speculation business $5 a day, including Sundays.[4] In 1915, Banks placed his net worth at $100,000.[5] Scott and Washington often referred Tuskegee students to Banks for work in Mound Bayou. This arrangement benefited not only Banks but also Tuskegee, because it provided employment opportunities for its graduates. While Tuskegee was their training ground, Mound Bayou became the place Tuskegee graduates could apply the skills they learned at the institute.

Many people outside of Mississippi also respected Banks as a businessman. Scott often congratulated Banks on "the fine standing you have with all of the business men whom you have to touch."[6] Scott's words were true; Victor H. Tulane, cashier of the Alabama Penny Savings Bank in Montgomery went to Banks for advice about his bank's financial statement. After analyzing the statement Banks found only one mistake: "I beg to ask did you not over-look the item 'capital paid in' in your published statement. I take it that you have some capital paid in. This should show, otherwise it looks good to me." That he could give this advice illustrates that Banks had knowledge of finance and accounting principles.[7]

Another example of the respect accorded Banks for his business knowledge is his election as secretary-treasurer of the MBA. E. F. Perkins held the job prior to Banks, but he died in March 1910. The secretary-treasurer had considerable responsibility; the association had 17,000 members, and the secretary-treasurer handled $15,000 to $20,000 a month for the organization. Edward W. Lampton, A.M.E. bishop and head of the Masonic lodge in Mississippi, along with many others, wanted Banks to run for the position. Reluctant at first, Banks changed his mind after he considered the benefits to his town and the bank. "For Mound Bayou's sake I have decided to stand for the place," Banks told Scott.[8]

Founding the Bank of Mound Bayou

Inspired by stories of business success he heard at the 1903 Nashville meeting of the NNBL, Banks met with the leading businessmen of Mound Bayou, and they organized the Bank of Mound Bayou in 1904, initially capitalized at $10,000.[9] Banks purchased sixty-six of the bank's initial one hundred shares at $100 each. From the beginning, he was the majority stockholder.[10] One observer commented, "It was due to the initiative, persistence, financial strength and popularity of Mr. Banks that the Bank of Mound Bayou was organized and put into operation." Another contemporary said that "in the promotion of the banking idea and in the marshaling of the necessary forces and finances to set the wheels of the important venture in motion, Chas. Banks . . . was the leading spirit, the very genius of the organization." Banks became the bank's cashier, while Francis became its president.[11]

The heart of the business community in Mound Bayou was its bank. White bankers frequently exploited black clients since they knew many Negroes had no alternative.[12] Before the establishment of Mound Bayou's bank, residents paid large mortgage payments to white financiers and many of Mound Bayou's farmers found themselves in perpetual debt. Some owed from $600 to $1,200 per annum, while others paid interest at 25 to 30 percent for supplies purchased on credit.[13] The creation of Negro banks forced whites to be more competitive with interest rates and to be mindful of their treatment of black customers. Banks's organizing the bank placed him in a very powerful position. Always working for the success of the town, Banks gave advances on crop loans to help area farmers and he provided the community with a circulating medium of exchange.[14]

The Bank of Mound Bayou initially operated out of a three-hundred-square-foot wooden building. In a little over two years, the bank relocated to a two-story red brick building, which cost $5,000. It had a fireproof vault equipped with a time lock. And it was "fitted out with solid oak tables, plate-glass windows, and brass grills."[15] When the new brick building was completed, Banks sent pictures to Washington and others so they could see the progress taking place in Mound Bayou. The new building "is a most creditable one," Washington told Banks after seeing these pictures. "I do not know when I shall exhaust my store of congratulations, because you are always doing something to draw from us the best wishes and continued success."[16] Washington considered Banks "the leading Negro banker in Mississippi."[17]

Banks frequently reminded his fellow citizens of the bank's significance: "the Bank of Mound Bayou has been the greatest factor in building up and holding together our town and community." In addition, he said, "without the influence and help of the Bank . . . our community could not have gained the attention of the world nor attained its present enviable position." More important, the town could not continue to be "a factor in the progress of the Negro, or hope to grow into the fullness of its power, without such an institution," Banks asserted. He realized the people in Mound Bayou benefited tremendously from having their own bank and he charged them with the responsibility of supporting the enterprise. "You who certainly will be benefited directly or indirectly by the development of the town and community," Banks told his fellow citizens, "owe it to yourself to see that a part at least of your money is deposited and all of your moral support is given to this worthy institution."[18] Encouraging the citizens to invest in the town's bank he asked:

What are you going to do with your surplus money? Are you going to hide it about the house where fire or [a] robber may consume it? Or, are you going to deposit it in a safe bank?[19]

His pleas seem to have worked, because the bank operated profitably for many years.

In the article "Financiering By Negroes," Banks explained what he considered the primary focus of the bank in his town. "Besides doing the commercial business of a bank for the Negro farmers and merchants in this section," Banks noted, the purpose of the bank was "to form a nucleus for the savings of those who have learned to save, and to teach . . . the benefits and advantages accruing from a constant and systematic saving to those who have not made a beginning."[20] There were certainly other advantages, which Kenneth Hamilton clearly identifies. The bank, he says, "enabled them to finance their own endeavors locally, and, by providing capital for new local businesses, it helped upgrade the range of locally available goods and services." Moreover, "as a successful black-owned and -operated institution that used money invested by blacks to support other black-sponsored endeavors, the bank also became a tremendous source of racial pride."[21]

Scott began investing in the Bank of Mound Bayou in November 1907. He opened an account with a $200 deposit after Banks informed him how well the bank had performed. Scott had an interest in the success of the enterprise as well as in other businesses in which he invested in the town, such as the Mound Bayou cotton oil mill.[22] Indeed, the bank made an impressive showing soon after it opened, earning 17 percent during the first eight months of operation. During the bank's first six years, it earned annual dividends of at least 7 percent.[23] By November 1908, the bank had increased its authorized capital to $50,000, from $10,000 when it first opened, and its total resources to $100,000.[24] In 1908, the bank handled transactions totaling as much as $200,000 in one month.[25]

Early on, the bank paid its bills and met its other obligations in a timely fashion. Thomas Owen, attorney for the bank, was pleased to receive an $81 check from the bank close to Christmas 1909: "It seems that this near Christmas, you are the only client that we have who responds to our urgent appeal. We have sent out quite a number of bills, and this is the only answer." He thanked Banks for "being the first and the best," of all his clients.[26] And Eugene Snowden, a white banker in Memphis, told Washington that it had been a pleasure lending the Bank of Mound Bayou "$30,000 each year and their business had been handled to our entire satisfaction."[27]

In January 1910, Scott became a member of the board of directors of the Bank of Mound Bayou, succeeding the late William T. Montgomery. Flattered by his election, Scott joked that he had now become a "banker." There was more in it than flattery for Scott. As a director, he received $5 for each board meeting, whether he attended or not.[28]

The bank continued to grow and prosper. According to a financial statement dated November 9, 1910, the bank had increased its total resources to $150,000.[29] Riding on the wave of success of the bank, Banks made another move to help place Mound Bayou on sound footing. When he moved to the town, a large number of mortgages were held by white businessmen associated with the L, NO & T Railroad. When Isaiah Montgomery first settled the land, however, he had worked out a compact with the owners of the railroad in which they agreed not to foreclose on late mortgages. They also agreed to allow time for other Negroes to move onto the land and assume the note on the property in case of defalcation. Many landowners in Mound Bayou had some type of lien against their property. This complication did not become a problem, however, until the Y & MV Railroad bought the L, NO & T. Many residents believed the new landholders were going to immediately foreclose on their mortgages, since the purchase nullified the agreement with the L, NO & T. Fortunately, Banks and a few other town leaders convinced the new mortgage holders to renew the loans and cut the interest rates from 8 to 6 percent.[30]

Some of the mortgages were paid in full, but approximately 85 percent of the residents were still in debt because they took second mortgages on their property to finance businesses and other ventures.[31] So that these people, in particular the farmers, would not lose their property, Banks and other leaders affiliated with the bank formed the Mound Bayou Loan and Investment Company. Capitalized at $50,000, the company sold stock to the farmers in the community for $50 a share. One purpose of the company was to cover notes on mortgages if they could not be met by their due dates. Also, if a person left the town or could not pay at all, the company would assume the note until the land was sold to someone else who would then assume the responsibility. This plan ensured that the town could remain exclusively in the hands of Negroes. "In having taken the initiative in launching this great race enterprise," one observer said, "Mr. Banks has shown himself to be a real benefactor to his race."[32]

Although things were going well for Banks and the town, problems lurked in the shadows. Although Banks had tried to diversify the economy, he did this with only limited success. Like much of the rest of the South, the town's economy depended primarily on a single crop. The majority of citizens were engaged in farming, particularly cotton farming, so they were constantly at the mercy of nature and market demand. In 1905, Mound Bayou had stable cotton prices and high yields; therefore, the town prospered. By contrast, in 1906, when wilt disease destroyed two-thirds of the cotton crop, and in 1911, when a boll weevil infestation caused low yields and low prices, the town suffered tremendously. In brief, crop disease, the pre–World War I cotton crisis, bad weather conditions, and insect plagues played a significant role in the fortunes of the Bank of Mound Bayou and other town enterprises.[33]

Difficulties at the Bank

The Bank of Mound Bayou was rated A-1 by Dun and Bradstreet in 1910, but this changed about 1911 as Mound Bayou experienced difficulties, including short crops, low prices, and low operating capital in the bank.[34] The bank also had problems collecting from farmers. As a remedy, Banks proposed raising the bank's charter to $50,000. In his effort to secure such funds, he asked Scott to consider investing in another share of the bank's stock and to find at least five other investors.[35]

Nonetheless, by May 1912, the bank had problems cashing a check submitted to it in March. Banks explained to Scott that the bank was experiencing problems because of poor crops. However, he assured Scott he would get things in order, saying, "[I] remained at my post, because I never run away from battle."[36] However, problems at the bank persisted. Banks asked Washington for help in securing a line of credit for $25,000, to be guaranteed by local securities: "We have had this much and more credit in the past with less ability to repay and have paid."[37]

A month later, while on a trip to Virginia, Washington met J. J. Turner, a black banker and truck farmer from Exmore, Virginia. Washington believed Turner might assist Banks, because during the summer months, Washington said, Turner had "more money in his bank than he knows what to do with." It appears that Banks did not work out a deal with Turner, however.[38]

In a further effort to rehabilitate the bank, Banks asked Washington if the accountant at Tuskegee, William H. Carter, could help with auditing for a month. Washington approved the idea but said he could not release Carter for such a long time. He also told Banks that "to keep down jealousy," he would not be able to pay Carter from Tuskegee funds while he worked outside the institute. Banks accepted the terms. Carter eventually went to Mound Bayou and assisted at the bank for three weeks.[39] Expert help and advice were among the benefits members of the Tuskegee Machine received.

By October 1913, Banks believed the town's economy was beginning to stabilize because of good crop yields. "I am glad to report that we have excellent crops this year, and thereby will be getting pretty well on our feet and will be collecting a large part of [our] loans," Banks said.[40] However, Banks seems to have misjudged the situation, because there were still cash flow problems at the bank. On December 31, 1913, Scott wrote Banks, "A check was returned by the bank some days ago which concerned Malvin [Banks's nephew in school at Tuskegee], and now the Carter check for services has also been returned." He also informed Banks that Washington had become "rather seriously concerned about the fate of matters at Mound Bayou."[41] Banks wrote Washington a letter giving him a thorough report of matters in the town, which seemed to have satisfied Washington temporarily.[42]

Washington sympathized with Banks's plight and told him he had also "passed through such difficulties many times in my experiences and predict that you are going to come out all right." "If anything fails in connection with any of your enterprises," he continued, "it would be a calamity by which would tell in the most disastrous way upon all of us."[43] If Banks failed, it would reflect negatively on Washington's approach to racial uplift, especially since he had publicly lent his support to Banks and the Mound Bayou enterprise.

Perhaps sensing the possible demise of the bank and legal problems associated therewith, John W. Francis, who had been president of the bank since its inception, abruptly resigned, as did Richard H. McCarty, chairman of the board. W. P. Kyle replaced Francis, and Isaiah Montgomery replaced McCarty.[44] Notwithstanding these changes, the Bank of Mound Bayou continued to deteriorate.

More than one hundred banks failed in Mississippi during the pre–World War I recession. The closings resulted from fluctuations in the market and a lack of supervision of an over-extended banking industry. On March 9, 1914, during the term of Gov. Earl Brewer, the state legislature passed new banking laws. The legislature also established examiners to supervise and oversee the banks.[45]

These changes in the banking industry were consistent with the larger agenda of progressive reformers throughout the country. However, Banks and other black businessmen believed there were sinister motives behind the movement, particularly in Mississippi. Banks claimed the legislature had passed this "drastic banking law, specially framed to eliminate and wipe out any institution the authorities desired." He also said that when it came to banking, the whites in Mississippi "think there are some things to which we should not aspire."[46]

Banks told the editor of the *New York Age* that black bankers were "meeting with unwarranted hostility on the part of the State Banking authorities" and that he believed this was "opposition they would not dare show against members of their own race."[47] The examiners' overall perception of black people likely influenced how they valued the holdings at black banks. On another occasion Banks charged that "the method of depreciation of values as indicated by the Examiner would create a state of insolvency in any institution."[48]

To continue operations under the new state laws, banks had to submit to four major changes. First, each bank needed $500 to deposit for every $100,000 of its average daily deposits with the treasurer of the state, after which they would receive a certificate of guarantee of solvency. Second, they were to pay the state treasurer .05 percent of the bank's average deposit in cash. Third, they had to submit to examinations by the state board at least twice a year. And fourth, stockholders were required to pay off the bank's bad debts and restore the bank's capital.[49]

Some of Mound Bayou's difficulties rested with the fourth requirement. Almost half the bad debts sustained by the Bank of Mound Bayou resulted from a white-owned bank's paying only 30 percent of a $4,000 obligation before going out of business.[50] To meet the state requirement, according to Isaiah Montgomery, Banks "voluntarily met this responsibility" and covered the bank's losses with his own money.[51] Another factor affected the vitality of the bank. Banks had used the Bank of Mound Bayou to partially finance the new $100,000 Mound Bayou Oil Mill. He lent money to investors to purchase stock and then accepted the stock as security. This placed the bank's depositors, including Banks, who owned from two-fifths to one-half of the bank's total deposits, at risk.[52]

In all, Banks engineered the purchase of $40,000 of oil mill stock. That is, he lent $40,000 of the depositors' money (about half of which belonged to him), which made the Bank of Mound Bayou a 40 percent owner in the mill. Banks shifted resources from one enterprise to another. Ultimately, this was an imprudent decision from a banking perspective because hard assets, like property and equipment, are preferable to soft assets, like stocks, as collateral, especially for new enterprises. If Banks had asked himself the question, If things go bad, how do I get the bank's money back? he would have realized the danger. He decided to accept soft collateral on the assumption that the oil mill would be profitable. When the mill began to have financial problems, the consequences were catastrophic for the bank.[53]

Although the mill was not a proven venture, the officers and directors of the bank supported Banks's decision and "fully empowered" him to lend the money to invest in the mill. He began to work vigorously to acquire capital to meet the new banking requirements. He secured $10,000 from an unnamed person in Memphis.[54] On May 19, Banks reported to Scott that the bank "had a thorough audit again by men experienced in that line of work, with the view of having everything just right . . . when the State Examiner comes around." He also reported that he had hired accountants from Charles F. Wermuth and Company, a nationally respected New Orleans firm. He assured Scott he was doing all he could to make sure "there will be no reflection on any of us connected therewith."[55]

The state examiners visited Mound Bayou on June 2 and 3. According to Banks, the examiners "found things in better shape than they really expected." But conditions were not perfect and examiners informed the bank officers they would still have to raise at least $5,000 over the next thirty days to be approved.[56] The examiners also told the officers to "close up the Overdrafts, Pay off the collection account and reduce our holdings of Stocks and Bonds by $10,000," Montgomery said.[57]

On June 5, 1914, Banks told Washington he had raised $5,000, but needed his help to secure another $5,000. Banks wanted to stabilize the town's bank so badly that he informed Washington he could "arrange to put up collateral of crop and real estate mortgage[s] held by me or the Bank here to secure the loan. I can arrange to put up $75,000 worth of collateral for . . . $5,000."[58]

By June 13, 1914, Banks, with the assistance of Washington, received $5,000 for the bank from Julius Rosenwald.[59] By this time, he had also reduced the bank's holdings of oil mill stocks to $25,000. Moreover, he had reduced the bank's total liabilities from $160,000 in 1911–12 to $70,000 in 1914. Given more time, he might have reduced the debts even more.[60]

The cotton crisis of 1914 severely restricted Banks's cash flow and exacerbated his financial woes, as was the case with most businessmen who had investments in cotton farming throughout the South. Cotton prices fell from about eleven cents to about five cents a pound in early 1914. Faced with economic ruin, cotton farmers pleaded with the government to use its resources to stabilize cotton prices. In the end, very little was done to assist them, and cotton planters across the South lost about half the value of their 1914 crop.[61]

Despite Banks's efforts and Rosenwald's assistance, by August 1914, the state banking commissioners had forced the Bank of Mound Bayou into liquidation. Banks felt this action was unjust, but he said he would accept the decision without protest because the officers were given ninety days to get the bank's affairs in order.[62] To make matters worse, rumors began to circulate about Banks's mismanagement of the bank and of the MBA. On September 10, 1914, the *Cleveland (Mississippi) Enterprise* ran a front-page headline: "CHARLEY BANKS FLEES THE STATE; WANTED BY AUTHORITIES FOR ALLEGED FLEECING OF COLORED MASONIC FRATERNITY." A short while earlier, the *Vicksburg Herald* had published an equally troubling story. It alleged Banks had secured a loan of $10,000 (with Washington's help) to rescue the bank, but he only used a small portion for that purpose. The paper also charged that the MBA had unpaid death claims totaling more than $75,000.[63]

Banks believed these allegations were orchestrated primarily by Diamond Cox, Sidney D. Redmond, and others in Jackson who had opposed Banks's becoming secretary-treasurer of the MBA. Cox and Redmond had wanted Cox to control the finances of the association, which handled from $15,000 to $20,000 a month in transactions, but Cox lost his bid for secretary-treasurer to Banks in 1910. In 1911, the Redmond-Cox faction split from The Most Worshipful Stringer Grand Lodge, the oldest Negro fraternal order in Mississippi, and tried to start its own lodge. These men, said Banks, were now taking advantage of an "opportunity to strike at me through the columns of the paper."[64]

Nonetheless, the articles circulated, and Philip J. Allston, fourth vice president of the NNBL, wrote to Emmett Scott asking: "Is it all true that I hear about our associate Mr. Charles Banks. . . . If so we deplore it and as far as a hindrance it should spur us to greater efforts to a honorable business life." None of the rumors were true. Banks had been in Mississippi the entire time, and he even encouraged a full and impartial investigation of the allegations.[65] According to Banks, after the state examiners finished their audit, they "found not quite $6.00 as the total amount of discrepancies in the accounts." They also complimented the officers on the "honesty and integrity of purpose that seems to have characterized" their management. Regarding the MBA, Banks assured Scott that "the books are all straight and there is no reflection on me and no criminal proceedings liable."[66] Unfortunately, this was not the end of Banks's problems. Mary Turner, a hairdresser in Oakland, California, really became a thorn in Banks's side. She alleged she had been cheated by Banks and had not received any returns on her investments in Mound Bayou, so she started a campaign to discredit him and his coworkers. At one point, Turner even threatened to publish her experience "in the *New York World*, the Chicago papers and the best papers of the South," if she did not receive her money shortly.[67] Banks complained that Turner had done "all she could to destroy us and our usefulness."[68]

Turner even coerced the state examiners into bringing criminal indictments against the officers of the bank. Then it was discovered that George Mays Jr., a field agent for Mound Bayou enterprises, was the person who really had defrauded Turner. Mays, a Tuskegee graduate, was referred to Banks after he sent a request for an "energetic, intelligent, and reliable person to do the soliciting work."[69] Mays sold Turner property and stocks and pocketed her money.[70]

Armed with information from Turner and data obtained from their audit, state authorities charged the bank with selling worthless stocks. They believed the bank's collateral, like the oil mill stocks, had no market value. In addition, Banks stated, they wanted to "institute criminal prosecutions against the [officers] because of loss [to] the creditors."[71] Indeed, the authorities tried to prosecute officers and directors of the bank on this basis. In two letters to Washington, Banks gave his opinion on the arguments made by the banking authorities. In the first he stated:

We made advances on local securities that in ordinary times were considered good, except that it was taking a longer time to work them out than a small commercial bank could afford to do. The bank was closed at the time when the war broke out and brought on such conditions that made it practically impossible to realize on any kind of securities. [E]ven securities on Wall Street would have collapsed had not the financiers there shut down the Stock exchanges, and what could they expect of a country bank and especially one where the securities were only traded in by Negroes. It would be unfair to compare the value of our securities under these conditions with what they were at the time the advances were made by our people.[72]

About a month later he astutely explained:

The Examiners' complaint that the securities are worthless is based on the fact that they are in a Negro settlement, the Whites will not buy them as long as we protest and ask for a chance and the Negroes have not the money to take them over, therefore he cannot realize on them.[73]

However, Banks proudly asserted, after an all-white grand jury reviewed the matter, "they took the position that since our accounts were correct, no shortage or irregularities existed, we had committed no criminal act."[74] Banks believed that many of the claims the examiners leveled at them were due to prejudice.

Even though the Bank of Mound Bayou had its legal reserve and had been entitled to operate, Banks believed the "constant 'nagging'" from "sources that do not appear on the surface . . . caused the Banking Commissioners to arbitrarily decide to have us liquidated."[75] Referring to Turner, Banks said her "letters to the State Banking authorities gave us more trouble than any other." He had grown frustrated with Turner because he had made several conciliatory proposals to her previously and believed if she had accepted one of them she could have received all of her money. He also maintained that the banking examiners would have been more inclined to accept the bank's plan of reorganization if it were not for Turner's vituperative letters.[76]

After the Bank of Mound Bayou closed, examiners closed down two other Negro banks a short time later. "One redeeming feature as was true of our bank here," Banks said, was that the examiners did not find any irregularities at those banks either. Still the examiners charged that the banks' "collaterals were unsatisfactory and . . . could not be realized on in emergency cases." Therefore, Banks did not think people should be surprised to see so many Negro banks "going down under the discriminating regulations and rules."[77]

Washington continued to lend moral support to Banks. "There is nothing like not giving up. Every strong business man who has finally succeeded has had his reverses," he said.[78] On another occasion he told Banks, "I hope you will not become discouraged but go forward at any cost." Encouraged by Washington's support to stabilize Mound Bayou, Banks set out to establish a new bank. "[T]he greatest service I can do you, the League and the Race is to 'Come Back' on this Mound Bayou proposition," he told Washington, "and I am bending all my efforts to that end."[79]

After the Bank of Mound Bayou closed, white bankers raised interest rates and even required Negro patrons to bring their cotton and other goods to be ginned and sold in the white towns. Some even started dictating how much landowners could charge for rent. This spurred the citizens of Mound Bayou to continually support all efforts to open a new bank.[80] "Out of a total holdings of over $100,000.00 of my own," Banks told Washington, "I have personally assumed over $30,000.00 of liabilities and am fixed in my determination to use my income and resources of whatever nature to the end that those who have trusted us shall lose nothing." However, before the examiners would provide the charter for the bank, they stipulated that Banks could not be an officer or stockholder.[81] Nevertheless, Banks helped establish the new Mound Bayou State Bank, which began operations October 21, 1915. It was one of only two Negro banks operating under the new banking laws, with deposits guaranteed by the state.[82] "We are on the same footing and relatively as strong as any other bank in the State," Banks proclaimed.[83]

Banks believed he owed it to Mound Bayouans and Negroes throughout the country to rehabilitate the bank. Therefore, he personally provided $11,000 of the $12,000 needed to open the bank. "Mr. Montgomery did his full part, and without his co-operation," Banks noted, "I hardly feel that the work would have been so well done."[84]

Perhaps state authorities targeted Banks because he was the only original bank officer actively involved in the formation of the new bank.[85] Francis and McCarty, the former president and chairman of the board respectively, had cut their official ties with the old bank in February 1914, six months before it closed. The examiners also used other tactics to delay the new bank's opening. They probably believed these things would deter and ultimately prevent the leaders of the town from organizing a new bank. Banks surprised them, however, by agreeing to their terms while still providing the majority of the capital needed to open the new bank. Amazed, Scott told Banks the work he had done was "a story worth telling."[86]

In an open letter published in the *New York Age* to Georgiana Whyte of Chicago, an investor in the bank, Banks explained the possibilities of success for the new bank as well as the intended outcome for stockholders and depositors of the old bank. By March 1916, state-appointed receivers still held the stock for the old bank and they had not yet made a report. However, Banks said that if the officers of the bank were given time, "and our friends exercise patience and indulgence, the chances are that no one who has ever placed money in Mound Bayou will lose" their investment.[87]

Banks went on to explain that it never had been the "intention or motive on the part of those" who managed the bank "to, in any way, abuse the public." He said the bank officers had suffered because of "false representation on the part of agents and promoters representing Mound Bayou . . . who promised the public more than they could carry out or more than they were authorized to do."[88] Nonetheless, Banks said, "I shall never feel that my obligations are fully discharged to the race and to the public generally until every promise, expressed or implied, touching any enterprise here is fully redeemed."[89]

Banks felt an obligation not only to the individual investor but also to the race. He probably knew that if the stockholders in the old bank were not repaid, that would negatively reflect on him and the race overall. For some, such a failure would confirm the myth of black business incompetence. Banks may also have realized that such an occurrence would shake the confidence of future investors in black enterprises across the country. They would have another excuse for not supporting black businesses. So, Banks stated, he was "bending" his "best energy and thought" to make sure that all investors were paid.[90]

While Banks's words may have provided some consolation to Whyte, his confidante and best friend, Emmett Scott, was becoming more and more concerned about his investments in the town. It seems, at least, that Banks got that impression. However, to allay any concerns along that line by Banks, Scott told him that "there has not been a moment in the midst of the trying experiences through which we have passed when my confidence in you has been shaken in the slightest degree." "I confess that I have felt for you a great deal more than I have felt for myself," he continued, "because I have known just how you must have suffered in mind not to faithfully carry out your plans, purposes and promises, but I have known all along of the hard situation you have been contending with." In closing, he told Banks that as he entered the New Year it would be "with high hopes and faith unshaken." Though Scott denied losing confidence in Banks, he scrambled to find as many ways as possible to salvage his investments.[91]

By January 1916, Banks somehow managed to pay Scott $100 of his deposit from the old bank. Scott gave the money to his wife "as a reward for her patient waiting and her confidence in both of us to the effect that everything would work out alright." The state receivers still had control when Banks made this payment. In all likelihood, Banks paid Scott out of his own pocket. Whatever the case, Scott told Banks he appreciated the $100 because he felt "most anxious" to get out of his "present financial pickles."[92]

Scott believed Banks would do everything he could to protect Scott's financial interests. Still he was concerned that the stock certificates he held for the bank and other Mound Bayou enterprises were going to be deemed worthless by the state receivers. If that happened he might lose all his investments. To protect against this, Scott unsuccessfully tried to exchange his stock in the Bank of Mound Bayou for stock in the cotton oil mill.[93] He reasoned that if the state receivers invalidated his bank stock, he would have his interests covered by the oil mill.

By September 1916, Scott's optimism had begun to fade even more. At that time, he discovered that $500 worth of stock he owned in the Mississippi Beneficial Life Insurance Company, for which Banks served as a director, had been "invalidated." "You may certainly put your thinking cap on to advise your old friend how to save as much as possible out of the Mound Bayou situation," Scott told Banks. "It has been three years since our catastrophe, and I am still somewhat in the air as to just what station I shall have to get off."[94]

Scott certainly had cause for concern, as over $1,600 of his money was tied up in various Mound Bayou enterprises. He held two shares of stock in the old bank worth $200 and had $763.30 on deposit before it closed. His deposits and bank stock, alone, totaled almost $1,000. In December, Scott asked Banks to give him an honest appraisal. "Some time ago you indicated that when the new bank was organized you would probably be able to turn back to me my deposit in the Bank of Mound Bayou," Scott said. "You also indicated that you would see that my stock [in the old bank] was protected by stock in the Oil Mill, and that you meant to take care of the certificates of deposit." Scott said he understood Banks was "burdened with many cares," but he, Scott, was "practically 'up a tree' as a result of the Mound Bayou situation which has developed by the closing of the . . . Bank of Mound Bayou."[95]

It is unclear whether Scott recovered the money from his investment in the Bank of Mound Bayou. What is clear, however, is that he never gave up on Banks and the Mound Bayou proposition. For years, Scott continued to lend his support to Banks in solving his economic woes. Scott may have stayed beside Banks because he really had faith in him. He also may have been doing whatever was necessary to salvage his investments by keeping the operations functioning. He may have been doing both. According to a biographer, Scott did more than Washington to support Banks, "particularly when Banks seemed to fail repeatedly." Even when Scott should have made critical judgments about Banks's business activities, his blind loyalty to Banks caused him to stay the course.[96]

Meanwhile, the new bank started with $10,000 in capital and a $2,000 surplus, and the people in the town, according to Banks, were "depositing lots of money."[97] The examiners, said Banks, " have called for a great deal on my part, the road has been a long one, but I am glad to report the battle won."[98] But the victory was short-lived. The bank survived for another seven years, closing in 1922. That same year, Banks moved from Mound Bayou to Memphis. The only other Negro bank in the state, the Delta Penny Savings Bank, closed in 1926. According to Neil McMillen, after that point, "no other black banks were ever chartered" in Mississippi.[99] White supremacy had eliminated black banks in the Magnolia State.

Mound Bayou Cotton Oil Mill

*"The Largest and Most Serious Undertaking . . .
in the History of Our Race"*

Founding the Mound Bayou Oil Mill

More than any other endeavor, the Mound Bayou Oil Mill became
Banks's most ambitious undertaking, "the largest thing of the kind ever
under taken by Negro people."[1] Isaiah Montgomery came up with the
idea of a cotton oil mill in 1901, but it did not become a reality until Banks
moved to town and took up the matter. Early on, Banks planned to finance
the mill by selling shares of stock to Negroes throughout Mississippi for
$1 each.[2]

At the 1907 annual meeting of the MNBL, the executive committee
(which Montgomery chaired) suggested that the league sponsor the oil
mill proposition. In May 1908, the founders of the Mound Bayou Oil Mill
and Manufacturing Company met and organized under its new charter.
Banks and the other promoters worked around the clock. They selected a
site for the mill, secured architectural plans, and hired a contractor. Thomas Cook, a Mound Bayou builder and architect, designed the mill. Promoters believed even the poorest Negroes in the state would have the
opportunity to invest in the mill. "This enterprise is planned to specially
appeal to the working classes and industrial masses of Negroes generally,
and for this reason particularly, the shares have been fixed at one dollar
each," states the prospectus, "so as to facilitate the profitable investment
of a portion of their weekly and monthly earnings in the establishment
and operation of a great plant." To make the offer more appealing, stock
certificates were "tastily designed" and large enough to be framed. "Just

think of it," Banks said, "a hundred thousand dollar enterprise, owned and controlled by Negroes."[3]

Banks met with the Eastern Star Lodge at Clarksdale and convinced them to purchase two hundred shares of stock. Out of six hundred people in attendance, he said, only two objected.[4] When construction began on the mill several months later, funds were "coming in for it surprisingly," Banks said.[5] The mill was capitalized at $100,000 and chartered under the laws of Mississippi. The plant would be used to manufacture cottonseed into cotton meal, cotton oil, fertilizer, hulls and other products that could be obtained from cotton. Many officers of the Bank of Mound Bayou were also officers of the oil mill. Montgomery served as president and chairman of the mill; John W. Francis, president of the bank, served as treasurer; and Banks worked as the general manager. Interestingly, Banks hired Emmett Scott's father to work as a supervisor at the mill.[6] Banks promoted the oil mill because he realized Mound Bayou needed a more diversified economy. He also understood that cotton farmers in the area could make more money and more jobs would be created by the manufacture of cottonseed products.

By February 1910, Banks was experiencing difficulty in generating funds for the mill. Even some blacks who had the resources were reluctant to invest large sums. For example, one woman in Natchez, who had preserved her family's wealth accumulated during slavery, purchased only thirty shares. Banks asked Scott to "pop the question," by asking Andrew Carnegie to help finance the mill. Scott put the idea before Washington, but, Scott said, "he did not say anything to indicate his very earnest approval of the suggestion."[7] Eventually, Banks asked Washington directly if he could help "without in anyway embarrassing you or your own work."[8] Washington assured Banks he would keep the matter in mind.[9]

By April 1910, Banks and the other officers of the mill hired Tuskegee graduate George H. Mays Jr. to sell stock for the mill. Initially, Banks was pleased with his work. "Your services are eminently satisfactory to the management of the entire oil mill body and you are making the best agent we have ever had," Banks told Mays.[10] Banks also continued to seek investors for the mill. In February 1911, he solicited financial support from W. L. Park, vice-president of the Illinois Central Railroad.[11] Banks even asked Scott to provide him with the names of one hundred "substantial colored men" whom he might interest in the oil mill.[12]

On November 29, 1911, Banks told Washington he intended "to blow the whistle of our One Hundred Thousand Dollar Oil Mill about the first of January." Around the end of December, however, Banks no longer thought it wise to have a formal opening because of unfavorable weather and because of the mill's inadequate funding.[13] Washington continued to give Banks names of possible investors. He also suggested that Banks take a month to visit New York, Boston, and other cities to make a "personal canvass among people who have money to invest. There are people who have schemes not half so worthy as yours who are getting money in the North," Washington advised, "but they do so by personal visits to investors." Washington assured Banks that if he took this approach, he would help him as much as possible.[14]

Banks took Washington's suggestion, but he decided to have Montgomery travel north.[15] Montgomery met with Carnegie in New York, and Carnegie asked the founders to obtain letters of recommendation from people who were familiar with their work at Mound Bayou. Then, he said, he would consider helping them.[16] To comply with Carnegie's request, Banks had several people write letters of reference, including both U.S. senators from Mississippi. Banks also asked Washington to write a letter in support of their project. Washington, however, told Banks, "if Mr. Carnegie desires my personal opinion on the project he undoubtedly will write me, and I shall be very glad to write him at such length as may seem wise."[17] Washington may have been reluctant to ask Carnegie for money on Banks's behalf because of the problems with the Carnegie library in Mound Bayou.

Nonetheless, Scott produced a generic "To whom it may concern" letter and sent it directly to Banks for this purpose.[18] Banks emphasized he did not want philanthropic aid but rather a long-term investment. Though the founders did all Carnegie asked, he did not provide financing for the mill. In all likelihood, Banks and Montgomery had fallen out of his favor after he learned they were not using their library for its initial purpose and after they did not meet their maintenance requirement as agreed.[19]

Opening Ceremony

Although full financing for the mill had not been secured, Banks began to plan a dedication ceremony. He believed such a ceremony would generate racial pride as well as publicity for Mound Bayou. He also thought that showcasing the mill might entice more people to invest.

The dedication ceremony took place November 25, 1912. Those in attendance marveled at the brick structure, which measured 250 by 60 feet, with a two-and-a-half-story cottonseed shed that measured 350 by 90 feet. The oil mill could crush up to forty tons of cottonseed in twenty-four hours, and Thomas Cook designed it with enough space for two more presses, which would double its manufacturing capacity. Fifteen thousand people attended, including people from New Orleans, Memphis, and Jackson, and a number of whites from all areas of the Delta. It was a grand affair that had been four years in the making. Among the speakers were Montgomery and C. P. Mooney, the white editor of the *Memphis Commercial Appeal.* Mooney participated at the request of his friend Banks. During his presentation, Mooney "showed the striking importance of the Mound Bayou Oil Mill and Manufacturing Company to the development of peace and prosperity among the white and colored people in Mississippi." He also emphasized that the enterprise would be in the best interest of all farmers and manufacturers in the state.[20] Mooney intended to allay the fears of whites who believed the oil mill would take business away from them.

Booker T. Washington was the keynote speaker. During the planning stages, Banks asked Washington to make an appeal to those in attendance to invest. During his speech, Washington praised the Negroes for their accomplishments and credited whites for helping the Negro at Mound Bayou. His remarks about whites were strictly for white consumption, a black survival strategy he had used for years. Throughout his speech, Washington praised Banks more than anyone else and honored Banks's request to encourage investment.[21]

Here only 49 years after our freedom as a race, the black people have gathered and invested nearly $100,000 in this manufacturing enterprise. I am told that only about $20,000 is needed to free it from debt and put it thoroughly upon its feet. I shall be disappointed if there are not scores of prosperous and thrifty colored men throughout this region who will be glad to invest additional money in this promising business concern. Mr. Banks ought to have no difficulty in raising speedily from our own race all the money needed to put this business in first class shape. Money invested in this plant will not only bring in steady return in the way of dividends, but it will result in affording employment for a large number of the educated men and women of our race. I repeat then, that this oil mill should have the liberal financial support of that class of our people who have money to invest.[22]

Washington went on to say:

> I am glad that this oil mill, the first in the history of our race, is
> located in the heart of the South where it will be a perpetual demon-
> stration of the fact that our people can not only make progress, but
> whenever they make progress along legitimate and helpful lines that
> the white man is willing to stand back of them and encourage them
> right here in the heart of the South.[23]

Washington's speech seems to have served the purpose of generating
racial pride and calming white anxiety. The speech probably also encouraged people to invest who might not have done so otherwise. But the
dedication did not generate enough money to place the mill on sound
financial footing, as Banks had hoped.

Still, the event seems to have deeply affected Negroes who attended.
Typifying the pride and excitement, the *Commercial Appeal* reported the
remarks of one black woman: "Well, Lord, here I is. I are sho' ready to lef'
dese lowgrounds. I has hearn Booker T . . . [and] I has seen de ile mill, de
big wheels an' all dat," she gleefully stated. Futhermore, "what was ain't
now, fer us cullud folks is gwine ter see de cotton after it's done picked in
de fiel' and fo' we buys it back 'cross de counter."[24] This woman witnessed
something she probably never imagined she would see in her lifetime.
Negroes would no longer just pick cotton in the fields, they would also
manufacture the cottonseed in their very own mill. Another observer
noted that "strong men wept and the women cried for joy" after witnessing the oil mill ceremony.[25] Impressed by the enterprise, Washington
called the mill "the largest and most serious undertaking in a purely commercial and manufacturing enterprise in the history of our race."[26]

When he finished speaking, Washington pulled the cord that sounded
the whistle for the symbolic opening of the mill.[27] After the dedication
ceremony, "a County fair, with race track, exhibits of all kinds, every home
open, a special dinner served in the Bank of Mound Bayou for the White
visitors, and all the airs of a proud city," took place.[28] Indeed, the oil mill
had become the "pride of the community."[29] Despite the praise from
Washington, whites still viewed the mill as competition to their mills and
a threat to their livelihood.[30]

Operating the Mill

Montgomery continued to canvass the North for people to invest in the oil mill, and by February 1913, his efforts paid off. He, along with Banks and others, persuaded Julius Rosenwald, president of Sears and Roebuck, to consider investing. However, Rosenwald insisted he would have to confer with Washington before he took action.[31] The promoters of Mound Bayou had already raised $60,000, but they needed an additional $40,000 to get the mill operational. They needed belts, conveyors, scales, tanks, presses, railroad track, and money to purchase cottonseed.[32]

Rosenwald agreed to purchase $25,000 worth of bonds with a 6 percent interest rate if the mill promoters could find someone else to finance the other $15,000. He made it clear he would be making this investment with the understanding that the plant cost approximately $100,000 and had no other indebtedness. Rosenwald also required that mill promoters insure his investment by providing him with a first mortgage on the plant and equipment and that Banks personally guarantee $12,500 of his bonds. Moreover, Banks had to purchase a $45,000 insurance policy on the mill and name Rosenwald the beneficiary. Last, the mill promoters had to agree to prepay all the mill's operating expenses through a trust fund controlled by Rosenwald as long as he held at least $5,000 worth of bonds.[33]

After Rosenwald agreed to invest, Washington wanted to make sure Banks and other Mound Bayou leaders did not renege on promises, as they had done with Carnegie. "I wish to particularly advise that you take note of everything that you may promise in connection with your understanding with Mr. Rosenwald and that you see that it is carried out to the exact letter," because, Washington told Banks, "he is a rather exacting man."[34] Early on, Mississippi whites began a campaign to boycott the mill, so, Banks and the other promoters had to overcome this obstacle and make the venture work. They turned to Benjamin B. Harvey, a white cotton broker in Memphis who owned the Memphis Cotton Oil Company. He agreed to lease the mill from Banks for five years and purchase the other $15,000 in bonds. Banks realized whites would be less apt to boycott one of their own. Harvey also agreed to pay the Mound Bayou stockholders 50 percent of the profits from the mill and assume the terms set forth in Rosenwald's bond purchase and repayment plan. Rosenwald agreed, and the mill was on its way to becoming fully operational.[35]

Under the agreement, Harvey actually became the lessee and manager of the Mound Bayou mill, although Banks and others did not widely publicize this fact. If this became known, it would have weakened Banks's "all-Negro enterprise" rhetoric. As the mill's attorney read the agreement, "Harvey was to receive the $25,000 received from Rosenwald as a trust fund for operating purposes, and was to pay the outstanding debts from the remaining $15,000.00 of bonds."[36] This meant that when Rosenwald paid the $25,000 for the bonds, that money was given to Harvey, who was supposed to hold it in trust. The agreement also required Harvey to pay Rosenwald interest on the bonds on specified dates. This arrangement became critical to the success or failure of the plant. On the surface it seemed to have been a good business move. The Mound Bayou mill would reap the benefits of Harvey's experience and withstand the white boycott.

As the mill came closer to opening, Washington again emphasized to Banks the importance of meeting his obligations to Rosenwald: "Be very sure that every promise which you made to Mr. Rosenwald be strictly and fully carried out. If Mr. Rosenwald [is] disappointed in this investment he will lose faith in our entire race."[37] Washington understood that he personally had a lot resting on the success of Mound Bayou. Banks certainly did not want to disappoint Washington or Rosenwald. He told Washington he would "leave nothing unturned . . . so far as my ability goes to bring about the desired end." Moreover, he said, "I realize what it means to make good as suggested, both here and with our Mr. Rosenwald." Banks also announced that "the mill will be all that our friends can expect and will be running at full speed within the next thirty days."[38]

On October 9, 1913, Banks sent a telegram to Washington, stating the "Mound Bayou Oil Mill Began Manufacturing Today."[39] To announce the opening to the nation, the *New York Age* ran a story on October 22, headlined, "Cotton Seed Oil Mill Now Open." The article complimented Banks for his efforts in making the mill operational.[40] This was a tremendous accomplishment for Banks and Mound Bayou; of sixty-eight mills in Mississippi, this was the only one predominantly owned and operated by blacks. A visitor from Tuskegee a few days before the mill formally began operation was impressed with "the lone puffing of an engine, the opening and shutting of a boiler door . . . [and] the glare of red fire in the distance," from the mill.[41] The mill operated smoothly during its first months. "The mill is moving onward night and day, and we are agreeably surprised to find that the scare about not getting enough seed was unfounded," Banks told Scott.[42] But a few months later, problems started to abound, particularly after the cotton depression of 1914.

Problems Encountered

William C. Graves, secretary to Rosenwald, became somewhat alarmed when he discovered that as late as February 1914, Montgomery had been in Chicago and Saint Louis still trying to raise money for the mill. All financing was supposed to have been in place by that time. Graves asked Washington to look into the matter, "without having it appear that the request came from me."[43]

Washington disregarded Graves's request for anonymity and almost immediately forwarded his letter to Banks. Washington also asked Banks to apprise him of the full details of the situation. "It is important that everything be made definite and clear, as much is involved," Washington insisted. Then in typical Tuskegee Machine fashion, he told Banks, "Of course, do not mention that you have seen a copy of this letter; as a matter of fact I have no right to send it to you, but you know my deep interest in you and your work."[44]

Shortly after writing to Washington, Graves asked Scott for an auditor's report of the mill. This did not seem to be a problem, since Banks had already arranged to have the mill audited by a New Orleans firm.[45] Banks sent Graves a letter updating him on the mill. According to Banks, the mill began operating on October 9, 1913, and closed on March 10, 1914. This was not a surprise, because it had been expected that the mill would run on a seasonal basis. Banks also told him that during those months the mill ran day and night, except for part of January and February, when it operated only during the day. The mill employed about fifty full-time workers, and the estimated profit for the season, according to a preliminary financial statement, was expected to be a little over $12,000. Moreover, Banks informed Graves, "this [matter] is in the hands of our lessee, as our settlement is not to be made until July." Banks also related that, compared to other mills, Mound Bayou's had a fruitful run for its first season. Last, he assured Graves that he would send him the auditor's report as soon as it was completed.[46]

If Banks was determined to deal honorably with Rosenwald, Harvey was determined to ruin the operation.[47] On April 20, 1914, Banks reported to Scott that "our Memphis partner has not paid the interest on Mr. Rosenwald's bonds amounting to $750.00."[48] However, Banks said, if Harvey did not make the payment, he would do so out of his own pocket until the issue could be resolved. As it became apparent that Harvey had no intention of making the payment, Washington told Banks to go ahead and pay Rosenwald. "I cannot impress upon you too strongly the importance of paying at once those over-due coupons," he said.[49] Although Banks was experiencing financial difficulties himself, he made the $750 payment.

When another payment came due, Banks first consulted Washington, then explained to Graves that Harvey had failed to abide by the agreement. However, Banks said, he would cover the note again. Although Banks said he could pay the notes in full, he asked Graves if he could "take them up in small allotments until they are all retired," allotments in the amount of $15 each, rather than pay a lump sum.[50] At Washington's urging, Rosenwald worked out a payment plan with Banks.[51] On October 13, 1914, after realizing Harvey did not plan to make any payments, Washington suggested that Banks "put aside enough bales of cotton to meet" his obligation if he did not have the cash. "Mr. Rosenwald has ways, of course, of disposing of cotton," Washington said.[52]

About two weeks later, Washington reminded Banks that if he could not come up with the money to pay Rosenwald, "have the cotton to offer him, which I think will serve about the same purpose." Washington sympathized with Banks's plight and did not want him to become discouraged by this turn of events. "I am especially glad to know that you have not become in any way discouraged," Washington told Banks, because at one time "I feared perhaps you might."[53]

After the cotton crisis of 1914, Harvey suffered severe losses at his Memphis oil mill, which ultimately drove him into bankruptcy. Although financial documents show that the Mound Bayou mill generated profits of $12,567.02 during its first season, an audit showed that Harvey embezzled the money and put it into his own business to try and keep it afloat. He also illegally sold some of Rosenwald's bonds that were supposed to be held in trust. "The bonds which he had held as security [have] been placed by him with other concerns for debts which he owed and with which we had nothing to do whatever," Banks reported to Graves. "In other words, he abused his trust as holder and misappropriated them." In an effort to gain complete control of the Mound Bayou mill, Harvey even persuaded the people to whom he had sold the bonds to demand their investment back in cash. According to Banks, "these parties who hold these bonds took the position that they were innocent holders and demanded of us payment for same which we refused."[54]

The new bondholders then tried to get Banks to send them an acknowledgement of the indebtedness, but Banks felt that he, along with the other investors in the enterprise, had been "already sufficiently badly treated in the matter and we are not inclined to make any more concession[s] unless the law says so." The new bondholders in turn applied for a receiver in the federal court since they were nonresidents of Mississippi, and the court granted their request. This effectively made the receiver custodian of the plant instead of Banks. Banks believed this move really had nothing to do with "the validity of their position as bond holders."[55]

He further said:

> Our attorneys feel that they will be able to set aside their [the new bondholders] position as claimants and even if they do not, it would be sufficient time after that question is settled before attempting to make any concession to them as they would be still minority bondholders; Mr. Rosenwald having $25,000 of the $40,000.[56]

Banks seemed pleased the matter had gone to the federal court because he thought it would be fairer than the state courts in Mississippi.

Banks felt that Harvey knew about his financial difficulties and that he believed Banks would not be able to come up with the money to cover the bonds. Harvey wanted the mill to be forced into foreclosure and placed on the market for a nominal fee. If that happened, he, along with what Banks called "designing White men," planned to step in and purchase the mill below cost.[57]

As Harvey reneged on his obligation to Rosenwald and refused to submit financial records on his operation, Banks, Montgomery, and others had to assume responsibility for the interest, taxes, and insurance on Rosenwald's note. At the same time, Banks had Owen start proceedings against Harvey to nullify the contract and gain control of the mill. However, Harvey stayed out of Mississippi to avoid being served with a summons, which delayed court proceedings. He also obtained a change of venue into a federal court at Clarksdale, which delayed legal actions even more.[58]

Washington had counseled against filing the lawsuit:

> It is a pretty good policy to avoid a lawsuit and I am wondering if you could not accomplish the same results through some other method. A lawsuit is tiresome, long and expensive and I fear you in the end would get the worst of it. . . . I am sure Mr. Rosenwald would shrink from anything involving his name in a lawsuit.[59]

Banks was not as concerned as Washington because the mill's white attorney was handling the matter, and Banks believed Owen, unlike black lawyers, would be given a fair hearing in the courts. Harvey had clearly violated the terms of his lease, and this could be proven in a court of law.

Fortunately, Rosenwald understood Harvey was the real culprit in the oil mill affair and did not express disappointment in Banks. Washington told Banks that Rosenwald "seemed to manifest a great deal of sympathy with you during the trying time through which you are passing." Even more vindicating for Banks, Rosenwald intimated that "no one could have foreseen the difficulties that you are having to face."[60] At a later point, Rosenwald told Scott he had not lost confidence in Banks. However, Rosenwald thought Banks's problems resulted from the oil mill being too big an undertaking for a small town. He also believed the economic depression "had probably put you on the blink as it had many other institutions throughout the country, both North and South," Scott related.[61] This took a burden from Banks's shoulders. "It is some relief to know that our friends appreciate the situation and difficulties under which we are laboring," Banks said. By May 1915, Banks announced to Washington that through the lawsuit Harvey had been eliminated from the lease. Nonetheless, Banks and others still had to make payments to Rosenwald. Harvey's defalcation ultimately had deleterious repercussions for the oil mill and the bank in Mound Bayou, which was so heavily invested in the enterprise.[62]

In September 1915, Banks received more devastating news. He discovered that Mays, who had been working as the mill's traveling salesman for several years, had been selling bonds under false pretenses and pocketing the money. The news shocked Banks. Managers of the mill had been lenient with Mays because they trusted him. But he "very much abused his opportunities even to criminality" said Banks. Banks also told Washington:

> Some of the statements he made to people to get their money were ridiculous and then to make it worse, it, the money, never reached us. . . . Nearly every day we run across something he has done that puts us in a false light with the public, things and propositions we never heard or thought of. . . . He seems to have had no limit nor conscience.[63]

Banks contemplated having Mays criminally prosecuted. As a businessman, however, Banks tried to repay the people who had been defrauded "without letting the persons or public know of my real surprise at developments."[64]

There were options that could have relieved the mill from its indebtedness, but Banks refused them. Representatives of two Mississippi companies—the Buckeye Cotton Oil Company, a subsidiary of Proctor and Gamble, in Greenwood and the Leland Oil Works in Leland—approached him about leasing and taking over the operation of the mill.[65] Banks did not agree to the offers, especially from the Buckeye Company, because he thought "it would mean the loss of our identity as a race with the Oil Mill." Although the companies were willing to go to great lengths to work out an agreement, Banks said he had "no idea of accepting this however, and would rather have an honorable defeat, than the kind of procedure which their proposition carries."[66]

Even if from a business perspective Bank's refusal seems imprudent, it shows his firm commitment to preserving the all-black legacy of Mound Bayou. Although, as he explained to Washington, turning over the mill would place him "squarely on my feet from a financial standpoint," he refused to do so lest it meant the loss of Mound Bayou's identity.[67] He also believed he would be able to guide the mill out of its predicament without having to revert to such drastic measures. Also, the fact that these were white-owned companies, like Harvey's, could have aroused Banks's suspicion.

During the litigation, the mill was not allowed to operate, which worked to Mound Bayou's detriment. And during this trying time, another event devastated Banks—the death of his mentor and friend Booker T. Washington on November 14, 1915. The day before Washington died, Banks had sent a desperate request to Tuskegee for more support for the oil mill.[68] But there was no relief in sight. In February 1916, he was still paying Rosenwald out of his pocket. Banks's cash flow was so tight he told Graves that for February he was not "in a position to take care of the principal, but will pay the interest."[69] Meanwhile, Scott, who was having his own problems at Tuskegee after Washington's death, could only give Banks moral support. "I hope you . . . find him [Rosenwald] sympathetic in your efforts to get straight," Scott told Banks.[70]

In a detailed letter to Graves, Banks explained the status of the mill "from a layman's viewpoint." Banks mentioned that because the case was going to federal court, Harvey could be forced to bring his company's books into court for all to see. "We are satisfied that a case of embezzlement will develop and thereby lay the foundation for criminal proceedings against him in the Federal Court," said Banks, "which we feel will result in Harvey's coming around to effect a compromise settlement with us rather than go to trial for embezzlement." Until that time, Banks and others had not been able to force Harvey's hand because of a lack of jurisdiction. In closing, Banks remarked, "We accept the battle as launched, [and] will fight it out with them."[71] In the same spirit, Scott wrote Banks, "I trust that the lessee may get all that is coming to him."[72]

Reviving the Oil Mill

Some scholars have asserted that the oil mill was a failure. For instance, Louis Harlan concludes that Harvey "milked" the oil mill into disaster and that ultimately the oil mill represented "black enterprise in reverse gear." He also implies that Banks became involved in some underhanded dealings, "obscuring" from Washington and Rosenwald the reality of his agreement with Harvey.[73] To the contrary, records show Banks communicated openly and honestly with Washington, Rosenwald, and Scott all along. In fact, Rosenwald did not agree to invest in the mill until all these matters were clear. By that time, he clearly knew of Harvey's full involvement in leasing the mill. To suggest otherwise not only casts Banks in a negative light but also raises questions about Rosenwald's business savvy. Moreover, Rosenwald did not express surprise in his correspondence to Banks when Harvey's trickery was discovered. On a few occasions, he even told Scott and Washington he did not fault Banks for Harvey's deeds.[74]

Similarly, McMillen states that Banks's "vigorous efforts" to reopen the mill failed, and the mill became a dance hall.[75] However, the only written evidence of that came from a study done in Mound Bayou in 1937, fourteen years after Banks died. Maurice Jackson, a graduate student at the University of Alabama at the time, did not expressly say the oil mill became a dance hall but that "the huge brick oil mill building is used as a ballroom, *upon rare and special occasions* [author's emphasis] when an out-of-town Negro orchestra is engaged for a night's engagement."[76] This does not suggest that even at that point the mill was used solely for dances, even if it had become inoperable. Oral sources suggest the mill may have operated into the 1930s.[77]

Though the mill may have become a dance hall at some point, neither Harlan nor McMillen mention that Banks along with Isaiah Montgomery eventually freed the mill from debt and made it fully operational again. The mill ended up being a quasi-philanthropic endeavor for Rosenwald, but Banks continued to work to have the mill functioning profitably well after Washington's death. Banks's plan for the oil mill could have worked if it were not for the scoundrel, B. B. Harvey; the mill generated roughly $12,600 in profits during its first season of operation. However, Harvey's actions choked the life out of the plant.

By July 12, 1919, Banks and Montgomery had arranged to have the mill operational again. Banks asked Tuskegee principal Moton for help in publicizing the accomplishment. He asked Moton to send a reporter to Mound Bayou to write a story about the mill and the overall progress of the town.[78] Eventually, the *Advance-Dispatch*, the official organ of the General Baptist Convention in Mississippi, did a story. "It is but fair to state that the Mound Bayou Oil Mill is in full operation and everything is moving smoothly or satisfactorily along," the newspaper reported. "Mr. Chas. Banks, manager, certainly deserves much credit for having taken care of this concern which speaks for itself as a race enterprise."[79]

On February 28, 1920, the *New York Age* ran a similar story. According to the article, the oil mill had been dormant for several years, but now "the wheels of the oil mill are whirling day and night, turning out a class of oil and other products equal to that of any factory in the country." By 1920 Banks apparently relented from his earlier convictions about the "identity" of the mill and leased it "to responsible parties and neighbors on a basis of 51 percent for the lessee and 49 percent for the stockholders." George C. Michie, the mill's new lessee, and O. A. Holmes, the superintendent, were white. Because the mill had been defunct for some years, it needed considerable repairs. But, the *Age* stated, the old stockholders were "not required to put up any additional money for operation or repairs." No dividends were to be paid the first year of operations so all profits could be put back into the business to strengthen it more.[80]

After realizing that his investment in the mill was partially philanthropic, Rosenwald voluntarily agreed to a 50 percent payout, which certainly pleased Banks and other town promoters. "A northern friend who owns and has carried bonds of the Company's for several years out of a spirit of helpfulness for the Race has decided to take $.50 on the dollar for his holdings," Banks told Moton. If the money could be raised, Banks's group would pay Rosenwald $20,000, which would give them the "first and only mortgage on the property here."[81]

To pay off Rosenwald, Banks started a campaign to have twenty Negroes invest $1,000 each in the oil mill. He wanted them to pay $500 in April and another $500 in November. Banks promoted this as a golden opportunity; although the mill cost $100,000 to construct before the war, he estimated it would cost from $200,000 to $250,000 to replicate it in the postwar era.[82] In a letter to Moton outlining the campaign, Banks denied his letter was solicitous, but he obviously wanted Moton to invest. However, Moton informed Banks he could not do so. "I am worse off financially than I have been for some time," he told Banks. "It looks like now as if I am in the neighborhood of three thousand dollars out, because a young man, the secretary of the Hampton Building and Loan Association absconded a year ago with it [and it] looks as if he disposed of my shares and everything else."[83] While that may have been the case, Moton was not as supportive of Banks's business efforts as Washington and Scott. Ultimately, by June or July 1919, Banks managed to secure the funds needed to pay off Rosenwald.[84]

Next, Banks wanted to pay off the original investors. He and Montgomery planned to issue $50,000 worth of new bonds that were to be secured by a first mortgage on the plant, assessed at more than $200,000. The new bonds would be sold for $500 each. Banks's and Montgomery's overall desire, according to the *New York Age*, was "to place the entire issue in the hands of colored men. They hope to interest one hundred men who will take one bond each." Banks's optimism had reached new heights because the mill had passed the "experimental stage," and the men claimed it was "one of the best in the State of Mississippi."[85] Whether these plans came to fruition is unknown. Also unknown is the exact closing date of the mill, but evidence clearly shows it still operated well into February of 1922. If the oil mill did eventually become a dance hall, it seems to have happened after Banks died in 1923.[86]

Banks realized he had made mistakes in running the affairs of the bank and the oil mill. Perhaps the most egregious thing he did from a business perspective was to intertwine the affairs of the bank with the mill. When he engineered the purchase of $40,000 worth of oil mill stocks through the bank, he placed the assets of the bank in jeopardy. Because he served as the town banker and was a major depositor in the bank, he easily persuaded others to go along with him. Banks may have had a conflict of interest, but under the banking laws of the time, all of Banks's maneuvers were legal. Banks believed his reputation and credibility were inextricably bound to the mill's success. Thus, ambition and ego played a role in his decision to use the bank to finance the mill. It also appears that Banks's pride kept him from making what might have been a prudent decision to later lease the mill to one of the companies that approached him. He insisted on maintaining the "identity" of the mill when he could have cleared the mill of debt, assuming the company would have dealt honorably.

A few months before Washington died, Banks confessed to him that in the efforts to support Mound Bayou he and others had "counted too strongly upon the loyalty and support of our constituency and resources at our command and did not properly discount the chances for reverses and general depression."[87] But in terms of the chicanery alleged by Mary Turner and others, Banks maintained that while he would "confess to having made mistakes, . . . [I] insist that they were of the head and not the heart."[88] In truth, his actions were more of the "heart" than of the "head." Racial pride and ego guided Banks when it came to the mill. Rather than let the mill sit idle until he could secure proper financing, he used the bank to purchase substantial shares of the mill's stock so it could become operational. This effectively placed the funds of the bank's depositors at risk. Again, Banks's "heart" and ambition got in the way of his good business sense. Instead of having it appear that the oil mill was dysfunctional after they disseminated so much promotional rhetoric throughout the country, Banks risked the resources of the bank to keep from losing his reputation as the "most influential businessman in the United States."[89] Thus, personal ego clearly played a role in his business decisions.

Although his hurdles were many, Banks remained committed to racial uplift and solidarity, and though he made mistakes, it does not appear that he ever tried to take advantage of his clients for his own gain. None of his letters to Washington, to Moton, or to his best friend Scott, indicate such a motive. Moton even recognized Banks's race consciousness, congratulating him for his work late in 1919. "You have been most courageous and most persistent in your efforts to make this project succeed," which will be looked upon, he said, "by our people as 'a big thing' put over by a member of our race."[90] Banks clearly capitalized on being in Mound Bayou during its Golden Age, but so did many other prominent citizens, and they all made lots of money from their investments. Still, Banks's wealth depended largely on the success of the town and to work against the larger interest would have ultimately destroyed him.

Mound Bayou's economic dependence on a single crop placed both the town and Banks in a precarious situation. Mound Bayou experienced some prosperity before World War I, when cotton prices were high for a short period. But by 1914, prices had dropped and the economic situation in the town had grown dismal. In fact, conditions became so bad that a number of families left Mound Bayou for the North. The exodus continued until the town's population dropped from about one thousand to about eight hundred. Many of the families who stayed continued to suffer financially. Many men were forced back into tenancy, while the women were increasingly thrust into domestic service. By 1922, even the Farmers' Cooperative Mercantile Company, the town's largest retail store, went out of business, indicating the travails experienced by many Mound Bayou businessmen by the early 1920s.[91]

Notwithstanding, Banks was a fairly successful businessman throughout his life. He was self-employed from about age sixteen until he died. He also provided jobs for many black people and paid some quite well. Moreover, any Negro who started life in extreme poverty, as Banks did, and who amassed $100,000 in net worth by 1915 through his business endeavors, should be appropriately credited. If this $100,000 were adjusted for inflation at 4 percent over eighty-five years, by 2000 his net worth would have been around $2,750,000. At a 5 percent rate of inflation over this same period, his net worth would have been around $6,289,000. Banks practiced what he preached. He not only advocated Washington's philosophy of economic uplift, he served as a shining example of it.

After Booker T. Washington

"A Tempest in the Teapot"

Losing the Favorite Guardian Angels

On November 14, 1915 Booker T. Washington, the Wizard of Tuskegee, died with family members at his bedside. Upon finding this out, Banks immediately wired Emmett Scott the following message: "With the entire race I am bowed in mourning—the loss of the greatest man the race has produced in any epoch. One of America's foremost citizens, regardless of race. The peer of any educator in any clime." Then he asked Scott to "convey to Mrs. Washington and the bereaved family" his "deepest sympathy."[1] A few days later, Banks and Isaiah Montgomery attended Washington's funeral and served as honorary pallbearers at his memorial service.[2]

The death of Washington significantly impacted the lives of many Americans, especially Banks and Scott. For years, both men had operated under Washington's leadership, and now he was gone. After his death, two major questions arose. First, who would lead the Tuskegee Institute? Second, who would head the NNBL? Since Scott had served as Washington's personal secretary for almost two decades, some believed he would automatically become president of Tuskegee.[3] Likewise, since Banks had been first vice-president of the NNBL for so many years, many people felt he would become its president. Scholars have touched on the first question, but none have adequately answered the second.

Four days after Washington's death, the *New York Age* published a story, "Three Spoken of to Succeed Washington." The paper referred to Warren Logan, treasurer of Tuskegee Institute; Robert R. Moton, commandant at Hampton Institute; and, of course, Scott. Based on the organizational structure of Tuskegee, Logan became acting principal pending selection of a successor. All the men had good connections to Washington or Tuskegee, which made them reasonable choices for the job.[4]

By December 9, rumors started to spread that forty-eight-year-old Major Moton would be Washington's successor. A newspaper reported that the white trustees of Tuskegee, as well as the faculty, favored him. The paper also noted that Washington had offered Moton the assistant principal position of Tuskegee two years earlier.[5] The longer it took for the board of trustees to make a decision, the more rumors spread. By December 16, it appears the field had been narrowed to two candidates, Moton and Scott.[6] Five days before Christmas, the board selected Moton to lead the institute. While they were not "unmindful of the long devotion and many qualifications of Emmett J. Scott for the position," board members said, they wanted to "bring to the work of Tuskegee another forceful personality."[7] The decision seems to have been in accordance with Washington's last wishes. In fact, Washington's wife, Margaret, later indicated he told her before he died that he wanted Moton to succeed him.[8]

The fact that Scott did not receive the principalship at Tuskegee had serious consequences for Banks. One month after Moton became principal, Scott began contemplating leaving the institute. The turn of events devastated Scott, although he tried to hide his disappointment publicly.[9] Banks suggested that Scott consider being appointed minister to Haiti if Roosevelt was elected president for another term. That opportunity did not materialize, so Scott remained in his position as secretary under Moton. Nevertheless, correspondence between Scott and Banks indicates that Scott did not plan on being at Tuskegee for long; as soon as the right opportunity presented itself, he intended to leave.[10]

Moton was inaugurated during the May 1916 commencement at Tuskegee, but he did not assume the helm until August. Banks did not attend the inauguration, but later extended "heartiest congratulations" to Moton, and wished him well in his new position. "If at any time you feel that my services will be of value to you," Banks said, "I hope you will feel free to command me."[11] Although Moton expressed disappointment at not seeing Banks at the inauguration, he said, "I always understand my friends." "I know if they do not do things, it is because of good reasons." It is hard to determine whether Banks and Moton were being honest when they wrote these notes. Moton knew how close Banks and Scott were and must have realized Banks would have preferred Scott for the position. Accordingly, Moton said the following about Scott in a letter to Banks:

"The workers here are most loyal and kind, particularly our mutual friend, Mr. Scott, who has been as kind and as thoughtful as heart could wish, but this is his nature and character anyhow. That sort of character has made the 'Tuskegee Spirit.'"[12]

Scott left Tuskegee less than two years after Washington's death. By October 15, 1917 he received a temporary appointment to serve as special assistant to Newton Baker, the secretary of war.[13] Scott's primary responsibilities were to generate plans that would boost morale among black soldiers and civilians and to make sure that the Selective Service regulations were impartially applied during the war. According to John Hope Franklin, Scott "was called upon to express an opinion regarding almost every phase of African-American life and was required to answer thousands of inquiries from blacks on every conceivable subject."[14] Although many members of the Tuskegee family were happy for Scott, they did not want to see him leave the institute, even temporarily.[15]

Banks rejoiced about Scott receiving the appointment. He realized his good friend had not recovered from losing his bid for the presidency of Tuskegee. Banks also believed that working for the War Department was a good career move for Scott. Meanwhile, Banks led Mound Bayouans in supporting the war effort. He boasted to Moton that Mound Bayou citizens exceeded their quota of $13,800 for the Third Liberty Bond call, subscribing instead for $18,250. Moton complimented Banks on the achievement: "Such a record, I am sure, [is] a credit in a large way to your leadership."[16] "The patriotism of the Negro at Mound Bayou has never been questioned," noted one observer. Indeed, during the war at least fifty men from Mound Bayou enlisted in the army. Fortunately, all the soldiers from the town returned, although some were seriously wounded. One source even reported that "Charles Banks and Rev. S. P. Felder were among the 'Four Minute Men.'" These Minute Men spoke at movie theaters to sell war bonds.[17]

Despite Banks's pleasure in Scott's appointment, Scott's absence from the school affected Banks. When Scott left for Washington, D.C., Albon Holsey temporarily replaced him as secretary at Tuskegee. Banks had known Holsey years earlier, and they had a cordial relationship. Banks had also worked with Moton in the NNBL, and Moton had traveled with Washington's entourage when he toured Mississippi in 1908. But while they respected and supported Banks, Moton and Holsey did not have the same "deep affection" for him as had Scott and Washington.

Perhaps one of the biggest limitations for Banks as a leader was his dependency on Washington and Scott. This became apparent after Washington died. It became even more apparent when Scott left Tuskegee. Banks could not count on Holsey to intercept or destroy complaints about him. Scott had done this for years, which helped Banks put a better image before the public and the Tuskegee Machine. It also helped Banks consolidate power as the premier Negro leader in Mississippi.

Internal Struggles

Because Mound Bayou's leaders respected him so much, Booker T. Washington had been the bonding agent holding the town together. "Outside of Tuskegee, I think I can safely say that there is no community in the world that I am so deeply interested in as I am in Mound Bayou," Washington told Isaiah Montgomery a few months before he died. The Tuskegee leader fully understood the problems that existed between Mound Bayou's leaders. In January 1915, he wrote Montgomery, stating how glad he was that the people in the town "are realizing the importance of getting together and working together." He also encouraged Montgomery to work out his differences with Banks. "I want to urge over and over again that at any cost and at any sacrifice all personal grudges and animosities be forgotten at once and for all and that all stand together with a determination to make Mound Bayou a good, clean, moral community. "[18]

Washington made it clear to Montgomery that he had the "fullest confidence" and "highest respect" for Banks. "I have worked with him under many difficult and trying circumstances and I have always found him to be loyal and true," he said. "I will go further, I have not only a respect for him but a deep affection for him." Nonetheless, after Washington died, internecine battles for leadership engulfed the town to such a degree that they ultimately brought Mound Bayou's Golden Age to a close. Montgomery's envy of Banks, which had been simmering for years, finally rose to the surface. However, Banks's most bitter foe in the town was not Montgomery but Eugene Booze, his brother-in-law. Booze became obsessed with trying to destroy Banks.[19]

One of the earliest manifestations of the struggle between Booze and Banks appeared at the end of June 1916, about one month before the annual convention of the NNBL at Kansas City. Booze wrote to Scott suggesting that he use his influence to help secure a successor to lead the NNBL who would reflect "credit upon the race and prove a worthy inspiration for generations to follow."[20] Although it had been decided the previous December that Banks would not run for the presidency of the league, Booze either did not know this or he wanted to make sure he ruined Banks's chances of doing so.[21]

In his letter, Booze also told Scott that "no man who lives openly and notoriously in adultery is fit to associate or to succeed Dr. Washington in any capacity." He also announced that when he arrived at the meeting in August he would "oppose in every honorable manner the selection of such a person to succeed Dr. Washington." Booze claimed that he was moved to lead this charge "from the highest grounds of principle and have no desire to do anyone an injury and hope that the necessity will not arise for me to take such a course in the meeting."[22]

Booze went on to say that there had already been too much toleration for moral weakness among black leaders and that he considered "the time propitious to check the growing immoral tendencies." "If we are going to place rewards upon those who revel in immorality, even though they be mentally and physically strong, what will be the ultimate result of our racial development?" he asked. In closing, he assured Scott he had no "motive other than the highest racial development." Scott, in his normal "guardian angel" fashion, forwarded the letter to Banks.[23] Banks told Scott he was "profoundly grateful" to be able to view the correspondance.[24]

When the NNBL meeting took place in August, proceedings were orderly. However, Booze was upset because Banks managed to retain his position as first vice-president. He later complained to Scott, who was secretary of the league, that he had sent Scott "certain documents" and requested they be turned over to the executive committee for their "information and action." "You can imagine my surprise when I found out through Mr. W. C. Gordon of St. Louis that the information had not been filed with the committee," Booze told Scott. Apparently to deter further action, Gordon had told Booze that even if the committee had received the material, it would not have acted on the complaint. "Of course, I didn't believe this," Booze asserted.[25]

Booze was angry that Scott ignored his letter charging Banks with adultery. "Knowing you to be a particular and close friend of Mr. Banks I did not expect or look for any encouragement from you in this matter," he complained, "but I felt it was your plain duty as an official of the League to acknowledge receipt of my correspondence." Whether Scott acknowledged receipt of the letters or not, he certainly received them, because he forwarded the letters to Banks. Without a formal acknowledgment, though, Scott could argue he never received a complaint from Booze.[26]

At the 1916 meeting in Kansas City, Booze said, he thought he would be called before the executive committee or at least hear from Scott about the complaint. But he was "greatly disappointed," he said, "and at one time in the early proceedings I thought to take the floor and ask for an explanation regarding my complaint." He later realized that Scott planned to ignore his correspondence and "push Mr. Banks as the presiding officer of the meeting without investigating the charges." Thus, he said, he decided "it would be best, not to take this approach out of respect for Washington and to keep from marring the proceedings of the meeting." Furthermore, he supported James C. Napier for the presidency, and he did not want to jeopardize Napier's chances in pushing charges against Banks.[27]

Booze did not want his acquiescence at the meeting to be misconstrued:

> . . .the cold blooded, steam roller political tactics which you allowed Charles Banks and his political henchman, Perry Howard, to put over on Major Moton thoroughly disgusted me, and compels me to believe that a complete exposure of the man, Banks, is absolutely necessary for the highest development and welfare of our race in this country, and I shall be glad to furnish you a copy of the information which I sent you as outlined above if you wish it and will promise to lay the matter before the Executive Committee.[28]

This time, Booze took precautionary measures so that Scott could not ignore his complaint: "In order to insure the safe delivery of this letter I am having it registered with request that it be delivered to the addressee only." [29] Scott's response to Booze is unknown, but it is certain he continued to share the letters with Banks and lend him his support. On October 9, 1916, Banks sent Scott a brief letter stating, "I am returning you herewith letters from Mr. Booze, and thank you kindly for having let me seen same."[30]

Booze eventually became more adamant in his attack on Banks, suggesting that Banks had been indicted for illegally selling whiskey while he ran his mercantile business at Clarksdale. Matters finally came to a point where Banks felt compelled to respond fully to the allegations. "Referring again to our mutual friend? Mr. Booze," Banks wrote to Scott, "you can now quite understand the mischief he has wrought in my family relations, especially when they [Eugene and Trenna] both are of the same blood." Banks went on to expound "how badly he gets along with the people." One of Mound Bayou's "best white friends" and a supporter of its enterprises, said Banks, lent Booze $1,000 to "prevent some embarrassment" about ten days before "he made his trip to Kansas City on his lofty mission in the interest of his race and humanity." According to Banks, this person ended up confronting Booze, and "threatened to shoot him down . . . because of uncalled for imposition that he did not feel like taking." According to Banks, the only reason the man did not shoot Booze was because "he did not want to embarrass us here by killing one of our supposed leading citizens."[31]

In November 1916, Banks told Scott that Booze had succeeded in "poisoning Mr. Montgomery as he did his sister and he [Montgomery] is about as rotten as his protégé." In response to the charge that he had been indicted for selling whiskey illegally in Clarksdale, Banks forthrightly said that "is all rot." "There has never been any indictment against me there or anywhere else," he claimed, "and I have never sold a drop of whiskey in my life which is more than he can say." Banks also assured Scott that the people of Clarksdale, black and white, "always give me first place among the list of our people, living or dead." In other words, whites held him in high esteem—if white people respected him, he was suggesting, he had to be respectable.[32]

Banks became so frustrated that he did not rule out physically assaulting Booze. "Were it not that I did not think the game is not worth the ammunition, I would take him to task personally for his continued iniquitous machinations against me," he said. But he realized such a move would not be prudent, because he had "all to lose and nothing to gain." However, he informed Scott that he would continue to ignore Booze, "unless it gets where it is a matter of self-defense."[33]

Banks was prevaricating when he denied the charge of illegally selling whiskey. Unbeknownst to Banks, Booze had secured copies of two indictments from the clerk of the Coahoma County Circuit Court, I. J. E. Montroy, which Booze forwarded to Scott to support his claim. Indeed, there were two indictments, made in May and in November 1902. The first charged Banks with "violating the Sabbath." Specifically the charge read: "Charley Banks being a shop keeper and not being a druggist, or apothecary did on . . . Sunday willfully and unlawfully keep open store and sell and dispose of goods wares and merchandise." Banks pleaded guilty and paid a $5 fine, plus court costs. The second indictment charged that

Banks did "willfully and unlawfully sell vinous, sourutous malt and intoxicating liquors," which was a retailing violation under Mississippi law. Again, Banks pleaded guilty and paid a $25 fine, plus court costs.[34]

It is unclear whether Banks knew Scott received the copies or whether Scott kept the information to himself to avoid embarrassing his friend even further. Nonetheless, the fact that Booze was able to prove his charge did not appear to shake Scott's confidence in Banks. While Banks did try to refute the charge that he had been indicted for illegally selling whiskey, he never denied living in "open adultery." Perhaps his conspicuous silence is an indication of the truth of the claim. It is worth noting, too, that these problems may have factored into Banks's decision to sell his business and leave Clarksdale for Mound Bayou at the end of 1903. Regardless, Banks told the truth when he asserted that the people in Clarksdale continued to hold him in high esteem.

New Problems with the Carnegie Library

If Banks thought he had seen the last of Booze's furor, he was sadly mistaken. About January 1917, Booze began to open old wounds in reference to the library.[35] He reported to James Bertram, Carnegie's friend and former secretary, that the library was still not being managed according to the agreement. With this move, it became apparent Booze's actions were not done out of "morality" or concern for the race but to carry out a personal vendetta. Bertram wrote Moton a letter expressing dismay about this news, and he asked Moton to get to the bottom of things.

Alarmed that Booze would go to such an extreme, Moton wrote Banks: "I am very much chagrined to receive such a letter as the enclosed from Mr. Bertram." Further, he said, "I am very sorry indeed that Mr. Booze has mixed in the library matter." In the meantime, he asked Banks to help him craft a response to Bertram. "Please let me hear from you very soon: the sooner, in my opinion, the better," Moton asserted.[36] Banks responded and suggested that Moton have Roscoe Simmons, a black reporter and Tuskegee man, visit Mound Bayou and write an article about the library. Banks actually believed that if Simmons visited, "the falsehoods and misrepresentations that come from one certain source can easily be shown up and the malice back of it."[37]

Surprisingly, Montgomery, who was Booze's usual ally, weighed in on this matter on the side of Banks. He stated that the town leaders had been derelict in meeting their responsibilities to the library, but he believed that given time they would make a marked improvement. Somewhat vindicating Banks, Montgomery noted: "In my opinion Mr. Banks does himself an injustice in trying to shoulder the whole responsibility." Though Banks now served as head of the board of directors for the library, someone else had managed it the previous four years.[38]

In April 1917, Booze went to New York. While there, he met with F. M. Coffin of the Carnegie Corporation. After discussing his concerns about the library, Booze agreed to make a report. "I am going to be as careful as I can in this report," he later told Moton, but "at the same time I think a free and frank statement will help all concerned."[39] Meanwhile, Banks sent a letter to Bertram explaining why the library was not being used as agreed. He reiterated that the MBA had only used a corner of the library for about fifteen months. He denied Booze's charge that the library had been rented to Mound Bayou Normal Institute for the 1915–1916 school term. In response to the charge that the library still had no books, Banks told Fred Moore, "You know it is a false[hood] . . . because you sent some here yourself." Nevertheless, Banks grew weary with Booze's campaign to smear his reputation. "He is a man bent on destruction and nothing constructive," Banks lamented. This may be why Banks asked Fred Moore to go to Bertram's office to "let him know that I have been misrepresented to him by this man, Booze."[40]

Banks's efforts to quiet Booze did not work. On May 2, 1917, Booze sent Coffin a detailed report on the library. Booze prefaced his report by telling Coffin he hesitated to make it because "Mr. Banks and his friends are doing everything they can to make it appear that my opposition to their method of handling public affairs, is based upon personal spite and ambition." And as he had done a year earlier, Booze claimed to be motivated strictly by the "continued mismanagement of public affairs, and the growing immoral tendencies" of Banks. Moreover, Booze stated, community members had come to him, as their leader, "to speak out against these evils," and he "could not honorably resist their wishes."[41]

Although he admitted he had not examined the town records to corroborate his claims, Booze reported:

there has not been a single dollar appropriated by the town council to buy a book or magazine, or to maintain the same according to their promise in securing the contribution from Mr. Carnegie. On the other hand, it can be shown that more than one thousand dollars have been collected as rent for the use of the building. It is true that the public generally have had the free use of the building for assembly purposes, when they happen to be in the good graces of the town Marshal, who carries the keys, but no effort at all has been put forward to keep the building open at anytime for reading purposes. Under the circumstances, I recommend: That you send in a representative to look into the situation without letting any one know about his coming or who he is until he has gotten the information he needs, and then have him call the people together to explain how the contribution was secured and the obligation they are under to operate the building for library purposes.[42]

Booze boldly sent a copy of the letter to Moton, which kept him involved in the matter. Maybe Booze assumed that by exposing Banks, his stature among Tuskegee men would increase. If so, he assumed wrong. Moton wrote Booze a pointed letter expressing displeasure with Booze's attempts to defame Banks, especially his turning to white men (people outside of the black community) to try to resolve his issues. He told Booze he wished that his problems "could be settled within the community, and at least within the race. You perhaps know how Mr. Bertram felt about the library situation." Moton scolded Booze, saying that because of his actions, "the Negro race suffers as well as the few individuals." Furthermore, Moton said, "while I do not believe in covering up or hiding anything, I do question how much we gain sometimes by going into too much detail with people outside of a local situation."[43] Although Booze vigorously tried to justify his actions, Moton rejected his arguments.[44]

Things Fall Apart

After Washington died, Banks's luck took a turn for the worse. On his way to the funeral of John E. Bush, a vice-president of the NNBL, around December 19, 1916, Banks was injured in a train wreck about fifteen miles from Memphis. Scott had asked him to attend the funeral as a representative of the NNBL. Banks was taken to Saint Anthony's Hospital in Memphis for treatment. While there, he received get-well wishes from Moton, Scott, and others. Despite his misfortune, Banks jokingly told Scott he would not "let this opportunity pass to share in the dividends of the Railroad Company." "I am not sure that I want to curse you or bless you for being responsible for this attempted trip," he said. Although confined in the hospital on New Year's Day 1917, Banks still wrote Scott his first letter of the year, as had been his custom for close to two decades.[45]

Relations between Banks and his wife had deteriorated by early 1917. Trenna Banks, who was doubtless upset about her husband's infidelity and the possibility that he might cut her out of his fortune if they separated, went into his office near the end of January, assaulted him, and "nearly sliced off one of his ears." Shortly after this ordeal, Banks filed for divorce. Trenna subsequently used her brother, Eugene, as legal counsel in the divorce proceedings.[46] The court dismissed Banks's suit, but Trenna won her countersuit. The court awarded her "the residence in the Town of Mound Bayou now occupied by her, together with all of the furnishing and fixtures." In addition to having to pay the costs for the court proceedings, Banks had to pay her $50 a month "for her support and maintenance."[47]

Meanwhile, Booze threatened to embarrass Banks at the annual business league convention planned for August 1917 in Chattanooga, Tennessee. Banks became aware of the threats through Moton, who, like Scott, forwarded Booze's correspondence to him. "The party to whom it all refers has made his efforts and attacks from every angle, both locally and nationally," Banks wrote to Moton, and yet Booze was now "in a more ridiculous position now than when he first began." Regarding the upcoming meeting, Banks stated, "I am not at all uncertain as to my footing, and, so far as I am concerned, have no fears of what he thinks he would be able to accomplish at the Chattanooga Meeting." Furthermore, "I stand ready to meet any reasonable and manly proposition" asserted Banks.[48] Booze convinced Fannie Knelland of Memphis, with whom Banks may have had an affair, to appear against him, which undoubtedly influenced the executive committee.[49] Charges were filed against Banks at the meeting, and a special investigative committee was to be established to look into the matter.[50]

Booze believed three people would be appointed to investigate the complaint. He and Banks would suggest one person each, and executive committee chairman Moton would choose the third party. Booze was suspicious of Moton, however, believing that he favored Banks. Booze presumed Banks would be allowed to handpick Moton's representative while Moton asked Booze to choose his own representative from a list pre-approved by Banks. In response, Booze told Moton, "neither of the names you mention would be entirely satisfactory to me." He also cautioned Moton to select a person who would be fair and impartial to head the committee. "To do otherwise would only mean to defeat the ends of justice and prove a waste of valuable time and money," he said. In his letter, Booze included the names of three men he found acceptable.[51]

Moton wrote Booze that he had previously selected some other men to represent him, but found out from Scott that the people charged with carrying out this investigation were supposed to be members of the executive committee. Only one of the names Booze proposed, Ernest Ten Eyck Attwell, who was Tuskegee's business agent and a member of the executive council, fit the criteria.[52] However, Booze doubted Moton's candor on this matter. "Now, Doctor," he began in a letter to Moton, "I have been reliably informed that before the selection of the names you sent me to serve on the committee, Mr. Banks had been requested to name his representatives and the names you sent to me had been approved by him before they were sent to me." "I submit, Sir, that this is not fair and unless a just investigation of the complaint is going to be made, what is the use of shaming?"[53]

Booze argued that he had not been informed that the investigators would have to come from the executive committee and that Scott had made an error on that score. He felt that as long as the investigators were reputable members of the league, they should be able to serve. By choosing only from the executive committee, Banks would have "a decided advantage." However, he agreed to the conditions set forth if Attwell could represent him and a Mr. Brooks, one of the first men proposed by Moton, could chair the committee.[54]

Although Moton appears to have favored Banks in the matter, he tried to convince Booze of his impartiality. Moton admitted to Booze that he had planned to send Banks the list of names for his approval but did not "because of my extreme anxiety to see that the whole matter was handled in a thoroughly fair and unbiased way."[55] Regardless of what Moton said, however, he probably did forward the names to Banks. Moton had done similar favors for Banks, a key lieutenant in the Tuskegee Machine. Ultimately, Booze continued to believe Moton favored Banks. "I know the cards have already been stacked against me," Booze said, "but I am going to accept anybody you want to appoint to make the investigation." Booze felt that at least league members would get a chance to learn the things he complained of were true, even though the committee might find otherwise to save a brother officer.[56]

Moton told Booze he had "nothing but the kindliest feelings" for him and Banks, but felt that "the development of Mound Bayou is of far greater importance than the success of any individual." This meant that even if he found Booze's charges to be true, he would not support him if it meant bringing harm to Mound Bayou. To his credit, Moton kept focusing on the big picture. He even tried to encourage Booze to meet with him, Banks, and a few others unofficially so they could bring the conflict to a close. "I am willing to be used in any way to further the best interests of our people," he told Booze.[57]

As the 1918 meeting where this matter was to be resolved drew near, a strange thing happened. Someone wrote Knelland, the woman who had appeared against Banks the previous year, a letter under Scott's name, inviting her to attend the NNBL meeting in Atlantic City. Banks believed some of Booze's allies at Tuskegee were responsible for this.[58] Although the details of the investigation are unknown, Banks does not appear to have been found guilty; he remained in his position as first vice-president for years afterward.

Political Turmoil

Another critical struggle between Mound Bayou's leaders erupted in 1917 when the Banks-Francis-Harris faction won Mound Bayou's municipal elections. B. Howard Creswell, whom the Banks faction supported, defeated Booze in the race for town mayor. Creswell, a longtime resident of Mound Bayou, owned a successful mercantile business and had served as mayor of the town for eleven years. He first became mayor in 1906 and handled his responsibilities so satisfactorily that one of the town's residents opined that he would "be permitted to occupy the honorable station as long as he may be disposed to desire it."[59]

In 1917 Creswell did not hold municipal elections. Consequently, Montgomery had Booze appointed mayor, along with a new slate of aldermen. This prompted Creswell to hold elections one month later, and he defeated Booze. Montgomery and his son-in-law, Booze, alleged fraud. Booze somehow arranged a second set of elections several weeks later, and he won the bid for mayor. George Moore was his marshal, John Jones his treasurer, and R. McCorkle, Edward Threadgill, Reuben Brooks, and H. H. Powell, his aldermen. Two governments attempted to rule the town for almost a year.[60]

When Booze visited New York in April 1917 to meet with Coffin about the library matter, he presented himself as mayor. Banks took steps to embarrass him in this regard. He told Moton that Booze in no way served as mayor of Mound Bayou, "aside from stationery he had printed to mislead the public." What is more, Banks asserted, "he is in no way exercising the functions of mayor and his little band are [a] laughing stock and not taken seriously by any well informed people on the situation." "The man's foolishness," said Banks, "makes me doubt his sanity."[61]

This situation placed Banks at odds not only with Booze but also with Montgomery. Eventually, Montgomery, whom some whites held in high esteem for having been Joseph Davis's "houseboy" during the antebellum period, persuaded avowed racist Governor Theodore G. Bilbo to intervene. In early 1917, Bilbo nullified the first election results and issued a proclamation recognizing the Montgomery-Booze faction as the legitimate government. However, the Banks faction refused to vacate. It filed suit against the Montgomery-Booze faction. This was a heated battle, and Banks definitely wanted to win. Booze later complained that Banks had hired as many as six attorneys, whom he characterized as "the most ablest and expensive attorneys in the state."[62]

Ultimately, Judge W. A. Alcorn ruled Booze's appointment illegal and sustained the election of Creswell.[63] The Montgomery-Booze faction appealed the decision to the Mississippi Supreme Court. Booze argued that the Banks-Creswell faction had refused to provide a legal voter registration system and election for Mound Bayouans, had mismanaged public affairs, and had not given a financial accounting of public funds. Perry Howard led the defense for the Banks faction, and on June 15, 1918, the *New York Age* reported that the Mississippi Supreme Court "decided in favor of the Banks-Creswell faction in the controversy for Mayor of Mound Bayou."[64] After this, Booze begrudgingly admitted that Banks's faction had defeated his faction "on technicalities" in both the circuit and supreme courts. Dissatisfied with the decisions, Booze ran for mayor in the next regular municipal election. Again, Creswell defeated him, "together with the entire administration ticket, by a vote of 2 to 1."[65]

Financial Turmoil

Political conflict between Banks and Montgomery was just part of their problems. Even more disturbing were the disputes over financial matters. Montgomery supported many businesses started by Banks, especially the town bank and oil mill. On June 13, 1919, he sent Banks a blistering letter, charging him with all sorts of unfair business practices regarding the oil mill:

> I have absolutely reached the conclusion that I have been pulling chestnuts out of the fire for you long enough. You have not come clean in this deal by a long shot, and have made due provisions for your own future and that of your particular friends, while I who have put more actual money and labor into the plant than anyone else, have only a bare pittance of $1,000 worth of stock to show for it.[66]

Montgomery stated he had stopped selling cottonseed to the Refuge Cotton Oil Company and started relations with Leland Oil Works and Port Gibson Oil Company at the request of Banks. He claimed he did this only because Banks assured him that the two companies were going to help put the local mill back in operation after the lawsuit with Harvey was settled. Montgomery complained that he stuck with these companies loyally, shipping them thousands of bales of seed, sometimes at a serious loss, for that reason. However, he became concerned after the lawsuit was won and the two companies failed to respond. When Montgomery became insistent, the companies had their representatives tell him, in the presence of Banks, that "they had never promised to help us." Even more disturbing, said Montgomery, during this same time Banks had worked with Leland and Port Gibson as a broker and had "received a cash commission of one dollar per ton amounting to altogether thousands of dollars." "You did not have even to turn your hand or supervise in anyway, the money just rolled in." Montgomery informed Banks that if he decided to help with rehabilitating the mill, he wanted "a definite and substantial prospect in its future." "We all may just as well understand this to start with," he declared.[67]

Montgomery unfairly lambasted Banks for having tied up oil mill stocks in the bank, because he had approved of these moves years earlier. He complained that "nowhere during all of our connections and dealings have I ever gotten a fee or bonus of any kind, not even a refund of traveling expenses." "From now on if you expect to go any further with me," he said, "you must lay down your cards and let me see the whole game, and if I care to go into it all right. Of course, I have some scruples about what kind of money I got."[68] Unfortunately, only Montgomery's side of the story is known. Banks and Montgomery apparently worked out their differences over the mill, because they jointly played key parts in reviving it.

A few years later another financial dispute developed between Montgomery and Banks after Moton's tour of Mississippi in 1921. As stated previously, certain black leaders in the state were asked to lend money to the finance committee because of a shortfall in raising the money needed. Indeed, when the tour reached Greenville, the members were short of funds. The Greenville Chamber of Commerce had agreed to provide them with the money, but the committee did not want to approach the chamber until after Moton spoke. The committee went to Banks and Montgomery, among others, and they jointly loaned them $150 to be re-paid as soon as the Greenville Committee received the money from Greenville's Chamber of Commerce. If the expense committee did not repay the loan in a few days, Montgomery and Banks were authorized to cover the expense by drawing directly on Tuskegee Institute's account. Also, while in Montgomery's office, committee members agreed to repay Banks the $150, and he was to give Montgomery his portion.[69]

The next day on October 26, 1921, Banks received the loan repayment, which he was supposed to split equally with Montgomery. But Banks kept Montgomery's portion. In June 1922, Montgomery ran into William H. Holtzclaw at the train depot in Jackson, and there he learned the loan had been repaid eight months earlier. Montgomery saw this as another effort by Banks to cheat him. He threatened to draw the money from Tuskegee's account if he did not receive his portion. One observer called this conun-drum "a tempest in the tea-pot."[70]

After Washington died and Scott left Tuskegee, Banks was charged more frequently with impropriety. Over time, these charges chipped away at the image Banks had taken so many years to build.

Turmoil over Land

Evidence suggests that Charles and Trenna Banks temporarily reconciled their differences and remarried. But the second marriage also ended in divorce. On March 4, 1921, Banks wrote Moton that Booze had gone to Memphis and employed a detective to testify against him "in the divorce case." Banks also reported that two other witnesses "testified that he [Booze] tried to get them to testify to things they knew to be false, which they refused to do."[71] Although Charles and Trenna stayed together for many years, a newspaper article reflecting on their relationship correctly concluded, "their married life was not happy."[72]

Around February 1921, Booze traveled to Tuskegee, pretending that the problems between him and Banks were over. "It is absurd for him to be pretending to my friends, such as you, that he is friendly to me or desires my good," Banks told Moton. Moton apparently had asked Booze about his views on a negative article published about Banks in the *Chicago Defender* on February 26.[73] Booze had claimed to be indignant about the matter and expressed remorse for Banks. However, Booze had stirred up the controversy in the first place.[74]

In an anonymous letter to the *Defender*, Booze charged that Banks had been indicted for mishandling funds from rent he collected from farmland owned by Campbell College, for which Banks served as a trustee. The letter charged that Banks had secured a loan of $9,000 on the rent notes without authority and that he used the funds for his personal business affairs. It also alleged that he failed to turn over the funds that were due the college.[75]

Booze even took the new A.M.E bishop of the Mississippi district, William Wesley Beckett, to his own lawyer, without the knowledge or approval of the trustees of Campbell College, and convinced him to bring a case against Banks. Beckett, who had been in Mississippi for less than a year and was probably unfamiliar with the battle raging between Banks and Booze, agreed. Still a judge found enough evidence to turn the issue over to a grand jury.[76]

According to Banks, Booze went so far as to have an "old man put in jail and frightened him into appearing as a witness against me." Booze even served as a chief witness against Banks. The letter published in the *Defender* was consistent with Booze's testimony against Banks. What is most telling about this entire affair is that Booze was not even a member of the A.M.E. Church.[77]

According to Booze, Banks had also charged Campbell College interest and a commission on money he collected and used for his own personal purposes.[78] Indeed, Banks worked as an agent for the school and received a 10 percent commission from the sale of the land. According to Banks, this arrangement had been in place for several years, and the parties involved had agreed to the terms. Banks testified that because of him, the "Jackson property had been saved from sale under the sheriff's hammer" and that "he had both spent and lost much money in taking care of" issues related to the land in 1920. That was why he charged $375 in interest. Banks believed the matter could have been handled amicably if it were not for "the malicious and mischief making agitators . . . who have opposed me for years." Ultimately, Campbell College declared it had no grievance against Banks and testified to that effect in court.[79]

11

Conclusion

"The Most Public-Spirited Citizen in the History of Mississippi"

Death of Banks

The years from 1919 to 1922 brought economic disaster for the town of Mound Bayou; its Golden Age had come to an end. Cotton prices in the postwar era rose, bringing profits to many but leading to rampant speculation. In 1920, farmers were being paid $.85 per pound. Consequently many decided to hold onto their cotton, anticipating that the price would increase to $1 per pound. But the market crashed, and cotton fell to a meager $.11 per pound. The crash forced so many people into debt that some farmers in neighboring Merigold, Mississippi, reportedly committed suicide. In addition, many black farmers who had been duped into purchasing commodities on credit during 1919 by white merchants could no longer afford to pay for them. These merchants instituted foreclosure proceedings against the farmers and took their land. Black farmers in the Mound Bayou vicinity reportedly lost around 4,000 acres of land by 1923.[1]

Conditions also continued to deteriorate between Banks and Montgomery and Booze. When Mound Bayou's thirty-first Founder's Day celebration took place in 1919, Banks's name was conspicuously missing from the program. A bitter and power-hungry Booze again lost his bid to become mayor in 1919, this time to Benjamin A. Green, a Harvard Law School graduate and the first child born in Mound Bayou.

The Mound Bayou State Bank closed for good on June 28, 1922, after it could not afford to pay off its loans. This was a result of the depressed cotton market and the farmers' inability to repay their loans. Likewise, the oil mill in Mound Bayou, already facing a product shortage from the drop in cotton prices, became the victim of a white boycott.[2]

In light of these circumstances, Banks moved to Memphis in 1922, and began carving out a new niche for himself, although he kept his official residence in Mississippi and maintained his financial interests in the all-black town. Banks continued to make regular visits to Mound Bayou and Clarksdale, where his mother had relocated sometime earlier. In Memphis he began managing a successful burial association.[3]

Many Mound Bayou settlers who had lost their land joined the exodus to Chicago and Saint Louis.[4] The situation became so alarming in Mississippi that the Jackson Chamber of Commerce called a meeting to ascertain why so many blacks were fleeing the state. Banks said that if the trend continued, he believed it would "threaten the stability of the economic structure of the South." Banks, however, realized that many blacks were leaving because of unjust treatment they received in the South. "The trouble lies along the path of economics, law and order, life, liberty and the pursuit of happiness in their fullest interpretations," he said. Nonetheless, he believed it would be better for most Negroes to remain in the South. "In the final analysis the nation, everywhere, must stand, in theory and practice, committed to the fullest and equal justice to all," he said.[5] Banks's words could not stem the tide of this great migration.

On November 17, 1922, his mother, Sallie Banks, died. The funeral took place the next day at the Friendship A.M.E. Church in Clarksdale and the interment was done at the Paw Paw Cemetery.[6]

Although Banks had experienced some occasional bouts with malaria, he maintained his health and optimism throughout much of his life. Banks, however, became ill in September 1923 and checked into Wilson Hospital in Memphis, a black-owned facility. He remained in the hospital for forty-two days, dying at 11:10 P.M. on October 18 at the age of fifty. The cause of death was "mitral insufficiency," meaning that his heart stopped pumping blood. However, ptomaine poisoning was a contributing factor. Ptomaine poisoning could cause severe diarrhea or vomiting, which after almost two months could have easily placed such a strain on his system that it caused his heart to stop functioning.[7]

Banks's funeral took place October 21 at Friendship A.M.E. Church in Clarksdale, the church of his youth, where he had served as Sunday school superintendent for almost twenty years. He was buried beside his mother in Clarksdale, not in Mound Bayou. Upon his death, the *New York Age* called him "one of the best known men of the race" and "a power in Mississippi affairs."[8] The *Jackson Daily News* said Banks was a man of "unusual ability." The white-owned newspaper stated that "the counsel of Banks given to his race was always sensible and conservative. He sincerely believed that the South was the natural habitat of the negro, and that his race would fare much better here than elsewhere in the country."[9]

This paper went on to say that "on all racial problems he was sane and far-seeing, and during the past two decades he had wielded a great influence especially in the delta section of the state." Although Banks had been active in Republican politics, the paper said, he "was more interested in the industrial welfare of his race than in matters political, and he had earned and deserved the respect and confidence of the white people of the commonwealth."[10]

The *Chicago Defender* reported that "one of the largest crowds ever gathered in Clarksdale paid a last and loving tribute to the most distinguished citizen of Clarksdale and the Delta." "Every society and fraternity in the state was represented at his funeral and lines of denomination were forgotten at his bier," the paper continued and noted that "no line of race or color was visible at the church and white and black, rich and poor sat side by side as mourners. The chief mourners, next to the kindred of the dead, were the Clarks, founders of the city, and under whose shelter Mr. Banks was born." "For almost 20 years," the paper stated, "he was a political power in the state." Those who knew him said "without division of opinion . . . the death of Charles Banks ends the life of the most public-spirited citizen in the history of Mississippi."[11]

When Maurice Jackson visited Mound Bayou in 1937, residents remembered Banks as a leader who could be credited with "the development of civic pride and consciousness in citizens of Mound Bayou in the first two decades of the century." "Banks had a personality which enabled him to mingle with the members of his race," Jackson wrote, and "he did not have that feeling of superiority usually associated with men of wealth. He had the happy faculty of being able to laugh and was always ready with a joke." The townspeople remembered Banks as being "honest in his dealings with his employees, and 'his word was as good as gold.'"[12]

Isaiah Montgomery died less than a year later, March 6, 1924, at the age of seventy-two. One writer commented that he died as he lived, "honored and dishonored, revered and despised."[13] The deaths of Banks and Montgomery, however, helped clear the way for Booze to seek preeminence in Mound Bayou. He continued to run for mayor of the town, but Green consistently defeated him. The split in Mound Bayou continued and was apparent to the most impartial observers during the Fiftieth Anniversary Founder's Day celebration in 1937. At that time, two celebrations were held, one by Mayor Green and the other by Booze.[14]

Mary Booze, Montgomery's daughter, became more popular than her husband, becoming a Republican National Committee member in 1924. Eugene Booze became administrator of the Montgomery estate after Isaiah's death. Booze claimed to have reduced its indebtedness from $91,000 to $50,000 over a three-year period. Simultaneously he said he provided for three Montgomery heirs "who were without visible means of support . . . without having to account to the other two heirs, who were my wife, and W. H. Mosby, my brother-in-law in St. Louis." After this three-year period, the heirs wanted to sell the estate and split the proceeds. At some point, the property went into foreclosure and Booze and his wife purchased the estate, paying $60,100 for the real estate and another $2,100 for personal property.[15]

Booze continued to manage the Montgomery estate along with his wife and his daughter, Eugene V. Wood. Ironically, Booze later moved his office into the Mound Bayou bank building. The Boozes now controlled about 800 acres of land inhabited by approximately thirty families, 210 people total. He also employed twelve day laborers. The average family of five worked about 20 acres of his land. Booze prided himself that "none of my families have ever been on relief," because he also found work for them during the winter months.[16]

The petulant Booze remained embroiled in bitter conflict with Isaiah Montgomery's children, especially Estella, a graduate of Oberlin College who married successful Saint Louis businessman, J. H. Kent. After a divorce, Estella reassumed her maiden name and moved back to Mound Bayou. The first conflict between Estella and Booze erupted shortly after Isaiah died in 1924. Estella accused Booze of poisoning her father and had charges brought against him. Although Booze was later exonerated in court, people in the community remained divided about his innocence. Next, Montgomery's heirs, led by Estella, accused Booze of stealing money from their father's estate, going through their father's mail before he died with intent to defraud the family, and illegally obtaining power of attorney. "He forced the heirs into poverty while he did use property and business from which some revenue might be derived," Estella complained, and he "refused the heirs wood, coal and food while he lived in luxury." Furthermore, she said, "he sold anything he wanted to, [and] cut all the timber from the estate without getting the heirs' consent . . . He is showing in every way that the heirs have no right that he is bound to respect." Last, Estella claimed ownership of the Montgomery estate by virtue of what she called a "federal patent."[17]

The dispute over the estate continued, and Booze had Estella and her sisters and their families removed at least three times from the beautiful mansion I. T. Montgomery had built in 1919. Estella even served time in jail because of disputes with Booze, in 1934, 1936 and 1937. In 1934, when Estella spent over a month in jail, Booze said he "wouldn't mind the other members of the family staying in the house but I don't want Stella there and since they let her stay, I'll put them all out." Booze secured a court order prohibiting Estella from entering the home after she allegedly conducted several illegal land deals pertaining to the Montgomery estate. After this, she moved back to Saint Louis, but returned to Mound Bayou for periodic visits.[18]

Estella had claimed possession of the mansion for years, and in early September 1939 a newspaper reported that the federal government upheld her claim to the patent for the property. With her claim to the property finally settled (at least in her mind), Estella arrived in town on the evening train on September 30, 1939 and went to the Montgomery mansion, which she thought was now hers, violating the court order Booze had against her. Booze, who viewed Estella as a troublemaker, got a warrant for her arrest for trespassing. He did not want to personally remove her, however, because he knew it would be viewed negatively by the community. Thus, he got two white officers from neighboring towns, "that didn't mind killing blacks," to remove her. Sheriff Clayton Dempsey of Cleveland and Marshal Fred Connor of Merigold accompanied Booze to the residence to take Estella into custody. On Sunday, October 1 at about 11:00 P.M., Booze and the officers arrived at the house and conflict ensued. When Estella refused to open the door, the police broke it down. They claimed she resisted arrest with a butcher knife, so they fired nine shots at close range, four of which struck and killed her. Booze fully supported the officers' story, stating that they were defending themselves. He contended that "if the officers hadn't acted instantly, they, instead of Stella Montgomery, would have been killed."[19]

Estella's son, Harvey M. Kent of Saint Louis, asked Mississippi governor Hugh L. White and the U.S. attorney general, Frank Murphy, to investigate the slaying. The governor responded that the state had no jurisdiction and that local authorities would have to carry out any investigation. According to some, Mary Booze did not appear overly troubled by the death of her sister. When Eugene told Mary, "we had to kill Estella," she reportedly responded with a cold and laconic: "oh, yeah?" Neither of the Boozes attended the funeral on October 8.[20]

While Mary and Eugene may not have been troubled by this turn of events, citizens of Mound Bayou certainly were. Many felt Booze thought he was above everyone else in the town and had gone too far by having Estella murdered. Thus, the citizens of Mound Bayou started holding meetings around town to decide "what to do about Booze." At one meeting, with 500 people in attendance, the slogan "Booze must go" was adopted. Some people even started holding fund-raising events, perhaps with intentions of using the money to pay someone to avenge Estella's death.[21]

Booze became more and more concerned about his safety and asked his chauffeur, Andrew Polk, to serve as his bodyguard. Booze received threats to "get out of town," but he did not heed them. On November 6, 1939, at about 7:30 P.M., he left his office in Banks's old bank building and started to enter his new maroon Dodge parked outside. Shots rang out. The car was riddled with twenty-six bullet holes, and five empty shotgun shells were found nearby. Booze took four shots in the abdomen and two in his chest.[22] His bodyguard also was shot in the hip.

Booze did not die immediately but was taken to the Greenville hospital, where blood transfusions were unsuccessful. The sixty-one-year-old Booze died November 7 at 2:00 A.M., from gunshot wounds. Many citizens believed Booze's murder was in retaliation for Estella's death, but Booze stated before he died that the shooting resulted from "political jealousy." Under orders from District Attorney Greek P. Rice, Fred Miller, a bookkeeper in Mound Bayou, was arrested about a week later in Clarksdale and questioned about the murder, but he apparently was not charged with the crime. Rice believed several assailants were involved in the murder, which had been "carried out in typical gangland fashion."[23] Some people believed the assassin(s) came from either Clarksdale or Saint Louis.

A little over a month after Booze's death, the National Guard raided Mound Bayou, supposedly because of corruption and vice. However, many townsmen thought it was because Booze, who was viewed by many blacks as being a "half-white niggah" and embraced by whites for being almost one of them, had been murdered.[24]

These vicious murders in Mound Bayou are quite intriguing. While serious crimes remained uncommon in the town, on those rare occasions when murders did occur, members of their upper-class were often the victims. Ben Green, Banks, Estella, and Booze all died somewhat peculiarly.[25] This turn of events with the irascible Booze and Estella may even shed some information on Banks's death. In light of the enemies he faced, it would not be unreasonable to assume that someone may have intentionally poisoned Charles Banks. One can only wonder if Booze had something to do with his death, especially since Estella charged that he killed her father the same way, just a few months after Banks's death.[26]

Despite Booze's most vigorous efforts, Banks remained a powerful figure who kept him from achieving the prominence he so desperately craved. Banks even realized this and told Moton that notwithstanding Booze's "efforts and attacks from every angle, both locally and nationally" he found himself "in a more ridiculous position now than when he first began."[27] More important, if Booze could so coldly have his sister-in-law killed, he had the potential to do the same thing to his brother-in-law, Banks, whom he had been feuding with unsuccessfully for years. Although Banks had moved to Memphis in 1922 he still frequented Mound Bayou because he had business interests in the town. Thus, the opportunity for poisoning his food surely could have presented itself over those several months.

Conclusion

It is an understatement that Charles Banks had a multifaceted career as a black leader during the Washingtonian era. Banks contributed to the struggle for racial uplift through his efforts at building Mound Bayou into a viable town, a place where Negroes could find refuge without having to leave the South. He contributed to the race by working to improve the educational resources in the town. Most of his achievements in these areas were due to his success in attracting white largesse. Banks received educational assistance for the farmers in Mound Bayou by securing the permanent placement of a farm demonstration agent for the town. As a leader, he demonstrated remarkable abilities as an organizer and promoter. He illustrated these talents when he organized Booker T. Washington's trip through Mississippi in 1908. Banks wielded some influence in politics, although he never ran for public office. More than any other endeavor however, Banks devoted his life to the principle of economic development. He owned a number of businesses and made many contributions to black uplift through his work in this area.

Banks performed a critical role in the Tuskegee Machine. As Washington's Mississippi lieutenant, he became the most powerful Negro in that state during the first fifteen years of the twentieth century. As leader of the MNBL, Banks exercised a considerable amount of influence and an equal amount of prestige. Moreover, as first vice-president of the NNBL, second in command only to Washington, he interacted, exchanged ideas, and hobnobbed with some of the most powerful men and women in the country.

Equally important, Banks's role as lieutenant in the Tuskegee Machine largely assured the success of Washington's agenda in Mississippi. Although Washington clearly reigned as the most prominent Negro leader of his day, he did not rise to this position by working alone. Banks made sure that the Negroes in his state embraced Washington's philosophy. If Washington's trip through Mississippi is any indication of the success of Banks's efforts, it is clear that the Negroes in the Magnolia State were avid and loyal followers of Washington, and viewed him as their leader. Thus, if it were not for lieutenants working in this capacity for the Tuskegee Machine, Washington probably would not have been nearly as popular, effective, or successful throughout the South. Key people like Banks, who were dealing with the masses of Negroes at the grassroots level on a daily basis, insured the success of Washington's program.

In return for their work, state lieutenants like Banks were given access to white philanthropy, professional expertise, notoriety and patronage power by Washington. Washington also made sure that his lieutenants wielded political and economic influence throughout their respective states. Indeed, these were some of the benefits received by members of the Tuskegee Machine. However, these lieutenants were not puppets of Washington. On several occasions Banks spoke his mind, acted independently, and disagreed with Washington without falling out of his favor. This contradicts the dictatorial image sometimes painted of Washington. While he may have been brutish with his enemies, he took good care of members of the Tuskegee Machine. Banks's role as lieutenant serves as a prototype of the kind of leaders Washington had in his organization and also shows the type of people he associated with.

Banks also used the black survival strategy to manipulate whites for his own purposes. At times he may have appeared deferential on the surface, but close examination of his correspondence with Washington and Scott shows that he intentionally "wore the mask" for ulterior reasons. Many members of the Tuskegee Machine used this strategy, especially Washington. This approach certainly had its benefits for black leaders, particularly those who were operating in the South. White patronage gave Banks a tremendous amount of support among the white people in Mississippi, especially in Bolivar County. For example, understanding that Negro attorneys would be accorded little or no respect in Mississippi courtrooms, Banks hired Thomas Owen, a white man, to serve as attorney for the Bank of Mound Bayou and the Mound Bayou Oil Mill and Manufacturing Company. At first glance this may seem contradictory to Mound Bayou's, "all-Negro" theme, but upon further analysis, Banks utilized the services of Owen because he knew that it would be the most feasible way of receiving justice in courtrooms throughout the South.[28]

Banks realized that since he lived in the South, the Du Boisian philosophy of civil and political activism would not be a practical alternative for black people in their communities who were only one or two generations away from slavery, particularly in an agrarian state like Mississippi. This is one reason why Du Bois never mustered a large following like Washington. Thus, Banks and other members of the Tuskegee Machine advocated economic uplift as the first step in elevating the Negro in the South.

Although members of the Tuskegee Machine did not totally discount political participation, as evidenced by their involvement in politics, they concentrated most of their efforts on helping black people develop an economic base. After they attained this, they believed that Negroes would be in a better position to fight for their political rights. Indeed, one scholar argues that other ethnic groups like the Japanese-Americans and Chinese-Americans focused on building an economic base first when they immigrated to this country. After building an economic base, they were grounded well enough economically to let future generations fight for their political rights. By contrast, groups like African Americans who emphasized political activism, especially after Washington died, have had to be more dependent on others for employment and their livelihood over the long term.[29] If this analysis is correct, it is precisely what Banks and Washington did not want to see happen.

Banks, Mississippi's foremost black businessman, became the "leading citizen" of Mound Bayou during its Golden Age and became responsible for facilitating much of its prosperity. After he moved to the town at the end of 1903, he quickly replaced Isaiah Montgomery as Mound Bayou's "leading citizen." After he started the Bank of Mound Bayou, the town flourished like never before. Several businesses as well as the farmers in the town reaped the benefits of Banks's efforts. Mound Bayou grew tremendously in terms of population and notoriety during this time. To be sure, after Banks left Mound Bayou his presence was certainly missed. From that point on, the prospects of realizing the Mound Bayou proposition became more of a dream than a reality and by 1924, the town had already begun to regress.

Although being in an all-black town afforded Banks an opportunity to engage in many ambitious business undertakings, the fact that he lived in the poorest state in the union, compounded with the weight of white supremacy, severely restricted his chances for success. What is more, being a small businessman with inadequate capital backing during an era of big business, made Banks all the more vulnerable during depression times such as the 1914 cotton crisis and the worldwide agricultural depression of the early 1920s. Simply stated, smaller businesses went down while larger ones remained afloat during these arduous economic times. Thus, the market forces as well as individual decisions played a major part in the outcome of Banks's enterprises. Against these tremendous odds few American businessmen, black or white, could have equaled Banks or done more.[30]

Perhaps Banks's dependency on Washington and Scott became one of his biggest limitations as a leader, and was apparent after Washington died. It became even more obvious when Scott left Tuskegee.[31] Because Mound Bayou's leaders respected him so much, Washington had been the bonding agent holding the town together. After he died, internecine battles for leadership engulfed the town to such a degree that they ultimately led to the demise of its Golden Age. Isaiah Montgomery's envy of Banks, which had been simmering for years, partially because Banks replaced him as the town's "leading citizen," finally rose to the surface after Washington died. Montgomery dissolved his different partnerships with Banks after syndicating his land holdings and started a battle for preeminence in the town. Montgomery began to concentrate more on building his personal wealth than looking at the big picture in terms of Mound Bayou's destiny.[32] His son-in-law, Eugene Booze, became even worse when it came to fighting Banks. On many occasions, Moton sought to mediate between the leaders of Mound Bayou, but unlike Washington, he met with only limited success.

Nevertheless, Banks, a person "more concerned with racial solidarity than Montgomery ever was," continued his vigorous efforts to help uplift Negroes in Mound Bayou and throughout the South.[33] After the deaths of John W. Francis in 1921, Banks in 1923, and Montgomery in 1924, the greatness the town had once experienced quickly began to fade away.[34] Other factors also caused the decline of Mound Bayou. Primary among these was the recurring problem of the single crop economy of the town. When the cotton crops produced low yields it devastated Mound Bayou's economy from top to bottom. Also, the pre-World War I recession and other national economic setbacks like the post-World War I depression hurt the town. Moreover, the Great Migrations of black people from the South eventually hindered the growth of Mound Bayou. Northern social, political and economic opportunities as well as an escape from the disadvantages black people had to deal with in Mississippi continued to fuel this exodus.[35]

In terms of an overall assessment of the Mound Bayou experiment, some authors have concluded that it failed. For example, August Meier, one of the first historians to write about the town, concluded that "Mound Bayou never fulfilled its expectations" and that "self-help and racial solidarity were not . . . a sufficient base upon which to erect a successful economy and community."[36] However, when Meier wrote his essay in 1953, the racial climate in America at the time deeply influenced his interpretation. Thus, he shied away from viewing racial separation as a viable alternative to racial uplift, and used Mound Bayou as an example to make his point. Nonetheless, this interpretation seems to be somewhat flawed in that it does not measure the benefits of Mound Bayou to the people who were living in that segregated community. Perhaps over the long term, Meier's view is correct in that the dream of Mound Bayou never became fully realized. However, in terms of its success for its founders and the people who built the community, over the short term, it seems to have been just the opposite. They were able to carve out a place for themselves by creating a community owned and operated by Negroes, which coincided with what they wanted.

Black people living in Mississippi during that time viewed Mound Bayou as a beacon of hope from "whitecapping" and other assaults frequently encountered by Negroes. Therefore, if the effectiveness of the town is assessed during its Golden Age, the experiment worked. It worked not only because it gave blacks some reprieve from the onslaught of white supremacy, discrimination, oppression, and exploitation throughout the South, but also because it allowed them to exercise freedoms not practiced by a number of blacks in the South until decades later, like the right to vote.[37] This turned out to be a unique experience for its residents and if they had an opportunity to change places with Negroes who lived in predominantly white communities, they undoubtedly would have refused. Thus to Banks, Montgomery, Francis, Green, and others, the Mound Bayou experiment worked during its prime, but later deteriorated because of a number of interior and exterior factors.

Although white supremacy certainly worked to destroy the economic competition Mound Bayou posed, some of the major problems that led to its downfall came from within. Unlike Rosewood, Florida, and the Greenwood community in Tulsa, Oklahoma, which were both raided and pillaged by whites, Mound Bayou fell apart internally. After the death of Booker T. Washington, too many people wanted to be the "leading citizen" in the town. This effectively split Mound Bayou into factions with Banks and Francis on one side and Montgomery and Booze on the other. Destroying Banks became virtually a pathological obsession for Eugene Booze, and he went to almost any length to try to ruin him. Booze took these steps even when it meant harm to the overall progress of the town. He obviously did not care as much about uplifting the race as he pretended. Montgomery's envy also boiled over, although not to the same extent as Booze's, and he became more concerned about his individual wealth than with Negroes in Mississippi.

Charles Banks, however, with all things considered remained unquestionably committed to trying to elevate the race throughout his life. He also firmly believed in elevating blacks through economic development and continued to cling to Washington's philosophy until he died. This became apparent when the NAACP chartered a branch in Mound Bayou in 1919. Isaiah Montgomery, Eugene and Mary Booze all signed up as charter members, but Banks refused to join the group led by Du Bois.[38]

Entirely consistent with Washington's philosophy of economic uplift, Banks served as a perfect example of what hard work and dedication could yield for Negroes. This was "constructionalism" at its best. Banks had indeed carved out a place for himself, his family, and many other Negroes in the South. Many people looked at his triumphs and gained hope as to what "pure blooded" black people could accomplish. Despite the vicissitudes he encountered, Banks remained dedicated and loyal to serving black people throughout his life. It seems that Washington had the correct impression of Banks. He became the leading Negro banker in Mississippi and one of the most influential black businessmen in the country. As Emmett Scott once told him, his work and dedication to racial uplift was certainly "a story worth telling."[39]

Abbreviations

AMA	American Missionary Association
AME	African Methodist Episcopal
BTWP	Booker T. Washington Papers
BTWPF	Booker T. Washington Papers Microfilm
GEB	General Education Board
L, NO & T	Louisville, New Orleans, and Texas Railroad
MBA	Masonic Benefit Association
MDAH	Mississippi Department of Archives and History
MNBL	Mississippi Negro Business League
MP	Robert Russa Moton Papers
MSF	Mississippi State Federation of Colored Women's Clubs
NAACP	National Association for the Advancement of Colored People
NACW	National Association of Colored Women
NNBL	National Negro Business League
SEB	Southern Education Board
SYF	Silone Yates Federation
Y & MV	Yazoo and Mississippi Valley Railroad

Notes

Preface

1. Harlan, *Booker T. Washington: Making of a Black Leader,* 254–55, 271.
2. Harlan, *Booker T. Washington: Wizard of Tuskegee,* 106.
3. See Rogers, *World's Great Men of Color,* 2: 383–98.
4. Harlan, *Booker T. Washington: Wizard of Tuskegee;* Harlan, "Booker T. Washington and the National Negro Business League," 98, 100.

Chapter 1. The Early Life of Charles Banks: "Where I First Saw the First Light of Day"

1. *Booker T. Washington Papers,* ed. Harlan and Smock, 12: 60 (hereafter cited as BTWP).
2. *Memphis Commercial Appeal,* November 27, 1912, in Harlan, *Booker T. Washington: Wizard of Tuskegee,* 222.
3. Hamilton, *Black Towns and Profit,* 58.
4. Quotes in Harlan and Smock, BTWP, 12: 55.
5. Logan, *Negro in American Life and Thought,* 52.
6. See Wharton, *Negro in Mississippi,* and McMillen, *Dark Journey.*
7. McMillen, *Dark Journey,* 11.
8. Trelease, *White Terror,* 275; Litwack, *Trouble in Mind.* To be sure, some Negroes did not always stay in their "place." See Goings and Smith, "'Unhidden' Transcripts," 372–94. These authors argue that many working-class blacks constantly "fought back," "talked back," and "shot back," and they were not deferential and submissive as Old South mythology suggested. Nonetheless, while rebellion of this sort certainly took place, it was not the general pattern followed by most southern blacks, especially in Mississippi.
9. McMillen, *Dark Journey,* 1–32; Wharton, *Negro in Mississippi,* 230–42.
10. McMillen, *Dark Journey,* 9.
11. Woodson, *Mis-Education of the Negro,* 192.
12. McMillen, *Dark Journey,* 233–34.
13. Ibid., 10; Wharton, *Negro in Mississippi,* 230–33. See also Rabinowitz, *Race Relations in the Urban South.*

14. Franklin, *From Slavery to Freedom*, 218; Asante and Mattson, *Historical and Cultural Atlas of African Americans*, 96–97; Lynch, *Reminiscences of an Active Life*, ed. John Hope Franklin; Foner, *Freedom's Lawmakers*, 40, 57, 104; Brock, "Thomas W. Cardozo," 183–206; Foner, *Reconstruction*, 353, 388, 562.

15. See Franklin, *Slavery to Freedom*, 220; Du Bois, *Black Reconstruction*, 431–51; Logan, *Negro in American Life and Thought*.

16. Franklin, *Slavery to Freedom*, 236; Wharton, *Negro in Mississippi*, 206–15.

17. See Woodward, *Strange Career of Jim Crow*, 71.

18. Litwack, *Been in the Storm*, ch. 8.

19. McMillen, *Dark Journey*, 73, 78; Wharton, *Negro in Mississippi*, 234–55.

20. McMillen, *Dark Journey*, 5.

21. Ibid., 31.

22. Ibid., 233–34; Oshinsky, *Worse Than Slavery*, 1–133; Cobb, *Most Southern Place on Earth*, 112–18.

23. *Houston Post*, June 11, 1900; Ginzburg, *100 Years of Lynchings*, 32–33. Ginzburg gives a partial listing of some five thousand black men and women who were lynched in the U.S. between 1859 and 1961. See also Aptheker, *Documentary History of the Negro People*, 2: 792–804.

24. Asante and Mattson, *Historical and Cultural Atlas of African Americans*, 93. Also see Tolnay and Beck, ch. 2, esp. pp. 39–45.

25. *Tenth Census, 1880*. Death Certificate, Charles Banks, October 18, 1923, State of Tennessee, Bureau of Vital Statistics. The certificate lists Virginia as Sallie Banks's birthplace, whereas the 1880 census lists Mississippi.

26. Tong, "Pioneers of Mound Bayou," 395; *Tenth Census, 1880*.

27. McMillen, *Dark Journey*, 158, 163; Jones, *Labor of Love*, 128–29.

28. Weeks, *Clarksdale and Coahoma County*, 27–29.

29. While it is possible Leavell could have been the owner of Daniel and Sallie Banks before emancipation, it seems unreasonable to assume this. Sallie Banks was born into slavery in Virginia a year before Leavell and his family moved to Clarksdale from Clarksville, Tennessee, in 1845. Banks never mentioned the names of his parents' owners.

30. Weeks, *Clarksdale and Coahoma County*, 29.

31. *Ninth Census, 1870*.

32. Jones, *Labor of Love*, 128–29.

33. See Charles Banks to Booker T. Washington, June 14, 1910, in *Booker T. Washington Papers*, microfilm (hereafter cited as BTWPF); Hamilton, *Black Towns and Profit*, 58; Crockett, *Black Towns*, 124.

34. Banks to Eliza Clark, December 2, 1911, BTWPF.

35. Hamilton, *Beacon Lights*, 205. See Church and Walter, *Nineteenth Century Memphis Families of Color*, 38–39; Nichols and Crogman, *Progress of a Race*, 258; *Tenth Census, 1800*.

36. Weeks, *Clarksdale and Coahoma County*, 142.

37. Ibid.

38. Washington noted Banks was "attached" to this family. Washington, *My Larger Education*, 210.

39. For an example of "favored slaves," see discussion on the family of Benjamin Montgomery in Hermann's *Pursuit of a Dream*.

40. Banks to Washington, June 14, 1910, BTWPF.

41. Ibid.

42. Ibid.

43. Washington, *My Larger Education*, 210.

44. Banks to Washington, June 14, 1910, BTWPF.

45. Ibid.

46. Banks to Eliza Clark, December 2, 1911, BTWPF.

47. Ibid.

48. Washington to Banks, November 1, 1912, BTWPF.

49. Ibid.

50. Ibid. John Clark died on July 23, 1892, and Eliza Clark died on December 30, 1915.

51. For a discussion on the black elite, see Gatewood, *Aristocrats of Color*, esp. ch. 6.

52. Washington, *My Larger Education*, 210.

53. Hamilton, *Beacon Lights*, 205; Wharton, *Negro in Mississippi*, 250; Jenkins, "Development of Black Higher Education in Mississippi," 274–75.

54. Wells, *Crusade for Justice*, xv–xviii; McMurry, *To Keep the Waters Troubled*, 12–14; McMillen, *Dark Journey*, 98–99; Wharton, *Negro in Mississippi*, 250; Mosley, *Negro in Mississippi History*, 68; Works Progress Administration, *Mississippi: A Guide*, passim.

55. Wells, *Crusade for Justice*, xv; McMurry, *To Keep the Waters Troubled*, 12–14; Church and Walter, *Nineteenth Century Memphis Families of Color*, 1–3.

56. Wells, *Crusade for Justice*, xv–xviii; Litwack, *Been in the Storm*, 477–85.

57. Hamilton, *Black Towns and Profit*, 58. Sources conflict about Banks's college education. Some state Banks "attended Rust," "was educated at Rust," or "received his education at Rust." However, Booker T. Washington wrote that Banks "seems to be one of the few Negro College graduates." August Meier also says Banks was a "graduate of Rust University at Holly Springs." Banks himself was unclear. One time he said he "attended Rust University," which does not mean he did not graduate. Another time he said, "Rust is my Alma Mater." Unfortunately, because of fires and other mishaps, there are no records at Rust to settle the issue. Hamilton, *Beacon Lights*, 205; Washington, *My Larger Education*, 210; Richardson, *National Cyclopedia of the Colored Race*, 401; Washington, "Charles Banks," 731; Meier, *Negro Thought in America*, 148; Banks to Washington, September 4, 1908, September 23, 1908, BTWPF.

58. Based on an assessment of the grammar, vocabulary, and financial statements of Banks's documents, the author has determined Banks had an extensive

vocabulary, knowledge of history, and knowledge of accounting and bookkeeping. This illustrates the soundness of his education. See Banks, "The Negro Question," 95–102.

59. Hiram Tong described Banks in comparison with what he considered the typical southern black. He wrote pejoratively of the "negro's shiftlessness, his laziness," and "his racial ineptitudes," when describing southern Negroes. See Tong, "Pioneers of Mound Bayou," 395.

60. Gatewood, *Aristocrats of Color,* 185.

61. Anderson, *Education of Blacks,* 240–41; Neverdon-Morton, *Afro-American Women of the South,* 7. Other missionaries in the South thought it would be best for black people to work rather than secure an education. See Litwack, *Been in the Storm,* 477–85.

62. Hamilton, *Beacon Lights,* 205.

63. Washington, *My Larger Education,* 210.

64. See Gatewood, *Aristocrats of Color,* ch. 9, esp. p. 258.

65. Ibid., 265.

66. This was a federal patronage position, which shows that Banks knew someone who had connections, perhaps the Clarks or other influential whites in or around Clarksdale.

67. Hood, *Negro at Mound Bayou,* 53.

68. Hamilton, *Beacon Lights,* 207.

69. McMillen, *Dark Journey,* 155–57; Litwack, *Been in the Storm,* 399.

70. Litwack, *Been in the Storm,* 338, 399. For a discussion of black Americans' struggle against the prevailing forces of labor, see ibid., ch. 8.

71. Douglass, "History of E. P. Booze," ms., n.d., Montgomery Family Papers.

72. *Tenth Census, 1880;* Douglass, "History of E. P. Booze," Montgomery Family Papers.

73. Jones, *Labor of Love,* 125; Hunter, *To 'Joy My Freedom,* 34.

74. *Tenth Census, 1880;* Douglass, "History of E. P. Booze," Montgomery Family Papers.

75. McMillen, *Dark Journey,* 21.

76. Berlin, *Slaves without Masters,* 253–54, 273–74. For more on Natchez, see Wayne, *Reshaping of Plantation Society.*

77. Gatewood, *Aristocrats of Color,* 16.

78. Rouse, *Lugenia Burns Hope,* 138.

79. For data on how Negroes were treated in Natchez, see Wharton, *Negro in Mississippi,* 232–33; Rouse, *Lugenia Burns Hope,* 138n.

80. *Tenth Census, 1880.*

81. Ibid. Douglass, "History of E. P. Booze," Montgomery Family Papers.

82. Wharton, *Negro in Mississippi,* 250, 251; Mosley, *Negro in Mississippi History,* 67; Works Progress Administration, *Mississippi: A Guide,* passim.

83. Hamilton, *Beacon Lights,* 212; McMillen, *Dark Journey,* 96–97; Wharton, *Negro in Mississippi,* 250–51.

84. Neverdon-Morton, *Afro-American Women of the South*, 2–3.

85. Giddings, *When and Where I Enter*, 101; Rouse, *Lugenia Burns Hope*, 6; Jones, *Labor of Love*, 110–12; Hunter, *To 'Joy My Freedom*, 34.

86. Jones, *Labor of Love*, 143.

87. Giddings, *When and Where I Enter*, 100–101; Rouse, *Lugenia Burns Hope*, 6; Neverdon-Morton, *Afro-American Women of the South*, 2, 6, 78–82, 103; Hunter, *To 'Joy My Freedom*, 111–12.

88. Lerner, "Early Community Work of Black Club Women," 160; Jones, *Labor of Love*, esp. pp. 131, 137, 144; Rouse, *Lugenia Burns Hope*, 58–59; Neverdon-Morton, *Afro-American Women of the South*, 68–77; Giddings, *When and Where I Enter*, 17–31. Also see Wells-Barnett, "Lynch Law in All Its Phases," 651–55; Hunter, *To 'Joy My Freedom*, 34.

89. Jones, *Labor of Love*, 137, 143–44, 146, 157; Margo, *Race and Schooling in the South*, 52–56.

90. Richardson, *National Cyclopedia of the Colored Race*, 401; *Tenth Census, 1880*; Neverdon-Morton, *Afro-American Women of the South*, 78–79.

91. Giddings, *When and Where I Enter*, 108. Alice Dunbar-Nelson never had children either, and she held a leading position among black club women. See Gaines, *Uplifting the Race*, 231.

92. Giddings, *When and Where I Enter*, 108–9.

93. Hamilton, *Beacon Lights*, 212.

94. Spear, *Black Chicago*, 54–56, 71–72; Frazier, *Black Bourgeoisie*, 113.

95. Frazier, *Black Bourgeoisie*, 113–15; Spear, *Black Chicago*, 54–56; Litwack, *Been in the Storm*, 513.

96. Spear, *Black Chicago*, 71–72; Frazier, *Black Bourgeoisie*, 113–15; Crockett, *Black Towns*, 65; Meier, *Negro Thought in America*, 207–47. Some members of the old black elite eventually came to terms with the new aristocrats, as can be seen with the wedding of Jessie Binga, a leading Chicago banker by 1910 and a member of the NNBL. Binga, a reportedly "rough-hewn" man, had a third-grade education. Nonetheless, his elaborate wedding showed that the "new black elite" had replaced the old elite as Chicago's social leaders. Binga married the sister of one of Chicago's gambling lords, and the wedding was reportedly "the most elaborate and the most fashionable wedding ever held in the history of the Afro-American race." At the wedding, the old black elite "vied with each other in admiration of the grandeur of the surroundings and occasion." This "vying" confirms the adjustments they were making as they mingled with their new counterparts. At one time, members of the old elite would not have been caught dead at such an affair. However, as the economic position of the black middle class improved, the old elite had little choice. *Chicago Defender*, February 24, 1912; *Chicago Broad Ax*, February 24, 1912; Spear, *Black Chicago*, 74–75.

97. Charley's name was spelled *Charly* in the 1880 census; however, an affidavit and sporadic letters from his friends used *Charley*.

98. Washington, *My Larger Education*, 206–7.

99. Ibid.

100. Washington, "Charles Banks," 731.

101. Hamilton, *Beacon Lights*, 214; Crockett, *Black Towns*, 102–3. For references on the parentage of Douglass and Washington, see Harlan, *Booker T. Washington: Making of a Black Leader*, 3–8; McFeely, *Frederick Douglass*, 8; Douglass, *Narrative of the Life of Frederick Douglass*, 21; Douglass, *Life and Times of Frederick Douglass*, 29.

102. Washington, *My Larger Education*, 213; Washington, "Charles Banks," 731. Like Hamilton, many leaders in the black community refuted claims by whites that blacks with visible amounts of white blood were more intelligent than their darker brethren. Black leaders frequently pointed to poet Paul Lawrence Dunbar and Howard University professor Kelly Miller to illustrate that the "pure Negro" was as intelligent as persons of any other race. See Gatewood, *Aristocrats of Color*, 155.

103. McMillen, *Dark Journey*, 19–21; Giddings, *When and Where I Enter*, 115. T. Thomas Fortune, editor of the *New York Age*, stated that "those Black men who clamor most loudly and persistently for the purity of Negro blood have taken themselves mulatto wives." Nannie Helen Burroughs also commented on this phenomenon: "many Negroes have colorphobia as badly as the white folk have Negrophobia." She also stated that many black men married mulattos for their complexion, not their character. She scolded black men for getting angry when they saw black women with white men while at the same time "coveting the half-white daughters of such liaisons." It is unclear whether Charles Banks had this mindset when he married Trenna. Nonetheless, the "upwardly mobile" Banks, like many successful dark-skinned men of his day, chose a wife, nearly "white" in color. See Thornbrough, *T. Thomas Fortune*, 128–29, 131–32; Gaines, *Uplifting the Race*, 221–22. For more on Burroughs, see Barnett, "Nannie Burroughs and the Education of Black Women," 97–108.

104. McMillen, *Dark Journey*, 20–21; Litwack, *Been in the Storm*, 513–14; Gaines, *Uplifting the Race*, 229–31; Williamson, *New People*.

105. McMillen, *Dark Journey*, 20, 21; Douglass, "History of E. P. Booze," Montgomery Family Papers. Color was a complex phenomenon in the black community at that time. Dark-skinned blacks often felt bitter toward those of lighter hue. They felt the behavior of many "high tone" blacks showed they believed light skin was better than dark skin. Sometimes blacks viewed this dissension as divisive and harmful to the progress of the race. Other times much of the resentment from darker-skinned blacks derived from stereotypes. For a historical analysis, see McMillen, *Dark Journey*, 19–21; Giddings, *When and Where I Enter*, 115–16; Litwack, *Been in the Storm*, 513–14. For a psychological analysis, see Akbar, *Chains and Images of Psychological Slavery*, 31–35. He states that the color complex was so ingrained during slavery that it not only persisted during Banks's lifetime, but also persists today. In the black community, he says, "there is an unnatural equation of Caucasian physical features with beauty, intelligence, authority, and so forth. A

disproportionate number of . . . so-called 'beautiful' African-Americans have prominently Caucasian features." See also Baldwin, *African Personality in America*, ch. 6, esp. pp. 142–46.

106. Giddings, *When and Where I Enter*, 113; Williamson, *New People*, 61–139.

107. Williams, "Woman's Part in a Man's Business," 545; Giddings, *When and Where I Enter*, 112–13.

108. Hamilton, *Beacon Lights*, 213.

109. According to Michael Porter, a typical home of well-to-do blacks in Atlanta had two floors with about eight rooms, plus spacious parlors and a bathroom. Porter, "Black Atlanta: An Interdisciplinary Study of Blacks on the East Side of Atlanta."

110. Litwack, *Been in the Storm*, 541–42; Frazier, *Black Bourgeoisie*, 128.

111. See Banks to C. C. Buel, August 28, 1909, BTWPF; Crockett, *Black Towns*, 126.

112. Hamilton, *Beacon Lights*, 213; Hood, *Negro at Mound Bayou*, 55.

113. Fannie B. Williams stated that "a beautiful home built by a man is a tribute, not only to his own wife and family, but is also a tribute to womanhood elsewhere." Gatewood, *Aristocrats of Color*, 202; Giddings, *When and Where I Enter*, 112; Crockett, *Black Towns*, 67.

114. Wedding invitation, BTWPF.

115. Hood, *Negro at Mound Bayou*, 33.

116. Litwack, *Been in the Storm*, 541–42.

117. Hamilton, *Beacon Lights*, 212.

118. Redding, *No Day of Triumph*, 303; Crockett, *Black Towns*, 67, 72.

119. Woodson, *History of the Negro Church*, 232–33; Frazier, *Black Bourgeoisie*, 114, 128.

120. *Birmingham Age-Herald*, March 31,1899, 8.

121. Woodson, *History of the Negro Church*, 226, 228; Frazier, *Black Bourgeoisie*, 129.

122. Gatewood, *Aristocrats of Color*, 274, 294.

123. Hood, *Negro at Mound Bayou*, 11.

124. Ibid.; Redding, *No Day of Triumph*, 303; Crockett, *Black Towns*, 72.

125. *Chicago Defender*, October 27, 1923.

126. Hamilton, *Beacon Lights*, 210; Lee, "Mound Bayou, the Negro City of Mississippi," 41.

127. Hood, *Negro at Mound Bayou*, 53; Hamilton, *Beacon Lights*, 210.

128. Gaines, *Uplifting the Race*, 214, 217; Neverdon-Morton, *Afro-American Women of the South*, 3.

129. Gatewood, *Aristocrats of Color*, 242–46, 269; Giddings, *When and Where I Enter*, 95; Shaw, "Black Club Women and the Creation of the National Association of Colored Women," 433–47.

130. Giddings, *When and Where I Enter*, 108; Gatewood, *Aristocrats of Color*, 237–46; Jones, "Mary Church-Terrell and the National Association of Colored

Women," 20–33; Lerner, "Early Community Work of Black Club Women," 158–67; Davis, *Women, Race, and Class,* 127–36. See also Jones, *Quest for Equality;* Lerner, *Black Women in White America,* 433–58; Neverdon-Morton, "Black Woman's Struggle for Equality in the South," 43–57; White, *Too Heavy a Load,* 21–141.

131. Gatewood, *Aristocrats of Color,* 243.

132. Lerner, "Early Community Work of Black Club Women," 160.

133. Giddings, *When and Where I Enter,* 97, 98; Lerner, "Early Community Work of Black Club Women," 167; Gaines, *Uplifting the Race,* 220–22; Terborg-Penn, "Discrimination Against Afro-American Women in the Woman's Movement," 17–27.

134. Rouse, *Lugenia Burns Hope,* 4; Neverdon-Morton, *Afro-American Women of the South,* 6; Shaw, *What a Woman Ought to Be and to Do,* 166–88; White, *Too Heavy A Load,* 21–141.

135. For details of the work done by a local club affiliated with the NACW, see Rouse, *Lugenia Burns Hope,* ch.4. See also White, *Too Heavy A Load,* 21–141.

136. Mrs. Laurence C. Jones to Robert Russa Moton, October 18, 1921, Moton Papers (hereafter cited as MP). See letterhead of Mississippi State Federation.

137. *New York Age,* November 12, 1921.

138. Grace Allen was married to Laurence C. Jones, and she signed her name (and had it printed on MSF stationery) as Mrs. Laurence C. Jones. Mrs. Laurence C. Jones to Robert Moton, October 18, 1921, MP; Sewell, *Mississippi Black History Makers,* 174.

139. Josephine Yates was born in Mattituck, New York, in 1859 to a prominent family. She later became the first black person to receive teacher certification in Rhode Island. Noted for her work as an educator and a writer, she also helped organize the Kansas City Women's League in 1893, which became part of the national organization in 1896. See Hine, Brown, Terborg-Penn, *Black Women in America,* 2: 1297–98.

140. Hood, *Negro at Mound Bayou,* 33. See Lerner, *Black Women in White America,* 450–58.

141. Hood, *Negro at Mound Bayou,* 33.

142. Ibid. See also Higginbotham, *Righteous Discontent,* 16–17.

143. Neverdon-Morton, *Afro-American Women of the South,* 3, 6, 7; Shaw, *What a Woman Ought to Be and to Do,* 119.

Chapter 2. History of Mound Bayou: "A Negro Metropolis"

1. Banks et al., circular, March 19, 1915, BTWPF. Although Banks did not name the poet, it is R. W. Glover. See Felleman, *Best Loved Poems,* 103.

2. Sewell, *Mississippi Black History Makers,* 3.

3. Swingler, "Jewel of the Delta," 9; Sewell, *Mississippi Black History Makers,* 3–4; Everett, *Brierfield,* 75–88.

4. Washington, *Negro in Business,* 85.

5. Hamilton, *Black Towns and Profit*, 46.

6. For Negro affection for the South, see Litwack, *Been in the Storm*.

7. Richardson, *National Cyclopedia of the Colored Race*, 304; Washington, "A Town Owned by Negroes," 318–19; Crockett, *Black Towns*, 10. See also Rose, *Rehearsal for Reconstruction*.

8. For more on the "Kansas Hegira" see Painter, *Exodusters*; Cox, *Blacks in Topeka, Kansas*; Athearn, *In Search of Canaan*.

9. Washington, *Negro in Business*, 87; Crockett, *Black Towns*, 10.

10. Crockett, *Black Towns*, 10–11.

11. Richardson, *National Cyclopedia of the Colored Race*, 304; Hamilton, *Black Towns and Profit*, 89.

12. Washington, *Negro in Business*, 88–89; Summerville, *Educating Black Doctors*, 92–95; Crockett, *Black Towns*, 12. See also Savitt, *Medicine and Slavery*; Numbers and Savitt, *Science and Medicine*, 147–355; Savitt and Young, *Disease and Distinctiveness in the American South*, chs. 1, 2, 6.

13. Black health and immunity stereotypes were a factor for McGinnis; Sillers et al., *History of Bolivar County, Mississippi*.

14. Montgomery quoted in Washington, *Negro in Business*, 90.

15. Crockett, *Black Towns*, 12.

16. Jackson, "Gone but Not Forgotten," 6; "Darktown—Mound Bayou," June, 1937, Prominent Persons File, Mound Bayou Collection, MDAH.

17. Newton, "Country of the Yazoo Delta," 112–16. Charles Banks said the town was named after a "creek running through it bearing that name." Banks, "A Negro Colony," ms., BTWPF.

18. See Banks, "Negro Colony."

19. See Willey, "Mound Bayou—A Negro Municipality," 161.

20. See Richardson, *National Cyclopedia of the Colored Race*, 304.

21. See Tong, "Pioneers of Mound Bayou," 395.

22. Washington, "A Town Owned by Negroes," 309.

23. Holmes, "Whitecapping," 166; Montgomery to Washington, September 6, 1904, in Harlan and Smock, BTWP, 8: 61–63.

24. Montgomery to Washington, September 6, 1904, in Harlan and Smock, BTWP, 8: 61–63.

25. McMillen, *Dark Journey*, 120–21; Hood, *Negro at Mound Bayou*, 20. See Holmes, "Whitecapping," 165–85, for discussion on whitecapping in Mississippi. See also Banks to Washington, February 18, 1907, BTWPF; Washington to Montgomery, September 16, 1904, Washington to Edward H. Clement, September 21, 1904, in Harlan and Smock, BTWP, 8: 69–70.

26. Hood, *Negro at Mound Bayou*, 20.

27. Tong, "Pioneers of Mound Bayou," 393.

28. Crockett, *Black Towns*, 14.

29. Litwack, *Been in the Storm*, passim; Hunter, *To 'Joy My Freedom*, 124.

30. On the Montgomerys' avoidance of politics, see Hermann, *Pursuit of a Dream*, 123–24.

31. Quoted in McMillen, *Dark Journey*, 43. See also Kirwan, *Revolt of the Rednecks*, 58–84; Satcher, "Blacks in Mississippi Politics," 161–76; Sallis, "Color Line in Mississippi Politics."

32. Wharton, *Negro in Mississippi*, 206–15.

33. Redding, *Lonesome Road*, 103–6.

34. *New York Age*, October 11, 1890. For more on Fortune, see Thornbrough, *T. Thomas Fortune*.

35. Wharton, *Negro in Mississippi*, 206–15; Meier, *Negro Thought in America*, 38; Henry F. Downing to Washington, September 27, 1890, in Harlan and Smock, BTWP, 3: 84–85. See also *Cleveland Gazette*, February 15, 1902.

36. Montgomery to Washington, April 5, 1907, BTWPF. See also Loewen and Sallis, *Mississippi*, 188.

37. Hamilton, *Black Towns and Profit*, 51, 52; Redding, *Lonesome Road*, 106.

38. Redding, *No Day of Triumph*, 296, 300; Crockett, *Black Towns*, 15.

39. J. A. Welling to Stuyvesant Fish, September 1, 1897, and James Edwards to Fish, March 20, 1902, Illinois Central Railroad Papers; Hamilton, *Black Towns and Profit*, 52–53; Silver, "In the Eye of the Storm," 66–67.

40. Silver, "In the Eye of the Storm," 66–67; Redding, *Lonesome Road*, 106–7. Redding says Green's wife, who he married in 1890, may have encouraged the rift between Green and Montgomery and also encouraged him to dissolve his holdings with Montgomery; "Wonderful Mound Bayou," 427.

41. Jackson, "Mound Bayou," 62.

42. Hood, *Negro at Mound Bayou*, 64, 65; Redding, *Lonesome Road*, 102, 106–7.

43. Washington to Theodore Roosevelt, in Harlan and Smock, BTWP, 6: 358.

44. Banks to Washington, June 25, 1903, BTWPF.

45. Scott to Washington, June 21, 1903, in Harlan and Smock, BTWP, 7: 179–81.

46. See Harlan and Smock, BTWP, 3: 84–85n. Hermann suggests Montgomery became the target of powerful white Mississippi Republicans "who wanted to purge all black officeholders" and that Montgomery was set up by the racist special agent leading the investigation. Hermann, "Isaiah T. Montgomery's Balancing Act," 299–300.

47. Scott to Washington, June 21, 1903, in Harlan and Smock, BTWP, 7: 179–81.

48. Francis E. Leupp to Washington, June 27, 1903, in Harlan and Smock, BTWP, 7: 185; Roscoe C. Simmons to Washington, October 25, 1903, in Harlan and Smock, BTWP, 7: 310–11.

49. Washington to Scott, July 21, 1903, in Harlan and Smock, BTWP, 7: 215.

50. Washington, *Negro in Business*, 92; Willey, "Mound Bayou—A Negro Mu-

nicipality," 163; Hood, *Negro at Mound Bayou*, 10–45; Hamilton, *Black Towns and Profit*, 63, 68.

51. Washington, *Negro in Business*, 92; Hood, *Negro at Mound Bayou*, 10–45.

52. Hood, *Negro at Mound Bayou*, 10–45; "Wonderful Mound Bayou," 417–27.

53. There were several other black towns, such as Rosewood, Fla.; Nicodemus, Kans.; Allensworth, Calif.; Clearview, Boley, and Langston City, Okla.

54. Crockett, *Black Towns*, 142.

55. Ibid., 65, 142.

56. Ibid., 67–68.

57. Giddings, *When and Where I Enter*, 95–117; Gatewood, *Aristocrats of Color*, 237–46.

58. Crockett, *Black Towns*, 64, 142.

59. Ousley, "A Town of Colored People in Mississippi," 3.

60. Ibid.

61. Hood, *Negro at Mound Bayou*, 103–5.

62. Ibid.

63. Crockett, *Black Towns*, 6, 7, 15.

64. Tong, "Pioneers of Mound Bayou," 392.

65. McMillen, *Dark Journey*, 168. See also ibid., 166–77, where McMillen notes that in 1900 there were twenty-four black attorneys in Mississippi, yet by 1935 there were only five. The decrease can be attributed largely to harassment of black lawyers in the state. See also Mollison, "Negro Lawyers in Mississippi," 52–59.

66. Willey, "Mound Bayou—A Negro Municipality," 164; Crockett, *Black Towns*, 65–66; Washington, "A Town Owned by Negroes," 318–19.

Chapter 3. Charles Banks, Booker T. Washington, and the Mound Bayou Connection

1. See Spivey, *Schooling for the New Slavery*, 8–12, 16–38.

2. See Washington, *Up from Slavery*, 42–79; Franklin, *From Slavery to Freedom*, 244–46; Harlan, *Booker T. Washington: Making of a Black Leader*, 52–77; Washington, "Industrial Education Is the Solution," in Foner and Lewis, *Black Workers*, 277–79; Meier, Rudwick, and Broderick, *Black Protest Thought*, 6–7.

3. Washington, *Up from Slavery*, 217–37. See also Du Bois, *Souls of Black Folk*, 80.

4. Franklin, *From Slavery to Freedom*, 244–46. On Washington's philosophy, see Asante, *African American History*, 319–24.

5. Franklin, *From Slavery to Freedom*, 244–48. The Bailey case is an example of Washington fighting against peonage. See Daniel, "Up from Slavery and Down to Peonage," 654–70; Daniel, *Shadow of Slavery*, 65–81; Harlan, "Secret Life of Booker T. Washington," 403.

6. Franklin, *From Slavery to Freedom*, 249–50. If flaws in his strategy were as

apparent then as they are now, Washington was shrewd enough to have carefully considered other alternatives. See also McPherson, *Abolitionist Legacy*, where he discusses how the descendants of the old white abolitionists realized the flaws in Washington's approach early on and shifted their support from him to the NAACP. See also Goings, *The NAACP Comes of Age*, 3–8.

7. Dailey, "Neither 'Uncle Tom' nor 'Accommodationist," 25–28.

8. Ibid.

9. *New Orleans State*, June 7, 1910, quoted in Crockett, *Black Towns*, 104. See Banks, "The Negro Question," 101, where he argues that Negroes are not inferior to whites.

10. Tong, "Pioneers of Mound Bayou," 398.

11. Ibid. Crockett, *Black Towns*, 103–4; "Wonderful Mound Bayou," 426–27.

12. "Whites, Blacks Join to Stop Lynching," *Memphis Commercial Appeal*, ca. December 13, 1913.

13. Ibid.

14. "White Firemen Give Aid to Mound Bayou," *New York Age*, October 22, 1921.

15. Banks, "Negro Town and Colony," 11.

16. Charles Banks to Robert W. Taylor, June 22, 1908, Banks to Robert Parks, April 25, 1907, BTWPF.

17. Wiggins, *Life and Works of Paul Lawrence Dunbar*, 184.

18. Banks to W. L. Park, February 6, 1911, BTWPF.

19. Banks, circular letter to whites in adjoining counties, ca. October 5, 1912, BTWPF.

20. Banks, circular letter to MNBL members, ca. April 15, 1909, BTWPF. Banks understood that whites might also read this circular. Therefore, his references to them are generous.

21. Banks to Washington, November 2, 1912, BTWPF.

22. Ibid.

23. Crockett, *Black Towns*, 106; Banks to Washington, July 9, 1914, in Harlan and Smock, BTWP, 13: 84–85.

24. Banks to Washington, July 9, 1914, in Harlan and Smock, BTWP, 13: 84–85.

25. Washington to Banks, July 16, 1914, in Harlan and Smock, BTWP, 13: 93.

26. Banks to Washington, October 20, 1907, BTWPF.

27. Crockett, *Black Towns*, 103; Banks, "The Negro Question," 101.

28. Ellsworth, *Death in a Promised Land*; D'Orso, *Like Judgment Day*; Colburn, "Rosewood and America," 175–92; Jones, "Rosewood Massacre," 193–208; Jones, Rivers, et al., "Documented History of the Incident which Occurred at Rosewood, Florida in January 1923."

29. Harlan, "Secret Life of Booker T. Washington."

30. Thomas Owen to Charles Banks, March 24, 1912, BTWPF.

31. L. K. Salsbury to Banks, April 1, 1912, Leroy Percy to Andrew Carnegie, April 8, 1912, BTWPF.

32. Banks to Scott, February 10, 1910, BTWPF.

33. Banks to Robert Taylor, June 22, 1908, BTWPF.

34. Du Bois, "The Talented Tenth," in Lewis, *W. E. B. Du Bois: A Reader,* 261–69, 347–53; Aptheker, *Afro-American History,* 57; Jackson, *America Is Me,* 222. See also Fox, *Guardian of Boston;* Rudwick, "W. E. B. Du Bois," in Franklin and Meier, *Black Leaders of the Twentieth Century;* Lewis, *W. E. B. Du Bois: Biography of a Race.*

35. Gatewood, *Aristocrats of Color,* 302–6; Berry and Blassingame, *Long Memory,* 162–65; Meier, *Negro Thought in America,* 207–47.

36. Du Bois, *Souls of Black Folk,* 87.

37. Du Bois, "The Talented Tenth," quoted in Franklin, *From Slavery to Freedom,* 249; Du Bois, *Souls of Black Folk,* 87; Meier, *Negro Thought in America,* 190–206.

38. Du Bois, "The Hampton Idea," in Aptheker, *Education of Black People,* 15.

39. Gatewood, *Aristocrats of Color,* 302–6; "Washington's Leadership Repudiated," newspaper clipping, n.d., n.p., BTWPF.

40. Washington, *My Larger Education,* 200.

41. Banks to Washington, May 29, 1903, BTWPF.

42. Crockett, *Black Towns,* 134–35. See also Anderson and Moss, *Dangerous Donations;* Spivey, *Schooling for the New Slavery.*

43. Banks to Washington, December 21, 1905, Washington to Banks, December 27, 1905, BTWPF.

44. Banks to Washington, October 26, 1907, BTWPF.

45. "Washington's Leadership Repudiated," BTWPF.

46. Banks to Washington, June 7, 1907, Washington to Banks, June 10, 1907, BTWPF.

47. Banks to Washington, September 20, 1907, BTWPF.

48. Washington to Banks, February 25, 1909, BTWPF.

49. Washington to Banks, August 26, 1909, BTWPF.

50. Banks to Washington, December 1, 1909, BTWPF.

51. Washington to Banks, January 14, 1910, BTWPF.

52. Washington to Montgomery, January 25, 1915, in Harlan and Smock, BTWP, 13: 233–34.

53. Washington, *My Larger Education,* 207–8; Scott to Banks, June 15, 1911, BTWPF.

54. Washington, "Charles Banks," 731–33.

55. Ibid.

56. Washington, *My Larger Education,* 213.

57. Nationally, Banks wielded power through the NNBL as first vice-president. See Banks to Scott, July 7, 1913, Scott to Banks, July 10, 1913, BTWPF.

58. Banks to Scott, December 31, 1903, BTWPF.

59. Banks to Scott, January 1, 1909, Scott to Banks, January 5, 1911, Scott to Banks, January 3, 1913, BTWPF.

60. Scott to Banks, December 31, 1913, BTWPF.

61. Scott to Banks, September 5, 1916, BTWPF.

62. Scott to Banks, September 13, 1916, MP.

63. Banks to Scott, September 7, 1916, MP.

64. Scott to Banks, September 18, 1916, MP.

65. Scott to Banks, May 11, 1907, MP; Harlan, *Booker T. Washington: Making of a Black Leader*, 304–9; Baker, *Following the Color Line*, 219–25.

66. Banks to Baker, ca. May 11, 1907; Harlan, *Booker T. Washington: Making of a Black Leader*, 306–7; Baker, *Following the Color Line*, 219–25.

67. Scott to Banks, September 22, 1913, BTWPF.

68. See Scott to Banks, January 20, 22, 26, 1912, Banks to Scott, January 23, 1912, BTWPF.

69. Scott to Banks, July 15, 1904, BTWPF.

70. Scott to Banks, January 23, 1913, BTWPF.

71. Banks to Washington, October 4, 1906, Banks to Scott, October 30, 1906, Scott to Banks, October 19, 1906, Scott to Banks, November 12, 1906, Banks to Scott, November 15, 1906, N. J. Thompson to Banks, November 20, 1906, Banks to Scott, November 22, 1906, BTWPF; Banks, "The Negro Question," 95–103.

72. Banks repaid past favors by hiring Scott's father. Dailey, "Emmett Jay Scott," 227–28. See also Hamilton, *Black Towns and Profit*, 94n.

73. Banks to Scott, October 4, 1912, October 13, 29, 1913, Scott to Banks, October 9, 1913, November 3, 1913, ca. December 31, 1913, Washington to Banks, October 10, 1913, BTWPF. The goodwill between Banks and the leaders at Tuskegee is exemplified by Scott's response when Banks requested some chickens and roosters from Tuskegee: "I am writing to say that it will give me personally very great pleasure to send these with my compliments to you and Mrs. Banks at any time . . . you desire them." Gifts of this nature between the two were fairly common. Scott had already spoken to G. W. Greene, head of the Poultry Division, and Greene had assured him that since these animals were going to Banks "he will make the best selection possible for you." See Scott to Banks, August 18, 1914, BTWPF.

74. Washington, *My Larger Education*, 208.

75. Washington to Montgomery, January 23, 1915, in Harlan and Smock, BTWP, 13: 233–34.

76. Meier, "Booker T. Washington and the Town of Mound Bayou," in Meier and Rudwick, *Along the Color Line*, 218; Washington, *My Larger Education*, 212.

Chapter 4. Leader, Organizer, and Promoter: "On My Job All the Time and Doing the Best that My Ability Will Allow"

1. Hamilton, *Black Towns and Profit*, 59.

2. "Refuse to Leave Deposits in Bank," newspaper clipping, April 9, 1907,

n.p., BTWPF. On Atwood, see James, James, and James, *Mississippi Black Bankers*, 67.

3. James, James, and James, *Mississippi Black Bankers*, 83.

4. H. J. Hutton to Banks, January 30, 1908, BTWPF.

5. Washington to Banks, June 2, 1910, BTWPF.

6. Banks to Scott, July 7, 1913, Scott to Banks, July 10, 1913, BTWPF. On Perry Howard, see Lisio, *Hoover, Blacks, and Lily-Whites*, esp. ch. 8; McMillen, "Perry W. Howard," 205–24.

7. See also Banks to Scott, July 5, 1916, Scott to Banks, July 10, 1916, MP.

8. Perry Howard to Banks, September 15, 1915, BTWPF.

9. Banks to Scott, September 16, 1915, BTWPF.

10. Banks to American Express Company, May 24, 1907, BTWPF.

11. Ibid.

12. H. R. Beale to Columbus R. Stringer, April 8, 1909, BTWPF.

13. Banks to Oliver Chilled Plow Works, April 16, 1909, BTWPF.

14. Banks, circular letter to Mound Bayou farmers, January 12, 1910, BTWPF.

15. Ibid.

16. Ibid.

17. Washington to Banks, October 25, 1911, BTWPF.

18. Harlan, *Booker T. Washington: Wizard of Tuskegee*, 207–9.

19. Hood, *Negro at Mound Bayou*, 113–14; Jones, "The Role of Tuskegee Institute in the Education of Black Farmers," 263–66.

20. Washington to Banks, December 2, 1907, BTWPF.

21. Harlan, *Booker T. Washington: Wizard of Tuskegee*, 209.

22. Banks to Washington, December 9, 1907, BTWPF.

23. Hood, *Negro at Mound Bayou*, 72.

24. Banks to James A. Booker, February 25, 1908, BTWPF.

25. Hamilton, *Beacon Lights*, 211.

26. Banks to James Booker, May 23, 1908, BTWPF.

27. Harlan, *Booker T. Washington: Wizard of Tuskegee*, 207. See also Hamilton, *Black Towns and Profit*, 94; Jones, "The Role of Tuskegee Institute in the Education of Black Farmers,"263.

28. Dillard also directed the Jeanes Fund.

29. Banks to Seaman A. Knapp, January 23, 1909, BTWPF.

30. Washington to Banks, May 28, 1910, BTWPF.

31. Washington to Banks, May 31, 1910, BTWPF.

32. James A. Booker to Washington, May 31, 1910, BTWPF.

33. Banks to Washington, October 21, 1910, BTWPF. See also Banks, circular letter to members of the MNBL, August 31, 1909, BTWPF. Campbell assisted Mound Bayou again in 1914. See "Big Farmers' Meeting Held Here Monday," *Mound Bayou Demonstrator*, March 15, 1914, Tuskegee News Clippings File.

34. Banks to James A. Booker, October 24, 1910, BTWPF.

35. Banks to Washington, April 10, 1911, BTWPF.

36. Washington to Banks, July 8, 1911, BTWPF.

37. Banks to [?], n.d., BTWPF.

38. Banks to Washington, June 23, 1911, BTWPF.

39. Banks to Thomas M. Campbell, March 11, 1912, BTWPF.

40. Ibid.

41. Banks told Campbell he was sending Washington a copy of the letter so as not to undercut him in Washington's eyes.

42. Very little is written about Banks's involvement in establishing this town. See Nichols and Crogman, *Progress of a Race*, 259; *New York Age*, February 28, 1920.

43. Washington to Banks, March 8, 1907, BTWPF.

44. Washington to Banks, October 23, 1907, BTWPF; Washington to J. T. Harahan, September 16, 1908, BTWPF. See Washington, *My Larger Education*, 183–84, and ch. 3.

45. *Jackson Evening News*, ca. August 28, 1908, BTWPF.

46. Banks to Washington, September 4, 1908, BTWPF.

47. Banks to Washington, August 31, 1908, BTWPF.

48. Washington to Banks, September 17, 1908, BTWPF.

49. Banks to newspaper editors, September 23, 1908, BTWPF.

50. Banks to Perry Howard, September 23, 1908, BTWPF.

51. Banks to Scott, September 5, 1908, BTWPF.

52. Scott to Banks, September 8, 1908, BTWPF.

53. Banks to Washington, September 10, 1908, BTWPF.

54. Ibid.

55. Scott to Banks, September 16, 1908, BTWPF.

56. Banks to Washington, September 18, 1908, BTWPF.

57. Banks to J. T. Harahan, September 16, 1908, BTWPF.

58. *New Orleans Picayune*, October 6, 1908; *Memphis Commercial Appeal*, October 6, 1908; Kealing, "Booker T. Washington's Tour through Mississippi," 20–27; Moton, "Significance of Mr. Washington's Lecture Trip in Mississippi," 691–95.

59. Kealing, "Booker T. Washington's Tour through Mississippi," 20–27; Hemmingway, "Booker T. Washington in Mississippi," 30, 42. Isaiah Montgomery does not appear to have been with Washington's contingent during the trip.

60. Scott and Stowe, *Booker T. Washington: Builder of a Civilization*, 130–31; F. E. Miller, report, October 3–12, 1908, in Harlan and Smock, BTWP, 9: 640–45.

61. Washington, "Cheerful Journey through Mississippi," BTWP, 10: 60–68; Washington, *My Larger Education*, 196.

62. Washington, *My Larger Education*, 196–197; Hemmingway, "Booker T. Washington in Mississippi," 36; Reports of Pinkerton Detective F. E. Miller, October 10, 1908, in Harlan and Smock, BTWP, 9: 645. The Pinkerton report says that he spoke to about 3,000 in Mound Bayou.

63. Washington, "Cheerful Journey through Mississippi," BTWP, 10: 60–68;

Hemmingway says, "Observers claimed that he spoke to an estimated 68,000 to 80,000 people," Hemmingway, "Booker T. Washington in Mississippi," 36.

64. Washington to Banks, October 18, 1908, BTWPF.

65. Washington, "Cheerful Journey through Mississippi," BTWP, 10: 60–68. See also Washington, *My Larger Education*, 197; Moton, "Significance of Mr. Washington's Lecture Trip in Mississippi," 691–95. On the progress of Mississippi Negroes, see also Woodard, "Negro Progress in A Mississippi Town," 3–8.

66. Scott to Banks, October 15, 1908, BTWPF.

67. *New York Age*, July 9, 1908; Roscoe C. Simmons to Banks, n.d., BTWPF.

68. Harlan, *Booker T. Washington: Wizard of Tuskegee*, 263.

69. Miller, report, October 4, 1908, in Harlan and Smock, BTWP, 9: 641.

70. Miller, report, October 6, 1908, in Harlan and Smock, BTWP, 9: 642–43.

71. Residents of Lula said the bodies were left hanging because no family members claimed them that day. See the *Memphis Commercial Appeal*, October 12–13, 1908. See also Holmes, "Whitecapping," 165–85; Hemmingway, "Booker T. Washington in Mississippi," 39–42.

72. Scott to Banks, October 15, 1908, BTWPF.

73. Moton to Banks, July 1, 1920, MP.

74. Banks to Moton, May 29, 1920, MP.

75. Moton to Banks, May 5, 1920, MP.

76. Banks to Moton, July 21, November 9, 1920, Moton to Banks, August 3, 1920, MP.

77. Banks to Moton, July 21, November 9, 1920, Moton to Banks, August 3, 1920, MP.

78. *New York Age*, July 17, 1920.

79. Montgomery to Moton, June 30, 1920, MP.

80. Banks to Moton, July 2, 1920, MP.

81. Albon Holsey to Banks, July 4, 1920, MP.

82. Holsey to Banks, July 6, 1920, MP.

83. Moton to Montgomery, July 6, 1920, MP.

84. Banks to William H. Holtzclaw, September 1, 1921, MP.

85. Banks to Holtzclaw, September 2, 1921, MP.

86. Ibid.

87. Holtzclaw to Holsey, September 12, 1921, MP.

88. Holsey to Holtzclaw, September 15, 1921, MP.

89. Holtzclaw to Holsey, September 15, 1921, MP.

90. Holtzclaw to Holsey, September 22, 1921. The origin of this letter is unknown. Banks could have sent it to the paper to generate publicity for himself. More likely, some of Banks's enemies sent it as a press release to create friction between Banks and other committee members.

91. Sidney D. Redmond to Banks, September 28, 1921, MP.

92. Banks to Holtzclaw, September 28, 1921, MP.

93. Moton or Holsey to Holtzclaw, October 13, 1921, MP.

94. Holtzclaw to Holsey, September 28, 1921, MP.

95. *Jackson Daily Clarion-Ledger*, September 24, 1921.

96. Moton to Banks, October 15, 1921, MP. Moton also sent the same letter to Isaiah Montgomery. See Moton to Montgomery, October 15, 1921, MP.

97. Holtzclaw to Holsey, October 16, 1921, MP.

98. Holtzclaw to Moton, October 17, 1921, MP.

99. T. S. Morris to S. D. Redmond, October 19, 1921, MP.

100. Holtzclaw and R. S. Grossly to the Central Committee, December 23, 1921, MP.

101. Grace Allen Jones to Moton, October 18, 1921, MP. See also *New York Age*, November 12, 1921.

102. Holtzclaw to Holsey, September 20, 1921, MP.

103. *New York Age*, November 5, 1921. See also Aery, "Dr. R. R. Moton Makes 'Good-Will' Tour," MP.

104. Moton to Banks, November 7, 1921, MP.

Chapter 5. The Business League: "Being Worked to the Limit"

1. Hamilton, *Beacon Lights*, 208; Washington, "Negro in Business," 120–22, 268–75. For life membership listing, see souvenir program of NNBL for August 18–20, 1909.

2. See Banks to Scott, April 5, 1905, Scott to Banks, April 8, 1905, BTWPF. For history of the NNBL, see Burrows, "Necessity of Myth."

3. See Scott to Banks, June 10, 1914, Banks to K. W. Brown, June 15, 1914; Banks to Scott, July 29, 1914, BTWPF.

4. Program, Third Annual Session of the NNBL, August 25–27, 1902, National Negro Business League Papers (hereafter cited as NNBL Papers).

5. See Washington, circular letter to Local Negro Business Leagues, September 24, 1915, BTWPF. Also see Burrows, "Necessity of Myth."

6. Banks to Robert C. Owen, May 7, 1910, Scott to Banks, May 9, 1910, BTWPF.

7. Scott to Banks, January 3, 1916, March 6, 1916, BTWPF.

8. Banks to W. D. Frazee, May 23, 1910, BTWPF.

9. Ibid.

10. Banks to Washington, May 27, 1910, BTWPF.

11. Washington to Banks, May 31, 1910, BTWPF.

12. Banks to Washington, August 1, 1910, BTWPF.

13. Scott to Banks, June 12, 1914, BTWPF.

14. Banks to Scott, June 16, 1914, BTWPF; Report of the Fifteenth Annual Convention of the NNBL, NNBL Papers, 61–66.

15. Scott to Banks, July 11, 1914, BTWPF. See also Banks to Scott, July 15, 1914, BTWPF.

16. Banks to Scott, May 4, 1914, BTWPF.

17. Souvenir Program, NNBL Eleventh Annual Meeting, New York, August 19, 1910, BTWPF.

18. Scott to Washington, July 17, 1914, BTWPF.

19. Banks, circular letter to members of the NNBL, July 13, 1914, BTWPF.

20. Banks to Washington, January 27, 1912, BTWPF.

21. Washington to Banks, October 21, 1914, BTWPF.

22. Banks to Washington, November 2, 1914, BTWPF.

23. Banks to Washington, October 30, 1911, Washington to Banks, November 7, 18, 1911, BTWPF.

24. Washington to Banks, December 5, 1911, BTWPF.

25. Washington to Scott, December 28, 1910, Holsey Papers; Burrows, "Necessity of Myth," 95, 96, 99, 106–9.

26. Washington to Banks, November 10, 1913, BTWPF.

27. Banks to Washington, December 8, 1913, Washington to Banks, December 19, 1913, Banks to Perry Howard, December 16, 1913, BTWPF.

28. Washington to Banks, December 12, 1913, BTWPF.

29. Moton to Banks, September 12, 1917, MP.

30. Scott to Banks, December 29, 1915, BTWPF.

31. Scott to Banks, January 10, March 6, 1916, BTWPF.

32. Banks, circular letter to men and women in Mississippi, ca. March 13, 1905, BTWPF.

33. Scott to Banks, ca. May 1905, BTWPF.

34. Banks, circular letter, ca. April 15, 1909, BTWPF.

35. Montgomery to Washington, May 31, 1905, BTWPF.

36. Banks to Scott, April 5, 1905, Scott to Banks, April 8, 1905, BTWPF.

37. Washington to Banks, May 15, 1905, BTWPF.

38. Banks to Washington, May 24, 1905, BTWPF.

39. Washington to Banks, May 27, 1905, BTWPF.

40. Hemmingway, "Booker T. Washington in Mississippi," 30.

41. *Advance Matter*, newspaper clipping, n.p., n.d., BTWPF.

42. Banks to Scott, July 29, August 3, 1914, Scott (for Washington) to the Reverend A. J. Hall, ca. August 3, 1914, BTWPF.

43. Banks to Scott, June 5, 1905, BTWPF.

44. Banks to Scott, March 10, 1908, BTWPF.

45. S. K. Kinwood to Banks, July 22, 1913, BTWPF.

46. H. A. Wisher to Banks, October 4, 1907, BTWPF.

47. H. J. Hutton to Banks, January 30, 1908, Washington to Banks, June 2, 1910, BTWPF.

48. Burrows, "Necessity of Myth," 94–95.

49. Scott to Banks, April 8, 1905, BTWPF; Hamilton, *Beacon Lights*, 207–8.

50. *Galley Proof*, newspaper clipping, ca. June 25, 1910, BTWPF.

51. Banks to Scott, March 10, 1908, BTWPF.

52. Banks to Washington, November 5, 1908, BTWPF.

53. Washington to Banks, November 2, 1908, BTWPF.

54. Moton, "National Negro Business League at Louisville"; Report of the Tenth Annual Session of the NNBL, 91–131, NNBL Papers.

55. "Mississippi Day at the Convention," newspaper clipping, n.d., n.p. BTWPF; Report of the Tenth Annual Session of the NNBL, 92–100, NNBL Papers.

56. "Mississippi Day at the Convention"; Report of the Tenth Annual Session of the NNBL, 100–9, 114–18, NNBL Papers.

57. Report of the Tenth Annual Session of the NNBL, 118–27.

58. Ibid., 127–31.

59. Scott to Richard W. Thompson, December 30, 1915, in Harlan and Smock, BTWP, 13: 488.

60. Banks to Scott, May 27, 1916, BTWPF.

61. Washington to Napier, July 7, 1903, Napier to Washington, August 6, 1903, BTWPF.

62. Scott to Banks, July 26, 1916, BTWPF.

63. Scott to Banks, June 21, 1916, BTWPF.

64. Scott to Banks, July 3, 1916, Banks to Scott, July 5, 1916, Minnie M. Cox to Scott, July 21, 1916, BTWPF.

65. Report of the Seventeenth Annual Session of the NNBL, NNBL Papers, 3–17, 36–193.

66. Ibid., 63–64.

67. Ibid., 8.

68. Ibid., 8–9.

69. Scott to Banks, September 6, 1916, MP.

Chapter 6. Fund-Raiser for Negro Education: "Going Ahead Endeavoring to Meet the Conditions as Best We Can"

1. McMillen, *Dark Journey*, 72–75.

2. Ibid.

3. Hamilton, *Beacon Lights*, 209. See also "Chas. Banks, Trustee Campbell College," *New York Age*, December 16, 1915.

4. Richardson, *National Cyclopedia of the Colored Race*, 401; Banks to W. P. Thirkield, June 17, 1907, BTWPF.

5. Scott to Banks, May 15, 1913, BTWPF.

6. Scott to Banks, May 30, 1913, BTWPF.

7. Washington to Banks, May 30, June 16, 27, 1910, Banks to Washington, June 3, 1910, BTWPF.

8. See Banks to Robert J. McMullen, July 15, 1914, BTWPF; Holtzclaw, *Black Man's Burden*, 226. For more on Holtzclaw, see Cooper, "'We Rise upon the Structure We Ourselves Have Builded,'" 15–33.

9. Banks to W. J. Buck, April 6, 1912, BTWPF.

10. See Adams, *Great Negroes*, 136–37.

11. Crockett, *Black Towns*, 130.

12. Washington to Banks, December 27, 1905, BTWPF.

13. Banks to J. A. Miller, April 23, 1910, BTWPF.

14. See Washington to Banks, January 2, 1909, May 2, 1913, April 17, 1914, Banks to Washington, December 28, 1908, December 23, 1909, February 27, 1914, BTWPF.

15. Moton to Banks, October 24, 1918, MP.

16. Banks to Scott, March 15, September 8, 1906, BTWPF.

17. Scott to Banks, September 11, 1906, BTWPF.

18. Banks to Malvin Moore, September 20, 1910, BTWPF.

19. Banks to Scott, September 21, 1910, Scott to Banks, September 24, 1910, BTWPF.

20. Washington to Banks, November 26, 1910, BTWPF.

21. Scott to Banks, November 28, 1910, BTWPF. Banks had already heard about Charles's behavior from Malvin before he received Washington's and Scott's letters. See Banks to Scott, December 2, 1910, BTWPF. This behavior confirmed the fears of the old black elite that using money as a major criteria for determining status would allow "unpolished" people like Banks's nephew to enter the elite and would ultimately bring dishonor to their group.

22. J. B. Ramsey to Washington, February 22, 1912, BTWPF.

23. Scott to Banks, ca. February 26, 1912, BTWPF.

24. Scott to Banks, February 29, 1911, BTWPF.

25. Scott to Banks, March 21, 1912, BTWPF.

26. Banks to Scott, March 26, 1912, BTWPF.

27. Scott to Banks, March 30, 1912, BTWPF. There is no indication Charles Moore returned to Tuskegee after being suspended, though Scott had spoken of this possibility.

28. Scott to Banks, June 1, 1914, BTWPF.

29. Ibid.

30. Banks to Moton, June 25, 1917, MP.

31. Moton to Banks, June 28, 30, 1917, MP.

32. See Banks to Moton, September 24, 1920, Moton to Banks, September 28, 1920, Banks to Holsey, September 19, October 5, 1920, Holsey to Banks, September 25, October 13, 1920, MP.

33. See Scott to Banks, July 12, 1917, Scott or Moton to Banks, September 27, 1917, Banks to Holsey, n.d., September 5, 1919, September 1, December 16, 1921, Holsey to Banks, September 10, 1919, September 23, December 19, 1921, Moton or Holsey to Banks, October 25, 1920, MP.

34. Banks, "History of Mound Bayou," BTWPF.

35. Banks to Scott, August 28, 1908, BTWPF.

36. Ogden, Peabody, and Baldwin were white philanthropists who supported education for blacks. The Peabody Education Fund provided more than $3.5 mil-

lion to advance southern education between 1867 and 1914. See Franklin, *From Slavery to Freedom*, 240–43; Anderson and Moss, *Dangerous Donations*.

37. Harlan, *Booker T. Washington: Wizard of Tuskegee*, 186–94; Harlan, *Separate and Unequal*, 75–101; see also Anderson and Moss, *Dangerous Donations*, 39–62.

38. Banks to Scott, June 10, 1907, BTWPF.

39. Scott to Banks, June 15, 1907, BTWPF.

40. Banks to Robert Ogden, June 11, 1907, BTWPF.

41. Banks to Washington, July 15, 1907, BTWPF.

42. Banks to Washington, September 16, 1907, BTWPF.

43. Scott to Banks, October 16, 1907, BTWPF.

44. Scott to Banks, November 5, 1907, BTWPF.

45. Banks to Scott, October 25, November 12, 1907, BTWPF.

46. Robert E. Park to Banks, April 22, 1910, BTWPF.

47. Harlan, *Booker T. Washington: Wizard of Tuskegee*, 194.

48. Banks to Scott, November 27, 1908, Scott to Banks, December 1, 1908, BTWPF.

49. Murphy to Banks, December 17, 1908, BTWPF.

50. Ibid.

51. Washington to Banks, [?], Scott to Banks, March 2, 1910, BTWPF.

52. Washington to Banks, December 3, 1908, BTWPF.

53. Banks to Washington, December 7, 1908, BTWPF.

54. Washington to Banks, December 13, 1908, BTWPF.

55. Scott to Banks, December 7, 1908, BTWPF.

56. Banks to Washington, December 16, 1908, BTWPF.

57. Scott to Banks, December 31, 1908, BTWPF. See also Washington to Banks, January 5, 1909, BTWPF.

58. Banks to Andrew Carnegie, December 25, 1908, BTWPF.

59. Washington to Banks, February 10, 1909, BTWPF.

60. Scott to Banks, February 11, 1909, BTWPF.

61. Banks, circular letter, February 16, 1909, BTWPF. See also Montgomery [?] to James Bertram, February 16, 1909, BTWPF.

62. Banks to Washington, October 23, 1909, Washington to Banks, ca. October 28, 1909, BTWPF; Hood, *Negro at Mound Bayou*, 50–51, 84.

63. Banks, circular letter, March 1, 1910, BTWPF.

64. Scott to Banks, March 4, 1910, BTWPF.

65. Banks, circular letter to members of the MNBL, April 30, 1910, BTWPF.

66. Scott to Banks, May 3, 1910; Washington to Banks, May 3, 1910, BTWPF.

67. See invitation, December 23, 1910, BTWPF.

68. Scott to Banks, January 20, 1912, BTWPF.

69. Ibid.

70. Ibid.

71. Scott to Banks, January 22, 1912, BTWPF.

72. Banks to Scott, ca. January 22, 1912, BTWPF.

73. Scott to Banks, January 25, 1912, BTWPF.

74. Scott to Banks, January 26, 1912, BTWPF.

75. Ibid.

76. Banks to Scott, January 23, 1912, BTWPF.

77. Ibid.

78. Ibid.

79. Ibid.

80. Hamilton, *Black Towns and Profit*, 67–68.

81. Harlan, *Booker T. Washington: Wizard of Tuskegee*, 193.

82. Hamilton, *Black Towns and Profit*, 68.

83. Banks to Thomas S. Owen, December 29, 1909, BTWPF.

84. Banks to [?], ca. April 7, 1911, BTWPF.

85. Ousley, "A Town of Colored People in Mississippi"; "Wonderful Mound Bayou," 423.

86. Ousley, "History of Mound Bayou Normal Institute."

87. Hamilton, *Black Towns and Profit*, 67.

88. Ousley, "History of Mound Bayou Normal Institute."

89. Banks to Washington, September 1, 1912, BTWPF; Harlan, *Booker T. Washington: Wizard of Tuskegee*, 197.

90. Banks to Washington, September 2, 1912, BTWPF.

91. Washington to Banks, September 6, 1912, BTWPF.

92. Banks to Washington, October 2, 1912, BTWPF.

93. My research did not conclusively find that Rosenwald contributed $1,000 to Mound Bayou's school although he gave much more money to them for other investments. Some scholars have concluded that Rosenwald made the $1,000 contribution, but they may be in error. See August Meier, "Booker T. Washington and the Town of Mound Bayou," 398; Norman Crockett, *Black Towns*, 131; Hamilton, *Black Towns and Profit*, 67. For opposing view see Harlan, *Booker T. Washington: Wizard of Tuskegee*, 197; Franklin, *From Slavery to Freedom*, 241; Banks to Washington, September 1, 1912, September 2, 1912, October 2, 1912, BTWPF.

94. Hine, *Black Women in White*, 68.

95. Harlan, *Booker T. Washington: Wizard of Tuskegee*, 194–96.

96. Scott to Banks, January 27, 1909, BTWPF.

97. Banks to James Dillard, February 22, 1909, BTWPF.

98. Banks to Dillard, March 18, 1909, BTWPF.

99. Banks to Scott, March 21, 1909, BTWPF.

100. Scott to Banks, March 26, 1909, BTWPF.

101. Banks to Dillard, May 14, 1909, BTWPF.

102. Hood, *Negro at Mound Bayou*, 107.

103. Banks to Scott, September 3, 1910, BTWPF.

104. Banks to Dillard, April 7, 1911, BTWPF.

105. Banks to Washington, April 10, 1911, BTWPF.

106. J. R. E. Lee at Tuskegee provided Washington with Thomas's name. See

Lee to Scott, May 9, 1911, Washington to Banks, May 9, 1911, Banks to Scott, May 11, 1911, BTWPF.

107. Banks to Scott, August 9, 1911, BTWPF.

108. Scott to Banks, September 9, 1911, BTWPF.

109. Banks to Dillard, September 11, 1911, BTWPF.

110. Ibid.

111. Ibid.

112. Banks to Scott, ca. September 14, 1911, BTWPF.

113. Scott to Banks, September 16, 1911, BTWPF.

114. Scott to Banks, September 19, 1911. Lee also provided Scott with names for Banks. See Lee to Scott, September 20, 1911, BTWPF.

115. Banks to Dillard, March 4, 1912, BTWPF. Gertrude Bryant did not attend high school or college, but according to one observer, "you know this only after you are told and not by any apparent or discernible defect on her part." See Hood, *Negro at Mound Bayou*, 90–91.

116. Banks to Moton, May 30, 1912, BTWPF.

117. R. K. Bruff to Banks, April 14, 1913, BTWPF.

118. Banks to Dillard, April 16, 1913, BTWPF.

119. Scott to Banks, July 29, 1913, BTWPF.

120. Banks to Dillard, August 12, 1913, BTWPF.

121. Washington to Banks, May 5, 1914, BTWPF.

122. Banks to Scott, August 3, 1914, BTWPF.

123. Dillard to Banks, July 27, 1914, BTWPF.

124. Banks to Dillard, August 3, 1914, BTWPF.

125. Hamilton, *Black Towns and Profit*, 66, 67. See also Crockett, *Black Towns*, 131.

126. Eugene Booze to Moton, March 11, 1917, MP.

127. Montgomery to Moton, July 4, 1919, MP.

128. Ibid.; Banks to Moton, March 5, 1920, MP.

129. Banks to Moton, March 5, 1920, MP.

130. "Darktown—Mound Bayou," Mound Bayou Collection, MDAH.

Chapter 7. On Matters Political: "I See that 'Sambo' Is Left Out"

1. Banks to Scott, March 30, 1912, BTWPF.

2. Banks was probably exaggerating. Washington, *My Larger Education*, 211.

3. Hamilton, *Beacon Lights*, 210.

4. Richardson, *National Cyclopedia of the Colored Race*, 401; Hamilton, *Black Towns and Profit*, 59; Nichols and Crogman, *Progress of a Race*, 259; "Negro Republicans to Be Delegates," *Memphis News-Scimitar*, April 21, 1908.

5. Sherman, *Republican Party and Black America*, 28.

6. See Theodore Roosevelt to Carl Schurz, December 24, 1903, in Morison et al., *Letters of Theodore Roosevelt*, 3: 680–82; *Washington Bee*, October 19, 1901. On Washington's dinner at the White House, see Gatewood, *Theodore Roosevelt and the*

Art Of Controversy, ch. 2. See also Grantham, "Dinner at the White House," 112–30; Severn and Rogers, "Theodore Roosevelt Entertains Booker T. Washington," 306–18.

7. Mark Hanna controlled the lily-white and some Negro delegations of the Republican Party. See Franklin, *From Slavery to Freedom*, 278–79; Brands, *T. R.: The Last Romantic*, 421–24.

8. Franklin, *From Slavery to Freedom*, 278–79. See also Gatewood, *Theodore Roosevelt and the Art of Controversy*, ch. 4.

9. *Congressional Record*, 57th Cong., 2d sess., vol. 36, part 2, 1174–83; Scheiner, "President Theodore Roosevelt and the Negro," 171–72, 175.

10. *Washington Evening Star,* January 5, 6, 7, 1903; *Atlanta Constitution,* January 5, 6, 7, 1903; Gatewood, *Theodore Roosevelt and the Art of Controversy*, ch. 3. For a similar account, see Gatewood, "Theodore Roosevelt and the Indianola Affair," 48–69.

11. See *New York Times,* January 3, 6, 7, 1903; Jackson *Evening News,* January 5, 6, 7, 1903; *Indianola Enterprise,* January 16, 30, 1903; McMillen, *Dark Journey,* 61–62.

12. *Greenwood Commonwealth,* January 10, 17, 31, 1903; White, "Anti-Racial Agitation in Politics," 91–101; Lopez, "James K. Vardaman," 168–71; Holmes, "James K. Vardaman," 108–9, 97–115; Oshinsky, *Worse Than Slavery*, 85–106.

13. McMillen, *Dark Journey,* 62; Vardaman quote in Holmes, *White Chief,* 100.

14. *Cleveland Gazette,* February 7, 1903; Scott and Stowe, *Booker T. Washington,* 120–21; McMillen, *Dark Journey,* 184; Harlan, *Booker T. Washington: Wizard of Tuskegee,* 12.

15. See *Washington Bee*, October 12, 1901, January 11, February 1, 1902; Washington to Theodore Roosevelt, February 3, 1903, in Harlan and Smock, BTWP, 7: 28; Harlan, *Booker T. Washington: Wizard of Tuskegee,* 21, 319–20. For Roosevelt's perspective on blacks, see Scheiner, "President Theodore Roosevelt and the Negro," 169–82; Dyer, *Theodore Roosevelt and the Idea of Race,* ch.5, esp. pp. 104–5, 114–16. For alternative view, see Brands, *T. R.: The Last Romantic,* 423–24, 499–500.

16. Scheiner, "President Theodore Roosevelt and the Negro," 169–82; Dyer, *Theodore Roosevelt and the Idea of Race,* ch.5, esp. p. 109; Gatewood, *Theodore Roosevelt and the Art of Controversy,* 60, 86; see also Sherman, *Republican Party and Black America.*

17. On the Brownsville incident, see Weaver, *Brownsville Raid;* Berry and Blassingame, *Long Memory,* 310–11; Tinsley, "Roosevelt, Foraker, and the Brownsville Affray," 43–65; Thornbrough, "The Brownsville Episode and the Negro Vote," 469–93; Harlan, *Booker T. Washington: Wizard of Tuskegee,* 318.

18. *Memphis News-Scimitar,* October 28, 1907.

19. See Roosevelt to Banks, November 7, 14, December 3, 1908, Roosevelt Papers.

20. Scheiner, "President Theodore Roosevelt and the Negro," 169–82; Dyer,

Theodore Roosevelt and the Idea of Race, ch.5, esp. p. 109; Gatewood, *Theodore Roosevelt and the Art of Controversy*, 60, 86; see also Sherman, *Republican Party and Black America*.

21. Banks to W. W. Cox, November 19, 25, 1913, BTWPF.

22. See Washington to Banks, June 15, 1909, Banks to F. W. Carpenter, March 25, 1909, Banks to Washington, ca. March 25, 1909, April 5, 1909, BTWPF.

23. Hamilton, *Beacon Lights*, 210–11; Banks to Scott, May 2, 1908, August 28, 1909, BTWPF.

24. Washington to William H. Taft, June 7, 1908, in Harlan and Smock, BTWP, 9: 560–61.

25. Hamilton, *Beacon Lights*, 210–11; Banks to Scott, August 28, 1909, BTWPF.

26. Scott to Washington, June 15, 1908, in Harlan and Smock, BTWP, 9: 577.

27. Washington to Charles W. Anderson, June 19, 1908, in Harlan and Smock, BTWP, 9: 582.

28. Banks, circular, "As Ye Sow," BTWPF.

29. See Banks to E. D. Williston, January 30, 1909, Williston to Banks, February 5, 1909, BTWPF; Hamilton, *Beacon Lights*, 210.

30. Harlan, *Booker T. Washington: Wizard of Tuskegee*, 341.

31. Banks to Arthur I. Vorys, March 12, 1909, Banks to Fred W. Carpenter, March 25, 1909, Taft Papers; Scott to Washington, April 1, 1909, in Harlan and Smock, BTWP, 10: 81–82.

32. "Protest of Mississippians against Negro Census Enumerators Bears Fruit," newspaper clipping, April 12, 1909, n.p., BTWPF.

33. Washington to Banks, June 15, 1909, Banks to Fred W. Carpenter, March 25, 1909, Banks to Washington, ca. March 25, 1909, April 5, 1909, BTWPF. Banks also met with the president about December 26, 1911. See James Carroll Napier to Washington, December 26, 1911, in Harlan and Smock, BTWP, 11: 427.

34. Banks to Scott, July 22, 1909, BTWPF.

35. Casdorph, "The 1912 Republican Presidential Campaign in Mississippi," 4; *Twelfth Census, 1900*, 1: 545.

36. Banks to Scott, March 7, 1908, BTWPF.

37. Banks to Washington, August 6, 1909, Scott to Washington, June 15, 1908, BTWPF. Hitchcock served as Taft's presidential campaign manager in 1908, as chairman of the Republican National Committee from 1908 to 1909, as postmaster general from 1909 to 1913, and as presidential campaign manager for Charles Evans Hughes in 1916. See Harlan and Smock, BTWP, 9: 459.

38. Banks to Fred Carpenter, August 11, 1909; Banks to Scott, August 16, 1909, BTWPF.

39. Banks to Scott, August 28, 1909, BTWPF.

40. See Banks to Fred Moore, September 6, 1909, Banks to E. A. Fitzgerald, September 10, 1909, and Banks to C. P. J. Mooney, ca. September 10, 1909, BTWPF.

41. Banks to Scott, August 28, 1909, BTWPF.

42. Banks to James E. Landrum, January 10, 1910, BTWPF. For reply, see S. D. Chamberlin to Banks, January 15, 1910, BTWPF.

43. Banks to Washington, January 17, 1910, BTWPF.

44. Ibid.

45. Ibid.

46. Banks to Thomas Jesse Jones, February 11, 1910, BTWPF.

47. Washington to Banks, March 24, 1910, BTWPF.

48. Banks to Washington, March 25, 1910, BTWPF.

49. Edmund F. Noel was governor at the time. Banks to Washington, December 23, 1910, Washington to Banks, December 29, 1910, Banks to Scott, February 3, 1911, BTWPF. See recommendation letters from Sam C. Cook, Percy Bell, Sidney Smith, M. E. Denton, F. A. Montgomery, and J. T. Lowe, all ca. January 7, 1911, BTWPF.

50. Banks to Washington, December 23, 1910, Washington to Banks, December 29, 1910, Banks to Scott, February 3, 1911, BTWPF.

51. Scott to Banks, February 6, 1911, BTWPF.

52. Scott to Frank Cole, ca. February 6, 1911, BTWPF.

53. Banks to Washington, February 15, 1911, Washington to Banks, February 22, 1911, BTWPF.

54. Scott to Banks, April 10, December 14, 1911, BTWPF.

55. Banks to Scott, April 19, 1911, BTWPF.

56. Scott to Banks, April 24, 1911, BTWPF.

57. Ibid.

58. Banks to Charles D. Hilles, March 11, 1912, BTWPF.

59. Ibid.

60. Banks to Scott, ca. September 20, 1912, BTWPF.

61. Harlan, *Booker T. Washington: Wizard of Tuskegee*, 16–17.

62. William H. Lewis to Scott, September 24, 1912, BTWPF.

63. Phillip A. Rush to Scott, September 30, 1912, BTWPF.

64. Banks to Scott, October 5, 14, 1912, BTWPF.

65. Banks to Moton, September 28, 1918, Moton to Banks, October 5, 1918, MP.

66. Moton to Banks, October 8, 1918, MP.

67. Banks to Moton, October 15, 1918, MP.

68. Banks to Scott, January 2, 3, 1909, BTWPF.

69. Banks to Scott, February 3, 1911, Scott to Charles D. Hilles, February 3, 1911, BTWPF.

70. Banks to Hilles, February 25, 1911, BTWPF.

71. Banks to Scott, March 20, 1911, BTWPF.

72. Banks to Fred Carpenter, June 18, 1909, Thomas I. Keys to Banks, January 31, 1910, BTWPF.

73. Banks to Scott, March 9, 1911, BTWPF.

74. Keys to Banks, January 13, 1910, BTWPF.

75. Scott to Banks, ca. February 5, 1910, Banks to Scott, February 8, 1910, BTWPF.

76. Banks to Washington, February 5, 1910, BTWPF.

77. Banks to Vorys, February 8, 1910, BTWPF.

78. Washington to Hilles, February 9, 1910, BTWPF, 10: 269–70.

79. Vorys to Banks, February 12, 1910, BTWPF.

80. Washington to Banks, February 19, 1910, BTWPF.

81. Banks to Fred Moore, July 28, 1910, BTWPF.

82. Ibid.

83. McMillen, *Dark Journey*, 63.

84. Ibid.

85. Anderson to Washington, May 10, 1912, in Harlan and Smock, BTWP, 11: 535.

86. Fred Moore to Washington, May 13, 1912, in Harlan and Smock, BTWP, 11: 536–37.

87. Fred Moore to Banks, May 13, 1912, BTWPF.

88. Washington to Banks, May 20, 1912, Anderson to Washington, May 27, 1912, in Harlan and Smock, BTWP, 11: 539, 545.

89. Casdorph, "The 1912 Republican Presidential Campaign in Mississippi," 2–3. See also Kirwan, *Revolt of the Rednecks*; Sallis, "Color Line in Mississippi Politics."

90. Casdorph, "The 1912 Republican Presidential Campaign in Mississippi," 3–5; *Memphis Commercial Appeal*, March 29, 1912.

91. *Chicago Daily Tribune*, June 13, 1912.

92. Ibid.

93. Ibid.

94. *Memphis Commercial Appeal*, June 15, 1912; Casdorph, "The 1912 Republican Presidential Campaign in Mississippi," 9.

95. *Chicago Daily Tribune*, June 15, 1912.

96. Ibid.

97. Ibid.

98. Ibid.

99. Ibid.

100. "Charles Banks Again on the Mississippi Situation," ca. June 15, 1912, BTWPF.

101. Ibid.

102. *Chicago Daily Tribune*, June 19, 1912.

103. "Charles Banks Again on the Mississippi Situation," BTWPF.

104. Ibid.

105. Ibid.

106. See Taft, *Presidential Addresses and State Papers*, 63–66; Sherman, *Republican Party and Black America*, 88–89; Harlan, *Booker T. Washington: Wizard of Tuskegee*,

341–42. Sherman notes Roosevelt "read and approved Taft's inaugural address before it was delivered."

107. "Charles Banks Again on the Mississippi Situation," BTWPF.

108. Ibid.

109. Ibid.

110. Ibid.

111. Ibid.

112. Sherman, *Republican Party and Black America*, 111.

113. Washington to Banks, ca. May 18, 1912, BTWPF.

114. Dailey, "An Easy Alliance," 474–75; Sherman, *Republican Party and Black America*, 104–9; Casdorph, "The 1912 Republican Presidential Campaign in Mississippi," 1–19; Mowry, "The South and the Progressive Lily White Party," 237–47. See also Link, "Theodore Roosevelt and the South," 313–24; Link, "Correspondence Relating to the Progressive Party's 'Lily White' Policy," 480–90; Link, "The Negro as a Factor in the Campaign of 1912," 81–99; Brinkley, *American History*, 762; Conlin, *American Past*, 652–54.

115. McMillen, *Dark Journey*, 63–64. Washington's Tennessee lieutenant, James C. Napier, continued to support Taft and remain critical of Roosevelt, whom he apparently could not forgive for the Brownsville incident. See Clark, "James Carroll Napier," 251.

116. Washington to Banks, June 7, 1912, BTWPF.

117. Du Bois, "Politics,"180–81; Du Bois, "Last Word in Politics," 29; Blumenthal, "Woodrow Wilson and the Race Question," 1–21; Wolgemuth, "Woodrow Wilson and Federal Segregation," 158–73; Weiss, "The Negro and the New Freedom," 61–79.

118. See Harlan, *Booker T. Washington: Wizard of Tuskegee*, 412; Blumenthal, "Woodrow Wilson and the Race Question," 1–21; Weiss, "The Negro and the New Freedom," 61–79.

119. Banks to Washington, October 25, 1915, BTWPF.

120. Ibid.

121. Banks to Scott, January 3, 1916, MP.

122. Banks to Scott, February 19, 1916, MP.

123. Ibid.

124. Banks to Scott, February 19, 1916, MP. Also see Banks to Roosevelt, May 5, 29, November 18, 1912, April 17, 1913, January 19, 1918; Roosevelt to Banks, April 17, 1913, May 22, 1917, January 29, 1918, Roosevelt Papers.

125. Scott to Banks, February 24, 1916, MP.

126. *New York Age*, May 11, 1916; McMillen, "Perry W. Howard," 208; McMillen, *Dark Journey*, 64.

127. Sherman, *Republican Party and Black America*, 121–22; Dailey, "Emmett Jay Scott," 242.

128. McMillen, *Dark Journey*, 64; McMillen, "Perry W. Howard," 208.

129. *New York Age*, May 11, 1916; Sherman, *Republican Party and Black America*, 121–22; Dailey, "Emmett Jay Scott," 242.

130. Conlin, *American Past*, 670–71.

131. See Banks to Warren G. Harding, May 30, 1921, Harding's secretary to Banks, June 1, 1921, Harding Papers.

132. Banks to Moton, February 15, 1921, MP.

133. Ibid.

134. Moton to Banks, February 28, 1921, MP.

Chapter 8. "Wizard" of Finance: "Never Running Away from Battle"

1. Harlan, *Booker T. Washington: Wizard of Tuskegee*, 223–24; McMillen, *Dark Journey*, 189.

2. Washington probably meant Banks was the most influential Negro businessman. See Washington, *My Larger Education*, 207–8.

3. Hamilton, *Beacon Lights*, 209; Crockett, *Black Towns*, 125–26; Nichols and Crogman, *Progress of a Race*, 259; Lee, "Mound Bayou, the Negro City of Mississippi," 38–41.

4. Crockett, *Black Towns*, 126; *Chicago Daily Tribune*, June 15, 1912.

5. Banks to Washington, March 11, 1915, BTWPF. As early as 1912, Banks said his net worth was between $75,000 and $100,000. See the *Chicago Daily Tribune*, June 15, 1912.

6. Scott to Banks, February 21, 1911, BTWPF.

7. Victor H. Tulane to Banks, ca. May 20, 1910, Banks to Tulane, May 21, 1910, BTWPF.

8. Banks to Scott, March 14, 1910, BTWPF.

9. Washington, *Negro in Business*, 120.

10. Ibid., 120–21; Hamilton, *Black Towns and Profit*, 61.

11. Hamilton, *Beacon Lights*, 207; Hood, *Negro at Mound Bayou*, 22.

12. See Meier, "Booker T. Washington and the Town of Mound Bayou," 221; Harlan, *Booker T. Washington: Wizard of Tuskegee*, 224.

13. Hamilton, *Black Towns and Profit*, 61–63.

14. Crockett, *Black Towns*, 124–25; Hamilton, *Black Towns and Profit*, 61–63. On black banks in Mississippi, see Banks, "Negro Banks of Mississippi," 9–11.

15. Hood, *Negro at Mound Bayou*, 21–23; Tong, "Pioneers of Mound Bayou," 393; Lee, "Mound Bayou, the Negro City of Mississippi," 38, 41.

16. Washington to Banks, October 14, 1907, BTWPF.

17. Washington, *My Larger Education*, 208. See also Banks, "Negro Banks of Mississippi"; Schweninger, *Black Property Owners in the South*, 218.

18. Banks, circular letter, n.d., BTWPF.

19. Ibid.

20. Banks's essay quoted in Washington, *Negro in Business*, 120–21.

21. Hamilton, *Black Towns and Profit*, 62.

22. Scott to Banks, November 4, 1907, Banks to Scott, November 4, 1907, BTWPF.

23. Crockett, *Black Towns*, 125.

24. Banks to Scott, October 24, 1908, BTWPF.

25. Hamilton, *Black Towns and Profit*, 62.

26. Thomas S. Owen to Banks, December 23, 1909, BTWPF.

27. Eugene Snowden to Washington, December 22, 1910, BTWPF. See also Banks to Security Bank and Trust, January 4, 1911, BTWPF.

28. Banks to Scott, January 1, 13, 1910, Scott to Banks, June 15, 1910, BTWPF.

29. Bank of Mound Bayou Financial statement, November 9, 1910, Scott to Banks, November 26, 1910, BTWPF.

30. Washington, "A Town Owned by Negroes," 313.

31. Hamilton, *Black Towns and Profit*, 63.

32. Washington, "A Town Owned by Negroes," 313; Willey, "Mound Bayou—A Negro Municipality," 163; Hamilton, *Beacon Lights*, 209; Washington, *Negro in Business*, 122.

33. Hamilton, *Black Towns and Profit*, 61, 65; Link, *Woodrow Wilson and the Progressive Era*, 149–50.

34. Banks to A. J. Howard, January 18, 1912, Banks to Scott, January 19, 1912, BTWPF.

35. Ibid.

36. Scott to Banks, May 17, 1912, Banks to Scott, May 18, 1912, BTWPF.

37. Banks to Washington, April 11, 1913, BTWPF.

38. Washington to Banks, May 8, 1913; Banks to J. J. Turner, May 12, 1913, BTWPF.

39. Banks to Washington, September 18, 1913, Washington to Banks, October 2, 1913, Banks to Washington, December 1, 1913, BTWPF. See also William H. Carter to Washington, December 4, 1913, BTWPF.

40. Banks to J. A. Kearney, September 22, 1913, BTWPF.

41. Scott to Banks, December 31, 1913, BTWPF.

42. Scott to Banks, January 9, 1914, BTWPF.

43. Washington to Banks, January 23, 1914, BTWPF.

44. Banks to Scott, February 4, 1914, BTWPF. The bank closed down six months after Francis and McCarty departed.

45. McLemore, "James K. Vardaman," 9; Giroux, "Rise of Theodore G. Bilbo," 198; McMillen, *Dark Journey*, 181.

46. Banks to Washington, October 21, 1914, Banks to Scott, January 27, 1914, BTWPF; McMillen, *Dark Journey*, 181; Boyer et al., *Enduring Vision*, 644–45.

47. Banks to Fred Moore, July 14, 1915, BTWPF.

48. Banks to Washington, March 11, 1915, BTWPF.

49. Hamilton, *Black Towns and Profit*, 79–80; Rowland, *History of Mississippi*, 338; Isaiah T. Montgomery to Washington, June 5, 1914, BTWPF.

50. Hamilton, *Black Towns and Profit*, 80.

51. Isaiah Montgomery to Washington, June 5, 1914, in Harlan and Smock, BTWP, 13: 48–49.

52. Banks to Depositors of the Bank of Mound Bayou, August 22, 1914, Banks to Washington, August 23, 1914, BTWPF.

53. Banks to Washington, February 20, 1914, BTWPF; Crockett, *Black Towns*, 159.

54. Banks to Scott, April 19, 1914, BTWPF.

55. Banks to Scott, May 19, 1914, BTWPF; Montgomery to Washington, June 5, 1914, in Harlan and Smock, BTWP, 13: 48–49.

56. Banks to Washington, June 5, 1914, BTWPF.

57. Montgomery to Washington, June 5, 1914, in Harlan and Smock, BTWPF 13: 48–49.

58. Banks to Washington, June 5, 1914, BTWPF.

59. Banks to Scott, June 13, 1914, Banks to Washington, June 16, 1914, in Harlan and Smock, BTWP, 13: 63, 65.

60. Banks to Washington, March 11, 1915, BTWPF.

61. Link, *Woodrow Wilson and the Progressive Era*, 149–50.

62. Banks to Washington, August 22, 1914, Banks to Depositors of the Bank of Mound Bayou, August 22, 1914, BTWPF.

63. *Cleveland [Mississippi] Enterprise*, September 10, 1914; Crockett, *Black Towns*, 160–61.

64. *Cleveland [Mississippi] Enterprise*, September 10, 1914; Banks to Scott, March 14, 1910, BTWPF; Banks to Scott, September 8, 1914, in Harlan and Smock, BTWP, 13: 128–29; *Jackson Daily News*, December 16, 18, 1911, February 21, 1912.

65. Philip J. Allston to Scott, September 22, 1914, BTWPF; Crockett, *Black Towns*, 160–61.

66. Banks to Washington, August 23, 1914, BTWPF; Banks to Scott, September 8, 1914, in Harlan and Smock, BTWP, 13: 128–29.

67. Mary Turner to Washington, January 28, 1914, BTWPF.

68. Banks to Washington, March 11, 1915, BTWPF.

69. Banks to Washington, July 31, 1907, BTWPF.

70. See Mary Turner to Perry Howard, September 22, 1910, BTWPF; Banks to Washington, April 14, 1915, in Harlan and Smock, BTWP, 13: 271.

71. Banks to Washington, March 11, 1915, BTWPF.

72. Ibid.

73. Banks to Washington, April 14, 1915, in Harlan and Smock, BTWP, 13: 271.

74. Ibid.

75. Banks to Washington, August 23, 1914, BTWPF.

76. Washington to Banks, March 8, 1915; Banks to Washington, September 16, 1915, BTWPF.

77. Banks to Washington, October 21, 1914, BTWPF; Hamilton, *Black Towns and Profit*, 80.

78. Washington to Banks, January 16, 1915, BTWPF.

79. Banks to Washington, April 14, 1915, in Harlan and Smock, BTWP, 13: 271–72.

80. Meier, "Washington and Mound Bayou," 221.

81. Banks to Washington, March 11, 1915, BTWPF.

82. Washington to Banks, October 7, 1915, Banks to Washington, October 22, 1915, BTWPF. It seems Cox's support for the bank influenced the state banking authorities to allow it to reopen. Cox had been a longtime investor in the Mound Bayou Bank. See James, James, and James, *Mississippi Black Bankers*, 54.

83. *New York Age*, March 16, 1916.

84. Ibid.

85. Banks to Washington, September 30, 1915, BTWPF.

86. Scott to Banks, October 30, 1915, BTWPF.

87. *New York Age*, March 16, 1916.

88. Ibid.

89. Ibid.

90. Ibid.

91. Scott to Banks, ca. January 1916, MP.

92. Ibid.; Scott to Banks, February 14, 1916, MP.

93. Dailey, "Emmett Jay Scott," 226. It seems Banks suggested this as a remedy to Scott first. See Scott to Banks, December 24, 1916, Banks to Scott, April 17, 1916, MP.

94. Scott to Banks, September 13, 1916, MP.

95. Scott to Banks, December 24, 1916, MP.

96. Dailey, "Emmett Jay Scott," 227–28.

97. See "Notes on Racial Progress," compiled by the NNBL, n.d., Tuskegee Institute News Clipping Files; Banks to W. W. Cox, October 15, 1915, BTWPF.

98. Banks to Washington, September 30, 1915, BTWPF.

99. McMillen, *Dark Journey*, 181, 380. See also Banks to Fonda, November 3, 1921, MP. On black banks nationwide, see Harris, *Negro as Capitalist*. See also Frazier, *Black Bourgeoisie*, 38–42; James, James, and James, *Mississippi Black Bankers*, 46–56.

Chapter 9. Mound Bayou Cotton Oil Mill: "The Largest and Most Serious Undertaking . . . in the History of Our Race"

1. Banks to Robert Park, September 22, 1911, BTWPF.

2. Hamilton, *Black Towns and Profit*, 71; Banks to Washington, July 31, 1907, BTWPF; Montgomery, "Negro in Business," 734.

3. "Prospectus of the Cotton Seed Oil Mill—To be located at—Mound Bayou —Fostered by—Mississippi Negro Business League," Johnson Papers. Banks to [?], May 29, 1908, BTWPF.

4. Banks to Scott, ca.1908, BTWPF.

5. Banks to Scott, November 23, 1908.

6. Banks, cover letter for stock certificates, 1908, BTWPF; Dailey, "Emmett Jay Scott," 226.

7. Banks to Scott, February 14, 1910, Scott to Banks, February 18, 1910, BTWPF; "Prospectus of the Cotton Seed Oil Mill," Johnson Papers.

8. Banks to Washington, March 14, 1910, BTWPF.

9. Washington to Banks, March 23, 1910, BTWPF.

10. Banks to George Mays, April 20, 1910, BTWPF.

11. Scott to Banks, February 10, 1911, BTWPF.

12. Banks to Scott, August 26, 1910, Scott to Banks, August 29, 1910, BTWPF.

13. Banks to Scott, December 26, 1911, BTWPF.

14. Washington to Banks, February 3, 1912, BTWPF.

15. Banks to Scott, ca. March 1, 1912, BTWPF.

16. Banks to Washington, March 18, 1912, BTWPF.

17. Washington to Banks, March 28, 1912, BTWPF.

18. Scott to Banks, ca. March 28, 1912, BTWPF.

19. Banks to Washington, April 23, 1912, Washington to Banks, March 28, 1912, BTWPF.

20. Moton, "Mound Bayou Oil Mill," 66–67.

21. Washington, address, November 25, 1912, in Harlan and Smock, BTWP, 12: 56.

22. Ibid., 56–57.

23. Ibid.

24. *Memphis Commercial Appeal*, November 27, 1912.

25. Hamilton, *Black Towns and Profit*, 76.

26. Washington, address, November 25, 1912, in Harlan and Smock, BTWP, 12: 55; Walker, *History of Black Business in America*, 204–5. See also *New York Evening Post*, November 29, 1912; *New York Tribune*, November 30, 1912.

27. Hamilton, *Black Towns and Profit*, 76.

28. *Memphis Commercial Appeal*, November 27, 1912.

29. *New York Age*, April 25, 1912.

30. Williamson, "Mound Bayou History," 15.

31. Banks to Washington, January 6, 1913, BTWPF.

32. Banks to Scott, April 3, 1913, BTWPF.

33. Julius Rosenwald to Banks, February 25, 1913, BTWPF; Hamilton, *Black Towns and Profit*, 77.

34. Washington to Banks, ca. May 1912, BTWPF.

35. Thomas Owen to William Graves, October 4, 1915, BTWPF; Hamilton, *Black Towns and Profit*, 77; Williamson, "Mound Bayou History," 15.

36. Owen to Graves, October 4, 1915, BTWPF.

37. Washington to Banks, September 5, 1913, BTWPF.

38. Banks to Washington, September 10, 1913, BTWPF.

39. Banks to Washington, October 9, 1913, BTWPF.

40. *New York Age*, October 22, 1913.

41. Richardson, *Tuskegee Student*, October 4, 1913, quoted in Harlan, *Booker T. Washington: Wizard of Tuskegee*, 223.

42. Banks to Scott, November 25, 1913, BTWPF.

43. Graves to Washington, February 14, 1914, BTWPF.

44. Washington to Banks, February 17, 1914, BTWPF.

45. Banks to Charles F. Wermuth, February 12, 1914, Scott to Banks, February 5, 1914, BTWPF.

46. Banks to Graves, April 4, 1914, BTWPF.

47. After this matter became litigated, records show Harvey planned to ruin the Mound Bayou mill for his personal gain. See Banks to Graves, April 3, 1916, BTWPF.

48. Banks to Scott, April 20, 1914, BTWPF.

49. Washington to Banks, June 11, 1914, BTWPF.

50. Banks to Graves, June 15, 1914, BTWPF.

51. Banks to Washington, June 16, 1914, BTWPF.

52. Washington to Banks, October 13, 1914, BTWPF.

53. Washington to Banks, October 26, 1914.

54. Banks to Graves, April 3, 1916, BTWPF.

55. Ibid.

56. Ibid.

57. Hamilton, *Black Towns and Profit*, 78; Meier, "Washington and Mound Bayou," 220; Dailey, "Emmett Jay Scott," 224; Harlan, *Booker T. Washington: Wizard of Tuskegee*, 223–24; Banks to Scott, October 25, 1913, Owen to Graves, October 4, 1915, BTWPF.

58. Banks to Washington, November 30, 1914, February 11, 1915, Owen to Graves, October 4, 1915, BTWPF.

59. Washington to Banks, February 19, 1915, BTWPF.

60. Washington to Banks, ca. April 22, 1915.

61. Scott to Banks, November 13, 1915, BTWPF.

62. Banks to Washington, May 13, 1915, BTWPF.

63. Banks to Washington, September 30, 1915.

64. Ibid.

65. A. L. Aury to Banks, February 13, 1915, J. R. Jones to Banks, February 15, 1915, BTWPF; Walker, *History of Black Business in America*, 205.

66. Banks to Washington, February 15, 1915, BTWPF.

67. Ibid.

68. Scott to Banks, November 13, 1915, in Harlan and Smock, BTWP, 13: 436–37.

69. Banks to Graves, February 14, 1916, BTWPF.

70. Scott to Banks, February 17, 1916, BTWPF.

71. Banks to Graves, April 3, 1916, BTWPF.

72. Scott to Banks, April 8, 1916, BTWPF.

73. Harlan, *Booker T. Washington: Wizard of Tuskegee*, 223–24.

74. Washington to Banks, ca. April 22, 1915, Scott to Banks, November 13, 1915, BTWPF.

75. McMillen, *Dark Journey*, 189.

76. Jackson, "Mound Bayou," 80.

77. Crowe interview. Williamson says the mill closed in the mid-twenties and was torn down ten years later. Crowe, born in Mound Bayou in 1933, however, says he can remember his mother talking about the mill operating when he was growing up in Mound Bayou. See Williamson, "Mound Bayou History," 19.

78. Banks to Moton, July 12, 1919, MP.

79. *Advance-Dispatch*, October 17, 1919, Mound Bayou.

80. *New York Age*, February 28, 1920; *Advance-Dispatch*, October 17, 1919, Mound Bayou.

81. Banks to Moton, March 17, 1919, MP.

82. Banks to Moton, March 17, 1919, Banks and Montgomery to Moton, November 25, 1921, MP.

83. Banks to Moton, March 17, April 26, 1919, Albon Holsey to Banks, March 25, 1919, Moton to Banks, April 23, 1919, MP.

84. *New York Age*, February 28, 1920. See also Moton to Banks, January 26, 1921, MP.

85. *New York Age*, December 3, 1921; Banks and Montgomery to Moton, November 25, 1921, MP.

86. Banks and Montgomery to Moton, February 28, 1920, December 3, 1921; Nichols and Crogman, *Progress of a Race*, 259; To whom it may concern [?], to Tuskegee, ca. 1921, MP.

87. Banks to Washington, March 11, 1915, BTWPF.

88. Ibid.

89. Washington, *My Larger Education*, 207–8.

90. Moton to Banks, October 29, 1919, MP.

91. Banks, "State Should Study the Negro Exodus," *Jackson Daily News*, June 12, 1917; Ingham and Feldman, *African-American Business Leaders*, 49–50; Cobb, *The Most Southern Place on Earth*, 112–13; McMillan, *Dark Journey*, 189.

Chapter 10. After Booker T. Washington: "A Tempest in the Teapot"

1. Banks to Scott, November 14, 1915, BTWPF.

2. *New York Age*, November 25, 1915. There were also "active pallbearers" at the memorial.

3. On Scott's service to Washington and Tuskegee, see Lee, "Making Good," 8–9.

4. *New York Age*, November 18, 1915.

5. Ibid., December 9, 1915.

6. Ibid., December 16, 1915.

7. Ibid., December 23, 1915.

8. Imes, "To Tuskegee," 80.

9. Matthews, "After Booker T. Washington," 45–46.

10. Banks to Scott, January 28, 1916, BTWPF.

11. Banks to Moton, May 27, 1916, MP.

12. Moton to Banks, May 31, 1916, MP.

13. *New York Age*, October 4, 1917; William E. Wilcox to Newton Baker, October 15, 1917, MP.

14. Franklin, *From Slavery to Freedom*, 327–28.

15. William G. Wilcox to Scott, October 15, 1917, Wilcox to Newton Baker, October 15, 1917, Moton to Banks, June 16, 1919, MP.

16. Banks to Moton, April 8, 1918, Moton to Banks, April 13, 1918, MP; *New York Age*, April 20, 1918. Banks even supported Moton when Moton went to France and tried to persuade black soldiers that they should not expect the same sort of privileges and treatment from whites back home that they received overseas. Although Moton was criticized, Banks praised him and agreed with him: "I fully agree with you that you said nothing but what any man with common sense and sound mind would have said." See Banks to Moton, February 28, 1919, Moton to Banks, March 6, 1919, Scott to Moton, July 10, 1919, MP.

17. Souvenir Program of the Fiftieth Anniversary of Mound Bayou, Mound Bayou Files, MDAH.

18. Washington to Montgomery, January 25, 1915, in Harlan and Smock, BTWP, 13: 233–34.

19. Ibid.

20. Booze to Scott, June 29, 1916, MP.

21. Scott to Richard W. Thompson, December 30, 1915, in Harlan and Smock, BTWP, 13: 488.

22. Booze to Scott, June 29, 1916, MP.

23. Ibid.

24. Banks to Scott, September 28, 1916, MP.

25. Booze to Scott, September 19, 1916, MP.

26. Ibid. See also Booze to Moton, August 7, 1917, MP.

27. Booze to Scott, September 19, 1916, MP.

28. Ibid.

29. Ibid.

30. Banks to Scott, October 9, 1916, Scott to Banks, October 18, 1916, MP.

31. Banks to Scott, October 27, 1916, MP.

32. Ibid.

33. Ibid.

34. *State of Mississippi v. Chas. Banks*, case nos. 623, May 2, 1902 and 681, November 26, 1902, Second District, Coahoma County, Circuit Court, MP.

35. See Moton to Banks, January 19, 1917, MP.

36. Moton to Banks, March 26, 1917, MP.

37. Banks to Moton, March 30, 1917, Moton to Banks, April 2, 1917, MP.

38. Montgomery to Moton, April 3, 1917, MP.

39. Booze to Moton, April 23, 1917, MP.

40. Banks to Fred Moore, April 23, 1917, Booze to Moton, August 7, 1917, MP.

41. Booze to F. M. Coffin, May 2, 1917, MP.

42. Ibid.

43. Moton to Booze, June 6, 1917, MP.

44. Booze to Moton, June 8, 1917, MP.

45. Banks to Scott, December 19, 1916, January 1, 1917, Moton to Banks, December 21, 1916, Scott to Banks, December 21, 1916, January 5, 1917, MP.

46. Dailey, "Emmett Jay Scott," 228.

47. *Charles Banks v. T. O. Banks,* case no. 1341, July 13, 1917, Chancery Court, Bolivar County.

48. Banks to Moton, July 10, 1917, MP.

49. Banks to Scott, July 20, 1918, MP.

50. Booze to Moton, June 21, 1918, MP.

51. Ibid.

52. Moton to Booze, July 3, 1918, MP.

53. Booze to Moton, July 15, 1918, MP.

54. Ibid.

55. Moton to Booze, July 25, 1918, MP. See also handwritten note on Booze to Moton, July 15, 1918, MP.

56. Booze to Moton, August 2, 1918, MP.

57. Moton to Booze, ca. July 16, 1918, MP.

58. Banks to Scott, July 20, 1918, MP.

59. Hood, *Negro at Mound Bayou,* 86.

60. Banks, "Montgomery-Booze Faction Loses in Mound Bayou Municipal Suit," press release, November 19, 1917, MP; Hamilton, *Black Towns and Profit,* 84; Crockett, *Black Towns,* 84; *New York Age,* March 15, 17, 1917; *Indianapolis Freeman,* June 29, 1918; Williamson, "Mound Bayou, Mississippi." See also Williamson, "Mound Bayou History," 3–22.

61. Banks to Moton, March 31, 1917, MP.

62. Banks to Fred Moore, April 23, 1917, MP; Crockett, *Black Towns,* 84; *Indianapolis Freeman,* June 29, 1918. Banks hired lawyers from Owen and Clark of Cleveland, Miss., Wilkinson and Thompson of Shelby, Miss., and Perry Howard and Benjamin Green. Only the last two were black.

63. Banks, "Montgomery-Booze Faction Loses in Mound Bayou Municipal Suit," MP; *New York Age,* March 15, 17, 1917.

64. *Booze v. Creswell,* Superior Court (March 1918) 795–809, courtesy of Milburn Crowe; *New York Age,* June 15, 1918; *Indianapolis Freeman,* June 29, 1918.

65. *New York Age,* December 21, 1918; *Indianapolis Freeman,* June 29, 1918.

66. Montgomery to Banks, June 13, 1919, MP. Montgomery copied Moton on this letter.

67. Montgomery to Banks, June 13, 1919, MP.

68. Ibid.

69. Holtzclaw to Moton, December 23, 1921, MP. See also Montgomery to R.

S. Grossley, June 12, 1922, Grossley to Montgomery, June 17, 1922, Grossley to Holtzclaw, June 17, 1922, Holtzclaw to Moton, June 22, 1917, MP.

70. Holtzclaw to Moton, December 23, 1921, MP. See also Montgomery to Grossley, June 12, 1922, Grossley to Montgomery, June 17, 1922, Grossley to Holtzclaw, June 17, 1922, Holtzclaw to Moton, June 22, 1917, MP.

71. Banks to Moton, March 4, 1921, MP.

72. *New York Age*, October 27, 1923.

73. *Chicago Defender*, February 26, 1921.

74. Banks to Moton, March 4, 1921, MP.

75. *Chicago Defender*, February 26, 1921.

76. Ibid. On William Beckett, see Wright, *Bishops of the African Methodist Episcopal Church*, 92–93.

77. Banks to Moton, March 4, 1921, MP.

78. *Chicago Defender*, February 26, 1921.

79. *New York Age*, March 12, 1921; Banks to Moton, March 4, 1921, MP.

Chapter 11. Conclusion: "The Most Public-Spirited Citizen in the History of Mississippi"

1. Williamson, "Mound Bayou History," 18–19.

2. Mound Bayou Founder's Day Program, July 12, 1919, MP; Williamson, "Mound Bayou History," 18–19.

3. *New York Age*, November 25, 1922, October 27, 1923.

4. Williamson, "Mound Bayou History," 18–19.

5. *New York Age*, May 26, 1923.

6. *New York Age*, November 25, 1922.

7. Banks to Holsey, August 11, 1920, Holsey Papers; Charles Banks, Death Certificate, October 18, 1923, Tennessee Bureau of Vital Statistics.

8. *New York Age*, October 27, 1923.

9. *Jackson Daily News*, October 22, 1923.

10. Ibid.

11. *Chicago Defender*, October 27, 1923.

12. Jackson, "Mound Bayou," 88.

13. Sewell, *Mississippi Black History Makers*, 14; Hermann, *Pursuit of a Dream*, 242.

14. Williamson, "Mound Bayou History," 20. Ben Green remained mayor of Mound Bayou until he died in 1960.

15. Douglass, "History of E. P. Booze," Montgomery Family Papers.

16. Ibid.

17. Smith, Woodley, and Crowe interviews. Smith was born in Mound Bayou in 1922 and personally remembers Booze. Woodley, in her eighties, was also born in Mound Bayou and knew Booze and Montgomery personally. Memo from Isaiah Montgomery's heirs, "A Few of the Things E. P. Booze Has Done," n.d., provided by Milburn Crowe, copy in author's possession; Redding, *Lonesome Road*, 107. See

also "Police Kill Sister of Mississippi National Committeewoman," October 11, 1939, "Daughter of Mound Bayou Founder Named in Land," February 19, 1938, "Unknown Assailants Fire from Ambush—Death Car Riddled with 26 Bullets," November 10, 1939, "Quiz Bookkeeper as Police Probe Ambush Murder of E.P. Booze," November 15, 1939, in *The Claude A. Barnett Papers, The Associated Negro Press.*

18. See "Police Kill Sister of Mississippi National Committeewoman," October 11, 1939; "Daughter of Mound Bayou Founder Named in Land," February 19, 1938; "Unknown Assailants Fire From Ambush—Death Car Riddled with 26 Bullets," November 10, 1939; "Quiz Bookkeeper As Police Probe Ambush Murder of E.P. Booze," November 15, 1939, in *Claude Barnett Papers.*

19. Ibid.

20. Ibid. Smith, Woodley, and Crow interviews.

21. All in Ibid.

22. Ibid.

23. Ibid.

24. Smith, Woodley, and Crowe interviews; McMillen, *Dark Journey,* 21; Williamson, "Mound Bayou History," 20; Redding, *Lonesome Road,* 107.

25. Some residents seemed to believe Montgomery may have been murdered by Benjamin A. Green. Green supposedly was questioned about Montgomery's death, but after an investigation, he was not charged. Smith and Crowe interviews.

26. "Quiz Bookkeeper as Police Probe Ambush Murder of E. P. Booze," November 15, 1939, in *Claude Barnett Papers.*

27. Banks to Moton, July 10, 1917, MP.

28. Mollison, "Negro Lawyers in Mississippi," 52–59.

29. Sowell, *Ethnic America,* 274, 286.

30. McMillen, *Dark Journey,* 181; Link, *Woodrow Wilson and the Progressive Era,* 149–50, 169–72; Boyer et al., *Enduring Vision,* 644–45.

31. Matthews, "After Booker T. Washington," 45–50.

32. Hamilton, *Black Towns and Profit,* 84; Crockett, *Black Towns,* 84.

33. Hamilton, *Black Towns and Profit,* 84; Crockett, *Black Towns,* 84.

34. Taylor, "Mound Bayou—Past and Present," 105–6, 109–11.

35. See Marks, *Farewell—We're Good and Gone*; Trotter, *The Great Migration in Historical Perspective.*

36. Meier, "Booker T. Washington and the Town of Mound Bayou," 222.

37. Harlan, *Booker T. Washington: Wizard of Tuskegee,* 225.

38. Application for branch charter, Mound Bayou, March 9, 1919, NAACP Papers.

39. Scott to Banks, October 30, 1915, BTWPF.

Bibliography

Primary Sources

Government

Congressional Record. 57th Cong. 2d sess., 1903, vol. 36, pt. 2.

Tennessee Bureau of Vital Statistics. Death certificate, Charles Banks. Nashville, October 18, 1923.

U.S. Bureau of the Census, Washington, D.C. *Ninth Census of the United States, 1870: Population.*

———. *Tenth Census of the United States, 1880: Population.*

———. *Twelfth Census of the United States, 1900: Population.*

Works Progress Administration. *Mississippi: A Guide to the Magnolia State.* New York: Viking Press, 1943.

Manuscripts, Papers, and Collections

Douglass, Joseph H. "A History of E. P. Booze." Manuscript. Benjamin T. Montgomery Family Papers, n.p.

Harding, Warren G. Papers. Manuscript Division, Library of Congress, Washington, D.C.

Holsey, Albon. Papers. Tuskegee University Archives, Tuskegee, Ala.

Illinois Central Railroad. Papers. Newberry Library, Chicago.

Johnson, William. Papers. Special Collections. Hill Memorial Library, Louisiana State University, Baton Rouge.

Jones, Maxine, et al. "A Documented History of the Incident which Occurred at Rosewood, Florida, in January 1923." Submitted to the Florida Board of Regents, December 22, 1993.

Montgomery, Benjamin Thornton. Family Papers. Manuscript Division, Library of Congress, Washington, D.C.

Moton, Robert Russa. Papers. Tuskegee University Archives, Tuskegee, Ala.

Mound Bayou Collection, Mississippi Department of Archives and History, Mound Bayou. July 1937.

National Association for the Advancement of Colored People. Papers. Microfilm Collection. Ned R. McWherter Library, University of Memphis.

National Negro Business League. Papers. Microfilm Collection. Ned R. McWherter Library, University of Memphis.

Ousley, Benjamin F. "History of Mound Bayou Normal Institute." Manuscript. N.p., 1912.

Roosevelt, Theodore. Papers. Manuscript Division, Library of Congress, Washington, D.C.

Taft, William Howard. Papers. Manuscript Division, Library of Congress, Washington, D.C.

Tuskegee Institute News Clipping Files. Tuskegee University Archive, Tuskegee, Ala.

Washington, Booker T. Papers. Microfilm Collection. Ned R. McWherter Library, University of Memphis.

Published Works

Aery, William Anthony. "Dr. R. R. Moton Makes Good-Will Tour." Hampton Institute Press Service, ca. November 1921.

Aptheker, Herbert. *A Documentary History of the Negro People in the United States.* Vol. 2. New York: Carol Publishing Group, 1992.

Asante, Molefi K., and Abu S. Abarry, eds. *African Intellectual Heritage: A Book of Sources.* Philadelphia: Temple University Press, 1996.

Baker, Ray S. *Following the Color Line: An Account of Negro Citizenship in the American Democracy.* New York: Doubleday, Page, 1908.

Banks, Charles. "As Ye Sow, So Shall Ye Reap." Circular, n.d., BTWPF.

———. "Negro Banks of Mississippi." Pamphlet. Committee of Twelve for the Advancement of the Interests of the Negro Race. Philadelphia: Biddle Press, 1909.

———. "The Negro Question." *The Colored American Magazine*, February 1907.

———. "Negro Town and Colony, Mound Bayou, Bolivar Co., Miss., Opportunities Open to Farmers and Settlers." Pamphlet. Mound Bayou, Miss.: Demonstrator Print, n.d.

The Claude A. Barnett Papers: The Associated Negro Press, 1918–1967. Microfilm. Frederick, Md.: University Publications of America, 1986.

Clay, N. R. "40th Anniversary of Rust University," *Voice of the Negro*, July 1906.

Douglass, Frederick. *Life and Times of Frederick Douglass.* Reprint, New York: Collier Books, 1962.

———. *Narrative of the Life of Frederick Douglass, an American Slave.* Boston: The Anti-Slavery Office, 1845. Reprint, New York: Signet, 1968.

Du Bois, W. E. B. *Black Reconstruction in America, 1860–1880.* Introduction by David Levering. New York: Harcourt, Brace, 1935. Reprint, New York: Atheneum, 1992.

———. "The Hampton Idea." In *The Education of Black People: Ten Critiques, 1906–1960.* Ed. by Herbert Aptheker. New York: Monthly Review Press, 1973.

———. "The Last Word in Politics." *Crisis,* November 1912.

———. "Politics." *Crisis,* August 1912.

———. *The Souls of Black Folk.* 1903. Reprint, New York: Signet, 1969.

———. "The Talented Tenth: Memorial Address." In *W. E. B. Du Bois: A Reader.* Ed. by David L. Lewis. New York: Henry Holt, 1993.

Foner, Philip S., and Ronald L. Lewis, eds. *Black Workers: A Documentary History from Colonial Times to the Present.* Philadelphia: Temple University Press, 1989.

Ginzburg, Ralph, ed. *100 Years of Lynchings.* Baltimore: Black Classic Press, 1988.

Hamilton, G. P. *Beacon Lights of the Race.* Memphis: E. H. Clark, 1911.

Harlan, Louis R., and Raymond W. Smock, eds. *Booker T. Washington Papers.* 14 vols. Urbana: University of Illinois Press, 1972–89.

Holtzclaw, William H. *The Black Man's Burden.* New York: Neale Publishing, 1915.

Hood, Aurelius P. *The Negro at Mound Bayou.* Nashville: African Methodist Episcopal Sunday School Union, 1909.

Johnson, William. *William Johnson's Natchez: The Ante-Bellum Diary of a Free Negro.* Ed. by William R. Hogan and Edwin A. Davis. Baton Rouge: Louisiana State University Press, 1993.

Kealing, Hightower T. "Booker T. Washington's Tour through Mississippi, a New Form of University Extension." *A.M.E. Church Review,* October 1908.

Lee, G. A. "Mound Bayou, the Negro City of Mississippi," *Voice of the Negro,* December 1905.

Lerner, Gerda. *Black Women in White America: A Documentary History.* New York: Vintage Books, 1973.

Lewis, David L., ed. *W. E. B. Du Bois: A Reader.* New York: Henry Holt, 1993.

"Making Good: From Obscurity to International Fame." *Southwestern Christian Advocate,* July 12, 1917.

Montgomery, Isaiah T. "The Negro in Business," *Outlook* 69 (November 16, 1901).

Morison, Elting, et al., eds. *Letters of Theodore Roosevelt.* 8 vols. Cambridge, Mass.: Harvard University Press, 1951–54.

Moton, Robert Russa. "Mound Bayou Oil Mill." *Southern Workman,* February 1913.

———. "National Negro Business League at Louisville." *Tuskegee Student,* September 11, 1909.

———. "The Significance of Mr. Washington's Lecture Trip in Mississippi." *Southern Workman,* December 1908.

Newton, Elsie E. "The Country of the Yazoo Delta." *Southern Workman,* February 1907.

Ousley, Benjamin F. "A Town of Colored People in Mississippi." Pamphlet. New York: American Missionary Association, 1904.

Richardson, Clement, ed. *The National Cyclopedia of the Colored Race.* Montgomery: National Publishing, 1919.

Souvenir Program of the Fiftieth Anniversary of Mound Bayou, Mississippi. Mound Bayou Files. Mound Bayou, Miss.: MDAH, July 1937.

Taft, William Howard. *Presidential Addresses and State Papers of William Howard Taft, from March 4, 1909, to March 4, 1910.* New York: Doubleday, Page, 1910.

Tong, Hiram. "The Pioneers of Mound Bayou." *Century Illustrated Monthly Magazine,* January 1910.

Washington, Booker T. "Charles Banks." *American Magazine,* March 1911.

———. "A Cheerful Journey through Mississippi." *World's Work,* February 1909. Reprint, BTWP, vol. 10: 60–68.

———. "Industrial Education Is the Solution." In *Black Workers: A Documentary History from Colonial Times to the Present.* Ed. by Philip S. Foner and Ronald L. Lewis. Philadelphia: Temple University Press, 1989.

———. *My Larger Education: Being Chapters from My Experience.* Garden City, N.Y.: Doubleday, Page, 1911.

———. "The Negro in Business." *Gunton's Magazine,* March 1901.

———. *The Negro in Business.* Boston and Chicago: Hertel, Jenkins, 1907. Reprint, New York: AMS Press, 1971.

———. "The Negro Life in Slavery." *Outlook,* September 11, 1909.

———. "A Town Owned by Negroes." *World's Work,* July 1907.

———. *Up from Slavery.* New York: Doubleday, Page, 1901. Reprint, New York: Penguin, 1986.

Willey, Day Allen. "Mound Bayou—A Negro Municipality." *Alexander's Magazine,* July 15, 1907.

Williams, Fannie B. "The Woman's Part in a Man's Business." *Voice of the Negro,* November 1904.

"Wonderful Mound Bayou." *Colored American Magazine,* June 1907.

Woodard, D. W. "Negro Progress in A Mississippi Town." Pamphlet. Committee of Twelve for the Advancement of the Interests of the Negro Race. Philadelphia: Biddle Press, 1909.

Woodson, Carter G. *The Education of the Negro.* Washington, D.C.: Associated Publishers, 1919. Reprint, New York: A&B Publishers, 1999.

———. *The History of the Negro Church.* 1921. Reprint, Washington, D.C.: Associated Publishers, 1992.

———. *The Mis-Education of the Negro.* Washington, D.C.: Associated Publishers, 1933. Reprint, Trenton: Africa World Press, 1990.

Interviews

Crowe, Milburn J. Telephone interviews by author, June 22, 1996, October 25, 1999.

Dailey, Maceo Crenshaw. Telephone interviews by author, January 17, February 4, 1997.

Hamilton, Kenneth Marvin. Telephone interview by author, January 17, 1997.

Hemmingway, Theodore. Interview by author, Tallahassee, January 10, 1997.
Smith, Kemper. Interview by author, Mound Bayou, Miss., October 22, 1999.
Woodley, Willie T. Interview by author, Mound Bayou, Miss., October 22, 1999.

Newspapers

Advanced-Dispatch, 1919.
Advance Matter.
Atlanta Constitution, 1903.
Birmingham Age-Herald, 1899.
Birmingham Voice of the People, 1916.
Chicago Broad Ax, 1912.
Chicago Daily Tribune, 1912.
Chicago Defender, 1912, 1921, 1923.
Cleveland Enterprise, 1914.
Cleveland Gazette, 1902, 1903.
Greenwood Commonwealth, 1903.
Houston Post, 1900.
Indianapolis Freeman, 1908.
Indianola Enterprise, 1903.
Jackson Daily Clarion-Ledger, 1921.
Jackson Daily News, 1917.
Jackson Evening News, 1903, 1908.
Memphis Commercial Appeal, 1908, 1912, 1913.
Memphis News-Scimitar, 1907, 1908.
New Orleans Daily Picayune, 1908.
New York Age, 1909, 1912, 1915–18, 1920–21, 1923.
New York Evening Post, 1912.
New York Times, 1903.
New York Tribune, 1912.
Vicksburg Herald, 1909.
Washington Bee, 1901, 1902.
Washington Evening Star, 1903.

Secondary Sources

Unpublished Works

Burrows, John H. "The Necessity of Myth: A History of the National Negro Business League, 1900–1945." Ph.D. dissertation, Auburn University, 1977.
Dailey, Maceo C. "Emmett Jay Scott: The Career of a Secondary Black Leader." Ph.D. dissertation, Howard University, 1983.
"Darktown—Mound Bayou." Prominent Persons File. Mound Bayou Collection, Mississippi Department of Archives and History. June 1937.

Jackson Jr., David H. "Charles Banks: A Black Leader in Mississippi, 1873–1915." Ph.D. dissertation, University of Memphis, 1997.

———. "Gone but Not Forgotten: A Look at the Riveting Career of Charles Banks, 1903–1915." Research paper, University of Memphis, November 18, 1993.

Jackson, Maurice. "Mound Bayou: A Study in Social Development." Master's thesis, University of Alabama, 1937.

Matthews, Carl S. "After Booker T. Washington: The Search for a New Negro Leadership, 1915–1925." Ph.D. dissertation, University of Virginia, 1971.

Porter, Michael L. "Black Atlanta: An Interdisciplinary Study of Blacks on the East Side of Atlanta, 1890–1930." Ph.D. dissertation, Emory University, 1974.

Sallis, William C. "The Color Line in Mississippi Politics, 1865–1915." Ph.D. dissertation, University of Kentucky, 1967.

Satcher, Buford. "Blacks in Mississippi Politics, 1865–1890." Ph.D dissertation, Oklahoma State University, 1976.

Silver, David M. "In the Eye of the Storm: Isaiah T. Montgomery and the Plight of Black Mississippians, 1847–1924." Senior paper, Amherst College, 1993.

Williamson, Stephen. "Mound Bayou, Mississippi: The Growth of an Idea, 1865–1924," Senior paper, Brown University, 1971.

Published Works

Adams, Russell L. *Great Negroes, Past and Present.* Chicago: Afro-Am Publishing, 1984.

Akbar, Na'im. *Chains and Images of Psychological Slavery.* Jersey City, N.J.: New Mind Productions, 1991.

Anderson, Eric, and Alfred A. Moss, Jr. *Dangerous Donations: Northern Philanthropy and Southern Black Education, 1902–1930.* Foreword by Louis R. Harlan. Columbia: University of Missouri Press, 1999.

Anderson, James D. *The Education of Blacks in the South, 1860–1935.* Chapel Hill: University of North Carolina Press, 1988.

Aptheker, Herbert. *Afro-American History: The Modern Era.* New York: Citadel Press, 1971.

Asante, Molefi K. *African American History: A Journey of Liberation.* Maywood, N.J.: Peoples Publishing, 1995.

Asante, Molefi K., and Mark T. Mattson. *The Historical and Cultural Atlas of African Americans.* New York: Macmillan, 1991.

Athearn, Robert G. *In Search of Canaan: Black Migration to Kansas, 1879–1880.* Lawrence: Regents Press of Kansas, 1978.

Baldwin, Joseph. *The African Personality in America: An African-Centered Framework.* Tallahassee: Nubian Nation Publications, 1992.

Barnett, Evelyn B. "Nannie Burroughs and the Education of Black Women." In *The Afro-American Woman: Struggles and Images.* Ed. by Sharon Harley and Rosalyn Terborg-Penn. 1978. Reprint, Baltimore: Black Classic Press, 1997.

Berlin, Ira. *Slaves without Masters: The Free Negro in the Antebellum South.* New York: New Press, 1992.

Berry, Mary F., and John W. Blassingame. *Long Memory: The Black Experience in America.* New York: Oxford University Press, 1982.

Blumenthal, Henry. "Woodrow Wilson and the Race Question." *Journal of Negro History* 48 (January 1963): 1–21.

Boyer, Paul S., et al. *The Enduring Vision: A History of the American People.* Vol. 2, 4th ed. Boston: Houghton Mifflin, 1999.

Brands, H. W. *T. R.: The Last Romantic.* New York: Basic Books, 1997.

Brinkley, Alan. *American History: A Survey.* 10th ed. Boston: McGraw-Hill College, 1999.

Brock, Euline W. "Thomas W. Cardozo: Fallible Black Reconstruction Leader," *Journal of Southern History,* 47 (May 1981): 183–206.

Casdorph, Paul D. "The 1912 Republican Presidential Campaign in Mississippi." *Journal of Mississippi History* 33 (February 1971): 1–19.

Church, Roberta, and Ronald Walter. *Nineteenth Century Memphis Families of Color, 1850–1900.* Memphis: Murdock Printing, 1989.

Clark, Herbert L. "James Carroll Napier: National Negro Leader." *Tennessee Historical Quarterly,* 49 (winter 1990): 243–52.

Cobb, James C. *The Most Southern Place on Earth: The Mississippi Delta and the Roots of Regional Identity.* New York: Oxford University Press, 1992.

Colburn, David R. "Rosewood and America in the Early Twentieth Century." *Florida Historical Quarterly* 76 (fall 1997): 175–92.

Conlin, Joseph R. *The American Past: A Survey of American History.* 5th ed. Fort Worth: Harcourt Brace, 1997.

Cooper, Arnie. "'We Rise upon the Structure We Ourselves Have Builded': William H. Holtzclaw and Utica Institute, 1903–1915." *Journal of Mississippi History* 47 (February 1985): 15–33.

Cornelius, Janet D. *"When I Can Read My Title Clear": Literacy, Slavery, and Religion in the Antebellum South.* Columbia: University of South Carolina Press, 1991.

Cox, Thomas C. *Blacks in Topeka, Kansas, 1865–1915: A Social History.* Baton Rouge: Louisiana State University Press, 1982.

Crockett, Norman L. *The Black Towns.* Lawrence: Regents Press of Kansas, 1979.

Dailey, Maceo D., Jr. "An Easy Alliance: Theodore Roosevelt and Emmett Jay Scott, 1900–1919." In *Theodore Roosevelt: Many-Sided American.* Ed. by Natalie Naylor, Douglas Brinkley, and John A. Gable. Interlaken, N.Y.: Heart of the Lakes Publishing, 1992.

———. "Neither 'Uncle Tom' nor 'Accommodationist': Booker T. Washington, Emmett Jay Scott, and Constructionalism." *Atlanta History* 38 (winter 1995): 20–33.

Daniel, Pete. *The Shadow of Slavery: Peonage in the South, 1901–1969.* Urbana: University of Illinois Press, 1972.

———. "Up from Slavery and Down to Peonage: The Alonzo Bailey Case." *Journal of American History* 57 (December 1970): 654–70.

Davis, Angela Y. *Women, Race, and Class.* New York: Vintage Books, 1983.

D'Orso, Michael. *Like Judgment Day: The Ruin and Redemption of a Town Called Rosewood.* New York: Boulevard Books, 1996.

Dyer, Thomas G. *Theodore Roosevelt and the Idea of Race.* Baton Rouge: Louisiana State University Press, 1980.

Ellsworth, Scott. *Death in a Promised Land: The Tulsa Race Riot of 1921.* Baton Rouge: Louisiana State University Press, 1982.

Everett, Frank E., Jr. *Brierfield: Plantation Home of Jefferson Davis.* Hattiesburg: University and College Press of Mississippi, 1971.

Felleman, Hazel, ed. *The Best Loved Poems of the American People.* Garden City, N.Y.: Doubleday, 1936.

Foner, Eric. *Reconstruction: America's Unfinished Revolution, 1863–1877.* New York: Harper and Row, 1988.

Fox, Stephen. *The Guardian of Boston: William Monroe Trotter.* New York: Atheneum, 1970.

Franklin, John Hope. *From Slavery to Freedom: A History of Negro Americans.* 6th ed. New York: Knopf, 1988.

———, ed. *Reminiscences of an Active Life: The Autobiography of John Roy Lynch.* Introduction by John Hope Franklin. Chicago: University of Chicago Press, 1970.

Frazier, E. Franklin. *Black Bourgeoisie: The Rise of a New Middle Class.* Glencoe, Ill.: Free Press, 1957.

Gaines, Kevin K. *Uplifting the Race: Black Leadership, Politics, and Culture in the Twentieth Century.* Chapel Hill: University of North Carolina Press, 1996.

Gatewood, Willard B. *Aristocrats of Color: The Black Elite, 1880–1920.* Bloomington: Indiana University Press, 1990.

———. *Theodore Roosevelt and the Art of Controversy: Episodes of the White House Years.* Baton Rouge: Louisiana State University Press, 1970.

———. "Theodore Roosevelt and the Indianola Affair," *Journal of Negro History* 53 (January 1968): 48–69.

Giddings, Paula. *When and Where I Enter: The Impact of Black Women on Race and Sex in America.* New York: Bantam Books, 1985.

Giroux, Vincent A. "The Rise of Theodore G. Bilbo, 1908–1932." *Journal of Mississippi History* 43 (1981): 180–209.

Goings, Kenneth W. *The NAACP Comes of Age: The Defeat of Judge John J. Parker.* Bloomington: Indiana University Press, 1990.

Goings, Kenneth W., and Gerald L. Smith. "'Unhidden' Transcripts: Memphis and African-American Agency, 1862–1920." *Journal of Urban History* 21 (March 1995): 372–94.

Grantham, Dewey W., Jr. "Dinner at the White House: Theodore Roosevelt, Booker T. Washington, and the South." *Tennessee Historical Quarterly* 17 (June 1958): 112–30.

Hamilton, Kenneth M. *Black Towns and Profit: Promotion and Development in the*

Trans-Appalachian West, 1877–1915. Urbana: University of Illinois Press, 1991.

Harlan, Louis R. *Booker T. Washington: The Making of a Black Leader, 1856–1901.* New York: Oxford University Press, 1972.

———. "Booker T. Washington and the National Negro Business League." In *Booker T. Washington in Perspective: Essays of Louis Harlan.* Ed. by Raymond W. Smock. Jackson: University Press of Mississippi, 1988.

———. *Booker T. Washington: The Wizard of Tuskegee, 1901–1915.* New York: Oxford University Press, 1983.

———. "The Secret Life of Booker T. Washington." *Journal of Southern History* 37 (August 1971): 393–416.

———. *Separate and Unequal: Public School Campaigns and Racism in the Southern Seaboard States, 1901–1915.* Chapel Hill: University of North Carolina Press, 1958.

Harris, Abram L. *The Negro as Capitalist: A Study of Banking and Business among American Negroes.* Philadelphia: American Academy of Political and Social Science, 1936.

Hemmingway, Theodore. "Booker T. Washington in Mississippi, October 1908." *Journal of Mississippi History* 46, (February 1984): 29–42.

Hermann, Janet Sharp. "Isaiah T. Montgomery's Balancing Act." In *Black Leaders of the Nineteenth Century.* Ed. by Leon Litwack and August Meier. Urbana: University of Illinois Press, 1988.

———. *The Pursuit of a Dream.* New York: Oxford University Press, 1981.

Higginbotham, Evelyn B. *Righteous Discontent: The Women's Movement in the Black Baptist Church, 1880–1920.* Cambridge, Mass.: Harvard University Press, 1993.

Hine, Darlene Clark. *Black Women in White: Racial Conflict and Cooperation in the Nursing Profession, 1890–1950.* Bloomington: Indiana University Press, 1989.

Hine, Darlene Clark, Elsa Barkley Brown, and Rosalyn Terborg-Penn, eds. *Black Women in America: An Historical Encyclopedia.* 2 vols. Bloomington: Indiana University Press, 1994.

Holmes, William F. "James K. Vardaman: From Bourbon to Agricultural Reformer," *Journal of Mississippi History* 31 (May 1969): 97–115.

———. "Whitecapping: Agrarian Violence in Mississippi, 1902–1906." *Journal of Southern History* 35 (May 1969): 165–85.

———. *The White Chief: James Kimble Vardaman.* Baton Rouge: Louisiana State University Press, 1970.

Hunter, Tera W. *To 'Joy My Freedom: Southern Black Women's Lives and Labors after the Civil War.* Cambridge, Mass.: Harvard University Press, 1997.

Imes, G. Lake. "To Tuskegee." In *Robert Russa Moton of Hampton and Tuskegee.* Ed. by William H. Hughes and Frederick D. Patterson. Chapel Hill: University of North Carolina Press, 1956.

Ingham, John N., and Lynne B. Feldman. *African-American Business Leaders: A Biographical Dictionary.* Westport, Conn.: Greenwood Press, 1994.

Jackson, Kennell. *America Is Me: 170 Fresh Questions and Answers on Black American History.* New York: HarperCollins, 1996.

James, Arthur, Jimmie James, Jr., and Robert James. *The Mississippi Black Bankers and Their Institutions* (n.p., 1996).

Jenkins, Robert L. "The Development of Black Higher Education in Mississippi, 1865–1920." *Journal of Mississippi History* 45 (November 1983): 272–86.

Jones, Allen W. "The Role of Tuskegee Institute in the Education of Black Farmers." *Journal of Negro History* 60 (April 1975): 252–67.

Jones, Beverly. "Mary Church-Terrell and the National Association of Colored Women, 1896 to 1901." *Journal of Negro History* 67 (spring 1982): 20–33.

———. *Quest for Equality: The Life and Writings of Mary Eliza Church Terrell, 1863–1954.* Vol. 14. *Black Women in United States History,* ed. by Darlene Clark Hine. Brooklyn, N.Y.: Carlson Publishing, 1990.

Jones, Jacqueline. *Labor of Love, Labor of Sorrow: Black Women, Work, and the Family from Slavery to the Present.* 1st Vintage ed. New York: Vintage Books, 1995.

Jones, Maxine. "The Rosewood Massacre and the Women Who Survived It." *Florida Historical Quarterly* 76 (fall 1997): 193–208.

Kirwan, Albert D. *Revolt of the Rednecks: Mississippi Politics, 1876–1925.* Lexington: University of Kentucky Press, 1951.

Lerner, Gerda. "Early Community Work of Black Club Women." *Journal of Negro History* 59 (April 1974): 158–67.

Lewis, David L. *W. E. B. Du Bois: Biography of a Race.* New York: Henry Holt, 1993.

Link, Arthur S. "Correspondence Relating to the Progressive Party's 'Lily White' Policy in 1912." *Journal of Southern History* 10 (November 1944): 480–90.

———. The Negro as a Factor in the Campaign of 1912." *Journal of Negro History* 32 (January 1947): 81–99.

———. "Theodore Roosevelt and the South, 1912." *North Carolina Historical Review* 23 (July 1946): 313–24.

———. *Woodrow Wilson and the Progressive Era, 1910–1917.* New York: Harper and Brothers, 1954.

Lisio, Donald J. *Hoover, Blacks, and Lily-Whites: A Study of Southern Strategies.* Chapel Hill: The University of North Carolina Press, 1985.

Litwack, Leon. *Been in the Storm So Long: The Aftermath of Slavery.* 1st Vintage ed. New York: Vintage Books, 1980.

———. *Trouble in Mind: Black Southerners in the Age of Jim Crow.* New York: Vintage Books, 1998.

Loewen, James W., and Charles Sallis, eds. *Mississippi: Conflict and Change.* New York: Pantheon, 1974.

Logan, Rayford. *The Negro in American Life and Thought: The Nadir, 1877–1901.* New York: Dial Press, 1954.

Lopez, Claira. "James K. Vardaman and the Negro: The Foundation of Mississippi's Racial Policy." *Southern Quarterly* 3 (1965): 155–80.

Margo, Robert A. *Race and Schooling in the South, 1880–1950: An Economic History.* Chicago: University of Chicago Press, 1990.

Marks, Carole. *Farewell—We're Good and Gone: The Great Black Migration.* Bloomington: Indiana University Press, 1989.

McFeely, William S. *Frederick Douglass.* New York: Norton, 1991.

McLemore, Nannie P. "James K. Vardaman, A Mississippi Progressive." *Journal of Mississippi History* 29 (1967): 1–11.

McMillen, Neil R. *Dark Journey: Black Mississippians in the Age of Jim Crow.* Urbana: University of Illinois Press, 1989.

———. "Perry W. Howard, Boss of Black-and-Tan Republicanism in Mississippi, 1924–1960." *Journal of Southern History* 48 (May 1982): 205–24.

McMurry, Linda O. *To Keep the Waters Troubled: The Life of Ida B. Wells.* New York: Oxford University Press, 1998.

McPherson, James. *The Abolitionist Legacy: From Reconstruction to the NAACP.* Princeton: Princeton University Press, 1975.

Meier, August. "Booker T. Washington and the Town of Mound Bayou." In *Along the Color Line: Explorations in the Black Experience.* Ed. by Meier and Elliott Rudwick. Urbana: University of Illinois Press, 1976.

———. *Negro Thought in America, 1880–1915: Racial Ideologies in the Age of Booker T. Washington.* Ann Arbor: University of Michigan Press, 1963.

Meier, August, Elliott Rudwick, and Francis L. Broderick, eds. *Black Protest Thought in the Twentieth Century.* 2d ed. Indianapolis: Bobbs-Merrill, 1971.

Mollison, Irvin C. "Negro Lawyers in Mississippi." *Journal of Negro History* 15 (January 1930): 38–71.

Mosley, Charles C. *The Negro in Mississippi History.* Jackson, Miss.: Hederman Brothers, 1950.

Mowry, George E. "The South and the Progressive Lily-White Party of 1912." *Journal of Southern History* 6 (May 1940): 237–47.

Neverdon-Morton, Cynthia. *Afro-American Women of the South and the Advancement of the Race, 1895–1925.* Knoxville: University of Tennessee Press, 1989.

———. "The Black Woman's Struggle for Equality in the South, 1895–1925." In *The Afro-American Woman: Struggles and Images.* Ed. by Sharon Harley and Rosalyn Terborg-Penn. 1978. Reprint, Baltimore: Black Classic Press, 1997.

Nichols, J. L., and William H. Crogman. *Progress of a Race.* Naperville, Ill: J. L. Nichols, 1920. Reprint, New York: Arno Press, 1969.

Numbers, Ronald L., and Todd L. Savitt, eds. *Science and Medicine in the Old South.* Baton Rouge: Louisiana State University Press, 1989.

Oshinsky, David M. *Worse Than Slavery: Parchman Farm and the Ordeal of Jim Crow Justice.* New York: Free Press, 1997.

Painter, Nell I. *Exodusters: Black Migration to Kansas after Reconstruction.* New York: Knopf, 1976.

Rabinowitz, Howard, N. *Race Relations in the Urban South, 1865–1890.* Urbana: University of Illinois Press, 1980.

Redding, J. Saunders. *The Lonesome Road: A Narrative History of the Black American Experience*. Garden City, N.Y.: Anchor Press, 1973.

———. *No Day of Triumph*. Introduction by Richard Wright. New York: Harper and Brothers, 1942.

Rogers, Joel A. *World's Great Men of Color*. Introduction, commentary, and new bibliographical notes, ed. by John Henrik Clarke. Vol. 2. New York: Macmillan, 1972.

Rose, Willie L. *Rehearsal for Reconstruction: The Port Royal Experiment*. Introduction by C. Vann Woodward. New York: Vintage Books, 1967.

Rouse, Jacqueline A. *Lugenia Burns Hope, Black Southern Reformer*. Athens: University of Georgia Press, 1989.

Rowland, Dunbar. *History of Mississippi: The Heart of the South*. Chicago and Jackson, Miss.: S. J. Clark, 1925. Reprint, Spartanburg, S.C.: Reprint Company, 1978.

Rudwick, Elliott. "W. E. B. Du Bois: Protagonist of the Afro-American Protest." In *Black Leaders of the Nineteenth Century*. Ed. by Leon Litwack and August Meier. Urbana: University of Illinois Press, 1988.

Savitt, Todd L. *Medicine and Slavery: The Diseases and Health Care of Blacks in Antebellum Virginia*. Urbana: University of Illinois Press, 1978.

Savitt, Todd L., and James H. Young, eds. *Disease and Distinctiveness in the American South*. Knoxville: University of Tennessee Press, 1988.

Scheiner, Seth. "President Theodore Roosevelt and the Negro, 1901–1908." *Journal of Negro History* 47 (July 1962): 169–82.

Schweninger, Loren. *Black Property Owners in the South, 1790–1915*. Urbana: University of Illinois Press, 1997.

Severn, John K., and William W. Rogers. "Theodore Roosevelt Entertains Booker T. Washington: Florida's Reaction to the White House Dinner." *Florida Historical Quarterly* 54 (January 1976): 306–18.

Sewell, George A. *Mississippi Black History Makers*. Introduction by Margaret Walker. Jackson: University Press of Mississippi, 1977.

Shaw, Stephanie J. "Black Club Women and the Creation of the National Association of Colored Women." In *"We Specialize in the Wholly Impossible": A Reader in Black Women's History*. Ed. by Darlene Clark Hine, Wilma King, and Linda Reed. Brooklyn, N.Y.: Carlson Publishing, 1995.

———. *What a Woman Ought to Be and to Do: Black Professional Women Workers during the Jim Crow Era*. Chicago: University of Chicago Press, 1996.

Sherman, Richard B. *The Republican Party and Black America from McKinley to Hoover, 1896–1933*. Charlottesville: University Press of Virginia, 1973.

Sillers, Florence W., et al., eds. *History of Bolivar County, Mississippi*. Jackson: Hederman Brothers, 1948.

Smock, Raymond W., ed. *Booker T. Washington in Perspective: Essays of Louis Harlan*. Jackson: University Press of Mississippi, 1988.

Sowell, Thomas. *Ethnic America: A History*. New York: Basic Books, 1981.

Spear, Allan H. *Black Chicago: The Making of a Negro Ghetto, 1890–1920*. Chicago: University of Chicago Press, 1967.

Spivey, Donald. *Schooling for the New Slavery: Black Industrial Education, 1868–1915*. Westport, Conn.: Greenwood Press, 1978.

Summerville, James. *Educating Black Doctors: A History of Meharry Medical College*. Foreword by Lloyd C. Elam. University: University of Alabama Press, 1987.

Swingler, Lewis O., ed. "Jewel of the Delta." Souvenir Bulletin. N.p., 1962.

Taylor, Joseph. "Mound Bayou—Past and Present." *Negro History Bulletin* 3 (April 1940): 105–11.

Terborg-Penn, Rosalyn. "Discrimination against Afro-American Women in the Woman's Movement, 1830–1920." In *The Afro-American Woman*. Ed. by Sharon Harley and Rosalyn Terborg-Penn. 1978. Reprint, Baltimore: Black Classic Press, 1997.

Thornbrough, Emma L. "The Brownsville Episode and the Negro Vote," *Mississippi Valley Historical Review* 44 (December 1957): 469–83.

———. *T. Thomas Fortune: Militant Journalist*. Chicago: University of Chicago Press, 1972.

Tinsley, James A. "Roosevelt, Foraker, and the Brownsville Affray," *Journal of Negro History*, 41 (January 1956): 43–65.

Tolnay, Stewart E., and E. M. Beck. *A Festival of Violence: An Analysis of Southern Lynchings, 1882–1930*. Urbana: University of Illinois Press, 1992.

Trelease, Allen W. *White Terror: The Ku Klux Klan Conspiracy and Southern Reconstruction*. Baton Rouge: Louisiana State University Press, 1995.

Trotter, Joe William, Jr., ed., *The Great Migration in Historical Perspective: New Dimensions of Race, Class, and Gender*. Bloomington: Indiana University Press, 1991.

Wade, Richard C. *Slavery in the Cities: The South, 1820–1860*. New York: Oxford University Press, 1967.

Walker, Juliet E. K. *The History of Black Business in America: Capitalism, Race, Entrepreneurship*. New York: Twayne, 1998.

Wayne, Michael. *The Reshaping Of Plantation Society: The Natchez District, 1860–1880*. Illini books ed. Urbana: University of Illinois Press, 1990.

Weaver, John D. *The Brownsville Raid*. Foreword by Louis L. Gould. College Station: Texas A&M University Press, 1992.

Webber, Thomas L. *Deep Like the Rivers: Education in the Slave Quarter Community, 1831–1865*. New York: Norton, 1978.

Weeks, Linton. *Clarksdale and Coahoma County: A History*. Clarksdale, Miss.: Carnegie Public Library, 1982.

Weiss, Nancy J. "The Negro and the New Freedom: Fighting Wilsonian Segregation." *Political Science Quarterly* 84 (March 1969): 61–79.

Wells-Barnett, Ida B. "Lynch Law in All Its Phases." In *African Intellectual Heritage: A Book of Sources*. Ed. by Molefi K. Asante and Abu S. Abarry. Philadelphia: Temple University Press, 1996.

Wharton, Vernon L. *The Negro in Mississippi 1865–1890.* New York: Harper Torchbooks, 1965.

White, Deborah G. *Too Heavy a Load: Black Women in Defense of Themselves, 1894–1994.* New York: Norton, 1999.

White, Eugene E. "Anti-Racial Agitation in Politics: James Kimble Vardaman in the Mississippi Gubernatorial Campaign of 1903." *Journal of Mississippi History* 7 (1945): 91–110.

Wiggins, Lida K. *The Life and Works of Paul Laurence Dunbar.* Naperville, Ill., and Memphis: J. L. Nichols, 1907. Reprint, Nashville: Winston-Derek Publishers, 1992.

Williamson, Joel. *After Slavery: The Negro in South Carolina during Reconstruction, 1861–1877.* New York: Norton, 1975.

———. *New People: Miscegenation and Mulattoes in the United States.* Baton Rouge: Louisiana State University Press, 1995.

Williamson, Stephen. "Mound Bayou History." *The Voice* 4 (July 1971): 3–22.

Wolgemuth, Kathleen L. "Woodrow Wilson and Federal Segregation." *Journal of Negro History* 44 (April 1959): 158–73.

Woodward, C. Vann. *The Strange Career of Jim Crow.* 3d rev. ed. New York: Oxford University Press, 1974.

Wright, Richard R. *The Bishops of the African Methodist Episcopal Church.* Nashville: A.M.E. Sunday School Union, 1963.

Index

Accommodationist, 42
Advance-Dispatch, 183
Africa, 38, 121
Alabama Penny Savings Bank, 155
Alabama Supreme Court, 139
Alcorn A&M College, 104, 121, 124
Alcorn, Eliza Jane. *See* Clark, Eliza
Alcorn, W. A., 200
Allen, Richard, 35
Allen Endeavor League, 35
Allston, Phillip J., 91, 164
Alsop, M. M., 88, 128
A. M. E. Church Review, 70, 72
American Bank, 59
American Express Company, 61
American Magazine, 55
American Missionary Association, 121
Anderson, Charles H., 95
Anderson, Charles W., 133
Anna T. Jeanes Fund, 55, 123–27, 233n.28
Armstrong, Samuel Chapman, 41
Arrington, Mr., 107
Askew, Henry, 4
"Atlanta Compromise," 31, 33–34, 42
Atlanta race riot (1906), 55, 56
Attaway, W. A., 93
Atwell, Ernest Ten Eyck, 198
Atwood, Louis K., 59, 60, 75, 149

Baker, Newton, 189
Baker, Ray Stannard, 55, 56
Baldwin, William H., 111, 239n.36
Bank of Mound Bayou, 57, 85, 171, 174, 184, 212, 213; difficulties at, 159–69; founding of, 156–59

Banks, Charles: 33, 79, 80, 81, 83, 87, 89; appraisal of, 210–16; and Banks Prize, 105–6; business ventures of, 35, 36, 154–55, 205; and Carnegie Fund, 113–19; and Carnegie library, 117–19; as census enumerator, 12; church affiliation of, 20–22; and the Clarks, 7–10; and conflict with Booze, 190–94; and conflict with I. T. Montgomery, 200–202; as constructionalist, 42–43; and coordination of Moton's tour of Mississippi, 73–78, 235n.90; and coordination of Washington's tour of Mississippi, 67–73; criticism of, 45, 49–50, 117–18; death of, 204–6, 210; early education of, 7; early work experiences of, 12; and election of 1912, 142–50; and election of 1916, 150–53; family background of, 5–7; family problems of, 193, 197, 202; and farm demonstration agents, 63–67; and farmers, 62–63; and founding of Bank of Mound Bayou, 156–59; and GEB, 110–13; home of, 19–20, 82; and Jeanes Fund, 123–27; and land dispute, 202–3; as leader of MNBL, 95–98; as leading citizen, 40, 213; and loss of guardian angels, 187–90; net worth of, 145, 155, 186, 248n.5; and NNBL, 90–95, 101–3, 196–99; 231n.57; and oil mill, 1, 170–74, 175–77, 177–82, 182–86; and orations for education, 104–5; and organization of Mississippi Day, 98–100; philosophy of, 41–49, 58; physical appearance of, 17–19; and political conflicts in Mound Bayou, 199–200; political

Banks, Charles—*continued*
involvement of, 129–32; political patronage of, 136, 137–42; 194–96; and
Rockefeller Fund, 113; and Rosenwald
Fund, 120–22; at Rust University, 10–
11, 221n.58; as state and local leader,
59–63; as supporter of war effort during
World War I, 189, 255n.16; and Taft,
132–36; and Tuskegee Machine, 50–58;
as Washington's lieutenant, xi, xii, 53,
54, 140, 211–12; and youth achievement, 106–10
Banks, Daniel, 5, 7, 220n.29
Banks, G. Joseph, 5
Banks, Joeannia, 5, 7
Banks, Mary, 5
Banks, Sallie, 5, 6, 7, 9, 205, 220n.25,
220n.29
Banks, Trenna O., 57, 90, 93, 232n.73;
appearance of, 18, 224n.103; church
affiliation of, 20–22; education of, 14–
16; family background of, 13–14; family
problems of, 193, 197, 202; home of,
19–20, 82; works with Mississippi
women's clubs, 23–24, 37; works with
NACW, 22–23. *See also* Banks, Charles
Banks-Creswell faction. *See* Banks-Francis-
Harris faction
Banks-Francis-Harris faction, 199–200
Banks & Bro., 12, 154
Baptist Women's Union, 35
Baptist Young People's Union, 35
Barber, Jesse Max, 51
Beale, H. R., 61, 62
Beck, Mr., 66
Beckett, William W., 203
Beito, David, 258n.17
Bertram, James, 194–96
Bethel A.M.E. Church, 20–21, 84
Bilbo, Theodore G., 200
Binga, Jessie, 223n.96
Black aristocrats. *See* Elite
Black attorneys, 229n.65
Black Belt, 138
Black survival strategy, xii, 46, 47, 48, 92,
173, 212
Black towns, 229n.53

Black Victorians, 16, 19
Bolivar County Negro Fair, 65
Bolivar County Public Schools, 128
Booker, James A., 35, 64, 65
Bookerites, xiii, 128
Booze, Eugene P., 14, 35, 37, 93, 152, 154,
215, 257n.17; and Banks, 190–94, 213–
14; and Carnegie library, 194–96; con-
flict of, with Montgomery heirs, 207–10;
death of, 209–10; as "half-white niggah,"
18, 21, 210; provokes land dispute, 202–
3; and NNBL, 196–99; and politics in
Mound Bayou, 199–200
Booze, Henderson, 13, 14
Booze, Mary, 37, 207, 209, 215
Booze, Mayme L., 19, 36, 37
Booze, T. M. Louise, 13, 14
Booze, Trenna O. *See* Banks, Trenna O.
Boswell, Henry, 23
Boycott, 119, 175, 176, 205
Brewer, Earl, 161
Brooks, Mr., 198
Brooks, Reuben, 199
Brown, E. P., 100
Brown, Sydney J., 124–25
Brownsville affair, 131–32, 247n.115
Bruce, Blanche K., 3
Bryant, Gertrude A., 126, 242n.115
Buchanan, C. A., 29–30
Buckeye Cotton Oil Company. *See* Proctor
and Gamble
Buckley, Mr., 146–47
Buel, C. C., 19
Bull Moose Convention, 149
Bull Moose Party, 149. *See also* Progressive
Party
Burroughs, Nannie H., 224n.103
Burrows, John H., 98
Bush, John E., 196
Buttrick, Wallace, 111, 112

Campbell, Thomas M., 36, 64, 65, 66, 67,
233n.33, 234n.41
Campbell College, 104, 105, 203
Cardozo, Thomas W., 3
Carnegie, Andrew, 51, 94, 114–18, 171–72,
195

Carnegie Corporation, 195
Carnegie Fund. *See* Carnegie, Andrew; Carnegie library at Mound Bayou
Carnegie library at Mound Bayou, 85, 120, 172; problems with, 113–19, 194–96
Carpenter, Fred Warner, 135, 140
Carter, Leon, 106
Carter, William H., 160
Carver, George Washington, 63
Census: enumerators and supervisors, 134–36
Charles F. Wermuth and Company, 162
Charleston (West Virginia) *Advocate*, 72
Cherry Street Public School, 126
Chicago Daily Tribune, 143
Chicago Defender, 203, 206
Christian Recorder, 72
Clark, Eliza, 5–7, 9, 221n.50
Clark, James, 6
Clark, John, 5–7, 12, 221n.50
Clark family, 6, 11, 206, 222n.66
Clarksdale Daily Register, 9
Clarksdale Graded School, 55
Classical education, 11, 49, 105, 121, 128
Coahoma County, 6; school system of, 7
Coffin, F. M., 195, 200
Cohen, Walter, 147
Cole, Frank, 137, 139
Color complex. *See* Elite
Colored American Magazine, 57
Colored Medical Association of Mississippi, 52
Compromise of 1877, 3
Confederacy, 26
Connor, Fred, 208
Constructionalism, xiii, 42–43, 72, 97, 215
Cook, Thomas W., 35, 85, 86, 116–17, 170, 173
Coon, Charles L., 120
Cosey, Auger A., 35, 100
Cotton crisis: of 1914, 163, 176, 178, 185–86, 213, 214; post-WWI, 77, 176, 204, 214; pre-WWI, 159
Cotton oil mill. *See* Banks, Charles; Mound Bayou Oil Mill; Rosenwald, Julius; Scott, Emmett J.; Washington, Booker T.
Cottrell, Elias, 70, 89, 100

Covington, J. W., 36
Cox, Diamond, 164
Cox, Minnie M., 101–2, 130–32
Cox, S., 99–100
Cox, Wayne W., 70, 93, 132, 251n.82
Creswell, B. Howard, 35, 44, 199–200
Crowe, Milburn, 254n.77
C. R. Stringer and Company, 61
Crum, William D., 130, 131

Daly, M. H., 144
Davis, Alexander K., 3
Davis, Frank, 73, 235n.71
Davis, Jefferson, 26
Davis, Jim, 73, 235n.71
Davis, Joseph E., 26, 200
Davis, William H., 102
Davis Bend, 26, 27, 28, 38
Delta, 6, 19, 28, 62, 73, 74, 100, 112, 113, 121, 173, 206
Delta Penny Savings Bank, 70, 131, 169
Democrats, 130, 136, 138, 140, 141, 147, 148, 150, 153
Demonstrator. *See* Mound Bayou
Dempsey, Clayton, 208
Dillard, James H., 55, 65, 123–27, 233n.28
Dixon, Joseph M., 144
Dogan, M. W., 93
Douglass, Frederick, 17, 23
Downing, Henry F., 31
Du Bois, W. E. B., 49–50, 51, 105, 149, 153, 212, 215
Dun and Bradstreet, 159
Dunbar, Paul Lawrence, 45, 224n.102
Dunbar-Nelson, Alice, 223n.91
Dyer, Thomas, 121

Eastern Star Lodge, 171
Elite: and color complex, 224n.105; new black, 16, 17, 20, 24, 33, 37, 38, 50, 108, 223n.96, 225n.109; old black, 9, 10, 11, 13, 14, 16, 17, 20, 49, 223n.96, 239n.21
Exodusters, 26

Farm demonstration agent, 62, 63–67, 210
Farmer's Cooperative Mercantile Company, 154, 186

Felder, S. B., 110, 189
Felder, Tyree, 110
"Financiering By Negroes," 157
Fisk University, 121, 124, 130
Following the Color Line (Baker), 56
Foraker, Joseph B., 132, 133
Fortune, Timothy Thomas, 31, 51,
    224n.103
Francis, John W., 36, 37, 154–55, 156,
    161, 167, 171, 214, 249n.44
Francis, Mrs. John W., 101
Franklin, John H., 189
Fraternal associations, 35, 59, 67, 155. *See
    also* Masonic Benefit Association
Frazee, W. D., 91–92
Freedmen's Aid Society, 10
Freedmen's Bureau, 7
Friendship A.M.E. Church, 21, 205
Frissell, Hollis, 123

Gaiter, Annie, 38–39, 84
Gaiter, Simon, 38–39, 84
Garrett, James B., 35, 37
Gary, Daniel W., 143–44, 149
Gates, Frederick T., 63
General Baptist Convention, 183
General Education Board, 63, 111–13
George, Sumner, 114
Gilliam, C. W., 99
Glover, R. W., 25, 226n.1
Goldwire, John J., 114
GOP. *See* Republican Party
Gordon, James, 91–92, 104
Gordon, W. C., 191
Graves, William C., 177–78, 181
Great Migration, 205, 214
Green, Benjamin A., 36, 204, 207, 256n.62,
    257n.14, 258n.25
Green, Benjamin T., 26, 28, 31, 32–33, 35,
    121, 124, 210, 228n.40
Green, John St. Anthony, 124
Greene, G. W., 232n.73
Green Grove Baptist Church, 21
Greenville Chamber of Commerce, 202
Greenville Savings Bank, 100
Griffin, Riley, 43–44

Hall, A. J., 97
Hall, George C., 52
Hamilton, Green P., 17, 224n.102
Hamilton, Kenneth, 157
Hampton Building and Loan Association,
    184
Hampton Institute, 41
Handy, William C., 4
Hanna, Mark, 130, 243n.7
Harahan, J. T., 69
Harris, Arthur, 110
Harris, Scott, 36
Harvard University, 49; law school, 139,
    204
Harvey, Benjamin B., 175–83, 201, 253n.47
Harvey, Thomas, 29
Hayes, Rutherford B., 3
Henry, Richard, 33
Hill, James, 3, 27
Hilles, Charles, 137, 138, 141, 142
Hitchcock, Ethan A., 129
Hitchcock, Frank Harris, 133, 135, 141,
    142, 244n.37
Holley, Marriah, 5, 7, 9
Holmes, O. A., 183
Holsey, Albon, 74, 76, 77, 189–90
Holtzclaw, William H., 60, 75–77, 89, 105,
    202
Hood, Aurelius, 30
Household of Ruth. *See* Fraternal associa-
    tions
Houston Daily Post, 4
"How to Build Up Worn Out Soils," 63
Howard, Perry W., 60, 68, 100, 142, 143,
    144, 149, 152, 192, 200, 256n.62
Howard University, 49, 224n.102
Howe, Julia Ward, 102
Howell, E. D., 59
Hughes, Charles, 152, 244n.37
Hume, Leland, 8
Humphries, B. G., 112
Hunt, Nathan, 70
Hutton, H. J., 60

Illinois Central Railroad, 32, 45, 69, 171
Indianola affair, 130–32

Industrial education, 50, 105, 128

Jackson, Maurice, 182, 206
Jackson Chamber of Commerce, 205
Jackson Daily News, 206
James, George R., 74
Jeanes, Anna T., 123
Jeanes Fund. *See* Anna T. Jeanes Fund
Jesup, Morris K., 65
Jesup Agricultural Wagon, 65
Jim Crow, 2, 40, 51
Jinning, Dan, 5, 7,
Johnson, J. E., 76
Johnson, Jack, 17
Jones, E. P., 53, 100
Jones, Grace Allen, 23, 226n.138
Jones, John, 199
Jones, Mrs. Laurence C. *See* Jones, Grace Allen
Jones, Vannie, 140
Jones-Bryant, Gertrude, 35
Jordan, Minnie, 110

Kansas City Women's League, 226n.139
Kansas Hegira, 26
Kealing, Hightower T., 70
Kendall, J. C., 73
Kent, Harvey M., 208
Kent, J. H., 207
Kettering, G. C., 61
Keys, Thomas I., 140–42, 147
Kinwood, S. K., 97
Knapp, Seaman A., 63, 65
Knelland, Fannie, 197, 199
Knights of Pythias. *See* Fraternal associations
Knox Academy, 126
Kyle, W. P., 161

Lampton, Edward W., 155
Langston University, 114
Leavell, Napoleon B., 6, 220n.29
Lee, Clyde, 36
Lee, J. R. E., 241n.106, 242n.114
Lee, M. A., 36
Lee, Wilson, 110
Leland Oil Works, 181, 201

Lewis, William H., 133, 139
Liberal arts education. *See* Classical education
Lincoln, Abraham, 133
Logan, Warren, 187–88
Louisville, New Orleans, and Texas Railroad (L, NO & T), 27, 28, 32, 158
Lynch, John Roy, 3

MacKintosh, W. P., 99
Masonic Benefit Association, 57, 117, 119, 145, 155, 164, 195. *See also* Fraternal associations
Masonic lodge. *See* Fraternal associations; Masonic Benefit Association
Masons. *See* Fraternal associations; Masonic Benefit Association
Matony, J., 72
Mays, George, Jr., 164, 171, 180
McCarty, Richard, 33, 161, 167, 249n.44
McDonald, A. C., 10
McGinnis, George W., 27, 28, 227n.13
McKinley, William B., 142, 144–46
McLaurin, John L., 130
McMillen, Neil, 4
Memphis Commercial Appeal, 43, 56, 72, 74, 143, 173, 174
Memphis Cotton Oil Company, 175, 178
Memphis school system, 10
Methodist Episcopal Church, 10
Michie, George C., 183
Miller, F. E., 72–73
Miller, Fred, 209
Miller, Kelly, 224n.102
Millsaps, R. W., 112
Millsaps College, 112
Ministers' Union, 35
Minute Men, 189. *See also* World War I; Third Liberty Bond call
Missionaries, 222n.61
Mississippi Beneficial Life Insurance Company, 154, 168
Mississippi Constitutional Convention (1890), 3, 30, 139
Mississippi Day, 98–100. *See also* Mississippi Negro Business League

Mississippi Department of Education, 23
Mississippi Negro Business League, xii, 54, 69, 117, 170, 95–98, 211
Mississippi Negro State Fair, 60
Mississippi Plan, 30, 31, 139
Mississippi Republican Convention. *See* Republican State Convention
Mississippi State Federation of Colored Women's Clubs, 23–24, 76, 78
Mississippi Supreme Court, 200
Mississippi Women's Club, 23–24
Mollison, Willis E., 100, 134, 143–44, 149, 152
Montgomery, Dexter, 106, 107
Montgomery, Estella, 207–10
Montgomery, Isaiah T., 50, 53, 58, 80, 83, 96, 127, 143, 158, 187, 190, 213, 215, 228n.40, 234n.59, 257n.17; and Bank of Mound Bayou, 162, 166–67; and Carnegie library, 194–95; death of, 206–7, 258n.25; financial conflicts with Banks, 200–202; mansion of, 208; and Moton's tour of Mississippi, 74, 77–78; and Mound Bayou, 26–28, 32, 34, 35, 38–40; and Mound Bayou Normal, 120, 121; and oil mill, 170–72, 173, 175, 177–79, 182–84; philosophy of, 30–32, 43–44, 49; political involvement of, 30–31, 143, 149, 152, 199–200, 228n.46; on whitecapping, 29–30
Montgomery, Joshua P. T., 35
Montgomery, Martha, 27, 37
Montgomery, Mary. *See* Booze, Mary
Montgomery, William T., 35, 158
Montgomery-Booze faction, 200
Montroy, I. J. E., 193
Mooney, C. P. J., 74, 173
Moore, Charles, 107–9, 239n.21, 239n.27
Moore, Fred, 51, 77, 141–43
Moore, George, 199
Moore, Malvin, 107, 160, 239n.21
Morgan, S. A., 21
Mosby, W. H., 207
Mosely, Lonzo B., 135, 136, 140–47, 152
Most Worshipful Stringer Grand Lodge,

164. *See also* Fraternal associations; Masonic Benefit Association
Moton, Robert R., xiii, 17, 23, 70, 89, 101, 106, 110; and Carnegie library, 194, 196–99; on land dispute, 202–3; and NNBL, 192–94; and oil mill, 183–84; political involvement of, 139–40, 152–53; president of Tuskegee, 187–89; tours Mississippi, 73–78, 201–2; travels to France during World War I, 255n.16
Mound Bayou: and arrival of Banks, 25; cemetery at, 24; crime in, 32, 33, 210; and *Demonstrator*, 35, 36, 62; enterprises in, 34–36, 169; farmers in, 27, 28, 38, 61–63, 156, 159, 171, 213; Golden Age of, xii, 185, 186, 190, 204, 213, 215; history of, 25–40, 227n.17; leading citizen of, 40, 213, 215; as Negro Metropolis, 40, 48; social status in, 36–40
Mound Bayou Baptist College, 110
Mound Bayou Business League, 35
Mound Bayou Consolidated Negro School, 73, 78, 88, 127–28
Mound Bayou Loan and Investment Company, 159
Mound Bayou Normal and Industrial Institute, 111, 116, 120–22, 123, 127, 195. *See also* Ousley, Benjamin F.
Mound Bayou Oil Mill, 5, 57, 71, 88, 99, 100, 154, 158, 162, 169, 201, 212; dedication of, 1, 19, 86, 172–74; founding of, 170–72; operation of, 175–77; problems with, 177–82; revival of, 182–86, 205
Mound Bayou State Bank, 166, 169, 204
Mulattos, 9, 13, 14, 16, 20
Mulvihill, Michael J., 143–44, 152
Murphy, Frank, 209
My Larger Education, 53, 154

Napier, James C., 101, 192, 247n.115
Natchez Baptist College, 14–16
National Association for the Advancement of Colored People, 23, 215
National Association of Colored Women, 22–23, 24

National Bankers Association of Mississippi, 59
National Federation of Women's Clubs, 75
National Guard, 209
National Negro Bankers Association, 59
National Negro Business League, xi, xii, 17, 35, 50, 51, 76, 90–95, 97, 98, 126, 142, 164, 187, 189, 189, 190, 191, 196–99, 211, 223n.96; 1916 meeting of, 101–3; national organizer of, 94–95; purpose of, 91
National Negro Suffrage League, 51
National Review, 70, 72
Negro Day, 60, 75
Negro Educational Congress, 105
Negro lawyers. *See* Black attorneys
Negro Metropolis, 40, 48. *See also* Mound Bayou
Negrophobia, 224n.103
New Negro, 8
New Orleans Picayune, 72
New York Age, 31, 72, 119, 141, 161, 167, 176, 183, 184, 187, 200, 205
New York Times, 142
New York World, 164
Niles, Henry, 139
Noel, Edmund F., 105, 138, 245n.49
Normal education. *See* Classical education
Nugent, Lillie W., 140

Oberlin College, 207
Ocean Springs affair, 140–42, 147
Odd Fellows. *See* Fraternal associations
Odd Fellows Journal, 72
Ogden, Robert C., 111, 112, 239n.36
Ogden Movement, 111
Oliver, Alice Carter, 23
Oliver, George H., 55
Oliver Chilled Plow Works, 61, 62
Ousley, Benjamin F., 36, 38, 121–22. *See also* Mound Bayou Normal and Industrial Institute
Order of the Eastern Star. *See* Fraternal associations
Owen, Robert, 91

Owen, Thomas, 48, 120, 125–26, 137–38, 139, 140, 158, 179–80, 212, 256n.62

Palmer, W. J., 52
Park, Robert, 112–13
Park, W. L., 45, 171
Parker, Barry, 14
Patronage. *See* Banks, Charles; Moton, Robert R.; Republican Party; Scott, Emmett J.; Washington, Booker T.
Patterson, J. A., 67. *See also* Peace, Arkansas
Paw Paw Cemetery, 205
Peabody, George F., 111, 239n.36
Peabody Education Fund, 239n.36
Peace, Arkansas, 67, 234n.42
Pearman, Mr., 125–28
Peonage, 139
Peoples Bank, 59
Perkins, E. F., 155
Perkins, George, 151
Phelps Hall Bible Training School, 105–6
Piney Woods School, 23
Pinkerton Detective Agency, 72–73, 234n.62
Planters Journal, 62
Polk, Andrew, 209
Port Gibson Oil Company, 201
Postal appointments, 140
Powell, H. H., 199
Proctor and Gamble, 181
Progressive Party, 149. *See also* Bull Moose Party

Quaker, 123

Race riots, 47, 55, 56, 215
Racial etiquette, 48
Racial pride, 28, 91, 157, 172, 174
Racial stock, 9, 14
Racial uplift, 11, 16, 23, 41, 43, 48, 49, 54, 58, 96, 155, 161, 185, 210, 211, 214, 215, 216
Ramsey, J. B., 108
Randolph, Virginia, 123

Reconstruction, 1, 3
Redmond, Sidney D., 59, 76–77, 143, 144, 149, 164
Redmond-Cox faction, 164
Refuge Cotton Oil Company, 201
Republican Party: 129, 130, 132, 133, 142, 146, 148, 149, 150, 151, 152, 206; leaders of, xii, 64, 228n.46; lily-white, 129, 134, 135, 148, 149, 150, 152, 153; patronage power of, 136, 143, 149, 150, 152, 153, 211; patronage referee of, 130; regular faction of, 143, 144; Roosevelt faction of, 143, 144. *See also* Banks, Charles; Booze, Mary; Howard, Perry W.; Montgomery, Isaiah T.; Moton, Robert R.; Scott, Emmett J.; Washington, Booker T.
Republican Central Committee, 30
Republican National Committee, 152, 207, 244n.37
Republican National Convention, 129, 133, 144, 150, 151, 152
Republican State Convention, 143, 148, 150, 152
Revels, Hiram, 3
Rice, Greek P., 209
Robb, Martha. *See* Montgomery, Martha
Roby, J. H., 36
Rockefeller, John D., 51, 63, 113
Rockefeller Fund, 113
Roosevelt, Theodore, 52, 91, 115, 129–32, 141, 143, 145–47, 149, 151, 152, 188
Rosenwald, Julius, 51, 163, 175, 180, 182–84, 241n.93
Rosenwald Fund, 55, 122
Rosewood Race Riot, 47, 215
Rush, Phillip A., 138, 139
Russ, Ed, 4
Russell, S. Douglass, 46
Rust University, 10–11, 70, 93, 105, 221n.57

Saint Anthony's Hospital, 196
Salsbury, L. K., 48
Sambo, 41
Scott, Eleonora, 57

Scott, Emmett J., xiii, 34, 43, 49, 60, 89, 105, 155, 202, 213, 216; accompanies BTW on tour of Mississippi, 67–70, 73; assists Banks, 191–94, 196–99; assists students at Tuskegee Institute, 106, 108, 109, 239n.27; and Bank of Mound Bayou, 157–60, 164, 168–69; and Carnegie Fund, 115–19; election of 1916, 151–52; and GEB, 111, 112; and Jeanes Fund, 125–27; leaves Tuskegee, 187–89; and MNBL, 96–97; and NNBL, 90–95, 101–3; and oil mill, 171–72, 176, 177–80–82, 184, 185; political involvement of, 141; and political patronage, 137–39; and Tuskegee Machine, 51, 54–57
Scott, Emmett Jay, Jr., 109
Sears and Roebuck, 175
Second Mississippi Plan. *See* Mississippi Plan
Selective Service regulations, 189
Settle, Josiah T., 70
Sexton, J. S., 139
Shaw University, 10
Shumpert, W. H., 146
Silone Yates Federation, 19, 23–24, 35, 37
Simmons, Roscoe, 70, 72, 194
Slater Fund, 65, 127
Smith, Kemper, 257n.17
Snowden, Eugene, 158
Social etiquette, 2
Society of Renovators, 35
Southern Bank, 59
Southern Education Board, 111
Southern Letter, 117
Southern Workman, 72
Standard education. *See* Classical education
Star of Zion, 72
State banking examiners, 161–68
Stewart, Charles, 70
Stone, B. S., 110
Strauther, John W., 100
Stringer, Columbus R., 35, 61, 62
Stringer, L. E., 19
Stringer, Thomas W., 67
Sullivan, R., 13

Taft, William H., 132–36, 137, 140–42, 151; election of 1912, 142–50; southern policy of, 147

Talented Tenth, xi; defined, 49; philosophy of, 49–50

Terrell, Mary Church, 15, 18

Terry, Watt, 91, 95

"The Negro Question," 56

Theological and Industrial Institute, 70

Third Liberty Bond call, 189. *See also* World War I

Thirteenth Amendment, 26

Thomas, Jessie O., 124–26, 241n.106

Thomas, William H., 139, 140

Thompson, C. B., 23

Thompson, Richard W., 101

Threadgill, Edward, 199

Tong, Hiram, 222n.59

Tradesman, 57

Trinity Episcopal Mission, 21

Trotter, William M., 49, 51, 153

Trotterites, 55. *See also* Trotter, William M.

Truly, Jeff, 139

Tulane, Victor H., 155

Tulane University, 123

Tulsa Race Riot, 47, 215

Turner, Mary, 164–66, 185

Turner, J. J., 160

Tuskegee Executive Council, 109

Tuskegee Institute, 56, 64, 105–8, 110, 181, 187, 189, 190

Tuskegee Machine, xi–xii, 50, 54, 55, 56, 61, 66, 75, 90, 92, 101, 105, 115, 119, 132, 137–42, 149, 160, 177, 190, 198, 211, 212

Tuskegee Student, 117

Tuskegee Wizard, 102, 187. *See also* Washington, Booker T.

Tyler, Ralph, 94–95

Union Guaranty Insurance Company of Mississippi, 154

United States African News Company, 31

University of Alabama, 182

U.S. Department of Agriculture, 63, 66; Bureau of Plant Industry, 64; Farmers'

Cooperative Demonstration Work, 35, 64

U.S. Department of Justice, 138, 139

U.S. Department of War, 189

Utica Normal and Industrial Institute, 75, 104, 105. *See also* Holtzclaw, William H.

Vanbiber, Delia, 110

Vardaman, James K., 30, 120, 130–31

Vernon, Dr., 105

Vicksburg Herald, 163

Violence, 4, 29–30, 32–33, 73, 143–44. *See also* Race riots; Whitecapping

Vorys, Arthur I., 132, 141

Wall Street, 165

Washerwomen, 13, 15

Washington, Booker T., xi–xiii, 89; and "Atlanta Compromise," 31, 33–34, 42; Atlanta Exposition speech of, 8, 41–42; and Bank of Mound Bayou, 156, 158, 160–61, 163, 165–66, 169; on Banks, 17, 154–55; and Banks Prize, 105–7; and black elite, 16–17, 20, 49–50; and Carnegie Fund, 113–19; criticism of, 45, 52; death of, 187, 196; and election of 1912, 142–51; and farm demonstration agents, 63–67; and GEB, 111–12; and Jeanes Fund, 123–27; and Mississippi Day, 98–100; and MNBL, 96–98; on Mound Bayou, 57–58; and Mound Bayou Normal, 122; and Mound Bayou Oil Mill, 1, 171–83, 189; and NNBL, 90–95, 101–3, 190, 191; and Ocean Springs affair, 141; philosophy of, 41–43, 229n.6; political involvement of, 129–32; and political patronage, 137–39; struggles with Taft's administration, 133–36; tours Mississippi, 67–73, 189, 211; Tuskegee Institute after death of, 188–90; and Tuskegee Machine, 54, 55, 60, 61, 63, 65, 211–16; white father of, 17, 26, 29; visits White House, 130–31

Washington, Margaret Murray, 18, 57, 187, 188

Weaver, Fortune J., 102

Wells-Barnett, Ida B., 10, 18
West Virginia Colored Institute, 64
White, Georga, 5, 7
White, Hugh L., 209
Whitecapping, 29–30, 214
White House, 130, 131, 135, 141, 148
White supremacy, 42, 130, 169, 213, 215
Whyte, Georgiana, 167
Wilberforce University, 104, 124
Wiley University, 93
Williams, Fannie B., 18, 225n.113
Williams, Joe, 59
Williams, Thomas, 110
Williams v. Mississippi, 3
Wilson, Edgar S., 34

Wilson, Woodrow, 149, 152
Wilson Hospital, 205
Wisher, H. A., 97
Wizard of Tuskegee. *See* Tuskegee Wizard;
    Washington, Booker T.
Wood, Eugene V., 207
Woodley, Willie T., 257n.17
Woodson, Carter G., 2, 20
World War I, 10, 128, 165, 184–85, 189,
    214, 255n.16. *See also* Minute Men; Third
    Liberty Bond call; Moton, Robert R.

Yates, Josephine S., 23, 226n.139
Yazoo & Mississippi Valley Railroad, 32,
    73, 158

David H. Jackson Jr. is associate professor of history at Florida A&M University. He is the author of numerous articles on Charles Banks and other civil rights leaders of the Jim Crow era.